GOD

A BIOGRAPHY

GOD

A BIOGRAPHY

Jack Miles

SIMON & SCHUSTER

LONDON · SYDNEY · NEW YORK · TOKYO · SINGAPORE · TORONTO

First published in Great Britain by
Simon & Schuster Ltd. 1995

Simon & Schuster Ltd
West Garden Place
Kendal Street
London W2 2AQ

Simon & Schuster of Australia Pty Ltd
Sydney
A CIP catalogue record for this book is available
from the British Library.

ISBN 0-671-71178-4

Printed and bound in the United States of America

To Jacqueline
and for Kathleen

Contents

The spirit comes to guide me in my need,
I write, "In the beginning was the Deed."

—Goethe

GOD

A BIOGRAPHY

KEYNOTE

The Image and the Original

That God created mankind, male and female, in his own image is a matter of faith. That our forebears strove for centuries to perfect themselves in the image of their God is a matter of historical fact. During the long centuries when the God of the Jews and the Christians was the unchallenged ultimate reality of the West, European and, later, American men and women consciously sought to model themselves on him. They believed that by trying they could make themselves into better copies of the divine original, and they bent themselves diligently to the task. *Imitatio Dei*, the imitation of God, was a central category in Jewish piety. The imitation of Christ, God made man, was equally central for Christians.

Many in the West no longer believe in God, but lost belief, like a lost fortune, has effects that linger. A young man raised in wealth may, when he comes of age, give his fortune away and live in poverty. His character, however, will remain that of a man raised in wealth, for he cannot give his history away. In a similar way, centuries of rigorous, godly character-building have created an ideal of human character that stands fast even though, for many, its foundation has been removed. When Westerners encounter a culture with a different ideal, when we find ourselves saying, for example, "The Japanese are different," we discover, indirectly, the strangeness and durability of our own ideal, our inherited sense of what a human being should be. In innumerable external ways, Japan and the West have grown alike. Japan eats beef; the West eats sushi. Japan wears business suits; *kimono* has entered the Western vocabulary. Yet a deep difference abides, for Japan was looking into a different religiocultural mirror during the centuries when the God of the Bible was the mirror of the West. This book about God aims to place the biblical mirror, cleansed and polished, in the reader's hands.

For non-Westerners, knowledge of the God whom the West has worshiped opens a uniquely direct path to the core and origin of the Western ideal of character. But for Westerners themselves, a deepened knowledge of this God can serve to render conscious and sophisticated what is otherwise typically unconscious and naive. We are all, in a way, immigrants from the past. And just as an immigrant returning after many years to the land of his birth may see his own face in the faces of strangers, so the modern, Western, secular reader may feel a tremor of self-recognition in the presence of the ancient protagonist of the Bible.

How can an unbeliever enter the presence of God? From generation to generation, Judaism and Christianity have transmitted their knowledge of God in several ways. For the few, there have been and still are the demanding and sometimes esoteric disciplines of asceticism, mysticism, and theology. For the many, there is, remarkably perhaps, a book that an unbeliever no less than a believer may open and read. Knowledge of God as a literary character neither precludes nor requires belief in God, and it is this kind of knowledge that the book before you attempts to mediate.

Philosophers of religion have sometimes claimed that all gods are projections of the human personality, and so it may be. But if so, we must at least recognize the empirical fact that many human beings, rather than project their own personalities upon gods wholly of their own creation, have chosen to introject—take into themselves—the religious projections of other human personalities.

This is why religion excites so much fascination, envy, and (sometimes) rage in writers and literary critics who give the matter much thought. Religion—Western religion in particular—may be seen as literature that has succeeded beyond any writer's wildest dreams. Any character who "comes to life" in a work of literary art may have some degree of influence over real people who encounter the work. Miguel de Cervantes's *Don Quixote*, in which the title character models himself on the popular literature of his day, is an incomparably poignant and hilarious picture of this process in action. Cervantes surely thought about the influence that his own work would eventually have, and indeed he presents his "real" Don Quixote encountering people who know of a literary character by the same name. In our own day, millions fuse the real lives and the screen lives of movie actors, assign the combination an importance greater than any they concede to the real human beings whom they know, and then suffer the melancholy consequences. Their flesh is sad, alas, and they have seen all the movies.

No character, however, on stage, page, or screen has ever had the reception that God has had. God is more than a household word in the West; he is, welcome or not, a virtual member of the Western family. Parents who would be done with him cannot keep their children from him, for not only has everyone heard of him, everyone, even now, can tell you something about him. Playwright Neil Simon published a comedy, *God's Favorite*, some years ago, based on the biblical Book of Job. Few who saw the play had read the biblical book, but there was no need: They already knew what God was like well enough to get the jokes. If nothing is serious, nothing is funny, as Oscar Wilde once wrote. Whence came the serious God-idea in the minds of Simon's ready-to-roar Broadway audience?

It came almost entirely from the Bible and, in more specific human terms, it came from those who wrote the Bible. To the eyes of faith, the Bible is not just words *about* God but also the Word *of* God: He is its author as well as its protagonist. But whether the ancient writers who wrote the Bible created God or merely wrote down God's revelation of himself, their work has been, in literary terms, a staggering success. It has been read aloud every week for two thousand years to audiences who have received it with utmost seriousness and consciously sought to maximize its influence upon themselves. In this, it is certainly without parallel in Western literature and probably without parallel in all literature. The Qur'an comes immediately to mind, but Muslims do not regard the Qur'an as literature: It occupies, for them, a metaphysical niche all its own. Jews and Christians, by contrast, while revering the Bible as more than mere literature, do not deny that it is *also* literature and generally concede that it may be appreciated as such without blasphemy.

Religiously fostered appreciation of the Bible attends centrally and explicitly to the goodness of God. Jews and Christians have adored God as the origin of all virtue, a wellspring of justice, wisdom, mercy, patience, strength, and love. But peripherally and implicitly, they have also grown accustomed and then attached, over the centuries, to what we may call God's anxiety. God is, as I shall try to show in the book that follows, an amalgam of several personalities in one character. Tension among these personalities makes God difficult, but it also makes him compelling, even addictive. While consciously emulating his virtues, the West has unconsciously assimilated the anxiety-inducing tension between his unity and his multiplicity. In the end, despite the longing Westerners sometimes feel for a simpler, less anxious, more "centered" human ideal, the only people whom we find satisfyingly real are people whose identity binds several incompatible subidentities together. As Westerners get to know one another personally, this is what we seek to learn about one another. Incongruity and inner conflict are not just permitted in Western culture; they are all but required. People who are merely clever about playing various roles fall short of this ideal. They have personality—or a repertory of personalities—but lack character. Uncomplicated, simple people, who know who they are without ado and embrace an assigned role without struggle, also fall short of the ideal. We may admire their inner peace, but in the West we are unlikely to imitate them. Centered and all too centered, they have character but little personality. They bore us as we would bore ourselves if we were like them.

We make matters so difficult for ourselves because our forebears understood themselves to be the image of a God who, in effect, had made matters similarly difficult for himself. Monotheism recognizes only one God: "Hear, O Israel, the Lord is our God, the Lord is one." The Bible insists on nothing about God more than on his unity. God is the Rock of Ages, integrity in person. And yet this same being combines several personalities. Either mere unity (character alone) or mere multiplicity (personality alone) would have been so much easier. But he is both, and so the image of the human that derives from him requires both.

God is no saint, strange to say. There is much to object to in him, and many attempts have been made to improve him. Much that the Bible says about him is rarely preached from the pulpit because, examined too closely, it becomes a scandal. But if only some of the Bible is actively preached, none of the Bible is quite denied. On the improbably unexpurgated biblical page, God remains as he has been: the original who was the Faith of our Fathers and whose image is living still within us as a difficult but dynamic secular ideal.

1

PRELUDE

Can God's Life Be Written?

Can a literary character be said to live a life from birth to death or otherwise to undergo a development from beginning to end? Or is a literary character—fixed on the pages of a book, trapped forever in the same few words and actions—the very opposite of a living, developing human being?

Contention on this point has shaped a century of *Hamlet* criticism, according to a recent survey by William Kerrigan, who calls the two contending groups the critics and the scholars. The critics, he says, dominant at the start of the century, believed in character. They believed that to talk about *Hamlet* the play, you had to talk about Hamlet the man: what he said, what he did, and how he changed during the time between his first and his last words onstage. The scholars, dominant in the middle of the century, took as their motto Hamlet's own line "The play's the thing." They believed that, empirically speaking, there was no Hamlet, only Shakespeare's words on the page, and that therefore one could legitimately talk only about them. If one went beyond them, it could not be into the imagined rest of Hamlet, for the rest was silence, to borrow another line from the play. One could go only into the rest of Elizabethan drama and Elizabethan society, seeking other plays that Shakespeare might have known, deepening one's knowledge of the language he spoke, and so forth.

The dean of the critics was A. C. Bradley, whose still influential *Shakespearean Tragedy* was published in 1904. The turning point from criticism to scholarship and from character to dramaturgy as a focus may be dated to 1933, when L. C. Knights wrote a famous essay, "How Many Children Had Lady Macbeth?" mocking Bradley's assumption—naive in Knights's view—that literary character could ever be talked about in its own right. Knights believed that Bradley's approach was perhaps appropriate for biography but certainly inappropriate for literary criticism.

For decades, Kerrigan shows, the triumph of scholarship over criticism seemed complete. Most of those now teaching and writing about Shakespeare were trained by scholars. Yet criticism never quite folded its tent, and in the last years of the century an interesting bifurcation has occurred.

On the one hand, the kind of historicism whose rise may be dated to Knights's essay has been succeeded by a "New Historicism" with intellectual debts to French thought. Broadly, where the Old Historicism sought to understand the history that was embedded in the text of the play, the New Historicism seeks to understand the play as itself embedded in history. Thus, Kerrigan writes:

> Stephen Greenblatt [the best-known of the New Historicists] famously concludes his *Renaissance Self-fashioning* with the declaration that he had started to write a book on Renaissance individuals but discovered in the end that there are no individuals. One is somewhat amazed to learn at the beginning of his *Shakespearean Negotiations* that he started this book, too, in a quest for the writer's unique intensity but discovered in the end that there are no writers: "This book argues that works of art, however intensely marked by the creative intelligence and private obsession of individuals, are the products of collective negotiation and exchange."

The reign of scholarship continues, therefore; yet, on the other hand, at least a few erstwhile scholars are surreptitiously defecting to criticism, among them Kerrigan himself. "I was trained by scholars," he writes, "and speaking of 'character development' in *Hamlet* makes me uneasy. But I do not know how else to describe the shift from the self-loathing Hamlet of the final two soliloquies to the beautifully calm Hamlet of Act 5." Philosophically, Bradley was a

Hegelian, and the struggle between him and Knights was a literary version of the long-running contest between German (or Continental) idealism and British empiricism. But both traditions trace, ultimately, to classical antiquity, and Kerrigan ends his survey with Aristotle:

> So we need to understand Hamlet's beginning and his end, and need to put them together. Modern Aristotles puzzling out the mysterious tragedy of character, we must connect beginning, middle, and end.
>
> That's the way it's done.

THE BIOGRAPHY OF GOD

That is the way it will be done in this book. I have begun this foreword with a discussion of *Hamlet* because I want to situate my subject in literature. I write here about the life of the Lord God as —and only as—the protagonist of a classic of world literature; namely, the Hebrew Bible or Old Testament. I do not write about (though I certainly do not write against) the Lord God as the object of religious belief. I do not attempt, as theology does, to make an original statement about God as an extraliterary reality. I do not write as a historian and therefore do not focus, as historians do, on the successive Israelite and Jewish communities that believed in God. My interest goes not to those believing communities but, after the fashion of A. C. Bradley, to the God they believed in. And I believe with Bradley, and against Knights, that the biographical effect—the artistic suggestion of a life—is inseparable from the dramatic or literary effect itself. Unless the viewer of *Hamlet* can believe that Hamlet was born and will die, unless the viewer's imagination is carried offstage into the life for which there is no direct evidence onstage, the play dies with its protagonist. A character understood to have no life offstage can have no life onstage. And so it is also with God as the protagonist of the Bible.

If biography is seen narrowly as a branch of history, then there can be no biography of a nonhistorical character. But God does have a first and a last appearance in the Hebrew Bible. We see him first as the creator, outside history, prior to it, masterfully setting in motion the heavenly bodies by which historical time will be measured. We see him last as the "Ancient of Days," white-haired and silent, looking forward to the end of history from a remote and cloudy throne. This book becomes a biography of a special sort by dint of its determination to describe the middle that lies between so vigorous a beginning and so quiescent an end.

The beginning and the end of the Hebrew Bible are not linked by a single, continuous narrative. Well short of the halfway point in the text, the narrative breaks off. What then follow are, first, speeches spoken by God; second, speeches spoken either to or, in some degree, about God; third, a protracted silence; and, last, a brief resumption of the narrative before a closing coda. The narrative suspense that lasts from the Book of Genesis through II Kings is succeeded, past that point, by another kind of suspense, one more like the kind jurors experience in a courtroom as different witnesses take the stand to talk about the same person. A sequence of testimonies—each in its own distinctive voice, with its own beginning and end—can be as effective as narrative in suggesting that the person about whom the words are spoken does not stop where the words stop. This is the biographical effect in another form. And even in this form, it is an effect that can include a sense of forward movement, of "What next?"

After action yields to speech in the Hebrew Bible, however, speech yields in its turn to silence. God's last words are those he speaks to Job, the human being who dares to challenge not his physical power but his moral authority. Within the Book of Job itself, God's climactic and overwhelming reply seems to silence Job. But reading from the end of the Book of Job onward, we see that it is Job who has somehow silenced God. God never speaks again, and he is decreasingly spoken of. In the Book of Esther—a book in which, as in the Book of Exodus, his chosen people faces a genocidal enemy—he is never so much as mentioned. In effect, the Jews surmount the threat without his help.

What is the meaning of the long twilight of the Hebrew Bible, its ten closing books of silence? The twilight is not followed by darkness: God does not die. But he never again intervenes in human affairs, and by accumulating implication, no further intervention is expected of him. His chosen people, returned from exile, cherishes him more than ever as his life ends—more, certainly, than when he vanquished Pharaoh "with mighty hand and outstretched arm" and led them through the desert to the promised land. Back then, they were recalcitrant, and he called them, bitterly, "stiff-necked." Now they are devout, but he has nothing further to say to them or about them—or to or about anybody or anything else. God and his people are beautifully, movingly reconciled as the Hebrew Bible ends, but it scarcely seems blasphemy to say that his own life is over.

This broad movement from action to speech to silence yields an account that might be called theography, as distinct from either theology or biography. A medieval mystic once wrote, "God cancels the successiveness of men," meaning that while human beings experience their lives one day at a time, God sees their lives' time as a portrait on a wall, every moment visible to him at once. But human beings have returned the favor with a vengeance, canceling the successiveness of the protagonist of the Bible by a tradition of Bible reading that regards the entirety of the text as simultaneous to itself, so that any verse may be read as the commentary on any other verse and any statement true of God at one point is taken to be true of God at all points.

"Jesus Christ is the same yesterday and today and for ever," the New Testament reads at Hebrews 13:8; but that one late and questionable verse aside, there is virtually no warrant in the New Testament for any claim that God is immutable, and there is equally little in the Hebrew Bible. The origin of this view lies presumably in Aristotelian philosophy, with its view of God as the unmoved mover, existing in a single, eternal moment. True, the Lord God of Israel is the creator and ruler of time, and the Psalms delight in repeating that he lives forever. To that extent he is like Aristotle's unmoved mover. And yet, contradictory as this must seem, he also enters time and is changed by experience. Were it not so, he could not be surprised; and he is endlessly and often most unpleasantly surprised. God is constant; he is not immutable.

A strictly sequential reading of the Hebrew Bible is a way to recover the successiveness, the character development or theography, that "Aristotelian" exegesis has obscured. Thus, Christians pray "Our Father, who art in heaven . . . ," as Christ did, and imagine that the being who says, at Genesis 1:3, "Let there be light" is a father, but God does not refer to himself as a father at that point. Only several hundred pages later, in II Samuel 7, does he do this for the first time. Jews pray "Blessed art thou, O Lord, our God, King of the Universe" and imagine that the God of Genesis is a king, but he does not present himself as a king until even later, at Isaiah 6. "Later" in this context does not mean later in historical time but simply later in the exposition, further along in a start-to-finish reading of the book. Historically speaking, the "time" when God says

"Let there be light" lies outside time; but from the point of view of a reader beginning at the beginning of the Book of Genesis and reading straight on from there, we may still speak of "later" and "earlier." In this book, we often shall.

There is no pretending that a diachronic or straight-through reading of the Hebrew Bible is the only possible approach to the character of God as its protagonist. A synchronic reading is also possible. That is, instead of proceeding from beginning to end in quasi-chronological order, a critic may create a set of topical headings and gather under each all the texts that seem to belong there. But a self-consciously naive, start-to-finish approach, besides being more respectful of the integrity of the Bible as a work of literature, has, as we shall see, a surprising drama and pathos about it.

Because this is a literary rather than a historical study, deliberate naïveté of another sort becomes possible and indeed necessary. Critical historians of any period or subject are at pains to distinguish what really happened from what did not happen. Even when they are quite certain that they are dealing with a literary invention, their concern is not to appreciate the invention in itself as a work of literary art but to recover from it evidence about some real history, if only the intellectual history of its author. Myth, legend, and history mix endlessly in the Bible, and Bible historians are endlessly sorting them out. Literary criticism, however, not only can but must leave them mixed. The Book of Genesis says that God turned Lot's wife into a pillar of salt, an event that obviously has no status as history but one that for the purposes of this work must be counted as a moment in the life of God and as evidence, however minor, about his developing character. We may allow the historians to tell us what really happened. We may allow the theologians to tell us whether the real God would ever do a thing like that. For literary purposes, however, which are the only purposes of this book, the fact that the protagonist of the book does indeed perform this action on its pages is enough to bring it into the reckoning.

Skeptical readers may ask, of course, whether there is not, even in a secular era, something misbegotten about an attempt to understand God in terms so like those we use to understand human beings. Robert Alter writes in this vein:

> There is little to be gained, I think, by conceiving of the biblical God, as Harold Bloom does, as a human character—petulant, headstrong, arbitrary, impulsive, or whatever. The repeated point of

'cal writers is that we cannot make sense of God in human

But Alter exaggerates. One of the very earliest statements any biblical writer makes about God is that mankind, male and female, is God's image—an unmistakable invitation to make some sense of God in human terms. God rarely says of himself that he is mysterious and more than once implies the opposite, as when, speaking of whether his words are difficult to understand, he says:

> Surely, this Instruction which I enjoin upon you this day is not too baffling for you, nor is it beyond reach. It is not in the heavens, that you should say, "Who among us can go up to the heavens and get it for us and impart it to us, that we may observe it?" (Deut. 30:11–12)

At a certain point in the Hebrew Bible, God does begin speaking of himself as mysterious. But nothing prevents us from asking why he does so then and not earlier. There is certainly no warrant whatever within the Bible itself for regarding God as a subject to be passed over in respectful silence.

As for whether Bloom is right or wrong that God may be spoken of as a human character, we may at least ask in what ways God differs from the human creature that, by his own testimony, he resembles to some degree. In other words, granting that God and mankind are not identical, in what ways are they different? What makes God godlike? What is special about his character? And, above all, we may ask, staying always within the confines of the Bible as a work of literature, how his earlier actions relate developmentally to his later ones. This question need not lose its relevance even when we read the biblical books that come after the extended opening narrative. At those later points, one may listen as a biographer during an interview or (as suggested earlier) as a juror in a courtroom, not attempting to reconstruct events but simply receiving character testimony from a character witness. *How did he affect you? Did he frighten you? Did you love him? What was he after? Did he change much during the time you knew him? What most impressed you about him?*

These and similar questions are what move this biography forward.

One may find, of course, that there is no real development and that God is monotonously the same and impenetrably mysterious from first to last appearance. No outcome can be ruled out. What is required is only a fidelity to the humble and patient tactic by which any character gets to know any other. With sympathy and attention, the biographer must address apparent conflicts between an earlier statement by God and a later one, an earlier action and a later one, a statement at any given moment with behavior at the same moment, and so forth. Conflicts must be resolved either by identifying and sanctioning them as development in the character or by explaining why they are apparent rather than actual conflicts or—failing any other resolution—simply by acknowledging them: Knowledge of an unresolved conflict in a character may be the most crucial knowledge of all.

In real life, this is the most ordinary and necessary of interpersonal activities. We engage daily in an ongoing assessment of the people we live and work with. Someone does something out of character, and either we find a way to explain away the uncharacteristic action—"My son is ill," "My wife has just lost her job"—or we make a provisional revision of our understanding—"He always seemed so well-intentioned, but after this. . . ." This skill, so central to the living of life, is equally central to the appreciation of literature, an art made by an intensified reuse of human lives and human language. The Bible is unquestionably an unusual work of literature, and the Lord God is a most unusual character. But one of the two key premises of this biography is that neither the work nor the character is so inhuman that interpersonal appraisal is out of the question.

THE ORDER OF THE CANON AND THE COURSE OF GOD'S LIFE

The second premise of this biography is that the order in which the books of the Bible appear—the order of the canon—is a crucial artistic consideration. Earlier in this foreword I spoke of "a classic of world literature; namely, the Hebrew Bible or Old Testament," as if the two were interchangeable. But are they?

Jews and Christians alike have certainly regarded them as such. True, both groups know that the Christian Bible has two unequal parts: the Old Testament and the New Testament. Jews may take offense at having their sacred scripture referred to as "old" by comparison with the conclusion of the Christian Bible. But both groups, including sophisticated literary critics of either confession, have invariably spoken of the Hebrew Bible and the Old Testament as the same work under two different names.

But they are not quite the same work. The distinctive, broad movement of the Hebrew Bible from action to speech to silence is not matched in the Old Testament, whose movement is from action to silence to speech. The contents in either case are the same, but the arrangement is not. The Old Testament shifts the great prophetic collections—Isaiah, Jeremiah, Ezekiel, and the twelve minor prophets—from the middle to the end, leaving in the middle what we called earlier the books of silence, including Job, Lamentations, Ecclesiastes, and Esther. For the special purposes of a biography of God, the difference between the two arrangements is crucial.

One might wonder why this point should have to be made at all. Is the order of presentation not obviously crucial for all literary purposes? If Jews and Christians have combined traditional or received materials in such sharply different ways, is it not immediately clear that two different works have resulted? What must be stressed is how completely the Western tradition of regarding every verse in sacred scripture as simultaneous to every other verse—and therefore every book as simultaneous to every other book—has blinded modern critics to the importance of the artistic decisions by which, two millennia ago, two different editors or teams of editors arranged one collection of books into two different canons or tables of contents.

The story of how the Hebrew Bible and the Old Testament diverged includes, improbably enough, a chapter from the history of technology. Muslim tradition has called Jews and Christians alike "peoples of the book," honoring the divinely inspired scriptures that preceded God's revelation of the Qur'an to Muhammad. In the modern sense of the word *book*, however, the Jews might be more accurately called the people of the scroll. It is the Christians who are the people of the book as we know it.

At issue is no title or privilege but only the definition of a term. What we now call a scroll is a text storage device that the first centuries of the common era called a book. What we call a book—cut pages sewn together on one side—was then called a codex. The codex, invented sometime in the first century of the common era, was clearly distinguished at the time from a "real" book—that is, from a scroll. The pagan literary elite of the Roman Empire, the conservatives of their day, looked on the codex rather as some in our day look on an electronic publication. They were attached to the older format and adopted the newer one reluctantly. The Jews, who had been using the scroll for centuries, were only somewhat quicker to change, and for ceremonial purposes they have retained the scroll down to the present. The Christians of the Roman Empire—a poorly educated, lower-class group with no secular literary traditions to preserve and, as a new religion, with few sacred traditions to preserve either—adopted the new device immediately and universally. The codex may in fact be their invention. Whoever invented it, Christianity's enthusiastic adoption of it gave the new religion a technological advantage that undoubtedly fostered its spread.

The new medium had a message of its own, however. As smaller codices gradually yielded to larger ones, the possibility emerged for the first time of including all the Jewish scriptures in one textual "container." Because the standard thirty-foot scroll could hold no work longer than the Book of Isaiah, the various works that would become the Hebrew Bible had always been stored separately: many scrolls in many storage jars. By keeping the constituent parts physically movable, the older text-storage system tended to keep them mentally movable as well and to forestall any tendency to edit them into a single, large, closed anthology.

The Christian scriptures, though also an anthology, had a different history, for they were born just as the codex was being born. Perhaps it is because the codex at first was not felt to be a proper book that the separate works of the New Testament have not traditionally been called books. There is no "Book of Matthew" or "Book of Paul." (True, there is the Book of Revelation, but Revelation is a late, consciously antiquarian exercise by a writer who is, among other peculiarities, fairly obsessed with the scroll as a physical object.) In all probability, the component parts of the New Testament came to seem the functional equivalent of chapters in a single work far earlier in their history than the component parts of the Hebrew Bible did.

The decisive moment came when the mode of storage the Christians preferred began to be extended to the inherited Jewish scriptures. The Christians, having taken these scriptures as their own, took this step first; the Jews did so somewhat later. As editors from either group realized that the order of the contents would now be fixed and visible, both would naturally have thought in a new way about the potential aesthetic or polemic significance of the order. In the end, the Jews made one decision about the order, the Christians made another, and so it came about that the last step in the editing of an edited masterpiece took place twice. The Hebrew Bible and the Old Testament are not quite two different works but, to speak more precisely, two very different editions of the same collection.

What motivated the Christian editor to move the prophets to the end of the newly edited Old Testament? Presumably his hope was that in this position the prophets would better announce their relationship to the now immediately following Gospels. Christianity believes that the life of Christ is the fulfillment of prophecy. The Gospels, which open the New Testament, make this point repeatedly. The Christian editor edited the Hebrew Bible to reflect this Christian belief.

Or so, at least, we may speculate. A rival school of thought maintains that two ancient Jewish canons have been preserved—a Palestinian canon, surviving in the Hebrew Bible, and an Alexandrian (or diaspora) Jewish canon, surviving in the Old Testament. In my judgment, stronger evidence supports the view that the order found in the Christian Old Testament reflects a Christian editor's conscious revision, but I admit that this cannot finally be determined.

Whatever the origin of the two editions, the difference between them is large enough that a biographer of God must choose on which he will base his account. For reasons that will not be completely evident until the very end of this book, I have chosen to base my account on the Hebrew Bible or, to use the standard Hebrew word for the collection, on the Tanakh. The word *Tanakh* is a postbiblical acronym derived from the Hebrew equivalents of the letters *t*, *n*, and *k* (pronounced *kh* under certain phonetic conditions), standing, respectively, for the Hebrew words *torah*, "teaching"; *nebi'im*, "prophets"; and *ketubim*, "writings." If the Old Testament were renamed with a comparable acronym, it might be *Takhan*, for the Old Testament order is, roughly, teaching, writings, prophets. *Tanakh* is the name that I shall ordinarily use for the collection from this point forward. What is of decisive importance, of course, is not the name but the character of the collection itself.

The character of the Hebrew Bible/Old Testament is such, to state what must be obvious by now, that the collection can be taken apart and put together in more than one way. The same necessarily goes for the character of God as its protagonist. A skeptic might conclude that the collection is so without an ordinary plot or an ordinary protagonist that it is not at all amenable to the ordinary tools of literary appreciation. A close reading of the text, however, suggests that the Tanakh is partially plotted and partially not, while its protagonist is partially a genuine or "drawn" character and partially not. In short, we are faced with a kind of patchwork. Along the seams some of the patches may be pulled apart and put back together in a new configuration. But even at moments when literary intent is questionable, literary effect is undeniable. Indeed, a part of the enduring power of the Hebrew Bible arises from its partially aleatory or accidental character. In art, typically, nothing is left to chance. In the real world, chance accounts for a great deal. The air of reality within a work of art is enhanced, therefore, if chance is admitted or even feigned. Whether or not for conscious artistic reasons, chance has definitely been admitted to the Bible.

The order in which the life of the Lord God is told in this book is the order of the Tanakh (see Appendix, page 411); and, except where otherwise indicated, the translation quoted is that of the 1985 Jewish Publication Society TANAKH (JPS). I hasten to add, however, that though I am laboring just now to establish the differences between the Tanakh and the Old Testament, and though I do believe that we may speak of two classics rather than one, the similarities between them as regards their common protagonist are plainly enormous. The order of the books in the two canons does count, but by that very token the fact that the order is identical through the formative first eleven books means that from youth through young adulthood, so to speak, the Lord God is understood identically in the Tanakh and in the Old Testament. Only his middle and old age are understood differently. A biography-shaped modern interpretation based on the work of one ancient editor will necessarily be different from a comparable interpretation based on the work of the other. But there can be no doubt that the subject, God himself, is the same being in either case.

BIBLE SCHOLARS VERSUS BIBLE CRITICS

Like William Kerrigan, I have had scholars rather than critics as my teachers, and a brief word seems in order about the relationship of this work to the imposing body of historical scholarship about the Tanakh. As a branch of secular learning, this scholarship has taken the religion of ancient Israel rather than God himself as its proper object. In so doing, it has rarely if ever defined itself against literary criticism, as one branch of secular learning may define itself against another. On the contrary, its psychological and sociological "other" has always been understood to be established religious authority. When it thinks of an alternate approach to its own, it thinks of theology.

In spite of this, however, its results, attentively read, are of great literary interest. First, historical scholars, albeit for their own reasons, are typically far more attentive than the average critic of modern literature to "meaningless" details that sometimes turn out not to be so meaningless after all. Among these are many that bear on the character of the Lord God. Second, historical scholars have much that is valid and useful to say about the authors of the individual works that make up the Tanakh. Even a critic who wishes to focus on the effect of the work as a whole upon a modern reader will gain from being instructed as fully as possible about the ancient authorial agendas that he overrides.

The God whom ancient Israel worshiped arose as the fusion of a number of the gods whom a nomadic nation had met in its wanderings. A reader interested in tracking this process historically may do so through such impressive technical studies as *Yahweh and the Gods of Canaan* by William Foxwell Albright, *Canaanite Myth and Hebrew Epic* by Albright's student Frank Moore Cross, and *The Early History of God* by Cross's student Mark S. Smith. These are works of controlled imagination as well as massive erudition. But a more literary reader may be prompted by them to ask, "How did all this feel to God?" an absurd question within the methodology of historical reconstruction but an utterly ordinary one—in fact, an indispensable one—for literary appreciation. Unless a playgoer is constantly alert to Hamlet's changing feelings, *Hamlet* as a play is incomprehensible. A. C. Bradley has continued to be read because, in effect, once inside the theater—once, that is, in the spellbinding presence of Hamlet come back to life—every playgoer believes with Bradley that Hamlet does not stop at Shakespeare's words.

To repeat, the question How did all this feel to God? is not a historical question, but a reader of the Tanakh asking that question will find one set of answers if he has first spent some time with historical scholarship and another if he has not. In their historical "genealogy" of God, scholars such as Albright, Cross, and Smith find that various divine personalities whom they recognize from extrabiblical sources have left traces on the pages of the Bible. A literary critic who knows their work may read this objective multiplicity back into the character of the Lord God as a literary protagonist, turning their observed inconsistencies imaginatively into God's experienced inner conflict. In this way, the emergence of monotheism from polytheism can be recovered for literature as the story of a single God struggling with himself.

The Tanakh has never *not* been such a story. Nothing needs to be added—no heavy psychological speculations, no sensational revelations from the latest archaeological dig, no readings between the lines—to bring this reading about. The contradictions, latent in the text all along, have never failed to have a marked aesthetic effect on the reader or hearer: The Lord God has always been intermittently baffling or irritating or inconsistent or arbitrary because of them. Historical scholarship simply helps to make the conflicts patent, turning muddy shades of gray in the Lord's interior life into clearly distinguishable tints. Here the sky blue of El, there the earth tones of "the god of your father," over there the blood red of Baal or Tiamat or the evergreen memory of Asherah. If the Bible is finally a work of literature, these historically distinguishable personalities need to be read back into—and then back out of—the one God, the *monos theos,* who came into being as they fused. After God has been understood in his multiplicity, in short, he needs to be imagined again in his riven and difficult unity.

Only when this is done does the Bible come into focus as a work of art rather than merely a defective work of history. Historians have generally recognized the powerful originality of Israel's religious synthesis even when they did not also believe, on religious grounds, that this originality was a revelation from God himself. But by regarding the Bible as just the most important among many sources for their history of the religion of Israel, they have failed to see that the Bible's own way of combining several personalities into one complex character is to plot them across a story in which God—rather than Israel—is the protagonist. The plot begins with God's desire for a self-image. It thickens when God's self-image becomes a maker of self-images, and God resents it. From this initial conflict, others emerge. The plot reaches its crisis when God tries and fails to conceal his originating motive from a single physically ravaged but morally aroused exemplar of himself.

The key methodological move in this rereading of the Hebrew

Bible—and the reason why it may be called a biography—is a shift of focus away from the human actors and toward the divine actor. Without insulting or contradicting historical scholarship, his character must be allowed to emerge through another, critical but more subjective set of questions. Why did God create the world? Why, on flimsy grounds, did he destroy it so soon after creating it? Why, having for so long shown no interest whatsoever in the wars of mankind, did he suddenly become a warrior? Why, having attended slightly if at all to morality, did he become a moralist? As his covenant with Israel seemed to break down, what consequences loomed for him? What kind of life awaited him after that impending breakup? How did he adjust to his failure to keep the promises he made through the prophets? What is his experienced life as a being without parents, spouse, or children? Historical scholarship neither asks nor answers questions such as these. Criticism does. But historical scholarship, judiciously employed, can teach criticism to recognize what it is looking for when it sees it.

THE ONE AND THE MANY

A distinguished American publisher, asked how he had come to choose publishing as a career, answered: "My father was a reader; my mother was a striver." *I am my mother and my father,* he implied; *publishing permits me to live out my contradiction.* From the moment of conception, when twenty-three chromosomes from a male and twenty-three from a female become the first cell of a new human being, we are defined by our inner division. Our only identity is a lack of identity. We have nothing all our own. Upon that initial division of identity, other divisions intrude: racial, cultural, occupational, temperamental. "Eely Meely and a-Miley Mo"—a song sung by my nine-year-old daughter, Kathleen, and her classmates —includes the following very American quatrain:

> My mother was a doctor,
> My father was a spy,
> And I'm the little pip-squeak
> Who told the FBI.

As a boy of about fourteen, I heard a Chicago version of a verse made famous by James Joyce:

My mother was a Jewess,
My father was a bird,
And I'm the queerest fellow
That ever said a word.

Genetically speaking, everyone is the offspring of a mixed marriage, for, cloning aside, no other kind of marriage exists. As the children's jingles suggest, however, genetics is just the beginning.

The deepest justification for reading the Tanakh as the biography of God is that, in the way of a great many human biographies, it follows the divisions in a character as they find expression in a life's work. Before there was a successful publishing executive, in other words, there was a young man with contradictory inclinations. "Trying to find something to do with himself," we say, and the saying is exactly right: trying indeed not just to find something to do but to find something to do *with himself.* Not always, but often, that stage of interior division and quest ends in a life's work that permits the double or multiple personalities coexisting in a given immature character to find simultaneous expression and so to fuse in a mature and dynamic identity. Not always, but often, the work is eventually undermined by the very inner tension that initially made for its success. To pursue the publishing example, it may become impossible at some pitch of intensity to be both reader and striver. The achievement and the identity may then come crashing down. Or, more often, the achievement may pass, changed, into other hands, while the identity lingers.

The Lord God has no mother and father, but the otherwise engendered contradictions in his character do find an enactment in his life. His character fuses, explodes, and—just here the Tanakh differs most strikingly from the Old Testament—disintegrates without disappearing. Biblical Hebrew, interestingly enough, has no word for *story*, and the Tanakh does not end as a well-written story would end. But real lives never end that way. The Tanakh's failure here is its success. Death comes to many if not to most human beings as an interruption. The survivors are left thinking not about the story that is over but about the person who is gone.

So it is at the end of the Tanakh. A bewildering classic, produced by countless literary hands over many hundreds of years, it is held together by its central character far more than by any rigid structure or epic theme. The Lord God is at war with himself, but his war is our own, for culturally speaking we have been living with him for centuries. Before meeting him, everyone, absolutely everyone, has heard of him. Of whom else can that claim be made?

Asked if he believed in God, the psychologist Carl Jung answered, famously, "I do not believe. I know." Can God be known? I leave that question unanswered. What I claim is only that God's life as found on the pages of the Bible can be told. This book aims to be the telling.

2

Generation

He is talking to himself. No human being has yet been created to hear him, and the other divine beings whom he will address infrequently and almost in passing seem barely within his field of attention—bystanders at best, not collaborators.

When God began to create heaven and earth—the earth being unformed and void, with darkness over the surface of the deep and a wind from God sweeping over the water—God said, "Let there be light"; and there was light. God saw that the light was good, and God separated the light from the darkness. God called the light Day, and the darkness He called Night. And there was evening and there was morning, a first day.

God said, "Let there be an expanse in the midst of the water, that it may separate water from water." God made the expanse, and it separated the water which was below the expanse from the water which was above the expanse. And it was so. God called the expanse Sky. And there was evening and there was morning, a second day.

God said, "Let the water below the sky be gathered into one area, that the dry land may appear." And it was so. God called the dry land Earth, and the gathering of waters He called Seas. And God saw that this was good. And God said, "Let the earth sprout vegetation: seed-bearing plants, fruit trees of every kind on earth that bear fruit with the seed in it." And it was so. The earth brought forth vegetation: seed-bearing plants of every kind, and trees of every kind bearing fruit with the seed in it. And God saw that this

> was good. And there was evening and there was morning, a third day. (Gen. 1:1–13)
>
> God said, "Let there be lights in the expanse of the sky to separate day from night; they shall serve as signs for the set times—the days and the years; and they shall serve as lights in the expanse of the sky to shine upon the earth." And it was so. God made the two great lights, the greater light to dominate the day and the lesser light to dominate the night, and the stars. And God set them in the expanse of the sky to shine upon the earth, to dominate the day and the night, and to separate light from darkness. And God saw that this was good. And there was evening and there was morning, a fourth day.
>
> God said, "Let the waters bring forth swarms of living creatures, and birds that fly above the earth across the expanse of the sky." God created the great sea monsters, and all the living creatures of every kind that creep, which the waters brought forth in swarms, and all the winged birds of every kind. And God saw that this was good. God blessed them, saying, "Be fertile and increase, fill the waters in the seas, and let the birds increase on the earth." And there was evening and there was morning, a fifth day.
>
> God said, "Let the earth bring forth every kind of living creature: cattle, creeping things, and wild beasts of every kind, and all kinds of creeping things of the earth." And God saw that this was good. (Gen. 1:1–25)

He is talking to himself, but not about himself. He says nothing about who he is or what he intends, and the words he does speak are abrupt, not intended to communicate anything to anyone, least of all to explain anything, but only to enact. His first words are abrupt in the extreme. The sentence "Let there be light" (1:3), so stately in English, translates just two quick words in Hebrew: *yhi ʾor.* The one-word sentence "Light!" would be a defensible English translation; for, if the sentence is a command, it is not spoken commandingly: One does not speak commandingly to oneself. It is rather as if a carpenter reaching for his hammer were to speak the word *hammer* aloud. Compliance with such a "command" is not even remotely at issue.

The scene has no narrator. It is not presented as a vision vouchsafed to some prophet privileged to witness God at work. Yet the effect is that of eavesdropping or spying. We come upon work in progress, and what strikes us about the worker is that, though he talks to himself, he does so without the slightest hesitation. He is not musing. He has something precise in mind, and each stage in his project leads without haste but with extreme economy and directness to the next. Light, first. Then the dome of the sky, opening like a gigantic bubble in the chaos of water: water above it, water below. Then the parting of the lower waters so that dry land may appear. Then vegetation from the newly exposed land. Then, on the fourth day, sun, moon, and stars for more light and for the reckoning of time; on the fifth, the living creatures of the sea and the air; and on the sixth, the beasts of the earth.

Creator

"Where Are You?"

GENESIS 1–3

And then, when all seems to be in readiness, a wobble, a word of oblique explanation from this fellow who seems so above explanation:

> And God said, "Let us make man in our image, after our likeness. They shall rule the fish of the sea, the birds of the sky, the cattle, the whole earth, and all the creeping things that creep on earth." And God created man in His image, in the image of God He created him; male and female He created them. God blessed them and God said to them, "Be fertile and increase, fill the earth and master it; and rule the fish of the sea, the birds of the sky, and all the living things that creep on earth."
>
> God said, "See, I give you every seed-bearing plant that is upon all the earth, and every tree that has seed-bearing fruit; they shall be yours for food. And to all the animals on land, to all the birds of the sky, and to everything that creeps on earth, in which there is the breath of life, [I give] all the green plants for food." And it was so. And God saw all that He had made, and found it very good. And there was evening and there was morning, the sixth day. (Gen. 1:26–31)

The effective meaning of *image* is given in the immediately following instruction to master the earth. Why give mankind this version of the divine dominion? Because mankind makes, thereby, a better image of "us." And why fertility and increase? Because when human beings reproduce, they are the image of their creator in his creative act. Reproduction produces reproductions, images: Don't children resemble their parents? The motive for all that precedes the creation of mankind is, ultimately, provision for that culminating act by which God creates another kind of creator.

To repeat, God makes a world because he wants mankind, and he wants mankind because he wants an image. Other motives could have been operative. To choose one from the ancient Near East, he could have wanted a servant. To range later in his own story, he could have wanted a lover. He could even have wanted a worshiper.

But at this point, he is not—to judge from anything he says—a God who wants love or worship or anything that can easily be named. He wants an image. But then, why should he want that? At this point, we can only guess.

God is guarded in manner, but what is he hiding? We hear of "us" and "our" image and want to hear more. If "our" image is male and female, are "we" not male and female as well? This would be the most logical, immediate inference, but nothing that follows seems to bear it out. The text speaks of God as masculine and singular. And if this God has a private life or even, as we might say, a divine social life among other gods, he isn't admitting us to it. He seems to be entirely alone, not only without a spouse but also without a brother, a friend, a servant, or even a mythic animal. His life is about to become hopelessly entangled with the determination of his image to make images of its own. But if God's life lacked human entanglements, what kind of life would it be? We can only guess. There has been no hint of exertion in his activity. The Six Days of Creation are not like the Twelve Labors of Hercules, full of flexing muscle and dripping sweat. Unchecked, effortless sovereignty has been his defining trait. And yet, on the seventh day, he rests "from all the work of creation that He had done." Has it cost him more than we noticed at the time? Is he weaker than he lets on?

The sixth day of creation has had a slightly ambivalent outcome. His command to the male and the female he has just created is "Be fertile and increase, fill the earth and master it," and the text says, "And it was so." But it is not yet so. The male and the female have not, at this moment, shown themselves fertile, they have not increased. And God does not say of them directly, as he says directly of all his other creations, "And God saw that they were good." The final judgment, spoken by the narrator, mysteriously reading the mind of God, is rendered only on creation as a whole: "God saw all that He had made, and found it very good." "Very," for the first and only time here, but only after a faintly troubling elision where mankind is concerned. And then, suddenly, this fall into a full day of rest. God is already, at this earliest moment in his story, a mix of strength and weakness, resolve and regret.

SECOND DISTINCT ACCOUNT of creation from an originally independent source begins at Genesis 2:4. Here "God," *ʾelohim*, is replaced by "the Lord God," *yahweh ʾelohim*. The deity is called by his proper name, *yahweh*, with the common noun (rather than the alternative proper name) *ᵓelohim* added as a gloss. The English phrase "the Lord," which by convention translates *yahweh* in all English Bibles, is in fact a translation of the Hebrew word *ᵓedonay*, literally "my Lord." The word *ᵓedonay*, which is not found in the text, is what pious Jews in ancient times chose to speak rather than desecrate the sacred proper name of God by pronouncing it. At later points in his long story, God will sometimes be *ᵓelohim*, far more often *yahweh*, and on occasion one of his several less frequently used names or epithets. Though the text clearly regards all these names as referring to one and the same being, that being, as we shall see, conducts himself somewhat differently under his different names in the Book of Genesis.

The second account of creation—which, in a continuous reading, is, of course, the sequel rather than an alternative to the first account—shows a narrowing of the focus and a heightening of the tension between creator and human creature. Mankind is no longer situated on "the earth" as a gigantic natural paradise in which to be fertile and increase but only in "a garden in Eden, in the east," which God has planted and given to "the man" to till and tend. And the free mastery that mankind was to exercise as God's image is also restricted: "Of every tree of the garden you are free to eat; but as for the tree of knowledge of good and bad, you must not eat of it; for as soon as you eat of it, you shall die" (Gen. 2:17).

In the first account of creation, something is commanded but nothing is forbidden. Now, for the first time, there is a prohibition. It seems to be imposed in man's interest, but we wonder: If the man is to master the earth (recalling the first account of creation), why may he not be allowed the knowledge of good and evil? The man is offered no motive for his obedience other than one that makes no sense. And the Lord God in this second creation story seems noticeably more anxious in confrontation with his creature than God seemed in the first.

The air of anxiety grows more acute when the Lord God creates woman. In context, this second account of that event reads like the story of what really happened on the sixth day, an explanation of why God, in the first account, did not "see that they were good." The Lord God, unlike God, does not see the man as good even by inclusion. No, something is wrong with the man, and of the flaw the Lord God can only say: "It is not good for man to be alone; I will make a fitting helper for him." But all the Lord God's efforts to come up with an adequate helper fail. He brings to the man "all the wild beasts and all the birds of the sky," an extraordinary parade, and allows the man the power-laden privilege of naming them, but "no fitting helper [is] found." By clear implication, the man rejects the whole of God's labors in creating other living creatures: They may be "good," but they are not good for him. The Lord God, now genuinely laboring, driven to an extreme expedient, creates a woman from one of the man's ribs.

The man, in the first words in the Bible spoken by a human being, acclaims her with joy but without expressing any gratitude or otherwise acknowledging the Lord God:

> This at last
> Is bone of my bone
> And flesh of my flesh.
> Let this be called Woman,
> For from her man she was taken. (2:23)

In the first account of creation, the male and the female also say nothing in response to the God who has created them, but for his part God seems to expect nothing. His only expectation is that they should be, fruitfully, themselves, subduing the earth and serving, thereby, as his image. The first creation story thus contains no story whatsoever of human transgression.

How very different the expanded second account:

> The two of them were naked, the man and his wife, yet they felt no shame. Now the serpent was the shrewdest of all the wild beasts that the Lord God had made. He said to the woman, "Did God really say: You shall not eat of any tree of the garden?" The woman replied to the serpent, "We may eat of the fruit of the other trees of the garden. It is only about fruit of the tree in the middle of the garden that God said: 'You shall not eat of it or touch it, lest you die.' " And the serpent said to the woman, "You are not going to die, but God knows that as soon as you eat of it your eyes will be opened and you will be like divine beings who know good and bad." When the woman saw that the tree was good for eating and a delight to the eyes, and that the tree was desirable as a source of wisdom, she took of its fruit and ate. She also gave some to her husband, and he ate. Then the eyes of both of them were opened and they perceived that they were naked; and they sewed together fig leaves and made themselves loincloths. (2:25–3:7)

When the serpent tells the woman that, contrary to what the Lord God said, she will not die if she eats of the tree of the knowledge of good and evil, the serpent is telling the truth. She and the man do not die when they break the Lord God's command; certainly, they do not die, as the Lord God had warned, "as soon as you eat of it." Is the serpent's ability to foil the Lord God's plan a reflection on the Lord God's power? Is the serpent his rival? Or is the entire temptation episode, as we might put it, a setup? Is the serpent the Lord God's secret or unwitting agent?

One may escape all these difficulties and preserve the serpent's role as a deceiver by arguing that the couple did indeed die at once but that theirs was a spiritual rather than a physical death. This is the classic theological interpretation of "the fall of man," the "original sin." However, as we shall see again and again, the narrative we are reading is not much given to spiritualized or purely symbolic meanings but is extremely fond of deception stories of all kinds. Rather than eliminate the conflict by spiritualizing the threatened death or rationalizing the apparent deceit, we may trace the conflict back to the Lord God, a cause of both weal and woe in the lives of his creatures because good and evil impulses conflict within his character.

IN ANCIENT MESOPOTAMIA, creation was often presented as the creator divinity's victory over chaos, chaos being represented as a rival deity, a fearful watery dragon, a flood monster. Imagine the curves of a great river as the living, twisting body of a gigantic snake; imagine that this snake could engulf the land in its watery coils, as the Tigris and the Euphrates could indeed do, and you have the mythological mise-en-scène. There is undoubtedly an echo of that mythic battle in the Lord God's punishment of the serpent for tempting the woman, but scarcely more than an echo, for monotheistic editing has tamed the serpent into an opponent scarcely worthy of the Lord God. The ancient mythic materials have been rewritten so thoroughly that the serpent—the third personality absorbed in the emergent divine personality—is no longer a rival god but (recalling the first creation account) merely one of God's creatures.

As a result of this revision, the serpent's creator cannot escape responsibility for what the serpent does. But as a rarely noticed second result of the same revision, the Lord God will become a character with an interior conversation. He will rebuke the serpent; and when he does so, he will necessarily rebuke himself. What polytheism would allow to be externally directed anger against a rival deity, monotheism—even a monotheism speaking occasionally in the first person plural—must turn into the Lord God's inwardly directed regret. The appearance of divine regret, the first of its many appearances, is the first appearance of the deity as a true literary character as distinct from a mythic force or a mere meaning endowed with an allegorical voice. The peculiar, culturally determined interior life of Western man begins, in a way, with the divided interior life of the deity, and the deity's interior life begins with a creator's regret.

The turning point comes after the Lord God discovers that the man and his wife have disobeyed him:

> They heard the sound of the Lord God moving about in the garden at the breezy time of day; and the man and his wife hid from the Lord God among the trees of the garden. The Lord God called out to the man and said to him, "Where are you?" He replied, "I heard the sound of You in the garden, and I was afraid because I was naked, so I hid." Then He asked, "Who told you that you were naked? Did you eat of the tree from which I had forbidden you to eat?" The man said, "The woman You put at my side—she gave me of the tree, and I ate." And the Lord God said to the woman, "What is this you have done!" The woman replied, "The serpent duped me, and I ate." (3:8–13)

The language in which the Lord God imposes his one, unexplained command and then converses with the man and the woman after their disobedience is language that any human being might use when speaking to another. It has neither the majestic, almost abstract simplicity of the language of God in Genesis 1 nor any other poetic or rhetorical heightening. But this changes when the Lord God punishes the sin he has discovered. His condemnation of the serpent, the woman, and the man, in that order, is an explosion of fury and also, as it happens, the first extended poem in the Bible:

> Then the Lord God said to the serpent,
> "Because you did this,
> More cursed shall you be
> Than all cattle
> And all the wild beasts:
> On your belly shall you crawl

And dirt shall you eat
All the days of your life.
I will put enmity
Between you and the woman,
And between your offspring and hers;
They shall strike at your head,
And you shall strike at their heel."
And to the woman He said,
"I will make most severe
Your pangs in childbearing;
In pain shall you bear children.
Yet your urge shall be for your husband,
And he shall rule over you."

To Adam He said, "Because you did as your wife said and ate of the tree about which I commanded you, 'You shall not eat of it,'

Cursed be the ground because of you;
By toil shall you eat of it
All the days of your life:
Thorns and thistles shall it sprout for you.
But your food shall be the grasses of the field;
By the sweat of your brow
Shall you get bread to eat,
Until you return to the ground—
For from it you were taken.
For dust you are,
And to dust you shall return." (3:14–19)

This rhetorical explosion is too sudden, too massive, and too unopposed by the serpent, who never speaks or acts again, for the scene to function as a mythic battle. Any notion of cosmic conflict is further foiled by the fact that the serpent has spoken truly of a tree of which the Lord God has spoken falsely. The serpent seems to be the Lord God's dupe rather than his great enemy, and the Lord God's punishment of the human couple seems in consequence an almost wanton act. As God, rather than as the Lord God, the creator had given his human creatures all creation to live in. The Lord God, far less generous, had given them only a garden to tend. Now even that less munificent gift has been taken back.

Revoked with it, by implication, are all the earlier arrangements that were made with man in mind. If man has failed the Lord God, then, by implication, all that God put in place for man's sake, his six days' labor, is also less than a total success. But the size of the reversal is less overwhelming than its suddenness. Even if the Lord God has been playacting, even if he really did not need to ask the man and the woman where they were or then ask them "Who told you that you were naked?" we are still unprepared for the speed and ruthlessness of his vindictive reaction. Why must the Lord God, who patiently paraded all the animals of creation before the man in the attempt to find a partner for him, react with such brutal impatience to the disobedience of the woman and the seemingly innocent mistake of the man? In these utterly crucial opening moments, what kind of relationship to mankind is the Lord God seen to have?

In the first creation account, God created man to be God's own image. The second creation account is different. Here the Lord God creates man from the dust, not by the word of his mouth, and never describes his creature as made in his image. Moreover, the nakedness or otherwise of the first couple, a matter of no interest in the first account, is insisted on in the second, as also their sexual desire and their shame. However, because the second account comes as a sequel to the first and not its correction, the dust, the desire, the shame all become relevant information about the deity, the original of whom mankind continues to be the image.

And in the long, emotional outburst just quoted, the Lord God does indeed act as the original of a human creature made of dust and passion. In the first creation account, the relationship between the creator and creature is not about obedience at all. God is so magisterially powerful but also so splendidly generous that human misbehavior cannot possibly trouble his calm. His "be fertile and increase" is more a magnanimous invitation than a command. Barely two pages later, the Lord God seems not just less powerful and less generous than God but far more vindictive. Worse, he is as gratuitous in his wrath as God was gratuitous in his bounty. Everything, for the Lord God, hangs on obedience to his deceptive command.

As a character, the Lord God is disturbing as anyone is disturbing who holds immense power and seems not to know what he wants to do with it. The power of the Lord God seems rather smaller than the power of God, as far as that goes. But such as it is, this power disturbs us. The motives for its exercise are in conflict, and the relationship in which these motives conflict is uncomfortably intimate. Any frightening character is the more frightening when he stands near enough for him to touch you. The Lord God stands much nearer to his human creatures than God does. Unlike God, the Lord God touches them, physically. That touch—particularly when it occurs after their transgression—intensifies everything about him.

I have suggested that Eve's temptation by the serpent can be read as an incident in which the serpent functions as the Lord God's unwitting agent. But the text is ambiguous. Any reading of the temptation as the Lord God's cool manipulation of his creatures, one against another, must be set against the call of the Lord God in the garden, "Where are you?" (3:9). If in the first account of creation God made mankind because he wanted an image, the Lord God, in this second account, seems to have made human beings because he wanted company. And the innocent poignancy of his garden call becomes something deeper at Genesis 3:21: "And the Lord God made garments of skins for Adam and his wife, and clothed them." How can this line be read if not as the Lord God's regret about his regret? Having just inflicted labor in childbearing on her and toil in the fields on him, why should he now spare them the inconvenience of making their own clothing? Why if not because, to speak very simply, he feels bad about it all?

The Lord God might have performed any of a number of other parting services for the man and the woman as he drove them from the garden. He might have fed them, for example. Or he might have instructed them about what lay ahead. Though created as adults, they are newborn in the world and helpless. He might certainly have said something to them in mitigation of the curses still ringing in their ears. He might, above all, have explained why he had to do what he did. He does none of that. Yet there is an inherent tenderness and poignancy in what he does do, choosing to make his parting gesture the covering of their nakedness.

Some commentators—including some very modern commentators determined to have a sexually enlightened Bible—have insisted that the sin of Adam and Eve has nothing to do with sex. The words "good and bad" in the longer phrase "the tree of the knowledge of good and bad" (2:17) are taken to mean "things in general," as in the phrase "soup to nuts," and the knowledge that ensues is not taken to be a narrowly sexual knowledge. But this interpretation is undercut by what happens when the forbidden fruit is eaten: "Then the eyes of both of them were opened and they perceived that they were naked; and they sewed together fig leaves and made themselves loincloths" (3:7). It is not desire, in and of itself, but knowledge of one's desire that generates shame. Animals desire, but they do not know that they desire, or that they are the objects of desire, so they feel no shame. The man's exultant reaction on first seeing the woman (2:23) certainly implies that he desired her from the start; the use of the phrase "one flesh" (2:24) makes this even clearer. But there was a difference. The fact that "the two of them were naked . . . yet they felt no shame" (2:25), though it does not mean that the two, like little children, were without desire, does suggest that they were without knowledge of their own desire.

It is *understood* desire, *admitted* need, that shames. When the Lord God calls out "Where are you?" is he admitting his own need and consciously compromising the perfection of his sovereignty? As we might more simply put it, does he miss them? Are the two humans, in their now shameful desire for each other, all the more perfect an image of him, who desired them enough to create them but only understood what he was doing after the fact? Is it this—their presentation to him of himself not as exercising mastery but as experiencing need—that enrages him? And is he, his rage spent, ashamed of his own desire and moved to cover his shame by covering theirs?

More can always be read into an action than into a statement, but this particular action cries out for explanation. Fresh from the very paroxysm of his rage, why does the Lord God suddenly grow so tender, dressing, as it were, the wound he has just inflicted? Note that the Lord God does not simply provide garments of skins for his shamed, punished, and humiliated creatures; he himself puts these garments on their bare bodies. In its suddenness and intimacy, this quasi-parental gesture is, we shall have occasion to see later, characteristic of the Lord God.

The tenderness is disarming, but it only makes the inconsistency the more unnerving, for the same Lord God who is tender with his creatures says in the verse immediately following (3:22): "Now that the man has become like one of us, knowing good and bad, what if he should stretch out his hand and take also from the tree of life and eat, and live forever!" Proof is given again that the serpent was speaking the truth when he said: "You are not going to die, but God knows that as soon as you eat of [the fruit of the forbidden tree] your eyes will be opened and you will be like divine beings who know good and bad" (3:4–5). By the Lord God's own testimony, this is just what has happened. But why did the Lord God seek to conceal that this is what would happen? And why does the Lord God want to stop mankind from living forever? If God's only motive in making mankind was that mankind should be God's image, and if God himself lives forever, then why should mankind not live forever?

Would immortality—if the Lord God would but permit it—not facilitate obedience to God's only positive commands to mankind, "Be fertile and increase, fill the earth and master it"?

The Lord God's expressed worry throws us back on our earlier observation that his purposes ominously include the presumptively hostile purposes of the serpent. The Lord God, half-conscious as he is, seems to be playing a double game. He does not address his explanation, his determination that mankind not "become like one of us," to the first humans. No, though this is evidently the real truth of the matter, he regards this truth, anxiously, as not for their ears. God—lofty, unwavering, and sincere in his creative actions—has become as the Lord God intimate, volatile, and prone to dark regrets and darker equivocations. The Lord God *is* God. There are not two protagonists in this text, only one. But this one protagonist has two strikingly distinct personalities.

Destroyer

"I Regret That I Made Them"

GENESIS 4–11

Though the Lord God put the man in the garden of Eden "to till it and tend it," an antiagriculturalist tilt is discernible in the fact that agricultural rather than pastoral or other labor is singled out as the punishment for sin. Gatherers and hunters being the forebears of farmers and shepherds, echoes of the same tension may be heard in God's provision of only vegetable food at Genesis 1:29. But it is the story of Cain and Abel that historians read as the Bible's most explicit mythical presentation of the age-old conflict:

> Now the man knew his wife Eve, and she conceived and bore Cain, saying, "I have gained a male child with the help of the Lord." She then bore his brother Abel. Abel became a keeper of sheep, and Cain became a tiller of the soil. In the course of time, Cain brought an offering to the Lord from the fruit of the soil; and Abel, for his part, brought the choicest of the firstlings of his flock. The Lord paid heed to Abel and his offering, but to Cain and his offering He paid no heed. Cain was much distressed and his face fell. And the Lord said to Cain,
>
> "Why are you angry and downcast?
> Surely, if you do right,
> You ought to hold your head high.
> Sin crouches at the door
> Lusting for you,
> Yet you can master it."
> [Previous six lines: my translation]
>
> Cain said to his brother Abel, "Come, let us go out into the field," and when they were in the field, Cain set upon his brother Abel and killed him. The Lord said to Cain, "Where is your brother Abel?" And he said, "I do not know. Am I my brother's keeper?" Then He said, "What have you done? Hark, your brother's blood cries out to Me from the ground! Therefore, you shall be more cursed than the ground, which opened its mouth to receive your brother's blood from your hand. If you till the soil, it shall no longer yield its strength to you. You shall become a ceaseless wanderer on earth."

> Cain said to the Lord, "My punishment is too great to bear! Since You have banished me this day from the soil, and I must avoid Your presence and become a restless wanderer on earth—anyone who meets me may kill me!" The Lord said to him, "I promise, if anyone kills Cain, sevenfold vengeance shall be taken on him." And the Lord put a mark on Cain, lest anyone who met him should kill him. Cain left the presence of the Lord and settled in the land of Nod, east of Eden. (Gen. 4:1–16)

Whatever this brief episode may say about a prehistoric struggle between shepherds and farmers, or about archetypes of good and evil, it also makes a basic statement about the Lord; it says when the man and the woman—now called Adam and Eve—were driven out of the garden of Eden, he went with them. This could scarcely have been predicted from Genesis 1–3, whose last verse reads: "He drove the man out, and stationed east of the garden of Eden the cherubim and the fiery ever-turning sword to guard the way to the tree of life." The Bible could well have ended with that verse, such is its sense of finality. Genesis 1–3, rediscovered in modern times, could have been added to archaeology's treasure house as one more deciphered, recovered ancient Near Eastern text. Nobody, so to speak, would have been any the wiser.

In fact, however, when the Lord God dressed the man and his wife in skins, he was giving them not a parting gift but a clue that his relationship with them would continue. What is this relationship to be? On this cosmic morning after, they do not know, and neither do we. The commands about trees in the garden of Eden are now obviously moot. The earlier command to "be fertile and increase" has not been abrogated, but what else might the Lord God want? And what is he going to do? What, after so devastating a reversal, is mankind to expect of him?

God and the Lord God differ strikingly in their attitude toward mankind as created in the divine image or otherwise akin to the deity. God spoke of creating mankind "in our image"; the Lord God did not. In fact, the Lord God takes a diametrically opposed position when he warns the heavenly "us" (3:22) that the man might "become like one of us" in knowledge; this is very nearly to warn of man's being in God's image. The Lord God objects even more, however, to the prospect that the man might resemble God by living forever, and, consistently, he reduces mankind to mortality: "For dust you are,/ And to dust you shall return" (3:19). God's command to the male and the female to "be fertile and increase" was ungrudging and unqualified. The Lord God wants mankind to live, but not forever, and to multiply, but not without pain.

In Genesis 6:1–4, it is the sons of God, not any sons of the Lord, who are attracted by human females and lie with them. And it is the Lord who objects to this coupling. What he objects to is not miscegenation but simply that superabundance of fruitfulness which results from life spans lasting centuries. His earlier curse of mortality has not precluded this, so he adds a proviso to it. After the fact, again, the Lord—not God—decides on a maximum human life span of 120 years.

Though the deity thus seems different when he is the Lord and when he is God, it remains true that whatever is predicated of him under either name is predicated of him under both names. He is one character with, at this point in his life, two (or, counting his serpentine side, two times two) personalities. Just this ambiguity raises the level of emotional tension in the story of Cain and Abel.

Cain and Abel—the first two children of Adam and Eve—each bring the Lord (the text uses "the Lord" rather than "the Lord God" in this episode and either "the Lord" or "God" from this point on) an offering. Why? The Lord has asked for no offering. He likes Abel's offering but not Cain's, and Cain is angry. Why? What is Cain expecting? As in Genesis 2–3, the Lord speaks to Cain as a somewhat impetuous man might speak to a fellow man. As before, he speaks principally to condemn. But it is crucial to note that the condemnation does not arise from Cain's having broken any commandment of the Lord. The Lord has given no command not to kill. After the murder, when he says to Cain, "Hark, your brother's blood cries out to Me from the ground!" it is as if he has at that moment discovered that murder merits condemnation. There is a groping and tentative quality on both sides of this relationship. The metaphor—"your brother's blood cries out to Me"—may bespeak agitation rather than moral condemnation. Something is wrong, but does the Lord yet quite know what it is? The Lord acts and then infers his own intention from what he has done.

Cain's punishment is an intensification of Adam's. "Cursed be the ground because of you," the Lord God said to Adam; "by toil shall you eat of it/All the days of your life" (3:17). Cain's curse is that when he works the land it will yield nothing, and he will become a wanderer. Cain interprets his banishment as a severing of his relationship with the Lord: "I must avoid Your presence" (the New

Revised Standard Version reads, more literally, "I shall be hidden from your face"). But the value of this relationship, like the value of life, is discovered only after it has been lost. According to Genesis 4:26, it was only in the generation after that of Cain and Abel that "men began to invoke the Lord by name." Cain and Abel only discover as they make offerings that the Lord is a being to whom offerings may be made. And the Lord himself only discovers his role as a regulator of human affairs as he begins to regulate them. Mankind is discovering what its life will be after Eden, and the Lord is discovering or determining what his relationship will be to his image as the image reproduces itself in circumstances so different from those he planned. The "Elohist" ("God") account of the first act of human generation (5:1–3) differs in several ways from the "Yahwist" ("Lord") account that precedes the story of Cain and Abel. Alert readers will notice that the "God" account makes Seth, not Cain, the first child. But note also that the "God" account makes reproduction the image of divine creativity and, consistently, omits any mention of woman's role: "When God created man, He made him in the likeness of God; male and female He created them. And when they were created, He blessed them and called them Man. When Adam had lived 130 years, he begot a son in his likeness after his image" (5:1–3). The "Lord" account, by contrast, begins with sexual intercourse—"Now the man knew his wife Eve" (4:1)—and omits any mention of divine-human resemblance.

THESE INDICATIONS of divine ambivalence toward human sexual fertility and thereby toward mankind's status as image of the divine creator pale, however, by comparison with an action that exposes the deepest of all fault lines in the divine character. In the story of the flood, the creator—both as God and as the Lord—becomes an outright destroyer. For a brief but terrifying period, the serpent in him, the enemy of mankind, takes over completely.

The story of the flood, like the story of creation, is told twice; but, unlike the two creation stories, the two flood stories are interwoven. This is the more easily possible because the two versions are structurally identical. In both, the deity decides to destroy all human and animal life by drowning it in a great flood. In both, Noah and his family are spared, being warned to prepare an ark in which to ride out the flood. In both, after the flood recedes, there is a new divine-human beginning. The inconsistencies lie in the details. How many animals is Noah to take on the ark? The "God" version says two of every kind (6:19); the "Lord" version says seven pairs of the clean, one pair of the unclean (7:2). These "doublets" fatten up and slow down the typically lean and swift style that otherwise characterizes the Book of Genesis, but they do not obscure the common plot.

Of much greater importance is a striking difference in mood between the Lord and God in the two accounts. The Lord acts because of his own feelings, his regret; God acts because a cleansing destruction is what the world needs. Thus, in Genesis 6:5–8, the Lord is embittered, and it is out of this bitterness that the destruction arises: "I will blot out from the earth the men whom I created—men together with beasts, creeping things, and birds of the sky; for I regret that I made them" (6:7). An exception is made for Noah, but it is not for Noah's sake—not to make a fresh start at creation with Noah as the new Adam—that the earth is destroyed. The destruction is not a means, it is an end, an expressive not an instrumental act. Though the Lord will in fact make a covenant with Noah after the flood, he foresees no such covenant at the start. In Genesis 6:11–22, by clear contrast, God acts without anger and with perfect knowledge of what he is about. He foresees the new covenant, and the steps that lie between his decision to destroy the earth and his proclamation of a new covenant follow, each upon the last, with the same cool mastery on display during the seven days of creation.

Afterward, when the waters have receded and Noah and his company are back on dry land, Noah makes a burnt offering to the Lord, the first such burning mentioned in the Bible, and "the Lord smelled the pleasing odor, and the Lord said to Himself: 'Never again will I doom the earth because of man, since the devisings of man's mind are evil from his youth; nor will I ever again destroy every living being, as I have done' " (8:21). The Lord, who has never said that mankind, even by inclusion in the goodness of creation, was good, repeats even at this moment that "the devisings of man's mind are evil from his youth"; that is, mankind is born evil, incorrigible. And were it not for the pleasing odor of the burnt offering, what would the outcome have been? The Lord has not planned every step of the flood in advance. His anger, and the violence that arose from it, was an interpersonal outburst of temper; it was a morose reaction without any clear consciousness of just what that human evil consisted of. His promise to refrain from further catastrophic violence is altogether unpremeditated and still lacks any stipulation of what he wants mankind to do or refrain from doing.

In short, the Lord has to be seduced out of a recurrence of his rage by the scent of Noah's offering. God, by contrast, requires no offering from Noah. It is, rather, the other way around: God gives Noah a sign, the rainbow, that "never again shall all flesh be cut off by the waters of a flood" (9:11). And the covenant is not just with Noah but with all his descendants—that is, with the whole human race, since all will now be descended from him—and, beyond the human race, as always when God is speaking, the covenant is with all of physical reality. The Lord, as before, does not bless. God blesses copiously, exhorting Noah and "your offspring to come" with a warmth greater than we heard at the first creation: "Be fertile, then, and increase; abound on the earth and increase on it" (9:7).

God speaks with something like the Lord's passion at just one point; namely, the point at which he imposes his own first prohibition on mankind, stipulating, in effect, what mankind must do to avoid another destruction of the world. God indicated before the flood that it was human violence (6:11–13) that required the destruction of the world. After the flood, in what is perhaps the most lapidary single line in the Bible, he puts the same view in the form of an implacable command. The line—*šopek dam ha'adam ba'adam damo yišapek*—puns on the similarity in Hebrew of the words *dam*, "blood," and *'adam*, "human being." I would translate it "Shed man's blood, by man be your blood shed" (9:6).

Why does bloodshed matter so much to God? The full sentence seems to contain an explanation: "Shed man's blood, by man be your blood shed, for God made man in his own image." Unlike the Lord, God sees his creature as an image of himself. But just why this leads to a prohibition on interhuman violence is not quite self-evident. Do we infer that human beings must revere one another as they revere God, since to profane God's image is to profane God? This is the explanation that comes most readily to mind, but it is anachronistic: At this point in the Bible, God has not yet asked for reverence, much less for worship, from his human creatures. Neither has the Lord done so. Beginning Bible readers are sometimes charmed by the casual, person-to-person way that the deity—especially when he is called "the Lord"—speaks to mankind. He seems to expect no reverence at all. But if we take this point with full seriousness, we must ask whether he yet knows that he deserves reverence. But, again, if there is no indication that he does know it, and there is truly none, we may need to base his prohibition of murder on something other than a demand for reverence.

It is striking that the line "Shed man's blood, by man be your blood shed," which would make so appropriate a conclusion to the story of Cain and Abel, concludes, instead, the story of the flood. This prohibition of human bloodshed comes just after the Lord/God has shed a great deal of human blood or, at any rate, taken a great deal of human life. Just as the one command the Lord gave after God had created the world was a restriction on human procreative power, so the one command given after the Lord/God destroys the world is God's restriction on human destructive power. Destruction is forbidden because God is a destroyer as well as a creator. Reverence aside, a human being engaging in either destruction or creation becomes his rival.

A destroyer as well as a creator? Historical criticism has long since noted the similarity of the biblical flood story, in both its general structure and a number of salient details, to the comparable myth in Babylonia. In that myth, as in this one, ten generations lie between the creation of the world and its destruction; divine wrath summons up a flood; the hero seals his boat with pitch; the deity smells a burnt offering afterward; and so on. There are two differences between the Babylonian and the biblical myths, however. First, at least in its synthetic form, the biblical myth provides the deity with an ethical pretext for punishing mankind: His action is not gratuitous; mankind deserves it. Second, and far more important, the Babylonian myth pits Marduk against the watery chaos-monster Tiamat. In other words, one god starts the flood; another god—after an epic battle—ends it. There are not two gods in the Book of Genesis, despite my deliberate contrastings of the Lord with God: There is just one, called at some times the Lord and at other times God. But in each of the two biblical flood stories that have been edited into a single story—the "Lord" version and the "God" version—a serpentine, watery destroyer (elsewhere called, in Hebrew, Rahab) has been wholly absorbed into the Lord/God, the creator.

In the second creation story, we noted that the serpent had only a residually independent role. Obscurely, the serpent's purposes were also the purposes of the Lord. In the two flood stories, the destroyer lacks even that residual independence. Her hostile personality (Tiamat/Rahab is a goddess) has been absorbed into the personalities of the Lord and of God. Her watery physical reality has been reduced to an instrument in his hands. The Lord and God are different both as creators and as destroyers, but the equation that gives us the character of the deity as the floodwaters recede is not *yahweh* + *ʾelohim*. It is (*yahweh* + Tiamat) + (*ʾelohim* + Tiamat).

Under either of his principal names, the creator has proven to us that he has the capacity to be a destroyer. Each of the two (now interwoven) versions of the ancient Israelite flood story is a monotheistic appropriation of an originally polytheistic story. In each, two opposing deities—one the friend and the other the enemy of humankind—have fused. It might not be too much to say that in the brooding, vindictive Lord, Tiamat is ascendant, while in calm, majestic God, Marduk is ascendant. All the same, the Lord and God both seem too fully and freshly imagined for us to speak of them as merely two versions of the same "recipe." Each is the fruit of a distinct artistic and religious breakthrough.

Neither the Lord nor God nor the combination of the Lord and God yet includes all that will eventually be drawn into the divine character, but even now both—each with this radical fault between creator and destroyer running through him—are coherent and original quasi-human personalities. And to take the Bible at its word, each personality, thus doubled, belongs to one and the same character.

Once again, at Genesis 9:17, we have reached a moment that could easily have been the closing moment of the Bible. Creation has been followed by sin, then by violence and catastrophe, and then by a triumphant new creation and an eternal covenant against violence. But the story is not over, and as it continues the doubled and quadrupled memory of God in these essential opening chapters will linger.

Despite the rainbow, the Lord God cannot now cease to be an object of fear as well as admiration. Though he has sworn that he will never again destroy the world, he will eventually threaten to break his word. Even before the actual threats begin, however, he remains a permanently threatening presence. We realize what he is capable of, and we cannot forget it. He is not just unpredictable but dangerously unpredictable.

CREATOR/DESTROYER

"Do Not Raise Your Hand Against the Boy"

GENESIS 12–25:11

Ethically, there would seem to be an abyss of difference between parenthood and murder; the latter is a crime, the former simply an inframoral fact. Psychologically, however, the two are linked as life and death are linked. Fertility is to sterility as life is to death. Control over the positive term in either pair implies control over the negative. Thus, if God gives fertility to mankind, and if mankind thereafter —in the language of the Revised Standard Version translation of Genesis 1—"ha[s] dominion over" his own fertility, then mankind also has dominion over sterility. This power, the power to decide who will be born, is of the same order as the power to decide who will die.

The Lord, as we saw earlier, did not know that he wished to deny humankind the power to decide who would die until the first murder was committed and the blood cried out from the ground. Similarly, he did not know that he wished to restrict human dominion over life until he noticed mankind multiplying. Though the stated reason for the flood is mankind's corruption, the brief episode immediately preceding (Gen. 6:1–4), a kind of prelude to the flood story, suggests that the unchecked multiplication of humans also played a part.

In Genesis 12 and the remaining chapters of the Book of Genesis, we see the deity—both as the Lord and as God—in an ongoing struggle with mankind over control of human fertility. This is the subtly aggressive meaning of the Lord's statement to Abram at 12:1–3, opening the long narrative cycle:

> Go forth from your native land and from your father's house to the land that I will show you.
>
> I will make of you a great nation,
> And I will bless you;
> I will make your name great,
> And you shall be a blessing.
> I will bless those who bless you
> And curse him that curses you;

And all the families of the earth
Shall bless themselves by you.

The Lord's promise to make Abram a great nation, that is, to make him fertile, is a repossession of a power that earlier seemed to have been entrusted to mankind without the need of any further divine participation. This repossession of the power to give life parallels God's earlier repossession of the power to take life. No promise of fertility to Abram should be necessary, since God has already ordered all humankind to be fertile and increase. But, on the one hand, if Abram needs a special promise from the Lord to become a great nation, then he does not possess the power to become a great nation on his own; and, on the other hand, if the Lord has not made this promise to every nation, then humanity's overall reproductive autonomy is reduced.

The premise of the narrative, in other words, is that in human fertility, as in mortal combat, whatever gives life to you takes life from me, and vice versa. At 9:6 God's seeming command against murder merely turns the law of blood revenge into divine action by proxy: Yes, every murderer will be murdered in turn, and men will do the killing, but God lays claim to their action as, instrumentally, his own. What may seem revenge to them is actually his exercise of his exclusive prerogative to take life. Genesis 12:1–3 has the same utterly motiveless energy that both of the creation accounts have. And, as the Bible could have ended at two points before this one, so it could have started here. The narrative is a fresh beginning, and Abram never gives any indication that he has heard of Adam or Noah or of God's earlier words or deeds. Abram knows God only from what God says and does to Abram himself. The reader, however, may make the comparisons that Abram does not, and the comparisons will reveal a striking difference between this beginning and those earlier ones.

The Lord does not say to Abram, "Go to the land that I will show you and there *be fertile and increase*." No, it is the Lord who will give the fertility; it is he who will govern the multiplication. Abram's fertility will become such a byword that others will wish one another well by wishing likeness to him (this is the meaning of "you shall be a blessing"). The inference, however, is that, lacking comparable divine assistance, none will match Abram in fertility. In context, the Lord is taking back from mankind a large measure of the gift of life. But does he realize this about himself? Or will human action be necessary to force upon him an awareness of his own jealousy?

Abram obeys, but silently. He goes to Shechem in Canaan, a place whose eventual importance in the story of Abram's offspring will be matched only by Jerusalem. The Lord appears to him for a second time, this time to promise him that the land, though at that time the Canaanites still rule it, will be given to Abram's offspring. Abram moves on to a place between Bethel and Ai, builds an altar to the Lord, and invokes his name, but then his resistance begins.

There comes a famine in the land, and Abram with his wife Sarai goes to Egypt. Claiming that Sarai is so beautiful the Egyptians will kill him to possess her, Abram tells her to say that she is his sister and to join Pharaoh's household as a concubine. There is, in fact, no evident danger. The Lord afflicts Pharaoh's household with plagues because of Sarai's presence there; but when Pharaoh discovers what has happened, he merely remonstrates with Abram—"Why did you not tell me that she was your wife?"—and sends the husband and wife on their way. The conflict, in truth, is not between Pharaoh and Abram but between the Lord and Abram, who does not want fertility on the terms offered and attempts to give it away.

Abram gives his wife to Pharaoh to act out his displeasure with the Lord. Against the Lord's wishes, Abram is giving offspring to Pharaoh by giving Sarai to Pharaoh. The Lord intervenes to reassert his control. Abram, who gave no reply to the Lord, though he did obey, also gives no explanation to Pharaoh, though again, bowing to superior force alone, he obeys. Back at Bethel/Ai, the Lord appears to Abram for a third time, again promising him offspring and possession of the land of Canaan and ordering him, "Up, walk about the land, through its length and its breadth" (13:17). Again Abram obeys. Again he says nothing.

Abram's silence is even more striking in Genesis 13. Lot, Abram's nephew, who is living in Sodom, is taken captive by an alliance of four kings in a local war. Abram leads a successful war party to rescue him but without invoking the Lord. Afterward, having defeated the four kings, Abram accepts the blessing of the priest Melchizedek in the name of what appears to be another god, "God Most High" (*ʾel ʿelyon* in Hebrew). Abram declines to accept any spoils of war, saying that he has sworn to this god, this "Creator of heaven and earth," that "I will not take so much as a thread or a sandal strap of what is yours" (14:22–23). Are the Lord and this creator the same being? Did Abram swear any such oath before starting his military campaign, or is he merely improvising something politic on the spur of the moment? Either way, the Lord himself is little more than a bystander in this sequence of events.

Against the background of Abram's silence and the Lord's non-participation in Abram's battle, the words the Lord speaks at the beginning of Genesis 15 have an ironic effect:

> Fear not, Abram,
> I am a shield to you;
> Your reward shall be very great.

These words, coming to Abram in a vision, should have been spoken before, not after, the battle with the four kings. The Lord seems, after the fact, to be claiming Abram's victory as his own. Abram's reply, the first words we have ever heard him speak to the Lord, seizes the moment of potential embarrassment for the Lord to press his complaint: "Divine Lord, what use are your gifts? I am still childless, and a slave born in my house will be my heir" (my translation). The Lord's fourth promise to Abram follows, and for the first time we are told in so many words that Abram believed the Lord and that the Lord "reckoned it to his merit." In other words, the Lord thought Abram had done well to take the Lord at his word as regarded offspring. As for the land, Abram's first words are again an expression of doubt regarding a promise: "Divine Lord, how can I believe that I shall possess it?" (my translation). The Lord's promise is again renewed, along with a prediction of oppression in Egypt, but this time we are not told whether Abram believes the Lord. The silence is not deafening, but it is distinctly audible.

The effect of the Lord's four-times-repeated promise of fertility is to inspire not trust but doubt in the reader. Historical scholarship sees these promise stories as separately preserved versions of the same story edited into a single, synthetic account. Be that as it may, the effect of the repetition cannot be gainsaid. A promise that was superfluous in the first place is repeated, repeated, repeated again to what becomes, as it is not kept, an effect of mounting unease. The initial effect of the promise was to compromise an earlier gift, and now it seems that the promise is not being fulfilled. Does the Lord lack the power to keep his promise? Does he lack the will?

Ten more years go by, and no child is born. Sarai does not say that she is barren but rather, reflecting the fact that the Lord has installed himself as the custodian and guarantor of her fertility, says,

"The Lord has kept me from bearing" (16:2). She sends Abram to her Egyptian servant girl, Hagar, angrily, in defiance of the Lord, rather as Abram earlier sent her to Pharaoh. She too seeks to turn the Lord's coercive gift, by countercoercion, into offspring for the Egyptians. But Sarai is of two minds. When Hagar conceives and grows haughty, Sarai drives her into the desert—in effect, to her likely death. Ironically, "the angel of the Lord" (the expression means "an apparition of the Lord") comes to Hagar and promises her that she will bear a son, Ishmael, and that Ishmael's offspring will be a multitude—and then sends her back to Sarai. It is the timing that makes God's promise to Hagar ironic. The woman is already pregnant. The Lord's promise of fertility to her *after* she has conceived is rather like his promise of safety to Abram *after* Abram has been victorious in battle. In both cases, the Lord seems to be co-opting rather than causing. Moreover, he is more interested in foiling Sarai than in fostering Hagar. Or so at least it could be. His real intentions are obscure.

Thirteen more years pass. Abram is now ninety-nine years old. The Lord appears to him (Gen. 17) and repeats his promise for the fifth time. Each repetition to this point has been more elaborate: (1) brief speech, (2) somewhat less brief speech, (3) long speech, (4) longer speech plus ritual, and now (5) much longer speech plus circumcision for Abram and all the males of his household plus new, symbolic names, Abraham and Sarah, for Abram and Sarai. Abram, reacting to the announcement of all this, falls on his face laughing and says to himself (17:17): "Can a child be born to a man a hundred years old, or can Sarah bear a child at ninety?" Abram has already fallen on his face once in this chapter, at 17:3, when the Lord said: "I am El Shaddai. Walk in My ways and be blameless. I will establish My covenant between Me and you, and I will make you exceedingly numerous." The name *ʾel šadday* is of obscure origin. The word *šadday* may mean, or suggest, mountains. But the tradition in the use and earliest translation of this name, "God Almighty," makes it clear that, of all the titles applied to God in Hebrew, it is the one most intended to convey raw power. Abram's initial prostration seems to be an awestruck acknowledgment of that power, but his second, laughing prostration quickly calls that first one into question. Abram knows God not from the creation or the flood, we recall, but only from God's words and deeds toward him. From those alone, what is he to make of God?

Abram, still without an heir born of his wife, last heard from the Lord twenty-three years earlier, when he was seventy-six. On that by now perhaps only dimly remembered occasion, the promise was, as ever, offspring. But no offspring have been born. And now the divine promiser appears once again, calling himself this time by the most august and imposing title available, repeating for the fifth time the unkept promise, and demanding that the ninety-nine-year-old penis be bared to the knife. Is it any wonder that Abram laughs?

To say this is not to make a latter-day, extraneous kind of humor at the expense of the sacred text. The humor, no less than the human antagonist's bitter laughter, is in the text. While it is true that life spans in the early chapters of Genesis are of mythic length, Abram is still a very old man, and the text itself draws attention to his age. To make this clear, we can reduce the numbers without any reduction in the effect. Abram will die at the age of 175 (25:7). If we set 100 years as a contemporary upper limit, then, equivalently, Abram was 57 and childless when the Lord made his fourth promise and is now 70 and still childless as the Lord, not having been heard from in 13 (rather than 23) years, shows up promising fertility and demanding circumcision. The promise, made now for the fifth time and with rhetorical flourish to a man who has heard it all four times before, is ludicrous. The covenant itself is also little short of outlandish. Though "God Almighty" opens his address to Abram by saying "Walk in My ways and be blameless," blameless behavior is not required of Abram by the formal terms of the covenant that then follows. All that is asked is, humiliatingly, his foreskin, the foreskins of the males of his household, and, the supreme irony, the foreskins of all the promised males of his future progeny, no legitimate one of whom has yet been born.

Abram replies to "God Almighty" in one witheringly sarcastic sentence: "O that Ishmael might live by Your favor!" Ishmael! To bring up Ishmael, to wish long life for Ishmael, is to say, in effect, "I expect no other offspring than the one illegitimate son I now have." It is to greet God's latest grandiose promise with insulting skepticism. Twenty-three years earlier, Abram begged the Lord that Ishmael, the Egyptian slave's bastard, *not* be his only heir, and the Lord, taking him outside and pointing to the sky, said: "Look toward heaven and count the stars, if you are able to count them. . . . So shall your offspring be" (15:5). This time, Abram will not be led on. Ishmael is his only heir. He refuses to hope for others.

The Lord's demand for a piece of Abram's penis is vividly consistent with all the ambivalence he has previously shown toward human potency in general and Abram's in particular. Circumcision is not the sign of the covenant in some arbitrary and purely external way as if it were a tonsure or a ritual scar. Abram's penis—and the penises, the sexual potency, of his descendants—is what the covenant is about. God is demanding that Abram concede, symbolically, that his fertility is not his own to exercise without divine let or hindrance. A physical reduction in the literal superabundance of Abram's penis is a sign with an intrinsic relationship to what it signifies. Abram, to judge from his bitter laughter and reported skeptical thoughts, does not believe the Lord's promises. He does make the requested concession. But what is he thinking? We do not know. He does not add a word to his "O that Ishmael might live by Your favor!" He merely goes through the motions: He surrenders, as ordered, his own foreskin, his son's (Ishmael is now thirteen), and those of all the males in his household. The text does not conceal the strangeness of the moment.

THERE NOW follows, in Genesis 18–19, an episode that may illustrate why the Bible has been called a masterpiece of editing. Historians believe that an ancient redactor combined written and oral legends, some from varying Israelite sources, others from foreign sources, into a single narrative. This narrative, now the Book of Genesis, stretched from the beginning of the world to just before the birth of the nation. As a compendium of received answers to questions about origins, it addresses many queries. Its overriding question is: Where did Israel come from? But at Genesis 11:1–8 the redactor finds a place for an old legend answering the questions Why are people so scattered about the world, and why do they speak such different languages? So too at Genesis 18–19, the narrative includes answers to miscellaneous Israelite questions such as: Why are there such strange salt formations along the Dead Sea? How did the desert along its eastern shore get to be a desert when we know there were once cities there? and Why are the Moabites and Ammonites, who live so near us and seem related to us, so repugnant to us? But the story that answers these questions comes just after Abraham's trust in the Lord has turned to incredulous laughter, and by its placement—the redactor's brilliant move—the story occasions an extraordinary twist in the struggle between the Lord and Abraham over Abraham's sexual powers.

The story opens at Genesis 18, when the Lord appears to Abraham in the form of three men. Since God, in later theology, is understood always as a singular being, commentary has traditionally rationalized this apparition, defining the three as the Lord accompanied by two male, angelic attendants. But if the Lord may appear in the guise of one man, he may also appear in the guise of three. When Abraham first looks up, what he sees is explicitly "three men," as clear a sign as any in the Old Testament of how literally the creation of humankind "in our image" may sometimes be taken. Both the gender and the number count. The Lord is a singularity, but as to his appearance, he may look either like the one man who appeared to Hagar or, as here, like a group of men. Throughout the episode, the two designations "the Lord" and "the men" alternate, and there is no internally consistent way to separate them.

Abraham orders food prepared for "the men," and one of them, after inquiring "Where is your wife Sarah?" volunteers: "I will return to you next year, and your wife Sarah shall have a son!" (18:10). This is the sixth futile promise, and this time, from inside the tent, where she has been listening, out of sight, it is Sarah who laughs:

> And Sarah laughed to herself, saying, "Now that I am withered, am I to have enjoyment—with my husband so old?" Then the Lord said to Abraham, "Why did Sarah laugh, saying, 'Shall I in truth bear a child, old as I am?' Is anything too wondrous for the Lord? I will return to you at the time next year, and Sarah shall have a son." Sarah lied, saying, "I did not laugh," for she was frightened. But He replied, "You did laugh." (18:12–15)

Though Sarah is said to be afraid of the Lord, the Lord seems indignant that he is not being taken seriously. (It is such exchanges as these, by the way, that have led some critics to speculate that portions of the opening books of the Bible are the work of a woman.)

There follows an extraordinary conversation (18:16–33) in which, with elegant sarcasm on both sides, the Lord first mocks Abraham's righteousness and his very trust in the Lord and Abraham follows by mocking, at one and the same time, the Lord's power and his veracity. With Abraham's and Sarah's laughter still ringing in the air, the Lord says grandly, almost collegially:

> Shall I hide from Abraham what I am about to do, since Abraham is to become a great and populous nation and all the nations of the earth are to bless themselves by him? For I have singled him out,

> that he may instruct his children and his posterity to keep the way of the Lord by doing what is just and right, in order that the Lord may bring about for Abraham what He has promised him. (18:17–19)

Neither Abram/Abraham's own righteousness nor that of his uncountable promised offspring was mentioned as a *motive* for the Lord's earlier promises to Abram/Abraham. As now announced, this motive carries within it a tacit threat. The Lord is telling Abraham why the promise of offspring might *not* be kept: Abraham might not be righteous enough to deserve it.

Is Abraham righteous enough? Earlier, when Abraham believed in the Lord's promise of offspring, the Lord "reckoned it to his merit" (15:6). And now? Abraham seems no longer to believe the Lord's promise, and neither does his wife. Has he thereby forfeited his righteousness? Where we might expect the Lord to say, magnanimously, "Shall I hide from Abraham what I am about to do . . . ? No, *for he is righteous,* and I have singled him out . . . ," we read only, "No, for I have singled him out. . . ." In this context, it is a kind of toying cruelty for the Lord to take Abraham into his confidence about the judgment to be rendered on the unrighteousness of Sodom and Gomorrah.

How does Abraham react to this manipulation? "Abraham came forward": The narrative is bold, almost brutal in its economy. Mortal, fallen man, in a moment when Almighty God stands poised to destroy, should fall back, not step forward. Abraham comes forward and addresses the Lord with aggressive, sarcastic, insinuating flattery of his own, all playing off the Lord's invidious introduction of righteousness as a condition for Abraham's potency:

> Will You sweep away the innocent along with the guilty? What if there should be fifty innocent within the city; will You then wipe out the place and not forgive it for the sake of the innocent fifty who are in it? Far be it from You to do such a thing, to bring death upon the innocent as well as the guilty, so that innocent and guilty fare alike. Far be it from You! Shall not the Judge of all the earth deal justly? (18:23–25)

Abraham is not bound to Sodom by any particular ties of tenderness or loyalty. True, his nephew Lot lives there, but he and Lot have had a tense parting of the ways, and at their parting Abram renounced all claim on Sodom and the adjacent plains. For him, Sodom is a foreign city, one with which he has pointedly declined even to establish relations (14:22–24). No, against what some pious commentators have claimed, the point of Abraham's "bargaining" with the Lord in this passage is not to show either Abraham's or the Lord's mercy. The point of the dialogue is to show the depth of Abraham's resentment of the broken promise of fertility and his contempt for what seems an eleventh-hour attempt on God's part to abrogate the promise. Abraham is saying to the Lord, in effect: "You say you will, but will you? And when you don't, your excuse will be, will it not, some defect in my righteousness?"

Abraham's politeness to the God at whom he and his wife have just laughed is deliberately excessive: "Far be it from You to do such a thing. . . . Far be it from You!" Does the Lord, with pseudo-magnanimity, invite Abraham to participate collegially in the justice of divine judgment on Sodom? Very well! Abraham accepts the invitation, addressing his divine colleague hyperdeferentially as "Judge of all the earth" while implying that his judgment will never be carried out. Abraham argues the Lord down from fifty to forty-five to forty to thirty to twenty to ten. He does not go on, but therein lies the delicacy of the insult. "To one?" the reader hears in his mind, and so, surely, does the Lord. "To none?"

Abraham accompanies the "men" toward Sodom. And then they—the Lord is now described as two men—call on Lot in Sodom as the three had called on Abraham. The two are received with identical hospitality. But when evening falls the people of the town—*"to the last man"* in allusion to Abraham's bargaining—surround Lot's house and call out to Lot (NRSV translation): "Where are the men who came to you tonight? Bring them out to us, so that we may know them." The verb *to know* is in classical Hebrew a euphemism for sexual relations; in this case, obviously, homosexual relations. Lot remonstrates with them: "I beg you, my brothers, do not act so wickedly. Look, I have two daughters who have not known a man; let me bring them out to you, and do to them as you please; only do nothing to these men, for they have come under the shelter of my roof." The Sodomites then attempt to break down the door of Lot's house, the "men" strike them blind, and, after the rescue of Lot, Sodom and its neighboring cities and adjacent region are utterly destroyed: the cities "and the entire Plain, and all the inhabitants of the cities and the vegetation of the ground" (19:25). The horror of the judgment is rendered more horrible by the taunting levity of the dialogue between God and Abraham that preceded it.

What has happened in this episode is that the men of Lot's town have demanded access to God's genitals just as, in the circumcision episode, God demanded access to Abraham's genitals. Although it is only by a forced political correctness that the Bible as a whole can be read as neutral on the subject of homosexuality, what counts in this episode is not the difference between hetero- and homosexual but that between human and divine. The "men" whom the Sodomites want to "know" are God. The virginal daughters whom Lot offers them instead are human. Human sexual autonomy, always indirectly an affront to God's control over life, here becomes a direct affront; in fact, a literal sexual attack.

It is not morality that is at issue, in short, but power. In none of his interactions with humankind, in none of his covenants with Adam, Noah, and Abraham, has God required or prohibited sexual relations of any particular kind. (Fertility entails heterosexual relations, but the matter is never addressed in those terms.) Just as the crime of violence was only recognized as crime when Cain slew Abel, so here: The crime of illicit sexual relations is recognized as such only at its first occurrence. But in both cases, it is not that the action itself is intrinsically evil; it is that the action infringes a just-discovered divine prerogative. To put it another way, if God in the form of the two male visitors to Sodom had wished to "know" the Sodomites, he/they could have done so, just as God could have slain Abel had he wished to do so. And when God destroys the Sodomites, what he is doing—with spectacular force—is again analogous to what he did when he banished Cain: He is reclaiming a power that a human or humans had sought to seize, a power he fully grasped as his own only at the moment when he punished its attempted theft.

Early in the morning on the day following the destruction of Sodom, Abraham hurries "to the place where he had stood before the Lord" (19:27)—that is, where he had taunted the Lord about his promises and threats—to view the destruction. What has been laid waste is the entire region that had fallen to Lot when Abram and Lot divided the country between them. The division could so easily have gone the other way! Lot's townsfolk have battled the Lord in the most direct way possible over human and divine life force. In the verses immediately following, Lot's daughters, as if avenging themselves on him for exposing them to gang rape, will lure him into incest. But as Abraham contemplates all this, his penis is still healing from the wound of his recent circumcision, the sign of his surrender. His genital submission has been pointedly unlike Sodom's genital aggression, and the stage is now set for him to complete it by acknowledging that it is only by means of such submission that land and offspring will come to him. In the destruction of Sodom, the Lord has given him both a warning and a reassuring demonstration of his power: The one who has the power to take so much life so suddenly and violently surely also has the power to give life.

Yet Abraham tarries before taking the final step. He not only remains silent but in the following chapter (Gen. 20) attempts to give Sarah to King Abimelech of Gerar as earlier he had attempted to give her to Pharaoh, claiming, as on that previous occasion, that she is his sister. God (this is a "God" story) intervenes by telling Abimelech the truth in a dream, but Abraham has demonstrated, again, that he neither trusts the Lord/God's power to protect nor accepts the Lord/God's authority over his own reproductive powers. The episode is what scholarship calls a doublet, a quasi duplicate, of the earlier one. A form of editing that stressed economy above all other considerations would include one episode or the other, and many critics resist assigning any meaning to what they regard as an all but accidental inclusion. Still, by its placement Abraham's misbehavior in Gerar stands as defiance not just of the Lord's claims on Abraham's body but also of the Lord's demonstrative destruction of Sodom. By his behavior in Gerar, Abraham shows clearly enough that, past a certain point, he refuses to be impressed. Coming after so stunning a demonstration of divine power, this defiance has another meaning than it had when it followed merely on the Lord's opening summons to Abram.

GOD'S RESPONSE to Abraham's intransigence is told in one of the boldest, deepest fables in the Bible. In Abraham's hundredth year, Sarah bears him a son, Isaac; but some years after the boy is weaned,

> God put Abraham to the test. He said to him, "Abraham," and he answered, "Here I am." And He said, "Take your son, your favored one, Isaac, whom you love, and go to the land of Moriah, and offer him there as a burnt offering on one of the heights that I will point out to you." (22:1–2)

The *ʿaqedah* or "binding of Isaac," as it is commonly referred to in Jewish tradition, is rightly admired as a masterpiece of economy, psychology, and artistic subtlety. Abraham never actually agrees to God's request. He goes through all the murderous motions up to the moment when God cries out to him, "Do not raise your hand against the boy," but we never learn whether he would actually have gone through with the sacrifice.

At two points, Abraham conceals what he is ostensibly about to do, as if to indicate that he knows it is wrong. He lies—or does he?—to his attendants when he tells them to stay behind, saying: "The boy and I will go up there; we will worship and we will return to you" (22:5). Will Isaac return? We cannot know whether or not Abraham is feigning when the boy asks, "Where is the sheep for the burnt offering?" and Abraham answers, "God will see to the sheep for His burnt offering, my son" (22:8). The sacrifice of Isaac, if Abraham had gone through with it, would have been "worship." As for the sentence "God will see to the sheep . . . ," this is just what God eventually does. Is the sentence spoken past Isaac to God? Is it a plea? Is it a challenge? The verb form translated "will see to" may be either future or jussive; that is, either "God will see to" or "Let God see to." Abraham resists even as he goes through the motions of compliance. At the end of the test as at the beginning, his only statement to God is the ostensibly willing but ultimately opaque "Here I am." Thus, when God declares that Abraham has passed the test and, for the seventh and final time, promises him abundant offspring, it is as much God who concedes defeat as Abraham.

God says, "Now I know that you fear God, since you have not withheld your son, your favored one, from Me" (22:12) and, a moment later, "Because you have done this and have not withheld your son, your favored one, I will bestow My blessing upon you and make your descendants as numerous as the stars of heaven and the sands on the seashore" (22:16–17). But Abraham's action has actually been far more ambiguous than God chooses to believe. He has not, after all, slain his son, and perhaps he would never have done so. Abraham goes as far as he possibly can without actually doing the deed, and God chooses to be satisfied with this much. By the time he begins this test, there is no longer any question that God knows what kind of acknowledgment he wants from Abraham. That much of God's self-discovery is plainly in place. By the time he concludes this test, however, God knows how much acknowledgment he can get and how much he cannot get from Abraham. This too is a part of God's self-discovery. In the self-love of Abraham, clinging as he does, by bluff and ruse, to his own bruised and defining power to create, God may well see an image of himself.

From this point on, as God and Abraham are linked not just by a covenant but also, at a deeper level, by a truce, a subtle but profound change comes over their relationship and over the mood of the narrative itself. Sarah dies, and Abraham rises from mourning to purchase a burial cave from the Hittites who rule the region. The ruling etiquette dictates that whatever is sought by the buyer must be offered as a gift by the seller but that in the course of conversation the cash value of the property must be "accidentally" divulged. Abraham, operating smoothly as a man of this world, delivers the appropriate lines at the appropriate moments and concludes the purchase. This is the first piece of the divinely promised land that has actually come into his possession. Next, in a mood of comparable practicality, he turns to the matter of a marriage for Isaac, charging his servant to go to Aram-naharaim, Abraham's home region, to procure a bride for his son.

The narrative of how the servant does this is full of vivid but uncharacteristically humble details. We seem to have dropped a register below the high, grave, timeless tone of the creation and flood myths, below even the tone of the opening legends in the Abraham cycle. In those legends, God and Abraham are the principal characters—the protagonist and the antagonist—in a set of interactions that, as we have seen, amount to a cosmic struggle. In the story of the purchase of Rebekah, by contrast, the principal characters are Abraham's servant (unnamed), Rebekah, and Rebekah's father and brother, Bethuel and Laban. God does not appear in this episode either to speak or to act.

It is striking, however, that Abraham, who has never before seen fit to characterize God or his own relationship with God, now finally does so. Abraham's servant worries: "What if the woman does not consent to follow me to this land?" But Abraham reassures him: "The Lord, the God of heaven, who took me from my father's house and from my native land, who promised me on oath, saying, 'I will assign this land to your offspring'—He will send His angel before you" (24:6–7). Up to now, God has announced to Abraham what God will do. Now, Abraham announces to God what God will do. The Hebrew verb, as noted previously, has a jussive—that is, a command form—as well as a future form, but the future and the jussive are morphologically indistinguishable in the third person singular. If God himself had said, "My angel will go before you," context would have told us, even in the English translation, that a command had been given to the angel in question. When it is Abraham who says, "The Lord, the God of heaven . . . will send," the English translation conceals the possibility latent in the Hebrew that this is a command rather than a prediction: "Let God send," to use the nearest (but still too weak) English equivalent. In truth, the Hebrew is ambivalent; but to put no finer point on it, Abraham is speaking with a striking new freedom and, as it were, casualness about what God will do. To this point in God's story, God's actions have been all but motiveless and therefore numinously, ominously unpredictable. Suddenly, and this is a measure of the victory that Abraham has won over God by raising his knife against Isaac, God is beginning to become a known quantity, defined and constrained by his past commitments.

This change in God is reflected in Genesis 24, the story of the servant's purchase of Rebekah, by a revealing shift of nomenclature. As we have seen, the text of Genesis refers frequently both to *ʾelohim*, always translated "God," and to *yahweh*, in some translations simply transliterated as "Yahweh" but in most, including the Jewish Publication Society Tanakh, translated "the Lord." In addition to these two principal names, the name *ʾel*, "God," always with a following epithet, is sometimes used when Abraham is described as praying, performing a ritual, or offering a sacrifice. Thus, the ritual circumcision is performed for, and at the request of, *ʾel šadday*, "Almighty God"; and just before the binding of Isaac, Abraham plants a tamarisk in Beer-sheba and calls on *ʾel ʿolam*, translated in the Revised Standard Version as "the Everlasting God." The Semitic noun *ʾel*, like the English noun *G/god*, is both a common and a proper noun. As a common noun, it was the most general and widely diffused term for divinity throughout the ancient Near East. As a proper noun in the Canaanite pantheon, it named the sky god or "high god," him whose authority over nature and society was broadest but whose involvement in any individual human being's life was smallest. Canaanite El was, if you will, the divine chief executive; and many scholars believe that the name *yahweh* itself, which is morphologically a verb form, though always treated syntactically as a noun, was originally the predicate of a sentence-name in which the subject was *ʾel*. That possibility aside, when Abraham describes the Lord in the preceding passage as "the God of heaven" and, a moment earlier, as "the God of heaven and earth," he identifies the being who demanded his migration as, functionally, this highest of the gods.

The identification is a natural one to the extent that the formation and destruction of whole peoples, the giving and taking of entire lands, the construction and maintenance of the political order at the top, is an "executive" responsibility. What is surprising is that, just at this point in the narrative, we are to descend from that level to a far more private and personal one. The Lord, the God of heaven and earth, spoke as Canaanite El when he promised Abraham, to quote the seventh repetition of the promise: ". . . your descendants shall seize the gates of their foes. All the nations of the earth shall bless themselves by your descendants, because you have obeyed My command" (22:17–18). This is the decision-making level at which El ordinarily operates. But now Abraham tells his servant that this very deity will send his angel along to see to it that the servant successfully concludes his purchase of a bride for Isaac. Caricaturing just a bit, this is to send the secretary-general of the United Nations on a merely personal errand.

If Abraham is only now, as he nears the end of his long life, taking conscious possession of his relationship with the Lord God, Abraham's servant is even less sure of just what sort of god this is and what sort of claim can be made on him. In the first true prayer in the Bible, the servant says, as he arrives in Aram-naharaim:

> O Lord, God of my master Abraham, grant me good fortune this day, and deal graciously with my master Abraham: Here I stand by the spring as the daughters of the townsmen come out to draw water; let the maiden to whom I say, "Please, lower your jar that I may drink," and who replies, "Drink, and I will also water your camels"—let her be the one whom You have decreed for Your servant Isaac. Thereby shall I know that You have dealt graciously with my master. (24:12)

The servant's instructions to his master's God are remarkably detailed. No one, to this point in the Lord God's story, has come remotely this close to bossing the Lord around. The servant is polite in his dealings with the Lord, yet he does not blush to give him instructions. It is as if he imagines himself to be dealing with a different kind of being than the august and imperious one we have seen in action with Abraham, the one who deals in vast territories and aeons of time and who, when offended, sends down fire and brimstone from the sky.

Ancient Mesopotamian religion did know of a category of god

with whom dealings at this level and in this manner were standard. This was the personal god, typically referred to by the name of his client; that is, as "the god of X," "the god of Y," and so on. The authority of the personal god was small, but his degree of responsibility for his worshiper-client was large. Nothing in the devotee-client's life was too small, too humble, or too everyday to be brought to the god's attention, for he was a god with no other responsibilities. Abraham's servant knows that his master worships a god named *yahweh*, "the Lord," but he sees fit to address him doubly: "O Lord [*yahweh*], *God of my master Abraham*." This second phrase, which to us seems only to indicate whom Abraham worships, actually indicates something else to Abraham's servant: It identifies the man for whom this god is preeminently responsible. It names, in other words, a limitation that contemporary heirs of Jewish or Christian tradition no longer hear when they say "My God" or "Our God." Those phrases do not now suggest that the God mentioned is functionally divine only for "me" or "us." In the polytheistic religions of Mesopotamia before the emergence of Israel, some gods were functionally divine for everybody, but some were not. Israelite monotheism seems to have come into existence as a rupture of this functional division with a resulting fusion of features that polytheism had attributed to several divine personalities.

By the late twentieth century, very late indeed in the history of monotheism, this fusion has become so familiar that it no longer seems strange to us to refer possessively to a being whose proclaimed power and domain transcend human possession. Genesis 24 shows us an extremely early moment in this fusion. When Abraham, having described the Lord as, functionally, Canaanite El, orders him to cooperate (or at least predicts confidently that he will cooperate) in discharging duties more appropriate to the Mesopotamian personal god, Abraham makes a momentous inference from his religious experience. He infers that, in his case, El will act as if he were a personal god. Abraham thus creates something religiously new. Whether he does so by conscious combination or by simple misidentification we cannot know. It is certainly conceivable that nomads migrating from Mesopotamia into Canaan may have mistakenly identified the personal god of the region they had left with the high god of the region to which they had come. All a historian can do is note, after the fact, that, as monotheism emerges in Israel, Israel's God combines features otherwise best described as those of Canaanite El and the Mesopotamian personal god.

In this episode it is Abraham's servant, rather than Abraham himself, who actually puts the combination in so many words by the way he prays. The direct-address marker "O," as in "O Lord," does not appear as such in the Hebrew. Thus, "O Lord, God of my master Abraham" translates a phrase that could also be translated "O Lord, O god of my master Abraham." The last of these translations is the one that may indicate best what is taking place: Two originally separate deities are being addressed simultaneously with the suggestion that they can now be equated. To the divine character as we have hitherto seen it—*yahweh*, *ʾelohim*, and the serpentine destroyer in fusion—a fourth personality is now juxtaposed. The newcomer is a personal god (I use the lowercase by design), a modest, helpful deity rather like a patron saint or guardian angel, who may be entrusted with so humble a task as finding a suitable young woman for one's son.

That it is Abraham's servant who calls upon Abraham's personal god is doubly suggestive. On the one hand, the assistance of this serviceable personage is appropriately sought for an errand deputed to a servant. On the other, Abraham is no longer, if he ever was, the only person capable of talking about Abraham's God. Abraham's servant also has access. It is by just such shifts, as one person talks about another's god, that religion changes. Some of the changes are deliberate, others accidental.

When Abraham's servant addresses God in the words "O Lord, O god of my master Abraham," we must understand that the second name says more about the deity than it says about Abraham. The name "god of Abraham," rather than serving principally to include Abraham among the god's worshipers, serves principally to limit the god's allegiance and responsibility to Abraham. The actual, historical process by which the personality content of the four mentioned deities fused is not the task of this book. Whatever the interest of that account, it need not be a precondition to recognizing that elements such as these do indeed combine in the character of the protagonist of the Book of Genesis. The Lord God, according to the story being told about him, is both the creator of the world and, at any moment and for any reason he chooses, also its destroyer. The fate of nations, witness Sodom, is in his hands, but he can also stoop to direct involvement in the private life of an individual man.

At the beginning of the Abraham cycle, Abraham belonged to the Lord; by the end of it, the Lord belongs to Abraham, or at least he mysteriously acts as if he does at certain points. One of these points comes when the Lord is first referred to, by Abraham's servant, as "of Abraham" and is, in effect, sent on an errand for Abraham. Having sought to assert control over Abraham's sexual potency, and having succeeded to a point, the Lord God now finds his own power enlisted in the service of that very sexual potency. One need never have heard of the Mesopotamian personal god to sense a change.

Abraham's story ends with a passage of the sort that new or unpracticed readers of the Hebrew Bible tend to find particularly opaque:

> Abraham took another wife, whose name was Keturah. She bore him Zimran, Jokshan, Medan, Midian, Ishbak, and Shuah. Jokshan begot Sheba and Dedan. The descendants of Dedan were the Asshurim, the Letushim, and the Leummim. The descendants of Midian were Ephah, Epher, Enoch, Abida, and Eldaah. All these were descendants of Keturah. Abraham willed all that he owned to Isaac; but to Abraham's sons by concubines Abraham gave gifts while he was still living, and he sent them away from his son Isaac eastward, to the land of the East.
>
> This was the total span of Abraham's life: one hundred and seventy-five years. And Abraham breathed his last, dying at a good ripe age, old and contented; and he was gathered to his kin. His sons Isaac and Ishmael buried him in the cave of Machpelah, in the field of Ephron son of Zohar the Hittite, facing Mamre, the field that Abraham had bought from the Hittites; there Abraham was buried, and Sarah his wife. After the death of Abraham, God blessed his son Isaac. And Isaac settled near Beer-lahai-roi. (25:1–11)

Literary mastery? Scarcely, but one must hear the crucial silence in this passage, whose very banality carries a message. The Lord does not appear to Abraham and solemnly promise that Keturah will bear a child, as earlier, when Abraham was much younger (though still old!), he had solemnly promised that Sarah would bear a child. Yet Keturah bears not just one but six sons, two of whom, at least, go on to have sons and grandsons of their own. The names of Keturah and her offspring carry echoes of later geographic names. In etiological terms, the passage expresses the later Israelites' sense that they are related, but somewhat distantly, to tribes in South Arabia. But by its placement at the conclusion of the story of a struggle between the Lord God and Abraham over human reproductive powers, the story has the further effect of partially restoring the status quo ante, that is, the unconditional gift of fertility given by God to Adam and Eve and given again to Noah and his descendants. Reproduction at least for the family of Abraham is again, so to speak, merely a part of human life.

In the remainder of the Book of Genesis, the Lord God will be repeatedly spoken of (and on occasion will identify himself) as "of" one patriarch or another. The Lord, the god of Abraham, will become the god of Isaac, the god of Jacob, or "the god of your father." As this happens, he will come to seem, often enough, more like a busy friend of the family than like the Judge of all the earth, as Abraham called him at Sodom. His help will be sought for conception and other human needs, but, significantly, the initiative will be on the human side. He will not attempt again to assert the same sort of control over reproduction that we have seen him attempting to assert over Abraham's reproduction. He will claim only what Abraham has already conceded. Yet the modest storms and calms of the house of Abraham will not be quite his only concern. At times, the masterful, abrupt, inscrutable being we first met will return, for the radically unpredictable creator and destroyer personalities of *yahweh* and *ʾelohim* remain in him alongside the loyal advocate now called "god of your father." All are in him, in a combination whose explosive potential will only gradually be revealed.

Friend of the Family

"He Made Him Popular with the Warden"

GENESIS 25:12–50:18

At the beginning of Abraham's story, to repeat, Abraham belongs to the Lord; at its end, the Lord belongs to Abraham. The Lord God's attempt to reclaim control over human fertility has ended with his being, to a point, domesticated into the house of Abraham. This process continues through the rest of the Book of Genesis. Genesis 25–50 consists of the story of Jacob (25–36) and the story of Joseph (37–50). Jacob, as we shall see, takes liberties with the Lord God far beyond any that his grandfather risked, for all Abraham's ironic defiance. As for Joseph, Jacob's favorite son, he all but ignores the deity, never speaking to him and rarely speaking of him. By the end of the Book of Genesis, Jacob's dying words, invoking the Lord's blessing on Joseph and Joseph's two sons, have an almost nostalgic effect, for during the long and moving story of Joseph (fully a quarter of the book), the Lord God has gone into a brief eclipse.

One early sign of the Lord God's gradual domestication is that women now feel free to approach him directly. When Rebekah conceived, "the children struggled in her womb, and she said, 'If so, why do I exist?' She went to inquire of the Lord, and the Lord answered her" (Gen. 25:22–23). To this point in the Bible, no woman has spoken to God except in reply to a direct question from him. After the sin of Adam and Eve, God does not address himself to the pair; he addresses himself to Adam: "The Lord God called out to the man and said to him, 'Where are you?' " (3:9). Only after Adam blames Eve does God speak to her; and only then does she speak to him. So also with Sarah. None of God's seven promises is addressed to her; none is addressed even to the couple; all are addressed to Abraham. Even when God tells Abraham that Sarah will conceive and Sarah laughs, God takes the matter up with Abraham—"Why did Sarah laugh . . . ?" (18:13)—and only deigns to speak to her when she contradicts him from inside her tent. Twice, God speaks, directly and compassionately, to Hagar; but even on these occasions, she does not speak to him. Rebekah does speak to him, and she receives a substantial answer:

> Two nations are in your womb,
> Two separate peoples shall issue from your body;
> One people shall be mightier than the other,
> And the older shall serve the younger. (25:23)

The two are Esau and Jacob, whose descendants will be the Edomites and the Israelites.

Jacob will have two wives, Leah and Rachel; and as they give birth to, eventually, twelve sons, God's assistance is repeatedly mentioned. Thus, "The Lord saw that Leah was unloved and he opened her womb" (29:31) and "Now God remembered Rachel; God heeded her and opened her womb" (30:22). God, who once spoke exclusively to the men and addressed fertility at the nation-founding level, is now down with the women, managing the pregnancies one by one.

This is not the only liberty taken with divine power. As Isaac nears the end of his life, he summons his elder son, Esau, to receive his blessing (Gen. 27). That Isaac even thinks he can bestow a blessing on Esau is a change. Abraham did not summon Isaac to receive a blessing as his own life was ending. Rather, "After the death of Abraham, *God* blessed his son Isaac" (25:11, italics added). But if Isaac is subtly self-aggrandizing vis-à-vis the divine prerogative, Jacob is contemptuous. Isaac tells Esau: "Bring me some game and prepare a dish for me to eat, that I may bless you, with the Lord's approval, before I die" (27:7). But Rebekah prefers Jacob and tells him to slay two kids from his father's flock. She will make a savory dish of them herself and send Jacob in to masquerade as Esau and steal the blessing.

> He went to his father and said, "Father." And he said, "Yes, which of my sons are you?" Jacob said to his father, "I am Esau, your first-born; I have done as you told me. Pray sit up and eat of my game, that you may give me your innermost blessing." Isaac said to his son, "How did you succeed so quickly, my son?" And he said, "Because the Lord your God granted me good fortune." (27:18–20)

"The Lord *your* God"? Jacob crassly builds his father's God, whom he has not yet accepted as his own, into his lie. The lie works. The blessing—now Isaac's, evidently, rather than the Lord's to bestow, even though what it promises is the Lord's favor—gocs to guileful

Jacob rather than to guileless Esau. To speak plainly, the Lord is trifled with.

To protect Jacob from Esau's revenge, Rebekah raises a secondary consideration, Isaac's desire and hers that their younger son not, like his twin brother, marry a Canaanite. She induces Isaac to send Jacob to find a bride in their ancestral Paddan-aram (= Aram-naharaim). Privately, Rebekah promises to summon Jacob home once Esau has cooled off. Jacob sets out, and, en route, the Lord appears to him in a dream:

> He had a dream; a stairway was set on the ground and its top reached to the sky, and angels of God were going up and down on it. And the Lord was standing beside him and He said, "I am the Lord, the God of your father Abraham and the God of Isaac: the ground on which you are lying I will assign to you and to your offspring. Your descendants shall be as the dust of the earth; you shall spread out to the west and to the east, to the north and to the south. All the families of the earth shall bless themselves by you and your descendants. Remember, I am with you: I will protect you wherever you go and will bring you back to this land. I will not leave you until I have done what I have promised you."
>
> Jacob awoke from his sleep and said, "Surely the Lord is present in this place, and I did not know it!" Shaken, he said, "How awesome is this place! This is none other than the abode of God [Hebrew: *bet ʾel*], and that is the gateway to heaven." (28:12–17)

The Lord has appeared to Jacob in a dream as awe-inspiring as any experienced by Abraham, and Jacob, unlike Abraham, has immediately and explicitly acknowledged the Lord's power. Or so it seems until a moment later, when he adds:

> If God remains with me, if He protects me on this journey that I am making, and gives me bread to eat and clothing to wear, and if I return safe to my father's house—the Lord shall be my God. And this stone, which I have set up as a pillar, shall be God's abode; and of all that You give me, I will set aside a tithe for You. (28:20–22)

In these words, for which there is no parallel in anything Abraham has ever said, Jacob is spelling out the conditions under which he will *not* accept his grandfather's and his father's God as his own. Unlike Abraham's wrangle with the Lord before the destruction of

Sodom, this is not mock bargaining but real bargaining. And note how humble Jacob's demands are—food, clothing, and safe conduct—and how humble, correspondingly, is his offer of a stone pillar as "abode" and a tithe, a mere tithe, to the being who has just promised, grandly: "Your descendants shall be as the dust of the earth." (One may note, parenthetically, that in this episode the names *yahweh* and *ʾelohim*, "the Lord" and "God," alternate and clearly are beginning to seem simple synonyms.)

If the Lord—as the friend of the family of Abraham and Isaac—had promised such humble necessities as food, clothing, and safe conduct to Jacob, then Jacob's promise of a pillar and a tithe in exchange would have been appropriate. By the same token, Jacob's first response—"How awesome is this place!"—would have been both appropriate and adequate to the grandeur of what the Lord has actually promised. By going on to his second response, Jacob might seem to call his first one into question and with it the Lord's vision. Against that lofty vision, Jacob's concerns seem too aggressively pragmatic. In other words, the Lord speaks as El, but Jacob answers as to a friend of the family. But just this incongruity will, in the long run, become a distinguishing feature of the protagonist of the Bible.

As Jacob continues on his journey and enters upon various adventures in Paddan-aram and back in Canaan, a question, nonetheless, does hang in the air: Will things go well enough for Jacob that he will take the Lord as his personal god? Hard bargaining of this sort is far from unknown in the annals of ancient Semitic religion; yet it comes as something of a jolt, within this story, to find the God who began with such laconic mastery grown eager in his promises and, for his troubles, placed on probation by the likes of Jacob.

In the next three chapters (Gen. 29–31), moreover, the Lord seems to accept Jacob's terms. Jacob trades his labor to his uncle, Laban, in exchange for his cousins Leah and Rachel in marriage. Laban schemes to keep Jacob in service to him, but Jacob knows a trick to increase the fertility of his own flocks and, once he is rich and strong enough to return home, he explains to his wives that it was God who taught him the trick and God who now wants him to take his wealth and head home:

> Once, at the mating time of the flocks, I had a dream in which I saw that the he-goats mating with the flock were streaked, speckled, and mottled. And in the dream an angel of God said to me, "Jacob!" "Here," I answered. And he said, "Note well that all the he-goats

> which are mating with the flock are streaked, speckled, and mottled; for I have noted all that Laban has been doing to you. I am the God of Beth-el, where you anointed a pillar and where you made a vow to Me. Now, arise and leave this land and return to your native land." (31:10–13)

Perhaps Jacob is lying to his wives about God's assistance as, earlier, he lied to his father, using an invented story about God to overcome their reluctance to leave home. Taking this dream as an honest report, however, it shows God active at the humblest level we have yet seen: as animal husbandry counselor. Why is God doing this? His allusion to Jacob's vow and thereby to the demands made of him seems to contain the answer.

Laban attempts to prevent Jacob's departure but eventually consents to it and swears an oath of peace in the names of the god of Abraham and the god of Nahor, Nahor being Laban's father and Jacob's granduncle (Abraham's brother). If Jacob were to reciprocate and swear by the same two gods, then he would acknowledge that his grandfather's (Abraham's) deity is also his own. But, as we saw earlier, Jacob has placed more conditions on that commitment than have yet been met. He has not yet safely returned home. "And Jacob swore by the Fear of his father Isaac" (31:53). This phrase, *paḥad yiṣhaq,* "the Fear of Isaac," has commonly been read as simply another epithet of El, on a par with *ʾel šadday* and the like. But it is more opaque than that, in fact, and the opacity is intended. The wily Jacob wants a one-sided oath. He wants Laban to swear by a deity who counts, while he himself swears by an empty phrase, thus neither obligating himself nor releasing God prematurely from probation.

What the Lord must yet do before winning Jacob's allegiance is meet the third of Jacob's initial conditions by delivering him from revenge at the hands of his original dupe, Esau. As Esau approaches with a band of four hundred men, Jacob prays to his grandfather's and father's god:

> O god of my father Abraham and god of my father Isaac, O Lord, who said to me, "Return to your native land and I will deal bountifully with you"! I am unworthy of all the kindness that You have so steadfastly shown Your servant: with my staff alone I crossed this Jordan, and now I have become two camps. Deliver me, I pray, from the hand of my brother, from the hand of Esau; else, I fear, he may come and strike me down, mothers and children alike. Yet

> You have said, "I will deal bountifully with you and make your offspring as the sands of the sea, which are too numerous to count." (32:10–13)

In the comparably long prayer of Abraham's servant (24:12–14), the god of Abraham was asked to show kindness. Here kindness is attributed to the god of Abraham and of Isaac, but kindness is not a quality that the Lord God has ever claimed for himself. Kindness did not motivate his promise of offspring and land to Abraham. These were rather his own grand design than kindly assistance in any human plan. Kindness may be inferred to be more properly a quality of the personal god, a deity who, so to speak, will take requests and do favors. But by the process of fusion that creates the protagonist of the Bible, what is attributed to any component is attributed to the fusion.

Israelite monotheism in its fully developed form, while retaining one personal god—the "god of" Abraham, Isaac, and Jacob—and assigning his functions to its fusion deity, will deny the reality of all other personal gods just as it denied the reality of all high gods but its own. But the emergence of monotheism from polytheism is a matter of selective inclusion as well as wholesale exclusion. It would be wrong, wildly wrong, to suppose that anything ever predicated of any Semitic deity ends up being predicated of Israel's deity—the sole survivor, so to speak. But it would be almost equally wrong to suppose that there is no overlap between Israel's deity and his ancient rivals. In fact, the most coherent way to imagine the Lord God of Israel is as the inclusion of the content of several ancient divine personalities in a single character.

There is then more than a verbal connection between fusion and confusion. The story of how Jacob put the high God on probation by demanding that he perform a task proper to the personal god bespeaks an initial confusion but advances the eventual fusion. Historically speaking, did it happen this way? We cannot know. The Mesopotamian personal god does not appear in the Book of Genesis as such, as Mesopotamian, any more than the flood appears in it in a personalized form, as Tiamat. But leaving the history of this process to the historians, we may still confirm its literary result; namely, a character with a multiple personality.

To return to the story, Jacob's promise to take the Lord as his own God had a further condition: Jacob's safe return home. Can the Lord meet this last condition?

Jacob—with his two wives, his two maids, his eleven children, his servants, and his flocks—is traveling south along a route somewhat east of the Jordan River, which runs north–south. Esau is traveling north to meet him. When Jacob comes to the Jabbok, a tributary running west through a deep gorge into the Jordan, he sends huge appeasement offerings of flocks southward across the Jabbok for Esau. Finally, he sends his family across the Jabbok ford. He himself stays behind for one night on the north rim of the majestic gorge.

> Jacob was left alone. And a man wrestled with him until the break of dawn. When he saw that he had not prevailed against him, he wrenched Jacob's hip at its socket, so that the socket of his hip was strained as he wrestled with him. Then he said, "Let me go, for dawn is breaking." But he answered, "I will not let you go, unless you bless me." Said the other, "What is your name?" He replied, "Jacob." Said he, "Your name shall no longer be Jacob, but Israel, for you have striven with God and men and have prevailed." Jacob asked, "Pray tell me your name. But he said, "You must not ask my name!" And he took leave of him there. (32:25–30)

The "man" of this episode is traditionally taken to be, like the "men" who visited Sodom, an apparition of God. Jacob's wrestling with God or, as some translations have it, with an angel, is one of the most famous scenes in all Scripture. Essentially, however, all later interpretations rest on Jacob's own: "So Jacob named the place Peniel, meaning, 'I have seen God face to face, yet my life has been preserved' " (32:31). But Jacob's interpretation is not necessarily that of the author of the text, who may wish to suggest that Jacob has wrestled with a man and simply spoken of him as God after the fact. The text leaves tauntingly open the question of whether Jacob actually saw the wrestler's face: The wrestler's insistence on leaving before dawn may mean that he did not.

But even if it is a man who, barely visible perhaps in the dark before the dawn, says, "You have striven with God *and men* and have prevailed," the fact is that Jacob has indeed prevailed over both. His attempt to appease his brother succeeds, and by that success the Lord himself complies with Jacob's third condition. After crossing the Jordan and proceeding to Shechem, where Abraham arrived on his entry into Canaan and first built an altar and called on the name of the Lord, Jacob builds an altar and calls it "El, the God of Israel," building his own new name, the one given to him in the dark by the wrestler, into the name of God and thereby, finally, claiming and acknowledging his grandfather's God as his own. Later (35:14), at Bethel, where his first theophany had occurred, he completes his vow by building the promised pillar of stone.

We may well say, at this point in Jacob's story, that the Lord God has *survived* another generation. Jacob has acknowledged the Lord God, but the reader cannot fail to recall that at three different turning points, Jacob's victory has been transparently the result of his own resourcefulness, if not guile. It almost seems that it is Jacob, rather than God, who is showing a degree of steadfast love and faithfulness, attributing to divine assistance happy outcomes that, by the word of the narration, come from his energies alone. Whether in tricking his father, outwitting his uncle, or appeasing his hostile brother, Jacob acts, to all seeming, on his own. The Lord God does not intervene except to assist Jacob's wives in conception, and even this assistance is only sometimes necessary.

It is gratuitous, of course, to regard human effort and divine favor as mutually exclusive. But at these moments, there is in Jacob an element of something like cynicism in his use of the religious belief and practice he has received from his forebears. In all three instances, Jacob trades on others' reverence for what he merely manipulates. First, Jacob lies to his father about the kids his mother has disguised as game. Second, he seems to invent, after the fact, a divine vision to impress his wives (31:11–13). As for the third turning point, there is a heart-stopping pun at 33:10. Esau is attempting to decline Jacob's aggressively munificent gifts. Jacob insists: "No, I pray you; if you would do me this favor, accept from me this gift; for to see your face is like seeing the face of God, and you have received me favorably." Speaking of the "man" with whom he wrestled all night, Jacob equates his face with God's face, saying, "I have seen God face to face, yet my life has been preserved" (32:31). But speaking here, he equates Esau's face with God's face. Was Jacob's nocturnal visitor Esau himself, come to kill his brother as, years earlier, he had vowed to do (27:41)? Jacob, having fought his attacker to a draw, unexpectedly demanded of him his blessing. And from whom, more appropriately than from Esau, does Jacob have reason to wrestle for a blessing? In seeking Esau's blessing, Jacob would be seeking his long-estranged brother's acquiescence in the earlier loss of their father's blessing. Finally, is Jacob, as he greets Esau on the morrow, making a daring allusion to their night of struggle, one that Esau may hear and silently recognize? The primal, physically intimate power of two men wrestling in the darkness returns with a jolt when Jacob speaks to his brother in this code.

The plausibility of Jacob's daring way of referring to God at his meeting with Esau recalls the equally risky way he has employed references to the Lord in dealing with his father and his wives. Jacob need not be denying the reality of the Lord God to use the Lord God for his own purposes. What really happened that night? Wrestling in the blackness, Jacob and Esau did not admit to each other who they were: Esau called Jacob Israel, claiming that his brother had prevailed in combat with God, while Jacob spoke of Esau as if he were God. Their statements do not necessarily mock God. But when, in the light of day, Jacob says to Esau, "To see your face is like seeing the face of God," alluding to their night of mortal combat, his statement is ambivalent if not consciously ironic. Yet ironic and manipulative as Jacob has appeared in the beginning and middle of his story, he seems wholehearted—and the Lord God seems restored to his awe-inspiring self—at its end:

> God said to Jacob, "Arise, go up to Bethel and remain there; and build an altar there to the God who appeared to you when you were fleeing from your brother Esau." So Jacob said to his household and to all who were with him, "Rid yourselves of the alien gods in your midst, purify yourselves, and change your clothes. Come, let us go up to Bethel, and I will build an altar there to the God who answered me when I was in distress and who has been with me wherever I have gone." They gave to Jacob all the alien gods that they had, and the rings that were in their ears, and Jacob buried them under the terebinth that was near Shechem. As they set out, a terror from God fell on the cities round about, so that they did not pursue the sons of Jacob.
>
> Thus Jacob came to Luz—that is, Bethel—in the land of Canaan, he and all the people who were with him. There he built an altar and named the site El-bethel, for it was there that God had revealed Himself to him when he was fleeing from his brother. (35:1–7)

The closing allusion is to the appearance in which, as we have claimed, Jacob stipulated the conditions the Lord would have to meet to become Jacob's God. Now, the Lord God has met all those conditions. The Lord God—so real, at this point, that terror of him can paralyze the entire countryside—repeats his promise to Jacob and formally changes Jacob's name to Israel. Jacob, as he had promised on that first occasion, sets up a stone pillar in God's honor.

Jacob's story is over at this point, and Joseph's is about to begin, but what has been said about the Lord God? Jacob's cunning use of the Lord God, turned into a statement about the Lord God, is, minimally, that the Lord God's power, whatever it is, does not preclude such use. It is as if, since the Lord God is on Jacob's side, Jacob is free to lie about the Lord God or insult him when it is in his interest to do so. The Lord God seems willing to tolerate much so long as, in the end, he accomplishes his purposes.

This point is made in a striking way in an incident that, perhaps as another inspired piece of redactional placement, comes between Jacob's reconciliation with Esau and his final acceptance of the Lord God. The narrative does not pass from the nocturnal irony of Esau-as-God directly to the closing, liturgical celebration at Bethel. Instead, in Genesis 34, an episode of what seems blasphemous violence is interposed.

At the end of Genesis 33, having made peace with Esau east of the Jordan, Jacob, as we have already noted, crosses over to Shechem and, for the first time, addresses the Lord God as his own God: "El, the God of Israel" (33:20). Dinah, Jacob's daughter, then goes out to visit the women of Shechem, which is still a Hivite town, and is raped by Shechem, son of Hamor. (The younger man and the town have the same name.) Shechem does not simply take his pleasure and abandon Dinah: "His soul was drawn to Dinah . . . ; he loved the maiden, and spoke tenderly to her" (RSV; 34:3). Hamor asks Jacob to give Dinah to his son in marriage and then goes a step further: "Intermarry with us: give your daughters to us, and take our daughters for yourselves: You will dwell among us, and the land will be open before you; settle, move about, and acquire holdings in it" (34:9–10). The sons of Jacob accept the offer on condition that the males of Shechem accept circumcision. If they will do this, "then we will give our daughters to you and take your daughters to ourselves; and we will dwell among you and become as one kindred" (34:16). The Hivites accept the offer, and all the males are circumcised. But the offer proves a ruse:

> On the third day, when they were in pain, Simeon and Levi, two of Jacob's sons, brothers of Dinah, took each his sword, came upon the city unmolested, and slew all the males. They put Hamor and his son Shechem to the sword, took Dinah out of Shechem's house,

> and went away. The other sons of Jacob came upon the slain and plundered the town, because their sister had been defiled. They seized their flocks and herds and asses, all that was inside the town and outside; all their wealth, all their children, and their wives, all that was in the houses, they took as captives and booty. (34:25–29)

Whether Dinah was merely the pretext for a raid by a clan of nomads on a settled people or whether Dinah was genuinely avenged by her genuinely aggrieved brothers, it is striking that circumcision—the sign of the Lord's covenant with Abraham—is falsified in this episode. Though neither Abraham nor the Lord is mentioned when circumcision is demanded of the Hivites, the reader knows—and knows that Jacob's sons know—the meaning of this action. And, for that matter, even the Hivites are led to believe that this is the sign of the clan's identity: If they accept circumcision, they are told they will become "one kindred" with the sons of Jacob. Here, the sons of Jacob use a sacred symbol deceitfully to a genocidal end, just as earlier their father used the name of God deceitfully in defrauding Esau. Jacob regrets what they have done but only because he fears that the other Canaanites (the Hivites are a Canaanite tribe) will now turn against him. Jacob does not think the Lord God is offended; and, to judge from the Lord God's absence from this chapter, Jacob is right. (As with Abraham's foreign war in Genesis 14, there is never any question of invoking the Lord God's help against this potential enemy or of thanking him for a victory.)

When Jacob lied to Isaac about the Lord, we said that the Lord was trifled with. Here, we might say that circumcision as a sacred symbol is trifled with, used blasphemously for a purpose utterly unlike what the Lord had in mind when he required circumcision of Abraham and his offspring. But the Lord never complains to Jacob that he is being trifled with in the Hivite genocide, or that circumcision is being trifled with. The Lord God, at this point in his story, is unconcerned with what humankind—Jacob or his sons or anybody else—says or fails to say (or deceitfully or cynically says) about him. Human speech is left unregulated. Call this sovereign indifference, serenity, lack of jealousy, or what you will, the matter does not come up. At this point in his story, as we might fairly put it, the Lord God has not yet learned to care what is merely said about him. He cares about some things that are done. He is jealous of human reproductive capacity in particular. But human speech concerns him very little.

The Lord God's silence in the face of these potential provocations, though it might seem audible only for an interpreter determined to hear it, does have one loud-and-clear consequence: It smooths the path to his absence from the story of Joseph. The Lord God is active and articulate in his relationship with Abraham; it is Abraham, not the Lord God, who keeps silent. In the story of Joseph, by contrast, the Lord God is neither active nor articulate. Though reference is occasionally made to him, he subsides temporarily to something more like an assumption than a character. If the text went directly from Abraham to Joseph, that subsidence would be a jolt. As it is, Jacob has already seized much of the initiative from the Lord God. It would be a long step from Abraham to Joseph; it is a considerably shorter step from Jacob to Joseph.

THE LORD WHOM Joseph knows not only has a smaller role in Joseph's life than in Jacob's but also has a different one. The Lord's promise of land and offspring remains constant, but what Jacob asked of the God of Abraham and Isaac, when this God first appeared to him at Luz (renamed Bethel), was food, shelter, and safe conduct back from Paddan-aram to Canaan. What Joseph receives from the same God—he never asks for it—is a successful career in the Egyptian bureaucracy. Joseph's brothers, all of them sons of Jacob, resentful of their father's fondness for Joseph and of dreams in which Joseph foresees his own greatness, sell him into slavery in Egypt. But wondrous fortune follows this misfortune:

> The Lord was with Joseph, and he was a successful man; and he stayed in the house of his Egyptian master. And when his master saw that the Lord was with him and that the Lord lent success to everything he undertook, he took a liking to Joseph. He made him his personal attendant and put him in charge of his household, placing in his hands all that he owned. And from the time that the Egyptian put him in charge of his household and of all that he owned, the Lord blessed his house for Joseph's sake. (39:2–5)

Later, falsely accused by his master's wife, Joseph is thrown into prison, but the Lord rescues him again: "The Lord was with Joseph: He extended kindness to him and disposed the chief jailer favorably toward him" (39:21). Or, in the lively and idiomatic translation of this verse in the 1966 edition of the Jerusalem Bible, "Yahweh made him popular with the warden." This is a new role for *yahweh*. We see, again, the functions of the personal god attributed to the Lord God.

Pharaoh's cupbearer remembers that when he himself was briefly imprisoned, Joseph successfully interpreted a dream he had. At the cupbearer's suggestion, Joseph is summoned to interpret Pharaoh's dreams and again does so successfully. On both occasions, Joseph refers to God—"Surely God can interpret! Tell me [your dreams]" (40:8); "God has told Pharaoh what He is about to do" (41:25)—but he does not pray to God or receive any message from God. Impressed with Joseph's performance, Pharaoh says, "Could we find another like him, a man in whom is the spirit of God? . . . Since God has made all this known to you, there is no one so discerning and wise as you. You shall be in charge of my court . . ." (41:38–39). And so it happens: Joseph becomes second in Egypt only to Pharaoh himself and is reconciled with his brothers as he rescues them and his father from famine in Canaan. The Lord has made Joseph a success; and for Joseph (who never refers to the Lord, only to God), divinity of any kind is a matter of belief, even knowledge, but not of personal encounter of the kind Abraham, Isaac, and Jacob have experienced.

At one point (43:23) in the story of the reconciliation, Joseph says to his brothers, "Your God, the god of your father, must have put treasure in your bags for you." In fact, it is Joseph who, hiding his own tenderness, has done so; but, notably, this is the only reference Joseph ever makes to God in language at all like that of Abraham, Isaac, or Jacob. As Jacob, now called Israel, set out for Egypt,

> God called to Israel in a vision by night: "Jacob! Jacob!" He answered, "Here." And He said, "I am God, the god of your father. Fear not to go down to Egypt, for I will make you there into a great nation. I Myself will go down with you to Egypt, and I Myself will also bring you back; and Joseph's hand shall close your eyes." (46:2–4)

This has, by now, a familiar sound, but God is not speaking to Joseph. It is as if God is one kind of being for Jacob and another kind for Joseph. To Jacob, he speaks directly or in a dream or vision so unequivocal that it requires no interpretation. He never speaks thus to Joseph. The "spirit of God" that Pharaoh (not Joseph himself) says is in Joseph is a talent, a gift of God, but not one that requires communication with God for its functioning.

Moreover, though Joseph does prosper indirectly by being discerning and wise with the Lord's help, what he directly accomplishes is the rescue of an entire social order in which he is an outsider. The Lord's promises and interventions in the lives of Abraham, Isaac, and Jacob involved them and their families only. Here, the divinely aided dream interpretation saves all of Egypt, and only because of that larger success is Joseph, with his enhanced personal power, able to rescue his family. The Lord announces no intentions for Joseph and his offspring as he did for Abraham, Isaac, Jacob, and theirs, and, for that matter, God has no intentions for Egypt either. In deciphering Pharaoh's dream and so foreseeing a coming famine, Joseph does not infer any divine plan for Egypt that he then implements. The famine is not divinely sent; God has simply helped Joseph to foresee it. The famine preparation plan, too, is Joseph's, not God's. In short, modest, timely, indirect assistance to Joseph essentially exhausts the divine repertory. Both the natural and the social order are given and tacitly immutable; divine help from his personal god simply permits Joseph to function successfully within these orders.

The story of Joseph and his brothers is a moving and accessible one for modern readers not just because of its undeniable literary artistry but also because of this "modern" absence from it of a powerful, intrusive God. In the Joseph story as in modern, postreligious society, God is remote, but his remoteness matters little, for he is thought of only fleetingly, in crisis moments when his help is sought to escape from some dilemma or avert some catastrophe. Modernity, expecting no surprises from God, speaks of him calmly, as Joseph does, and assumes that, whatever God's power, his intentions are benevolent. God is kind, as Joseph is kind.

Joseph attributes his own enslavement to God's providence:

> Then Joseph said to his brothers, "Come forward to me." And when they came forward, he said, "I am your brother Joseph, he whom you sold into Egypt. Now, do not be distressed or reproach yourselves because you sold me hither; it was to save life that God sent me ahead of you." (45:4–5)

To some extent, Joseph's interpretation of his own misfortune as providential contradicts what we have just said about God's having no plan for Egypt or for Joseph's rescue of Egypt, much less of his own family. Certainly God has had no *announced* plan. The emotional point of this scene, however, is not that God has or lacks a plan but that Joseph has a kind and forgiving heart. To the extent that it is a statement about God, the Joseph story in such moments as these addresses not power but character. God would not so favor Joseph —a transparently good man, perhaps the only true saint in the Tanakh—if God were not himself like Joseph.

But if God is implicitly like Joseph in the closing chapters of Genesis, we can only note that he was not like Joseph in the opening chapters. The Lord who did not forgive Adam and Eve for their single act of disobedience was not like the forgiving Joseph. Neither was the Lord/God like Joseph when he sent a flood that "destroyed all flesh" in retribution for scarcely named offenses in Noah's generation. The Lord God in those scenes is maximally powerful and minimally kind, whereas the God mirrored in Joseph is maximally kind and minimally powerful. We have already noted that Joseph never addresses God and only rarely refers to him; we might add that he never so much as once refers to the Lord. Even in the interlude at 46:1–4, a scene in which Jacob is the protagonist, it is God, not the Lord, who speaks to him. The Lord, the less lawful, more willful, and more personal form of the deity, is absent from the last quarter of the Book of Genesis. He will return, but he is gone for now.

The God who stands quietly in the background in the Joseph story—a being in whom the bountiful *ʾelohim* of creation and the solicitous "god of . . ." dominate—is almost, if not quite, loving. Love was not God's motive for creating or destroying the world or for choosing Abraham or Isaac or Jacob. The Book of Genesis speaks only rarely of human love (cf. 29:18: "Jacob loved Rachel") and never of divine love. A kind of prelude to love may be seen, however, in three successive divine choices: of the younger Isaac over the elder Ishmael, of the younger Jacob over the elder Esau, and finally, most important, of the younger Joseph over his ten elder brothers, especially Judah. Social custom, repeatedly acknowledged in the text, dictated that the eldest son would be the father's heir. When God chooses against this custom, he expresses his love to the admittedly limited extent that he is choosing someone and rejecting someone else on unnamed subjective grounds. This is particularly clear in the choice of Joseph. What makes the choice of Joseph a bit different from that of Isaac or Jacob is that so much is known about Joseph by the time the choice is made. The text subtly suggests that God would not have liked Joseph if he were not like Joseph; and since Joseph has been shown to be loving, so perhaps is God. We are in the realm, needless to say, not of argument but of impression.

Ishmael was born to a slave mother. Esau lost his inheritance when Isaac blessed Jacob instead of him. In both cases, there was an external or formal reason for the Lord to prefer the younger brother over the elder. There is no comparable reason why God should prefer the younger Joseph over the elder Judah, the dominant figure among the twelve brothers. God does prefer Joseph, the text suggests, because—and here is the novelty—Joseph is the better man. In character and achievement, he is superior. That the text suggests this is the more remarkable because the Hebrew Bible, though not written entirely by the descendants of Judah, the Jews, has been preserved by them; and the Joseph story disparages the eponymous father of the Jews at no fewer than three points.

The first of these is Genesis 37:26–27, in which Judah proposes to his brothers that they sell Joseph into slavery. Under later law, such an action was a capital offense. It was also, more important, a heartless and violent act by the sons of Leah against Jacob, their father, who so loved Joseph and Benjamin, the sons of Rachel. The writer of the Joseph story (and here we must speak of a writer, not a redactor) deliberately puts Judah and Joseph onstage together as their drama comes to its climax. Judah, not yet recognizing Joseph, eloquently evokes for him the anguish of Jacob, who still grieves for Joseph and now fears the loss of Benjamin. Hearing this, Joseph can contain himself no longer: He bursts into tears and, in the lines quoted earlier, identifies himself to his brothers. Judah conducts himself honorably in these closing moments, but the very pathos of the scene is a defeat for him. Clearly, the man he wronged so many years before is his superior.

The second invidious comment about Judah comes in Genesis 38, just after the sale of Joseph. Now living with the Canaanites, Judah has taken a Canaanite wife and had three sons by her. When two of Judah's sons in succession marry the same Canaanite woman, Tamar, and die before she has conceived, the woman disguises herself as a cult prostitute, seduces Judah, and gives birth to twins by him. The polemical point of the story is not just that the Jews are the offspring of an incestuous union nor even that they are the offspring of an incestuous Israelite-Canaanite union but that they are the offspring of an incestuous union between an Israelite man and a Canaanite woman in the act of Canaanite cultic copulation. In the Tanakh, an origin in incest is a major signal of contempt. Thus, when Lot's daughters get him drunk and seduce him, the offspring become the despised Moabites and Ammonites (19:30–38). By Genesis 38, intermarriage with the Canaanites has twice been condemned: Abraham sends his servant to find a bride for Isaac in Aram-naharaim lest Isaac marry a Canaanite; Isaac and Rebekah send Jacob in the same direction lest he sadden them as Esau has done by marrying a Canaanite. The religious rituals of the Canaanites have not yet come in for condemnation, but they will, and this episode anticipates that condemnation. The story is placed, moreover, immediately before the story (Gen. 39) of Joseph's refusal to yield to the adulterous advances of an Egyptian officer's wife. The redactor (this episode is an insertion into the original Joseph story) clearly intends Joseph to gain by contrast with the offensive Judah.

The third moment of invidious comparison between Judah and Joseph comes at the end of the Book of Genesis, when Jacob adopts and blesses Ephraim and Manasseh, Joseph's sons by the Egyptian Asenath. Perez and Zerah, Judah's sons by Tamar, are ignored. Afterward, when Jacob begins a long, deathbed oracle on his twelve sons, his first words are an aside to Joseph: "Now, I assign to you one portion [Hebrew *shechem*] more than to your brothers, which I wrested from the Amorites with my sword and bow" (48:22). The allusion is to Shechem, the city that Simeon and Levi conquered and pillaged (whatever Jacob's weak remonstrances at the time), the city that was Abraham's first destination when he entered Canaan and Jacob's when he reentered it, and the city where Joseph innocently went in search of the brothers who then sold him into slavery. Much later, an Israelite monarchy will split into a northern kingdom dominated by the house of Joseph, with its capital at Shechem, and a southern kingdom, dominated by the house of Judah, with its capital at Jerusalem. Jacob's oracle, reflecting the perspective of the northern kingdom, contains a true blessing only for Joseph and mere predictions or comments about all his brothers. The oracle on Judah acknowledges his power in words of thrilling eloquence yet attributes his power to violence and nothing else:

> You, O Judah, your brothers shall praise;
>   Your hand shall be on the nape of your foes;
> Your father's sons shall bow low to you.
>   Judah is a lion's whelp;
> On prey, my son, have you grown.
>   He crouches, lies down like a lion,
> Like the king of beasts—who dare rouse him?
>   The scepter shall not depart from Judah,

Nor the ruler's staff from between his feet;
  So that tribute shall come to him
  And the homage of peoples be his.

He tethers his ass to a vine,
  His ass's foal to a choice vine;
He washes his garment in wine,
  His robe in blood of grapes.
His eyes are darker than wine;
  His teeth are whiter than milk. (49:8–12)

Like the Joseph story itself, the oracle of Jacob reflects the views of the anonymous apologist-historian of the northern kingdom, called in scholarship the Elohist for his exclusive use of *ʾelohim* to name God. The oracle's half-disguised and somewhat tangled polemic, like the polemical moments in the story, is of literary interest as one of the first moments when God is seen, however obscurely, to respond to human differences. To this point in the Bible, the Lord God's actions have never seemed to come in response to human qualities of any kind. Such distinctions as he has made among human beings have been gratuitous. There was nothing about Abraham, so far as we were told, to make the Lord select him to become a great nation. At the time when the Lord blessed Isaac and repeated to him the promise he had made to Abraham, Isaac too had done nothing of note. Joseph, by contrast, by the time Jacob blesses him, has an extraordinary career behind him. Though the blessing is not explicitly granted in recognition of Joseph's merit, the quiet, half-formed implication of the story as a whole is that Joseph deserves the blessing that comes at its end. God does seem, as Jacob breathes his last and is "gathered to his people," to have chosen Joseph for reasons that Joseph's story has put on display. Joseph—ardent, handsome, astute, commanding, and wonderfully kind—is the most appealing figure yet seen in the Bible. And God, for the first time, seems susceptible to the appeal.

3

INTERLUDE

What Makes God Godlike?

In Exodus, the second book of the Bible, the Lord will return with sudden, violent force, ending his relative absence from the last chapters of the Book of Genesis. Before looking in detail at the character he assumes on his return, we might pause to consider what it is, in literary terms, that makes God as we know him at this point godlike. What makes him different?

God—and in this brief interlude we intend the word *God* to mean not *ʾelohim* but the protagonist of the Tanakh in as much complexity as has appeared by the end of the Book of Genesis—is in the most basic sense of the word the protagonist, the *protos agonistes* or "first actor," of the Bible. He does not enter the human scene. He *creates* the human scene that he then enters. He creates the human antagonist whose interaction with him shapes all the subsequent action. This is his first and most obvious distinguishing feature.

If God's priority makes his human antagonist uniquely dependent on him, it is nonetheless also true that God is uniquely dependent on his human antagonist and that this dependence complicates the attempt to do what we are doing—namely, to read the Bible as God's story. For though human dependence on God is never denied in the Bible, in practice much of what humans are seen doing in it has a "natural" autonomy that is unmatched by anything that God is seen doing. By no means all the human action reported in the Bible joins mankind to God as antagonist to protagonist, but the reverse is not true: None of the divine action reported in the Bible is unlinked to human beings; none of it is, in that sense, purely divine. God takes no action that does not have man as its object. There are no "adventures of God."

This is, up to a point, the inevitable result of monotheism. Polytheistic Greek mythology includes some stories that tell of intervention by Zeus in human affairs but others that tell of Zeus's life among his fellow gods. In the Bible, God, being the only god, does not have that second kind of action through which to present himself. But the peculiarity of God's character does not end there. God could conceivably engage in some kind of demonstrative action that would serve his own self-presentation apart from any interaction with man: miraculous displays, cosmic disruptions, the creation of other worlds. But in fact he refrains from all such activity. Not only does he lack any social life among other gods but he also lacks what we might call a private life. His only way of pursuing an interest in himself is through mankind.

God's words show the same symbiotic character as his deeds. Even lacking, as he does, all divine companionship (he is, to begin with, without a consort), why does God never talk to himself? Surely the divine mind could open itself in discursive soliloquy. But it does not. In the opening scenes of the Book of Genesis—the creation and the flood—something close to soliloquy is heard. From that point on, however, all of God's speech is directed at man, and, in most cases, it is also directive *of* man. God is like a novelist who is literally incapable of autobiography or criticism and can *only* tell his own story through his characters. Moreover, he can only deal with his characters creatively; his only creative tactic with them is direction. He tells them what to do so that they will be what he wants them to be. He is not interested in them in their own right. He does not deal with them analytically. He is always directive, never appreciative.

As for the concrete particulars of what God wants mankind to be, this he only discovers as he goes along. His manner is always supremely confident, but he does not announce or seem even to know all his plans in detail or in advance. Again and again, God is displeased with man, but often enough it seems that he discovers only in and through his anger just what pleases him. To change the analogy slightly, he is like a director whose actors never seem to get it right and who is, as a result, often angry but who doesn't, himself, always know beforehand what getting it right will be. When the actors get it wrong, he too gets it wrong until, finally, they get it more or less right, and he calms down enough to admit it. Getting it right is, in the Bible, not just a matter of mankind's observing the law of God (at this point in the story, the law has not even been given). It is rather, and much more broadly, a matter of mankind's becoming the image of God. That quest, arising from the protagonist's sole stated motive, drives the only real plot that the Bible can be said to have. But that plot, God's attempt to shape mankind in his image, would be far more comprehensible if God had a richer subjective life, one more clearly separate from, more clearly prior to, the human object of his shaping.

As it is, the plot of the Bible is difficult and elusive in a way that is intimately related to the difficulty and elusiveness of God as its protagonist. Experience shapes character, and character determines action. A character totally without experience is all but a contradiction in terms. If such a character could exist at all, we would scarcely know what to expect of him or what it would mean to be shaped in his image. True, we are well enough accustomed—in life and in literature—to see an innocent character living through new, sometimes painful experiences and so undergoing a character development. But that innocence, that lack of experience, is always only a relative lack. A country boy come to the big city does, when all is said and done, have eighteen or so years of history behind him. It is that history that makes him comprehensible to us. How would we understand him if chronologically he were eighteen but characterologically, a parentless newborn babe? His character would then necessarily lie entirely in his future rather than in his past. He could only be what he would become, and so at the outset he could only be a kind of living question mark.

God, though we have managed to say a good deal about him in the Book of Genesis, is this kind of living question mark, a wholly prospective character. He has no history, no genealogy, no past that in the usual way of literature might be progressively introduced into his story to explain his behavior and induce some kind of catharsis in the reader. No human character could be so fully without a past and still be human, yet we may see that by giving this inhuman character words to speak in human language and deeds to do in interaction with human beings, the writers of the Bible have created a new literary possibility. God frustrates our ordinary literary expectations, shaped as they are by the expectations that we have of other human beings when we meet them. We expect to learn who they are by learning how their past has led to their present. This is, almost by definition, what makes any human character interesting and coherent.

God is not interesting or coherent in this way. That the Greek gods had recognizably human bodies was ultimately less important to their anthropomorphism than that they had genealogies and desires, pasts and futures. God has neither, and the stray anthropomorphisms of detail that appear in the Book of Genesis are dwarfed by that overwhelming fact. We must think of God as newborn and yet not a babe, his possibilities not confined within the boundaries of human experience and yet, paradoxically, not to be realized unless in relationship with human beings. His manner in the Book of Genesis is, very roughly, that of a man of unreflective self-confidence, intrusive-to-aggressive habits, and unpredictable eloquence but, above all, a man who discloses nothing about his past and next to nothing about his needs or desires. When the adjective *godlike* refers implicitly to this God—Adam's maker and Abraham's partner—rather than, say, to the youthful, physically beautiful, and brilliant Apollo, it signifies a set of qualities like those just mentioned; and if the type in question is a familiar one in the West, biblical influence must be presumed. What is most compelling about the type is an air of power coupled with the absence of any of the usual clues as to how the power might be used.

In the case of absolutely every human character, we know that, though he may disclose nothing about his past, he has had one, nonetheless, one that included a mother, a birth, and a mewling and puking infancy. As for his future, though he may disclose no intentions, we do not believe him to be without desires. A powerful manner can intimidate, but adults know that godlikeness resting on a denial of the past and the future can be nothing more than a pose. Just here, however, the analogy breaks down: God is not posing. He is not the Wizard of Oz. He is portrayed, with apparent sincerity and unwavering consistency, as truly without a past and, though not without intentions, as truly without desires except the desire that mankind should be his self-image. Otherwise, though his intentions, rudimentary at first, grow more complex, and though he is surprised by their effects and inclined to repudiate them, they are not the product of desire until very late in his story. At the start, and for a long while after the start, God relies on man even for the working out of his own intentions and is, to this extent, almost parasitic on human desire. If man wanted nothing, it is difficult to imagine how God would discover what God wanted.

ONCE WE RECOGNIZE God as dependent on human beings in this way, we may appreciate why, for him, the quest for a self-image is not an idle and optional indulgence but the sole and indispensable tool of his self-understanding. If no one has painted your portrait, you, as a human being, still know who you are. Even if you have never seen yourself in a mirror, the same will be true. The person in the portrait, the person reflected in the mirror, is already in existence, and you know that person. Your history has both made you and made you a fact evident to yourself. God, as the Bible begins, is as yet unmade by any history and is therefore less than evident to himself. Though he is, uniquely, a protagonist who gives life itself to his antagonist, he is also, uniquely again, a protagonist who receives his life story from his antagonist.

The story of God's life is the story of his lifework, the creation of mankind in his own image. Concretely, that act of creation is achieved through the human history that constitutes the plot of the Bible. But this plot not only does not but cannot begin in medias res because God himself, who begins it, is so without history. There is, strange as it may sound to say this, too little *to* God at the start of the Bible for his story to begin that way. How then does it begin? When he tells mankind to "be fertile and increase," God makes mankind's single defining action—the only positive action mankind is told to take—an image of the single action that, at the start, defines God himself. Mankind's fertility and self-multiplication then anger God, however, and a conflict is generated that moves the action forward. God discovers, after the fact, that unchecked fertility was not quite what he had in mind. He destroys creation with an enormous flood only to discover that destruction was not what he had in mind either. He vows to Noah and his family, the only human survivors, that he will never destroy the world again, but he is now so riven that his vow is not altogether convincing.

Then what? Historically speaking, as we noted in Chapter 2, *yahweh* and *ʾelohim* seem to have separately absorbed the personality of a destroyer god rather like Babylonian Tiamat, the flood dragon, whose defeat by Babylonian Marduk was Babylonia's creation myth.

By positing some such conflation of deities, historians can explain the origin of contradiction in the character of the God of the Tanakh. Yet whatever the explanation, the contradiction must then be confronted as a literary reality. It is as if to say, "Yes, I understand: Your father was a doctor, your mother was a spy, but now I must get to know *you*."

After the biblical flood, and despite his reassuring vow never to destroy the world again, God retains a radical and ominous creative/destructive ambivalence. But if God's fusion of the personalities of creator and destroyer has consequences for his character, it also has consequences for the plot of the Bible. What the divine rejection of, on the one hand, unchecked human fertility and, on the other, any further destruction of the world contributes to the plot is a compromise: a reproductive covenant with one part of mankind. Fertility is still promised, but it is no longer promised to mankind as a whole. Instead, it is promised exclusively or at least preeminently to Abraham and his descendants, and even this restricted fertility is not Abraham's sovereign possession. It is now a power exercised only in conjunction with God. In this new order, God's intervention permits Abraham and Sarah, yes, to conceive and bear in their old age, but Abraham's penis is no longer his own possession. As circumcision so well symbolizes, the organ and the power behind it now belong partly to God.

The story of God-as-creator and mankind-as-progenitor unfolds like a jejune two-part musical invention that by contrapuntal repetition and variation becomes an elaborate and magnificent fugue. The sexual obsession of the early narrative gives it an extraordinary, primal, almost animal power. And yet there is something abstract about that very narrowness, that very intensity. The Book of Genesis, at least until the story of Joseph, is a narrative of brutal single-mindedness. Barrenness, conception, birth; masturbation, seduction, rape; uxoricide, fratricide, infanticide—these are the terms of the action. The narrative is preoccupied with reproduction and threats to reproduction to the exclusion of nearly everything else in human experience. But the narrative art of the Bible lies not just in the often noted power of these first biblical stories but also, and even more, in the way it manages the emergence of subsequent, far more complex events from such schematic beginnings. And as the narrative grows more complex, it is able to contain and carry progressively more elaborate nonnarrative material: poetic, legal, and prophetic presentations of God as protagonist and of mankind as God's image and antagonist.

In the Book of Exodus, to which we turn next, the struggle between mankind and God over human reproductive power enters a decisive new phase. As this book opens, the reproductive covenant between the Lord and Abraham, which tamed the creator/destroyer conflict in the Lord God, has generated a new provocation and exposed a new conflict. This has happened because of the very success of the Abrahamic covenant. Abraham and his one son have become Isaac and his two, then Jacob and his twelve, then the twelve and their seventy, and finally, as the Book of Exodus opens, a nation large enough to rival mighty Egypt: "The Israelites were fertile and prolific; they multiplied and increased very greatly, so that the land was filled with them" (Exod. 1:7). As we noted earlier, the Lord's promise of fertility to Abraham was a clear, if implicit, revocation of his promise to the rest of mankind. But though its consequence might strike us as foreseeable, the Lord quite clearly has not foreseen it. (In the terms of the narrative, of course, all these things are happening for the first time; there is no past from which to draw lessons for the future, and there is also no claim of omniscience.) The Lord is caught off guard, as it were; he does not immediately respond when, as Israel begins to grow into a great nation on Egyptian territory, the Egyptians defend themselves by enslaving the Israelites. But the Egyptian defense is futile: With God's help, the Israelite numbers continue to grow, the Israelite women giving birth all but without labor. Finally, Egypt's ruler gives an order that directly contravenes God's wishes: "Every boy that is born [to the Hebrews] you shall throw into the Nile" (1:22).

God has faced disobedience before but never such outright defiance. His response to it will turn him, for the first time, into a warrior. But before we consider that change, we must consider the conflict that Pharaoh has exposed within God's own character. The outer, Israelite-Egyptian conflict arises from this inner conflict. It was God, after all, who promised fertility to all men equally at creation, and who did so again after the flood, but who then promised—and delivered—a greater fertility to Abraham and his descendants. God is now confronted with the results of his inconsistent action: A powerful fertility loser is fighting back against God's designated fertility winner. How can the conflict be resolved? Remember that at the creation and after the flood God told the Egyptians too, at least by inclusion, to be fertile and increase.

One way to resolve the conflict or, better, one condition under which it would not have arisen is polytheism. That is, a god who was "of" Abraham could coherently promise him superior fertility as well as the possession of the land of "the Kenites, the Kenizzites, the Kadmonites," and so forth. Other gods, comparably personal, comparably "of" the leaders of those other groups, could coherently promise their devotees the same. The results, it would be understood, would be settled on the field of battle. Meanwhile, the God of heaven, understood to be over all men as well as over all other gods, would refrain from making such narrow promises. And if the human rivals descended to outright warfare, the God of heaven could retain his universal jurisdiction by abstaining from battlefield alliance with the forces of any side.

If keeping the God of heaven above the fray is one way to resolve the fertility conflict, another way is to turn the one God into a divine warrior. The God who is God of all may then take sides as if he were a god "of," but he must pay the price of the contradiction by allowing a change to take place in his own character. He must assume another role in human affairs than would otherwise be his. In Genesis 24, we saw an early stage in the fusion of the high or sky God with the personal "god of" when Abraham referred to the god who was to assist Abraham's servant in finding a wife for Isaac—a humble, lower-level errand—as "the Lord, the God of heaven" (Gen. 24:7). Abraham's servant made the same identification when he prayed, "O Lord, O god of my master Abraham . . ." (24:12). At the beginning of the Book of Exodus, however, what was earlier only a tentative, implicit fusion becomes confident and explicit. The "of-ness" of the Lord God is extended to the now huge nation of Israel, formalized by a covenant, and backed by the action of *yahweh*, who now becomes an exceedingly warlike deity.

In short, as in any effective plot, one action leads to another. God's creation leads to mankind's reproduction, which leads to war, which leads to God's taking part in the war. And as in any great work of literature, the deeper "action" is interior. It consists of the profound spiritual changes that the action works in the characters. It is as a consequence of Israel's fertility in Egypt that *yahweh*, the Lord, the god of Abraham, Isaac, and Jacob, is drawn into battle for the first time in his career. As he wages war, he is changed by what he does. War transforms him, and he becomes, permanently, a divine warrior. For the decisive and effectively the last time in the Tanakh, he adds to his character another entire divine personality, this time that of the ferocious Canaanite war god, Baal.

The relationship between the plot of the Bible and the character of monotheism's God, a deity who was, historically, a precipitate of Semitic polytheism, is thus intricate but coherent. First, the creator/destroyer contradiction within this deity is resolved by a fertility covenant between God and one man. A focus on the private concerns of this one man effects a further fusion between, on the one hand, the still-cosmic creator/destroyer deity and, on the other, the far humbler and more terrestrial personal god. Then, as Israel—super-fertile, thanks to the covenant—threatens to dominate Egypt, the inherent tension in the high god/personal god fusion requires for its alleviation that the Lord become and remain a warrior in addition to whatever else he is. The equation is creator (*yahweh/ᵓelohim*) + cosmic destroyer (*Tiamat*) + personal god (*god of . . .*) + warrior (*Baal*) = GOD, the composite protagonist of the Tanakh.

HISTORICALLY SPEAKING, the several elements were not combined in this simple order. The plotting of these elements—their narrative presentation in the opening books of the Tanakh—represents the literary achievement of a number of writers in a process whose complexity historical scholarship will never be finished charting. However, this literary achievement rests on a prior intellectual synthesis, a feat of religious rather than literary creativity. It was only as a set of several gods was imagined into a unity dynamic with unresolved tensions that the path was broken for the writing of a story of God in which the full complexity of a character with multiple personalities could be presented and the tensions within that character could be coherently and progressively revealed.

Did the telling of the stories create the God, or did the God, imagined first, provoke the telling of the stories? By stressing how recalcitrant a subject for storytelling this being without history or desire is, how uninteresting in all ordinary human and literary ways, I have already suggested which answer I think the more plausible. A shared idea of God must have come first, not that it can have come all at once. Only the fact that it was shared can explain how so large a number of writers working separately over so long a period of time could have produced a work that, in all its variety, has a deep underlying unity. Historical critical scholarship, having assigned different parts of different biblical books to different writers as well as, more recently, different and vastly expanded roles to different later redactors, has changed forever the way the Bible is read. But the unity of the Bible was not imposed entirely after the fact by clever editing. That unity rests ultimately on the singularity of the Bible's protagonist, the One God, the *monos theos* of monotheism. This God arose as a fusion, to be sure, but not of *all* prior gods, only of several. The inner contradictions that were the result of the fusion took shape, quite early on, as a finite set of inner contradictions. It was the biblical writers' common intellectual grasp of this set of contradictions—this set and no other—that permitted them, working over centuries, to contribute to the drawing of a single character.

Literarily speaking, the Bible is unique on several counts, of which three may be mentioned at this point. First of all, it is a translated classic. Only a minority of those for whom it has functioned as a classic over the centuries have read it in the languages in which it was written. Second, in an oddly modern way, it is a classic with a choice of orderings and endings that depends on the reader. The reader must choose to read it either as the Tanakh, the Hebrew Bible, or as the Christian Bible with the Old Testament in its distinct order and with the New Testament as an alternate ending.

A third, more important, but less easily formulated count on which the Bible is literarily unique, however, is the character of its central narrative. The long narrative that fills the first eleven books of the Bible, stretching from the creation of the world through the fall of Jerusalem, has sometimes been called a saga but it is not. The word *saga*, though now often used of any long story of historical origins, refers paradigmatically to several works in classical Icelandic. Though, like the Bible, these tell the story of a nation's origins and though they contain various miraculous or supernatural episodes, no single being is their protagonist as God is the protagonist of the Bible. Nor is the biblical narrative like a classical epic. Though the Greek gods play a large role in the classical epics, classical epic and biblical narrative differ in their conception of time. The epics, vast as they seem, are understood to cover only a crucial period in a much longer temporal framework. All the gods, as well as all the human characters, have pasts, old grudges, vows to discharge, scores to settle, and destinies to fulfill as the action begins. The richly textured, densely populated feeling that characterizes the classical epics, right from their immortal opening lines, contrasts with the open weave, so to call it, the relative barrenness and emptiness, of the Bible in its opening moments. The biblical narrative, whose distinctness every reader or hearer immediately and intuitively senses, works as it does because God, its all-defining protagonist, is a character without a past. A protagonist without a past yields a narrative without a memory, a narrative that is radically forward-looking and open-ended because, given its protagonist, it has no other alternative.

The chain of events that turns *yahweh* into a warrior and all but catapults the Lord God forward begins when

> The Israelites were groaning under the bondage and cried out; and their cry for help from the bondage rose up to God. God heard their moaning, and God remembered His covenant with Abraham and Isaac and Jacob. God looked upon the Israelites, and God took notice of them. (Exod. 2:23–25)

It is to the continuation of this story that we now turn.

4

Exhilaration

Israel is in Egypt, a mighty throng under genocidal attack. Moses, an Israelite raised as an Egyptian after being rescued from Pharaoh's infanticide, has murdered an oppressive Egyptian overseer and fled to Midian. There, now married, he is shepherding his father-in-law's sheep near "Horeb, the mountain of God," when the Lord appears to him:

> An angel of the Lord appeared to him in a blazing fire out of a bush. He gazed, and there was a bush all aflame, yet the bush was not consumed. Moses said, "I must turn aside to look at this marvelous sight; why doesn't the bush burn up?" When the Lord saw that he had turned aside to look, God called to him out of the bush: "Moses! Moses!" He answered, "Here I am." And He said, "Do not come closer. Remove your sandals from your feet, for the place on which you stand is holy ground. I am," He said, "the God of your father, the God of Abraham, the God of Isaac, and the God of Jacob." And Moses hid his face, for he was afraid to look at God. (Exod. 3:2–6)

The angel of the Lord, equivalent to the Lord (*yahweh*), is referred to a few words later as God (*ʾelohim*). The two names are used interchangeably within a single sentence: "When the Lord saw that [Moses] had turned aside to look, God called to him. . . ." Here the identities of the Lord and God fuse completely. A further fusion between the two of them and the personal god(s) comes when God identifies himself to Moses as at one and the same time the god of Abraham, the god of Isaac, the god of Jacob, and the god of Moses' own father. Any residual sense that the gods "of" these different men were different gods—a sense that, as we saw, Jacob himself seemed to have at the beginning of his career (Gen. 27:20 and 28:20–22)—is eliminated at this moment. These three gods "of" have never been spoken of this way before—that is, in apposition to one another. Moses has an Egyptian rather than an Israelite name, and his father is not named in the Tanakh, a highly exceptional omission. Does the omission suggest that Moses was illegitimate? That he had an Egyptian father? Sigmund Freud's speculations in *Moses and Monotheism* aside, the voice from the burning bush subsumes "the God of your father," whoever Moses' father was.

But these changes, significant as they are, merely solidify an old, if complex, identity that we have already seen approaching this unity. What is novel in this apparition is that the Lord God speaks from amid flame and atop a sacred mountain. He has never done this before.

But someone else has. The history of ancient Semitic religion does know of a god whose signature is mountain and flame: Baal, the dominant deity in Canaan, the region to which Abram came when he left Ur. Baal was simultaneously a war god, a storm god, a fertility god, and a mountain/volcano god. Like the word *ʾel*, which we have already seen, the word *baʿal* can be both a common noun and a proper name. As a common noun in Hebrew and the other languages in the Northwest Semitic group, to which Hebrew belongs, *baʿal* means "owner, master" or "lord" in that sense: the "lord of the manor." As a proper name, the same word refers to a deity, Baal, who is the master of the universe but who, notably, has acquired his mastery by military force. In mythical terms, he is a young god, a rebel god.

Liberator

"Your Right Hand Shatters the Foe"

EXODUS 1:1–15:21

If the setting (the flame, the mountain) in which the Lord God speaks to Moses is unfamiliar, so is the action announced:

> And the Lord continued, "I have marked well the plight of My people in Egypt and have heeded their outcry because of their taskmasters; yes, I am mindful of their sufferings. I have come down to rescue them from the Egyptians and to bring them out of that land to a good and spacious land, a land flowing with milk and honey, the region of the Canaanites, the Hittites, the Amorites, the Perizzites, the Hivites, and the Jebusites. . . . I will send you to Pharaoh, and you shall free My people, the Israelites, from Egypt."
>
> But Moses said to God, "Who am I that I should go to Pharaoh and free the Israelites from Egypt?" And He said, "I will be with you; that shall be your sign that it was I who sent you. And when you have freed the people from Egypt, you shall worship God at this mountain."
>
> Moses said to God, "When I come to the Israelites and say to them 'The God of your fathers has sent me to you,' and they ask me, 'What is His name?' what shall I say to them?" And God said to Moses, "Ehyeh-Asher-Ehyeh." He continued, "Thus shall you say to the Israelites, 'Ehyeh sent me to you.' " And God said further to Moses, "Thus shall you speak to the Israelites: The Lord, the God of your fathers, the God of Abraham, the God of Isaac, and the God of Jacob, has sent me to you:
>
> This shall be My name forever,
> This My appellation for all eternity."
>
> (Exod. 3:7–15)

When Moses asks God for an answer to the question What is His name? God says something, but does he say his name or does he give another kind of reply instead? The JPS translation transliterates rather than translates God's words: *ʾehyeh ʾašer ʾehyeh*. The RSV translates: "I AM WHO I AM." The three words in question are extremely familiar Hebrew words: *ʾehyeh* ("I am") *ʾašer* ("who" or "that which") *ʾehyeh* ("I am"). The word *ʾehyeh* can mean "I shall be" as well as "I am." Context ordinarily determines which is the correct translation, but God gives no context. Thus, rather than saying that his name is "I Am Who I Am," God could be saying, "I am what I shall be"; in effect, "You'll find out who I am." The matter is interestingly complicated by the fact that, as originally written, the Hebrew text contained the consonants only: *ʾhyh ʾšr ʾhyh*. By changing just one letter, the third word in this sentence can be made a form of the archaic Hebrew root *hwh*, from which the name *yahweh* is derived. The difference between *ʾhyh ʾšr ʾhyh* and *ʾhyh ʾšr ʾhwh* is small even when the letters of our alphabet are used. In the Hebrew alphabet the graphic (written) difference between *y* and *w* is almost microscopic. Add slightly different vowels, making the sentence read *ʾehyeh ʾašer ʾahweh*, and the similarity of the last word, *ʾahweh*, to *yahweh* is immediately apparent.

What would *ʾehyeh ʾašer ʾahweh* mean? The root *hwh*, as noted, is archaic. Hebraicists have had to speculate about its meaning. But most likely it means "become," and in its causative conjugation, the one to which the name *yahweh* belongs, it would mean "cause to become" or "make happen" or simply "act." The sentence *ʾehyeh ʾašer ʾahweh* would then mean "I am what I do." As we have already repeatedly seen, God is indeed defined by what he does, defined this way even for himself. His actions precede his intentions, or at least they precede full consciousness about his intentions. It is no exaggeration (and it is certainly not intended to be any insult) to say that he does not know who he is. Even to himself, he is a mystery that is revealed progressively only through his actions and their aftermath. But the moment of his apparition to Moses is obviously one of relatively intense self-consciousness. The simultaneous application of so many names to himself is, on God's part, an action of gathering self-knowledge. And there is also a line in which God appears to speak with the special self-knowledge of confession. After seeming to evade Moses' question by saying, "I am what I do," God recovers and gives Moses an explicit answer to pass along to the Israelites. In the JPS translation: "Thus shall you say to the Israelites, 'ʾEhyeh sent me to you.' " Again changing *ʾehyeh* to *ʾahweh*, we can see a change in the meaning of God's instruction to Moses: "Tell the Israelites, ' "I Will Act" sent me.' "

Highly speculative as all this is in detail, it is quite likely, historically speaking, that the cryptic phrase *ʾehyeh ʾašer ʾehyeh* was in some way connected with the introduction of the name *yahweh*; in other words, as originally understood, the burning bush vision probably included a folk etymology of the name *yahweh*. This reading may be wrong; it certainly cannot be proven right. But it is borne out by the massively and uncharacteristically activist character of what immediately follows in the text:

> Go and assemble the elders of Israel and say to them: the Lord, the God of your fathers, the God of Abraham, Isaac, and Jacob, has appeared to me and said, "I have taken note of you and of what is being done to you in Egypt, and I have declared: I will take you out of the misery of Egypt to the land of the Canaanites, the Hittites, the Amorites, the Perizzites, the Hivites, and the Jebusites, to a land flowing with milk and honey." They will listen to you; then you shall go with the elders of Israel to the king of Egypt and you shall say to him, "The Lord, the God of the Hebrews, manifested Himself to us. Now therefore, let us go a distance of three days into the wilderness to sacrifice to the Lord our God." Yet I know that the king of Egypt will let you go only because of a greater might. So I will stretch out My hand and smite Egypt with various wonders which I will work upon them; after that he shall let you go. And I will dispose the Egyptians favorably toward this people, so that when you go, you will not go away empty-handed. Each woman shall borrow from her neighbor and the lodger in her house objects of silver and gold, and clothing, and you shall put these on your sons and daughters, thus stripping the Egyptians. (3:16–22)

In all his promises to mankind as a whole and to Israel in particular, the Lord has never before promised to stretch out his hand and smite Egypt or any other nation. This is particularly striking because it is *not* the case that the Lord's chosen people has never had to go to war before. In Genesis 14, as noted, Abram goes to war against an alliance of four kings, but the Lord is not invoked before battle or thanked afterward. At that point in his story, the Lord is simply not a warrior: Abram does not expect this of him; only ironically, if at all, does the Lord seem to expect it of himself. In Genesis 19, the Lord destroys Sodom, but the destruction does not come as an intervention by God in any human war but rather because of a direct, sexual affront by the citizens of the town to the Lord himself, who is visiting them in the guise of two men. And if the threat of divine violence is a surprise, so is the promise of Egyptian tribute. God wishes something more than that his people should be delivered from bondage; he also wishes a grossly material tribute on the part of the Egyptians. Nothing that the Lord God has ever claimed for himself or promised to Israel was to take this form—jewelry, silver, gold, et cetera—or come in this way as the spoils of victory.

Moses fears that the people will not believe him; God gives him the power to perform wonders to convince them. Moses fears that he lacks the necessary eloquence; God, angered, promises him his brother Aaron as spokesman. Moses and his wife, Zipporah, then set out for Egypt with their sons. En route, however, God reveals himself to them in a more paradoxical guise than ever:

> And the Lord said to Moses, "When you return to Egypt, see that you perform before Pharaoh all the marvels that I have put within your power. I, however, will stiffen his heart so that he will not let the people go. Then you shall say to Pharaoh, 'Thus says the Lord: Israel is My first-born son. I have said to you, "Let My son go, that he may worship Me," yet you refuse to let him go. Now I will slay your first-born son.' "
>
> At a night encampment on the way, the Lord encountered him and sought to kill him. So Zipporah took a flint and cut off her son's foreskin, and touched his [Moses'] legs [euphemism for genitals] with it, saying, "You are truly a bridegroom of blood to me!" And when He let him alone, she added, "A bridegroom of blood because of the circumcision." (Exod. 4:21–26)

The Lord, who starting with Abraham has engaged in selective creation, now begins to engage in selective destruction. The spoils that the Israelites are to take from Egypt are not all the Lord is after. He also wishes the Egyptians to see that Israel's victory is the Lord's victory, and for that purpose a simple consent will not do: There must be a victory and the taking of life. The Lord will harden Pharaoh's heart to assure this outcome. As for his attitude toward Moses, when Zipporah touches her son Gershom's foreskin to that of her evidently uncircumcised husband, she circumcises Moses symbolically and saves him from death by the hand of God. Her action reminds us that the covenant of which circumcision is the sign was an alternative to a repetition of the destruction visited upon the generation of Noah. The bleeding foreskin of the boy Gershom, touched to Moses' genitals, is the sign not just of promised life but of death averted by submission; namely, by the surrender of generative autonomy.

Israel is, yes, the Lord's "first-born son," but the expression is used only for Pharaoh's benefit. At this point, the Lord has never said to Israel or to any Israelite, "You are my son," and he will not take his first tentative step toward characterizing himself as Israel's father for centuries. He is asserting, rather, that what Israel's reproductive power produces, he owns. When, as predicted, he slays the firstborn of Egypt, the act will be linked to the Israelite practice of treating all firstborn, animal and human, as forfeit to the Lord. The rituals of forfeiture, like circumcision, are apotropaic; that is, they avert divine wrath by appeasing it. Because just at this moment the Lord is about to become a god of death as he has not been since the flood, and because all those who are not visibly with him will be counted against him, this weird episode of fathers and sons and murder averted by circumcision is not the indecipherable and irrelevant intrusion that it first seems. Circumcision, from the start, has had everything to do with foiling the divine murderer. And Israel's women are as much at risk as men. The women are brides of blood—brides in danger of death at God's hand—just as their husbands are bridegrooms of blood.

MOSES AND AARON'S first attempt to induce Pharaoh to free the Israelites is the ruse of a mere three-day trip into the wilderness. The ruler is not deceived and only oppresses the Israelites the more. They complain to Moses, who complains to the Lord and receives this response:

> "Say, therefore, to the Israelite people: I am the Lord. I will free you from the labors of the Egyptians and deliver you from their bondage. I will redeem you with an outstretched arm and through extraordinary chastisements. And I will take you to be My people, and I will be your God. And you shall know that I, the Lord, am your God who freed you from the labors of the Egyptians. I will bring you into the land which I swore to give to Abraham, Isaac, and Jacob, and I will give it to you for a possession, I the Lord." But when Moses told this to the Israelites they would not listen to Moses, their spirits crushed by cruel bondage. (6:6–9)

Never before when the Lord has wanted to speak has he spoken through an intermediary such as Moses. Never has he offered his action as a response to human skepticism.

If God is more remote in one way, however, he is more directly intrusive in another. He has not previously exercised any dominion over the human mind or heart. Thus, for example, Adam and Eve were ordered not to eat from the tree of the knowledge of good and evil, but God did not attempt to manipulate their minds or appetites so as to ensure their obedience. Here, while inflicting the "ten plagues," as they are traditionally called, the Lord repeatedly intervenes in Pharaoh's very mind to prevent him from acting in the best interests of Egypt. The Lord's motives are undisguised. Before sending the plague of locusts, he says to Moses:

> Go to Pharaoh. For I have hardened his heart and the hearts of his courtiers, in order that I may display these My signs among them, and that you may recount in the hearing of your sons and of your sons' sons how I made a mockery of the Egyptians and how I displayed My signs among them—in order that you may know that I am the Lord. (10:1–2)

The Israelites are to gloat over the disaster that befalls Egypt, and the very gloating will be an acknowledgment of the Lord's power. In a particularly chilling passage, Moses' ferocious last words to Pharaoh, the Lord's emissary makes it clear why Egypt must suffer:

> Moses said, "Thus says the Lord: Toward midnight I will go forth among the Egyptians, and every first-born in the land of Egypt shall die, from the first-born of Pharaoh who sits on his throne to the first-born of the slave girl who is behind the millstones; and all the first-born of the cattle. And there shall be a loud cry in all the land of Egypt, such as has never been or will ever be again; but not a dog shall snarl at any of the Israelites, at man or beast—in order that you may know that the Lord makes a distinction between Egypt and Israel. Then all these courtiers of yours shall come down to me and bow low to me, saying, 'Depart, you and all the people who follow you!' After that I will depart." And he left Pharaoh's presence in hot anger. (11:4–8)

The Israelites are not a small, oppressed minority seeking release from bondage. One of the reasons Pharaoh refuses to let them go is that they are already more numerous than the original inhabitants of the land (5:5). The census of Numbers 2 finds 603,550 adult males, not counting adult males of the Tribe of Levi. Counting wives, children, and servants, the number could be perhaps seven times that large. In short, the Israelites are a majority whom Pharaoh, a god in his own right, of course, according to Egyptian belief, was attempting to dominate. But their departure from Egypt is not, despite its later use in liberation movements, a victory for justice. It is simply a victory, a demonstration of the power of the Lord to pursue fertility for his chosen people and wreck it for their enemy, a proof that "the Lord makes a distinction" when and as he chooses. This is also the meaning of the "passover offering to the Lord" (Exod. 12:11). Moses instructs the Israelites to splash the blood of a ceremonially slain lamb on their doorposts and lintels and quotes the Lord's reason: "When I see the blood I will *pass over* you, so that no plague will destroy you when I strike the land of Egypt" (12:13, italics added). This, rather than any more conventionally benevolent sentiment, is what Moses instructs the Israelites to celebrate in generations to come (12:14–28). That the Lord could have slain the Israelite firstborn too—that they also belong to him—is the meaning of the legal duty, inserted into the narrative at this point, to consecrate all firstborn to the Lord.

No responsible historian believes that at the time of the Exodus the Israelites actually outnumbered the Egyptians or that a company of 4 or 5 million people made its way through the desert and into Canaan. Despite the lack of any historical record outside the Bible, most historians do not believe that the story of the Exodus is a total fabrication. But were it an event of the size that the Bible reports, the likelihood of its leaving no record outside the Bible would be small. For the literary effect of the Book of Exodus to be what its authors intended, however, it is essential that readers imagine the numbers that the text reports rather than the ones that historians may, on other evidence, have good reason to believe. Historians of England have good reason to believe that Richard III was not the monster that Shakespeare made him out to be in the play that bears his name. Nonetheless, if the play is to work as Shakespeare intended, the villain must be allowed to be a villain. The same, analogously, goes for the Book of Exodus. Cecil B. De Mille's *The Ten Commandments*, with its mighty throng crossing the sea, may be truer to the intended literary effect of the Book of Exodus than scholarship's reconstruction of a band of minor tribes slipping through the marsh.

Be that as it may, when the Lord of the Passover insists that the power to give life when and where he wishes and destroy it when and where he wishes is his, his attitude is fully and clearly consistent with all that we have seen of his past behavior. What is new is not that basic attitude but only war among whole nations as a setting for it and mind manipulation (the hardening of Pharaoh's heart) as a tactic in its service. As a hostile tactic, this kind of direct address to the human heart is scarcely seen again in the Bible; but in more benevolent ways, it will loom progressively larger: God as the searcher, knower, prompter of the human heart and as liege whose vassals owe him wholehearted interior devotion as well as careful exterior observance. Ironically, God's first attitudinal interventions have Pharaoh and the Egyptians in view; they result in Pharaoh's heart-hardened determination not to consent to the departure of the Israelites (against the cry of his own advisers that "Egypt is ruined" [RSV; 10:7]) and in the gifts that the deceived Egyptians shower on the Israelites on the eve of their departure:

> The Israelites had done Moses' bidding and borrowed from the Egyptians objects of silver and gold, and clothing. And the Lord had disposed the Egyptians favorably toward the people, and they let them have their request; thus they stripped the Egyptians. (12:35–36)

The favorable disposition of the Egyptians sounds almost like fondness, but this fondness is the equivalent of another plague. It is as much a mind-altering act of God as the hardening of Pharaoh's heart, and its aim, unabashedly, is the humiliation of Egypt.

At this and related moments, we see how strongly the text insists on the Lord as its protagonist. The Israelites are not to be blamed for engaging in this plunder. It was God's idea. Similarly, they are not to be credited with valor or love of freedom in their escape from slavery. After the slaying of the firstborn, the Lord hardens Pharaoh's heart yet again, and he sends his army in doomed pursuit. As the army approaches, the Israelites say to Moses:

> Was it for want of graves in Egypt that you brought us to die in the wilderness? What have you done to us, taking us out of Egypt? Is this not the very thing we told you in Egypt, saying, "Let us be, and we will serve the Egyptians, for it is better for us to serve the Egyptians than to die in the wilderness"? (14:11–12)

There are moments when the Tanakh speaks a language so strange it might have dropped from the moon, and moments when a sentence will appear that might have been overheard yesterday. "Was it for want of graves . . ." is the second kind of sentence. If there is a kernel of historical truth in the story of the Exodus, something of the sort may well have been spoken. We can never know. The point of the sentence just at this juncture, however, is to strip the Israelites of autonomous virtue, just as the point of the divine hardening of Pharaoh's heart is to strip him of autonomous vice. The Exodus is neither an Israelite victory nor an Egyptian defeat. From start to finish, from the Israelite women giving birth before the midwife arrives to the Egyptian charioteers drowning in the Red Sea, the Exodus is an act of God.

When Moses and the Israelites see the Egyptians dead on the shore and know that they have escaped, they sing one of the great, exultant victory songs in all literature, and its tone, heard now for the first time, will never entirely desert the Bible. Muted, transposed, the same tone is audible still even on the last page of the New Testament. If we were forced to say in one word who God is and in another what the Bible is about, the answer would have to be: God is a *warrior*, and the Bible is about *victory*. The meaning of victory will change, yet no substitute will ever be found for the language of victory:

> I will sing to the Lord, for He has triumphed gloriously;
> Horse and driver He has hurled into the sea.
> The Lord is my strength and might;
> He is become my deliverance.
> This is my God and I will enshrine Him;
> The god of my father, and I will exalt Him.
> The Lord, the Warrior—
> Lord is His name!
> Pharaoh's chariots and his army
> He has cast into the sea;
> And the pick of his officers
> Are drowned in the Sea of Reeds.
> The deeps covered them;
> They went down into the depths like a stone.
> Your right hand, O Lord, glorious in power,
> Your right hand, O Lord, shatters the foe!
> In Your great triumph You break Your opponents;
> You send forth Your fury, it consumes them like straw.
> At the blast of Your nostrils the waters piled up,
> The floods stood straight like a wall;
> The deeps froze in the heart of the sea.
> The foe said,
> "I will pursue, I will overtake,
> I will divide the spoil;

My desire shall have its fill of them.
I will bare my sword—
My hand shall subdue them."
You made Your wind blow, the sea covered them;
They sank like lead in the majestic waters. (15:1–10)

In this first half of the song that continues to Exodus 15:18, we see in a kind of ecstatic fusion the same mix of elements we saw when Moses stood before the burning bush. The God who is praised is a personal god: He is "*my* strength and might . . . *my* deliverance." He is also "the god of *my* father" as well as both "God" and "the Lord." But whether as God, as the Lord, or as the "god of," this is a deity who has not previously shown himself to be a warrior. Now, suddenly, unexpectedly, he has shown himself an invincible warrior, defeating the mightiest military power the Israelites knew. That this being was on their side they already knew. They also knew that he had immense power, power over nature, the power of life and death. But that he would wield this power on their behalf in a military way, this is the great surprise and the source of the exultation.

The language used in the song alludes to cosmic victory in evoking this military victory: the victory of order over chaos, of Mesopotamian Marduk over Tiamat or (a similar myth) Canaanite Baal over Yam. The verse

At the blast of Your nostrils the waters piled up,
The floods stood straight like a wall;
The deeps froze in the heart of the sea

may be set alongside Genesis 1:9: "Let the water below the sky be gathered into one area, that the dry land may appear." Power greater than the power of the sea is clearly a power none can withstand; and no Israelite doubted that Israel's deity, whether called God or the Lord, had this power. But at the Red Sea, this power is seen to have a battlefield application that no one expected it would ever have. What can such a power not achieve? And what will it next seek to achieve?

Who is like You, O Lord, among the celestials;
Who is like You, majestic in holiness,
Awesome in splendor, working wonders!
You put out Your right hand,
The earth swallowed them.

In Your love You lead the people You redeemed;
In Your strength You guide them to Your holy abode.
The peoples hear, they tremble;
Agony grips the dwellers in Philistia.
Now are the clans of Edom dismayed;
The tribes of Moab—trembling grips them;
All the dwellers in Canaan are aghast.
Terror and dread descend upon them;
Through the might of Your arm they are still as stone—
Till Your people cross over, O Lord,
Till Your people cross whom You have ransomed.

You will bring them and plant them in Your own mountain,
The place You made to dwell in, O Lord,
The sanctuary, O Lord, which Your hands established.
The Lord will reign for ever and ever! (15:11–18)

Philistia, Edom, and Moab are nations through whose territory Israel must pass en route to Canaan, Canaan being the name both of a region and of a group of nations whose land God has repeatedly promised to Israel. No one of the four named peoples has enslaved or otherwise abused the Israelites, but war between them and Israel will result from the same divinely fostered fertility that made for war between Israel and Egypt; and as Egypt was defeated, so will they be. Their intentions, good or bad, have no bearing on the matter.

To this point, the song anticipates nothing but what God seems already to have promised. But when the singers imagine that the Lord has already brought them "in love" to his own abode, that he will "plant them in [his] own mountain," they go beyond anything that God himself has yet said. On internal evidence, it seems clear that, at least in its final form, this song comes from a time later than the date of the event it celebrates, and the references to God's abode are easily enough understood as an allusion to the temple at Jerusalem. The construction of the temple on Mount Zion in Jerusalem became the occasion for the application to the Lord of imagery—notably that of a noble and peaceful mountain abode—borrowed from the cult of Canaanite Baal. But the song includes these allusions precisely to suggest that, in their joyous imagination, the Israelites have already completed their journey, already conquered Canaan, already constructed the temple.

It is reasonable to infer from the central place assigned to the Exodus in Jewish tradition that Israel did win liberation and a victory of some kind over Egypt and that its confidence in its God surged in consequence. But if we hear this song as the Lord might hear it, we hear more devotion to Israel attributed to him than he has expressed. God never promised to take Abraham, Isaac, or Jacob, much less all their descendants, into his abode on his holy mountain. Even Joseph, exceptional in so many ways, is promised no such intimacy. He is said to have enjoyed God's "kindness" ("steadfast love" is another acceptable translation), but the claim made for him is made for no one else, not even for Abraham.

Clearly, a change has taken place. God now has an entire people on his hands, camped out in the desert as the direct result of his military intervention, dependent on him in a new way, living with him in a new intimacy. If they are to be, collectively, his image, they must change; but given the peculiar relationship of divine protagonist and human antagonist in this narrative, so must he.

Lawgiver

"Stone Tablets Inscribed with the Finger of God"

EXODUS 15:22–40:38

Ethical monotheism is commonly named as ancient Israel's signal contribution to Western civilization. In an age of unbelief, however, just why monotheism should be an advance on polytheism is not immediately apparent. If the one God is no less a fiction than the many gods were, wherein lies the gain? And if it is specifically ethical monotheism that is claimed as a crucial cultural achievement, is the claim an ethnocentric boast? Hinduism is polytheistic to this day. Are Hindus less ethical than monotheistic, Bible-reading Jews and Christians?

A modest attempt to answer that question may help to ground the somewhat unusual kind of criticism that follows. The emergence of ethical monotheism in Israel deserves the honor it has received as a crucial step in the cultural history of the West, but there are alternate paths to an equivalent outcome. What counts is that, in one way or another, moral value shall have been placed above the other values that human beings properly recognize: power, wealth, pleasure, beauty, knowledge . . . the list is long. All these goods of human life must somehow be gathered into a single perspective and ranked, and moral goodness must be assigned the top rank.

Monotheism achieves this result by denying reality to all gods but one and then ascribing to that one god a supreme concern with morality. Polytheism typically achieves the same result by denying supreme importance to any of the gods, however many they may be, and assigning it instead to an impersonal necessity of some kind whose workings favor and enforce morality and affect gods and men alike. This is the Greek *ananke*, the Hindu and Buddhist *karma*. A pious Christian may say of some apparent misfortune, "It was the will of God," personalizing what under many a polytheistic world-view would not be personalized, or "It is not for us to judge," deferring to the divine judge for a correction that polytheism would expect to come as process rather than as verdict.

Among the dilemmas of modernity is that of the modern man or woman who wishes to live a moral life but believes that morality is not guaranteed in any way—neither by a judge rewarding the good and punishing the wicked nor by any process through which, somehow, after the passage of enough time, justice wins out. There are moments even in the Bible—the Book of Job, the Book of Ecclesiastes, perhaps some of the darker sayings of Jesus—when this "modern" dilemma finds ancient expression. And there is no refuting those who claim to be able to sleep at night no matter what they do during the day, who find no reason, in effect, not to pursue some other good at the expense of moral good.

Broadly, however, elevation of morality over other goods in human life has been honored, wherever it has been achieved, as a tempering of the otherwise unquenchable human appetites for power, wealth, pleasure, and the rest. Morality has been, in that way, the price of peace and the basis of civilization, and the form of morality dominant in the West has been decisively affected by the emergence of ethical monotheism in Israel. *Emergence* is the term of choice, for historians of religion do not believe that ethical monotheism was achieved at a stroke in ancient Israel. Though decisive moments and pivotal individuals may be named, its development was gradual. Accordingly, when we read the Bible as a work of literature in which God is the protagonist, it becomes the story of how he gradually became both more unitary and more ethical. It is to the crucial first stage in that part of God's story that we now turn.

UNTIL JUST AFTER the Exodus, God shows little sustained interest in ethics. His one command to Adam and Eve, that they not eat from the tree of the knowledge of good and evil, is not an ethical demand so much as it is the condition of a paradise in which ethics is unnecessary. God's prohibition of bloodshed after Cain's murder of Abel is a genuine ethical demand, and after the flood he repeats and slightly expands this prohibition. But generally speaking, through the Book of Genesis, God is concerned with reproduction, not with morality. With morality, it is as with war: He treats a matter that will eventually come to concern him intensely as of merely human and practical interest.

This is not to say that the subject does not come up. From the patriarchal narratives, one can recover a picture of at least some of the customs that governed the nomadic society to which Abraham, Isaac, and Jacob belonged, customs governing the bride-price, for example, and relations between a woman's husband and her servants. In the manner of nomads, the patriarchs are more or less acquainted with and patient of the laws and customs of the settled peoples among whom they move. Abraham takes the Hittite customs for granted when he purchases his own gravesite.

The point is not that there are no laws or customs but that observing them is not material to the patriarchs' relationship with God. Abraham wants Isaac to marry not a Canaanite woman but a woman from his own native region. God, however, expresses no opinion on this point. Isaac and Rebekah are unhappy when Esau marries two Hittite women and insist that Jacob not do the same. But they do not claim that God has forbidden Jacob to do so. As God makes his various appearances to the three patriarchs and repeats his promises of land and progeny, he does not even once make his promise conditional on observance of any existing, much less any new, laws. The assumption is that the existing arrangements are adequate, as far as they go, and that they need not go further.

All this changes once the Israelites leave Egypt. The several long passages of interpolated law in the Book of Exodus undeniably do break the momentum of the escape from Egypt and the march toward the Promised Land. This effect, however, is by no means the only one that should be named. A far more powerful effect is that of stark contrast—shock, one can legitimately say—as the ferocious, terrifying, and often seemingly anarchic behavior of God as warrior alternates with the careful, severe but measured, and sometimes relatively benign language of God as lawgiver. Both roles, as already noted, are new. The Israelites are prepared for neither. And as they are unprepared, so are we, the readers or hearers of the Bible.

Exodus 15:22–40:38, the remainder of the book, begins with a transition (15:22–18:27) covering the first days of Israel's journey into the desert. The Lord provides food and water for the chronically complaining Israelites and defends them against the attacking Amalekites. Moses, on his father-in-law's advice, sets up a simple system of administration. Then the real action begins:

1. The Lord reveals himself to Israel in a spectacular and terrifying display of volcanic and meteorological effects (19:1–25).

2. Having just made himself maximally frightening, he gives the immortal Decalogue (the Ten Commandments) and another set of regulations commonly called the Book of the Covenant (20:1–23:33) followed by a promise of victory in Canaan and

instructions on treatment of the vanquished (23:20–33). The people then undergo a blood ritual of submission to the Lord's laws (24:1–14).

3. Moses goes back up the mountain for forty days and forty nights, disappearing amid the smoke and fire, and there the Lord gives him detailed instructions for the construction of a *miškan* or dwelling for himself and for the provision of uniforms and equipment for his priests. The Lord, who came and went from the daily lives of the patriarchs, indicates that, in all his fearfulness, he has come to stay (24:15–28:43 and 30:1–31:18). Midway in these instructions, the Lord prescribes a ritual of unprecedented bloodiness for the investiture of his priests (29:1–46).

4. Moses comes back down from the mountain and finds that the people have sunk to idolatry. In his rage, he shatters the tablets of the law, then leads the Levites in bloody and deliberately indiscriminate reprisal against the Israelites. Thousands die, and in addition God strikes the nation with a plague (32:1–35). God proves that he can and will be, in action against his chosen people, as violent and dangerous as he appeared in his first, frightening appearance to them.

5. God gives the law again, but this time the people are not called on to submit to it. Instead, the revelation is given more privately to—and accepted more intensely by—Moses alone. For Moses' sake, God, who was about to "withdraw his presence" from Israel, refrains from doing so. As with the first giving of the law, the last instructions relate to the promised victory in Canaan (34:11–26).

6. Back down from the mountain, Moses directs the preparation of the ritual furnishings and ordains Aaron and the other priests in a much simpler ceremony. Generally, what in number 3 above was instruction concerning work to be done is here a narrative of the work actually being done (34:27–40:38). At its conclusion, Moses personally assembles the tent in which the Lord will dwell.

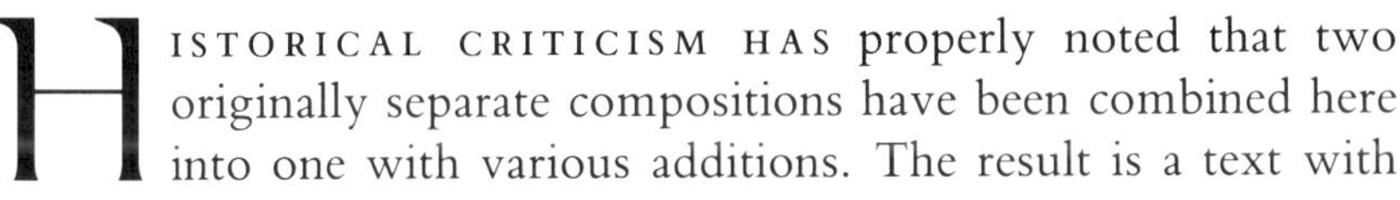

HISTORICAL CRITICISM HAS properly noted that two originally separate compositions have been combined here into one with various additions. The result is a text with duplications. Chapters 25–31 and 35–40, for example, contain various passages that are verbatim equivalents. Yet the plotting together of the two versions has made possible a quadruple crescendo that is particularly powerful as it affects the emerging character of God himself.

The first crescendo is that of Israelite suffering: groaning in Egypt, briefly exulting at their liberation, complaining after that event, timorously shrinking from and then meekly submitting to the Lord at Sinai, finally sinking into idolatry and suffering a horrendous punishment by the hand of the same God who rescued them. The second crescendo is that of divine militance: first waging war against Egypt, then warning Israel, then terrifying Israel with a display of unpredictable violence, then actually attacking Israel. The third crescendo, so strikingly opposed in mood to the second, is that of divine justice: from the grim warning of 15:26 (keep my statutes, or I will send plagues on you as I did on the Egyptians) to the majestic mercy before which Moses prostrates himself and adores: "The Lord! the Lord! a God compassionate and gracious, slow to anger, abounding in kindness and faithfulness" (34:6). The fourth crescendo is that of Moses' intensifying relationship with God. Moses, the frightened shepherd, "slow of speech and slow of tongue" (4:10), ends up speaking to God "face to face, as one speaks to a friend" (NRSV; 33:11) and, furthermore, successfully demands the privilege of looking upon the Lord's glory (33:17–23).

Since our concern is with God rather than with Israel, we may pass over the first crescendo and begin with the second. Many a man, as he comes home from war, seems utterly changed by the experience. Some are scarred; some, the kind who like to be called "colonel" or "general" for life, retain their wartime identity during peacetime. They *are* warriors; that is their new self-definition. The initial impulse may have come from without, but the change it occasioned is maintained from within. Similarly, the change in God's identity that begins when the Israelites cry to him from their oppression seems in short order to break free from that situation and erupt into an entirely new personality. Many a man, in war, discovers something he "didn't know he had in him." God never speaks of any such discovery, but a reader may note that, whatever its source, a stormy, volcanic personality bursts on the scene in the aftermath of the Exodus. Historically, as noted, the novel elements in God's personality match those of Canaanite Baal, a god of storm and volcano as well as of war. In the Lord God, however, these elements do not displace others whose source is elsewhere, and they are effectively plotted into the narrative by being made to emerge in response to Egyptian atrocities.

The plotting is skillful. Making a few allowances, we might even call it plausible. And yet for one who has known only the Lord God of the Book of Genesis, there is an unavoidable and profound sense of shock about the Lord's first actual appearance to his people:

> On the third day, as morning dawned, there was thunder, and lightning, and a dense cloud upon the mountain, and a very loud blast of the horn; and all the people who were in the camp trembled. Moses led the people out of the camp toward God, and they took their places at the foot of the mountain.
>
> Now Mount Sinai was all in smoke, for the Lord had come down upon it in fire; the smoke rose like the smoke of a kiln, and the whole mountain trembled violently. The blare of the horn grew louder and louder. As Moses spoke, God answered him in thunder. The Lord came down upon Mount Sinai, on the top of the mountain, and the Lord called Moses to the top of the mountain and Moses went up. The Lord said to Moses, "Go down, warn the people not to break through to the Lord to gaze, lest many of them perish. The priests also, who come near the Lord, must stay pure, lest the Lord break out against them." But Moses said to the Lord, "The people cannot come up to Mount Sinai, for You warned us saying, 'Set bounds about the mountain and sanctify it.' " So the Lord said to him, "Go down, and come back together with Aaron; but let not the priests or the people break through to come up to the Lord, lest He break out against them." (19:16–24)

No one remotely like this wild and thunderous being has yet been seen or heard in the Bible. And how strange a prelude this explosive passage makes for the great moral code that immediately follows. Some have claimed that the literary power of the Bible lies partly in incongruities and jolting transitions that force a reader or hearer to make some personal sense of the text. This is clearly one such passage.

The iconography of Canaanite Baal is derived from storm and volcanic mountain: thunder and lightning, clouds, smoke, earthquake, and unquenchable fire (see 24:17 and its anticipation in 3:2). Almost all those phenomena are in evidence here. But Canaanite Baal was not a lawgiver like the Lord God. It is one thing for the setting to be explosive, another for the protagonist himself to seem ready to erupt, to "break out" in the language of the translation. Is this the image of a legislator and judge? The Lord seems supremely amoral, impersonal, and physically anarchic—a force of nature on the point of escaping all control, a lethal danger at every moment to those he has just rescued from Pharaoh—and all this just as he is about to give the people his laws. Terrified, the people say to Moses, "You speak to us, . . . and we will obey; but let not God speak to us, lest we die." Moses replies, "Be not afraid; for God has come only in order to test you, and in order that the fear of Him may be ever with you, so that you do not go astray" (20:16–17). But we believe the people's fear more than we believe Moses' reassurance. True, God has scheduled this appearance. It is, clearly, *intended* to be a demonstration, but the demonstration seems to be out of anyone's control, including God's.

The description of what the Lord has in store for the Canaanites, though it comes as the concluding portion of the promulgated law, is consistent in mood with the sound and fury at Sinai. After giving Moses the Decalogue and the Book of the Covenant, the Lord describes just how he will go about clearing Canaan of its natives:

> I will send forth My terror before you, and I will throw into panic all the people among whom you come, and I will make all your enemies turn tail before you. I will send a plague ahead of you, and it shall drive out before you the Hivites, the Canaanites, and the Hittites. I will not drive them out before you in a single year, lest the land become desolate and the wild beasts multiply to your hurt. I will drive them out before you little by little, until you have increased and possess the land. I will set your borders from the Sea of Reeds to the Sea of Philistia, and from the wilderness to the Euphrates; for I will deliver the inhabitants of the land into your hands, and you will drive them out before you. You shall make no covenant with them and their gods. They shall not remain in your land, lest they cause you to sin against Me; for you will serve their gods—and it will prove a snare to you. (23:27–33)

Earlier in this passage, the Lord has said: "You shall serve the Lord your God, and He will bless your bread and your water. And I will remove sickness from your midst. No woman in your land shall miscarry or be barren. I will let you enjoy the full count of your days [that is, no one will die young]."

The terms of the engagement ahead in Canaan will be quite like those just seen in Egypt. The Israelites, in their divinely fostered fertility, will outbreed the Canaanites and so overwhelm them as they did the Egyptians. God will afflict the Canaanites with pestilence and terror as he did the Egyptians. The difference, a large difference, is that the physical separation between those inside and those outside the covenant—a distinction that, in Egypt, was imposed by the departure of the Israelites—will come about in Canaan by the expulsion of the Canaanites. As he announces his plans for the ethnic cleansing of Canaan, the Lord does not, to repeat, seem angry with the Canaanites, but the effect is genocidal, all the same, and there is no escaping it. Unlike the Egyptians, who provoked the Lord by enslaving the Israelites and sentencing all newborn Israelite males to death, the Canaanites' only offense is that they worship their own gods and live on land for which the Lord has other plans. No matter: They are doomed. They will not be offered the option of converting to the worship of the Lord, much less of coexisting with Israel and maintaining their own ways: "You shall make no covenant with them and their gods."

If this is a clear step beyond the level of violence the Lord was willing to inflict on Egypt, it is a universe away from the attitude he had toward the nations among whom the patriarchs lived. A mixing of peoples is taken for granted in the Book of Genesis; and even when the land of the Canaanite tribes is promised to Abraham and his family, the assumption, in the absence of any commentary to the contrary, is that they will receive it as they know it—that is, with its inhabitants. God in his new, more warlike guise revokes that assumption. Pharaoh's genocidal order to kill the Israelite boy babies has led the Lord, now that he has defeated Pharaoh, to become genocidal himself not just toward those who occupy the land on which the Lord wants to settle Israel but toward all of Israel's enemies. After a battle with the Amalekites in the desert, well outside Canaan,

> the Lord said to Moses, "Inscribe this in a document as a reminder, and read it aloud to Joshua: I will utterly blot out the memory of Amalek from under heaven!" And Moses built an altar and named it Adonai-nissi. He said, "It means, 'Hand upon the throne of the Lord!' The Lord will be at war with Amalek throughout the ages." (17:14–16)

By the blotting out of memory, we are to understand nothing less than extermination.

If the mood projected by the Lord God in the opening pages of the Book of Genesis is one of effortless mastery, the mood projected here is not just violent but also strenuously effortful and insistent. God is, at some level, *worried* about the non-Israelite nations and their attitude toward him, not just their threat toward Israel. Like the spectacular new theophany on Sinai, the merciless new attitude toward non-Israelites bespeaks a profound change. God is a warrior with, mysteriously, a military agenda on which Egypt seems to have been just the first entry.

The depth of the change is signaled in another way when the Lord prescribes to Moses the kind of animal sacrifice that he wants made to himself. The sacrifices the patriarchs offer, when they offer them at all, are extremely simple. Not all are quite as simple as in Genesis 22:13: "When Abraham looked up, his eye fell upon a ram, caught in a thicket by its horns. So Abraham went and took the ram and offered it up as a burnt offering in place of his son." But none can be called elaborate, and blood, per se, plays no part in them.

By contrast, blood is everywhere in the sacrifices called for by the Lord God, the Conqueror of Egypt. At the ratification of the covenant at Exodus 24, the blood is drained from twelve oxen—one for each of the twelve tribes of Israel—and collected in basins. Half of it is thrown at the altar, the other half at the people, as Moses says: "This is the blood of the covenant that the Lord now makes with you concerning all these commands" (Exod. 24:8). Similarly, the ordination ritual that the Lord tells Moses to require of Aaron and his sons, God's priests-to-be, is strikingly bloody. A bull is slaughtered at the entrance of the tent of meeting; some of its blood is smeared on the corners of the altar, the rest poured out at the base. Next a ram is slain and its blood dashed on the altar. Another ram is slain and its blood smeared on parts of the men's bodies as well as mixed with oil and sprinkled on their clothing. At the climax, the ordinands hold the dripping kidneys, fatty tails, and other parts of the rams' bodies as well as other ritual offerings aloft. The ritual is fairly awash in blood (29:10–28).

I do not linger over these details to condemn them or shrink from them as an animal-rights advocate might. Animal sacrifice has characterized an immense number of societies, and it is an intrinsically bloody business. At the same time, it should be noted that animal sacrifice is not a cultural universal. Within the history of Israel, it played a small role, then a large role, then no role at all. The question it is fair to ask about this ritual is What does it say about the God who requires it? What kind of divine personality would it suit? The answer is Just the kind of explosively violent god we have suddenly seen thundering from Sinai; just the kind we have seen maximizing, rather than minimizing, the loss of life in Egypt and grimly planning the annihilation of the Canaanites; and finally just the kind who would be willing to impose a reign of terror on his own people.

When Moses came down from Sinai and found the Israelites fallen into idolatry under Aaron,

> Moses stood up in the gate of the camp and said, "Whoever is for the Lord, come here!" And all the Levites rallied to him. He said to them, "Thus says the Lord, the God of Israel: Each of you put sword on thigh, go back and forth from gate to gate throughout the camp, and slay brother, neighbor, and kin." The Levites did as Moses had bidden and some three thousand of the people fell that day. And Moses said, "Dedicate yourselves to the Lord this day—for each of you has been against son and brother—that He may bestow a blessing upon you today." (32:26–29)

In other words, the bloodiness of the ritual ordination was far from unrelated to real, homicidal bloodiness. What commended the Levites to Moses was not that they had identified the ringleaders of the idolatry but precisely that they had been willing to kill "brother, neighbor, and kin." This looks like nothing so much as the demonstrative violence of gang members, proving their ability to kill and their willingness to place loyalty to the chieftain above all other values. In effect, the Levites do what Abraham may have been unwilling to do for God—namely, kill family to prove loyalty. And the Lord makes it clear that he does not disapprove: The next day, when Moses begs the Lord to forgive the people, the Lord refuses and, instead, sends a plague to further afflict the corpse-strewn camp (32:35).

SO MUCH FOR the divine warrior of the Book of Exodus. What of the divine legislator? What of what we called at the beginning of this chapter the third crescendo? It begins with a preliminary statement of the Mosaic covenant just before the theophany at Sinai:

> The Lord called to [Moses] from the mountain, saying, "Thus shall you say to the house of Jacob and declare to the children of Israel: 'You have seen what I did to the Egyptians, how I bore you on

> eagles' wings and brought you to Me. Now then, if you will obey Me faithfully and keep My covenant, you shall be My treasured possession among all the peoples. Indeed, all the earth is Mine, but you shall be to Me a kingdom of priests and a holy nation.' These are the words that you shall speak to the children of Israel."
>
> Moses came and summoned the elders of all the people and put before them all that the Lord had commanded him. All the people answered as one, saying, "All that the Lord has spoken we will do!" (19:3–7)

After this statement of what might be described as covenant goodwill on both sides, and after the Sinai theophany already described, there comes (20:1–23:33) the Decalogue or the Ten Commandments and a code of more particular regulations that scholars have come to call the Book of the Covenant. This longer code governs life in a settled, agrarian society with vineyards, livestock, and various kinds of property to attend to.

The Decalogue, in its extraordinary economy and lapidary strength, has proven itself to be the least culture-bound moral code ever written. But the Book of the Covenant is quite another matter. Historians correctly note that the regulations in this book reflect a later era: Many would simply be inapplicable to a nation migrating through a desert wilderness. Anachronism aside, moralists and others not reluctant to make value judgments may well find parts of the code barbaric at any time. The code is extremely free, for example, in imposing the death penalty. Thus, "He who insults his father or his mother shall be put to death" (21:17). And it is shockingly tolerant not just of slavery as an institution but of abuses within slavery. Thus, "When a slaveowner strikes a male or female slave with a rod and the slave dies immediately, the owner shall be punished. But if the slave survives a day or two, there is no punishment; for the slave is the owner's property" (NRSV; 21:20). Many of the regulations assume that interpersonal violence is a part of life and merely try to codify it, not forbid it. Thus, in a passage that contains one of the most quoted lines in the Bible:

> When men fight, and one of them pushes a pregnant woman and a miscarriage results, but no other damage ensues, the one responsible shall be fined according as the woman's husband may exact from him, the payment to be based on reckoning. But if other damage ensues, the penalty shall be life for life, eye for eye, tooth

> for tooth, hand for hand, foot for foot, burn for burn, wound for wound, bruise for bruise. (21:22–25)

The point of this *lex talionis* or "law of suchness" is that you shall not give two eyes for an eye or an eye for a burn. To that extent, the code may have been in its day a huge step in the right direction—that is, away from vindictiveness and revenge. And yet most modern readers would more easily see the many more steps waiting to be taken.

As a statement about the Lord, who has imposed these regulations through Moses ("These are the rules that you shall set before them" [21:1]), the Book of the Covenant is, in other words, something less than the best possible recommendation. But the step it takes in the right direction is, for him, a fateful first step. This is so because the giving of laws has an effect on the lawgiver as well as on the law receiver. God will never, in the course of the Bible, accept in so many words any obligations imposed upon him by mankind. However, he will impose obligations upon himself in function of those he imposes on mankind and, by this process, he will move out of the realm of the purely arbitrary and into the realm of the bounded and lawful.

In the distinctive double exposition of the Book of Exodus, Moses receives the laws once, smashes the tablets on which they are written, then ascends Sinai to receive them for a second time. On this second occasion, the giving of the law is not preceded by all the sound and fury that preceded it the first time. The only physical manifestations that occur are the cloud that surrounds the Lord as he comes to give Moses the law and the blinding light that radiates from Moses' face when he descends from the mountain having received it, "the two tablets of the Pact, stone tablets inscribed with the finger of God" (31:18). As immediate prelude to the giving of the law, Moses stands holding the still-blank stone tablets on which God will write the law. The Lord then passes before him, so that Moses may see his glory, and offers a glorious formulation of his own identity: "The Lord! The Lord! a God compassionate and gracious, slow to anger, abounding in kindness and faithfulness, extending kindness to the thousandth generation, forgiving iniquity, transgression, and sin; yet He does not remit all punishment, but visits the iniquity of parents upon children and children's children, upon the third and fourth generations" (34:6–7).

Historical scholarship has located the term *ḥesed*, translated above by the phrase "kindness and faithfulness," in ancient diplomacy rather than in personal relations. In the treaty between a suzerain and a vassal, *ḥesed* was the mutual promise of loyalty. Thus another translation sometimes seen is "covenant fidelity." At the most basic level, *ḥesed* is the virtue of one whose word can be relied on. Within the context of his covenant with Israel, the Lord has *ḥesed*, which is to say that, though he is free (as he endlessly insists) to break the covenant, he will not break it.

The Lord's stately description of himself as "abounding in kindness and faithfulness," however, contains a certain tension. As we shall see, his covenant relationship with Israel and his more nearly personal relationship with Moses are deliberately confounded toward the end of the Book of Exodus. Leaving that aside for the moment, there would appear to be an outright contradiction in the Lord's description of himself as "forgiving iniquity, transgression, and sin; yet He does not remit all punishment, but visits the iniquity of parents upon children and children's children, upon the third and fourth generations." Which is it? Is he forgiving, or is he vindictive?

Strange and offputting as the notion of "visit[ing] the iniquity of parents upon children" rings in modern ears, it is as much an ethical step forward as any practical regulation in the Book of the Covenant. First of all, it is worth noting that the Lord extends his kindness "to the thousandth generation" and visits iniquity only to the third and fourth. But to return to the discussion that opened this chapter, the rule of transgenerational punishment is, at a more basic level, ancient Israelite society's version of karma. In a worldview without an afterlife of rewards and punishments, the only punishment that could be inflicted on a criminal who died unpunished was through his children. The knowledge that revenge might be wreaked on one's children is a major deterrent to crime in some traditional societies even now. By placing the weight of his own power and authority behind that deterrent in Israel, God reassures his covenant partners that, as a part of his steadfast love toward them, he will do what it falls to the suzerain to do—namely, enforce justice.

And whatever the particular requirements of justice or the particular methods of its enforcement, it is of permanent and fundamental importance that it is by his justice rather than some other good that God, just at the moment when his power is least in question, chooses to define himself. By implication, if God's goal is still to make mankind in his image, then the human inclination to subordinate morality to power (rules applying only to those not strong enough to break them) receives here an implicit challenge. If morality is ultimate for God, then it must be ultimate for man. There must be no level of human power or human wisdom at which justice ceases to be the final goal and supreme criterion. Only once before, at the judgment and punishment of Cain, has God assumed anything like the role he assumes here. He assumes it because otherwise the laws he is about to write on Moses' tablets would be unenforced and therefore meaningless.

In a culture like ours, with an extremely strong sense of the individual and an ever weaker sense of family, enforcement by "visit[ing] the iniquity of parents upon children" is a repellent notion. By the same token, however, the promise of offspring as numerous as the stars in the sky is a somewhat puzzling one. "As numerous as the stars of the sky?" the modern reader asks. "And what good will they all do me?" I do not mean to make the modern reader sound crass, merely to point out that it is not only when it comes to justice that the early books of the Bible think transgenerationally. Clearly, for the patriarchs, a man who died with offspring had the only kind of immortality that it was possible to have. One who had many offspring, offspring as numerous as the stars, had not just immortality but also the equivalent of great renown: Children were the only magnification of the self that was commonly to be had.

Modern society believes that children are not just extensions of their parents, but imagine a society that believed the opposite: What if everyone thought of children as the true continuation of their parents? In that case it would be as reasonable for children to inherit punishment as in ours it is for them to inherit property. In Exodus 34:6–7, this is the view that obtains. Eventually, God will actively break with this intergenerational moral anthropology, so to call it; but even in this passage, what he means to reveal to Moses is the very opposite of wanton cruelty. He means to reveal as eloquently as possible that he is a God who attaches supreme importance to justice and will be utterly relentless in its pursuit.

THE FOURTH CRESCENDO in the latter half of the Book of Exodus is an intensification in Moses' personal relationship with God. What makes God's character distinctive, as we have noted repeatedly, is its combination of the lofty and relatively impersonal personalities of world creator and world destroyer with the humbler and more intimate one of personal advocate. God does not renounce any of these earlier personalities when he becomes warrior and lawgiver. Rather, by remaining a personal god, he personalizes his very lawgiving and war making. Concretely speaking, he inserts them into his relationship with Moses.

"Kindness and faithfulness," though the phrase may generally refer to reliability in keeping a covenant, has been used once, at this point in the Bible, to characterize God's relationship with an individual man. The man was Joseph. Significantly, Moses brings Joseph's bones with him from Egypt during the Exodus and will entrust them to his lieutenant Joshua. Like Joseph, Moses narrowly escaped early death and spent many years in the company of Egyptians. Moses, who has an Egyptian name and for whom, most unusually, no father's or mother's name is reported, is Joseph's spiritual heir.

God's unique bond to Moses comes to the fore after the Israelites' idolatry, during a long period when Moses is alone with the Lord on the mountaintop. The Lord announces that he will no longer dwell with Israel: He will send an angel to drive out their enemies, but, he says, "I will not go in your midst, since you are a stiffnecked people, lest I destroy you on the way" (33:3). Moses urges the Lord to change his mind: "For how shall it be known that Your people have gained Your favor unless You go with us, so that we may be distinguished, Your people and I, from every people on the face of the earth?" (33:16). The possibility that the Lord may no longer reside with Israel has the paradoxical but surely intended effect of drawing attention to the fact that he has taken up residence in the first place. The Lord visited the patriarchs, often by night or in dreams; he did not travel with them or have any symbolic dwelling place in their encampments. Post-Exodus, the Lord has declared his intention to occupy a meticulously appointed pavilion among the tents of Israel. As he now reconsiders this plan, attention is automatically focused on it.

The Lord relents: He will "go up" to Canaan with Israel after all. But he relents in a way that inscribes the law-bound relationship he has with Israel within a deepening personal relationship with Moses, a relationship that amounts to a more intense, greatly extended version of the "god of" theophanies that Abraham, Isaac, and Jacob experienced:

> The Lord said to Moses, "I will do the very thing that you have asked; for you have found favor in my sight, and I know you by name. . . . I will make all my goodness pass before you, and will

> proclaim before you the name, *Yahweh*; and I will be gracious to whom I will be gracious, and will show mercy on whom I will show mercy. But," he said, "you cannot see my face; for no one shall see me and live." And the Lord continued, "See, there is a place by me where you shall stand on the rock; and while my glory passes by I will put you in a cleft of the rock, and I will cover you with my hand until I have passed by; then I will take away my hand, and you shall see my back; but my face shall not be seen." (NRSV; 33:17, 19–23)

God's speech is riven by an emotional, if not quite a logical, contradiction. At the very moment when he is declaring something like love for Moses ("you have found favor in my sight, and I know you by name") and bringing Moses into a carefully protected physical intimacy with himself, God is insisting on his sovereign right not to do what he is doing. The words "I will be gracious to whom I will be gracious . . ." are, in effect, an ungracious and gratuitous boast coming just at this moment. But the action speaks louder than those words. We have read a moment earlier that "the Lord used to speak to Moses face to face, as one speaks to a friend" (33:11), and the intimacy of the scene that follows is matched in mood perhaps only by Jacob wrestling with his nocturnal visitor. The fact that the Lord wants to be seen only from behind may suggest that he is concealing his genitalia from Moses. The word *kabod* can have a spiritual meaning—its usual translation is "glory"—but also a visceral one: It is the standard word for "liver." According to the eminent linguist and Bible scholar Marvin H. Pope, *kabod* probably alludes to the male genitalia at Job 29:20, where "glory" is still the correct translation, even though genitalia are to be understood. The word *kabod* here may well have the same double meaning. That possibility aside, however, the scene confirms in the strongest possible way Moses' physical closeness to the Lord.

And so, in a fourth instance, the double exposition of the Book of Exodus has made possible something that single exposition would have precluded. At the first giving of the law, the covenant is between the Lord and Israel, and the law is merely transmitted through Moses. After the Israelites commit idolatry, however, the law is truly given to Moses. The Israelites are not asked to give their consent. It is as if, when the Lord looks at Israel, what he sees is Moses.

The personalization—or, as it almost seems, the repersonalization—of God's activity in his relationship with Moses is the note on which the Book of Exodus closes. As we have observed, many parts of 25:1–31:18, dealing with God's tabernacle or dwelling tent and with the priests who will serve him there, are repeated verbatim in 35:1–40:38. Much of the time, instructions given in the earlier section are actually enacted in the later one. One section that occurs only in the latter section, however, is 40:16–33, near the close of the book, in which Moses himself, rather than the craftsmen Bezalel and Oholiab, assembles God's tabernacle.

Having done that, he takes the tablets of the law, called in the text simply "the covenant," puts them in their cabinet, "the ark," and places the cover or "mercy seat" atop the ark inside the tabernacle. The Lord has forbidden the Israelites to make an image of him, but they are permitted to make a throne for him and to adorn it with the winged creatures or "cherubim" understood to attend him in heaven.

At the end of the Book of Exodus, after Moses, personally, has attended to all these arrangements, the Lord God finally seats himself on his throne:

> When Moses had finished the work, the cloud covered the Tent of Meeting, and the Presence of the Lord filled the Tabernacle. Moses could not enter the Tent of Meeting, because the cloud had settled upon it and the Presence of the Lord filled the Tabernacle. When the cloud lifted from the Tabernacle, the Israelites would set out, on their various journeys; but if the cloud did not lift, they would not set out until such time as it did lift. For over the Tabernacle a cloud of the Lord rested by day, and fire would appear in it by night, in the view of all the house of Israel throughout their journeys. (40:33–38)

Nothing in nature looks like cloud by day and fire by night except a volcano. The depth of the Lord God's compelling but contradictory power is well evoked by the extraordinary image of a volcano brought into a tent. The concern of the last, so-called priestly editors of the Book of Exodus for liturgical punctilio ends by heightening this very contrast. The power of a being who, by all that is personally and characterologically right, should be sweeping all law aside like the irresistible force of nature that he is has somehow been harnessed for the enforcement of law. And it is a personal relationship with one man that has brought this about. The volcano has come to live in the tent because the tent was built by the volcano's friend.

Liege
"The Foreskin of Your Heart"
LEVITICUS, NUMBERS, DEUTERONOMY

For a critic writing a literary biography of God, little compares in interest with the portions of his story that we have considered to this point, for, as in any ordinary life story, the beginning is crucial. The books of Genesis and Exodus are in some sense God's childhood. It is in them that his basic identity is formed. The changes that take place in such swift succession in these two books are, like the changes of childhood, large and dramatic. They deserve close attention. God changes less in the biblical books that immediately follow, and the literary biographer has less need to talk about them.

The first five books of the Bible are called, in Jewish tradition, the Torah, a Hebrew word meaning, roughly, "teaching," and in secular scholarship the Pentateuch, from a Greek word meaning "book of five." Genesis, the first book of the Pentateuch, begins as God creates the world. Exodus, the second book of the Pentateuch, ends one year to the day after the escape from Egypt. On that day, God moves into the tabernacle or dwelling prepared for him by Moses. "The cloud covered the Tent of Meeting," we read, "and the Presence of the Lord filled the Tabernacle. Moses could not enter the Tent of Meeting, because the cloud had settled upon it and the Presence of the Lord filled the Tabernacle" (Exod. 40:34–35).

The remainder of the story that the Pentateuch has to tell about the Israelites in the desert is told in Numbers, the fourth book of the Pentateuch. There we read that one month after the Lord has taken up residence in the tabernacle, he orders a census (whence the title, the Book of Numbers) of the Israelites encamped with him at Sinai. After the census, on the twentieth day of the second month in the second year, "the cloud lifted from the Tabernacle of the Pact and the Israelites set out on their journeys from the wilderness of Sinai" (Num. 10:11–12). The rest of the Book of Numbers recounts Israel's wanderings in the desert, the first sorties into Canaan (roughly, the area of present-day Israel) from the south, the subsequent decision to invade Canaan across the Jordan River from the east, and—en route to that invasion—the victories over Heshbon and Bashan, two small Amorite kingdoms on the east side of the Jordan River (in present-day Jordan). The narrative ends with Israel encamped in its newly conquered territory, preparing for the invasion of the Canaanite heartland.

Flanking this narrative are the third and fifth books of the Pentateuch, Leviticus and Deuteronomy, each a book-length speech by the Lord to Moses (Leviticus) or by Moses to the Israelites (Deuteronomy). The first is given at Sinai, just before the Israelites begin their trek toward Canaan; the second, Moses' last words before his death, is given on the plains of Moab, along the east bank of the Jordan River, opposite Jericho.

Leviticus

Like the far briefer "Book of the Covenant" section in the Book of Exodus, the Book of Leviticus reflects the customs of a later era, written down in a still later era. In 587 B.C.E., some six hundred years after the conquest of Canaan, Jerusalem fell to Nebuchadnezzar, king of Babylon, and the Israelites were carried into captivity. It was in Babylon that the priests of Jerusalem, the only effective Israelite leaders left after the conquest, attempted to codify the life that the nation had led in its lost homeland. The results, in a highly structured and at times almost abstract presentation, lay great stress, not surprisingly, on that part of the national life which was the priests' special province; namely, religious ritual. (The priests were all of the house of Levi, whence the title of the book.)

The religious rituals described are concerned with purification and exculpation, both of these being aspects of the same concern—that Israel as a nation and each individual Israelite remain in covenant with the Lord. A comparison of Leviticus 19, an expanded version of the Decalogue, with Exodus 20, the first statement of the Decalogue, may make the distinctive emphasis of Leviticus clear. In Exodus, at Mount Sinai, there is a clear, indeed overpowering sense of the "otherness," the numinous strangeness, of the Lord. The Israelites are no less excluded from that otherness than is the rest of mankind. Only Moses has access to it. In Leviticus, the line is differently drawn. God and Israel together are "other," and the rest of mankind—in some sense, the rest of reality—is excluded. The list of commands in Leviticus begins, "You shall be holy, for I, the Lord your God, am holy" (19:2).

Secularity as a tradition beginning with the Enlightenment is, of course, unknown in the Bible; and yet, in different books, at different moments, human relations may vary in the degree to which they are encased in the divine-human relation. Thus warfare was, for the patriarchs, a relatively secular undertaking. In the Book of Leviticus, by contrast, everything that sets Israel visibly apart from other nations—and a great deal is designed to do exactly that—concerns God, who set Israel apart in the first place. And, by the same token, everything that might divide one Israelite from another disturbs the perfection of the covenant between Israel and God and therefore, once again, concerns God. All the actions of ordinary living are sacralized by being interpreted as actions involving God, but all key, prescribed measures are predictable and efficacious, and all are ultimately benevolent. However repetitious and therefore tedious-to-read the many rituals may be for a modern reader, they do present, collectively, a distinctively serene and idealized picture of national life. Nothing goes wrong that cannot be set aright by the proper ritual; and since no tale is told of anyone declining to perform the ritual, the subtle implication is that no one ever did.

Historians postulate that the priestly redactors who produced the Pentateuch by combining and greatly supplementing earlier texts made the Book of Leviticus a long speech by the Lord at Sinai as a way of claiming the highest authority for their ritual practices. That will do as a historical explanation; but once the text is so placed, once God is the one who speaks it, it becomes a statement about him as well as one by him. Any speech, inevitably, characterizes the speaker. Following just after the storms of the Book of Exodus, the Book of Leviticus comes as a lull. The God whom the Book of Exodus presented was a frightening God. His presence among the tents of Israel—cloud by day and fire by night—was potentially menacing. But if the Lord's very consent to house himself in the tabernacle was a literal domestication, the Book of Leviticus suggests a much more elaborate and symbolic domestication. Though fearing the Lord at every turn, and building on that fear in others, the priests have contained the object of their fear in a complex set of rituals designed to guarantee Israel's purity, immunity, and safety. In the way of much liturgy, the very tedium soothes. One cannot be bored and terrified at once. Or, to put a somewhat less sharp point on it, one cannot simultaneously be paralyzed with fear and punctilious in observing the rubrics.

Leviticus thus comes as a kind of "breather" in God's story. The Lord's tone of voice as speaker is many registers away from the tone heard at Sinai. And, tone aside, the content of what he says, looking forward to the life his people will lead in the land he will give them, makes it clear that he will not always be as frightening as he has lately seemed. During the opening six chapters on sacrifice rituals, though he refers to himself frequently, he always refers to himself in the third person. During the long section on cleanliness and uncleanliness (chapters 11–16), even third-person references are missing: There is only the opening, formulaic "The Lord spoke to Moses, saying. . . ." For historical criticism, God's absence from the body of these speeches is a clear indication that the text was not originally written as divine speech. However, having now been rewritten to function as such, it cannot fail to interrupt the momentum of the rampant subjectivity that made the Lord so terrifying at Sinai. "Let not the priests or the people break through to come up to the Lord, lest He break out against them," we read at Exodus 19:24, and "I will be gracious to whom I will be gracious, and will show mercy on whom I will show mercy" at Exodus 33:19. In Leviticus, thanks to reliable procedures, the Lord no longer threatens to "break out" or to exercise his mercy (or vent his wrath) in any unexpected way. If at the end of the Book of Exodus the Lord is living uneasily in Israel (that is, among the Israelites), then in Leviticus Israel is living easily "in" a very considerably objectified and depersonalized version of the Lord.

The Book of Leviticus, the least dramatic, the least engaging book in the Bible, is also, as a result of all this, one of the gentlest. There is little talk here of punishments to be inflicted if Israel wavers in following the Lord. The familiar blessing

> The Lord bless you and protect you;
> the Lord make His face to shine upon you,
>   and be gracious to you;
> the Lord lift up his countenance upon you,
>   and grant you peace,

though it comes from Numbers 6:24–26, is of a piece with the priestly material that immediately precedes it in Leviticus. Though there is a section of curses in Leviticus (26:14–45), a standard feature in the promulgation of the ancient treaties on which, formally, God's covenant with Israel is modeled, the overwhelming assumption in the

Book of Leviticus is that Israel deserves and will receive only blessings. The tacit assumption is that the nation is at home and at peace, worshiping its own God and, in its security and prosperity, well-disposed not just toward the Israelite poor but also, within reason, toward the resident foreigners. Thus,

> When you reap the harvest of your land, you shall not reap all the way to the edges of your field, or gather the gleanings of your harvest. You shall not pick your vineyard bare, or gather the fallen fruit of your vineyard; you shall leave them for the poor and the stranger: I the Lord am your God.
>
> You shall not steal; you shall not deal deceitfully or falsely with one another. You shall not swear falsely by My name, profaning the name of your God: I am the Lord.
>
> You shall not defraud your fellow. You shall not commit robbery. The wages of a laborer shall not remain with you until morning.
>
> You shall not insult the deaf, or place a stumbling block before the blind. You shall fear your God: I am the Lord.
>
> When a stranger resides with you in your land, you shall not wrong him. The stranger who resides with you shall be to you as one of your citizens; you shall love him as yourself, for you were strangers in the land of Egypt: I the Lord am your God. (Lev. 19:9–14, 33–34)

This last motif—"for you were strangers in the land of Egypt"—has been heard before, in the Book of Exodus, but it has not been a ground, as it is here, for the Israelites to "love [the stranger] as yourself." Leviticus does not teach, here or elsewhere, that individual men and women should love all others with the force of their personal amour propre. As the adjacent phrases make clear, the instruction is simply that the foreigner should be treated as an Israelite would be treated, but just this much is much indeed.

It should go without saying, of course, that nothing like freedom of religion for the resident foreigner is envisioned. Leviticus, obsessed as it is with a holiness and purity that begin quite literally with the physical land itself, does not intend to accommodate on that land the polluting worship of foreign gods. Moreover, the text is inconsistent with regard to foreigners. At other points than this one, foreigners are clearly denied various kinds of equal treatment under the law. Thus, for example, nonresident foreigners near the border may be captured and enslaved, and the children of resident foreigners may be purchased for use as slaves, but not so Israelites or their children (25:44–46).

It is clear, however, that the foreigner is no longer regarded as a threat, above all not as a serious spiritual threat. Israel, in this vision, has its own God and its own thoroughly established way of managing relations with that God. The only relevant question about resident foreigners is to what extent they can or should be admitted to participation in Israel's life and worship.

To linger over the treatment of foreigners is not to single out one area of social relations from among many in which the assumptions of the seventh century B.C.E. might differ from those of the twentieth century C.E. As we shall see in the discussion of the Book of Numbers immediately following, this particular area of social relations is central by dint of its unique, inverse relationship to the notion of covenant ("pact" in the JPS translation). It is impossible —and it was impossible from the beginning—to think about God's special relationship with Israel without thinking about the absence of any such relationship between him and the other nations.

That much conceded in principle, the God who was only somewhat less ferocious with Israel than with the other nations in the Book of Exodus, and who will shortly seem even more ferocious toward both, appears in the Book of Leviticus only somewhat less benign toward the resident foreigner than toward the Israelite. If the Lord is still a volcano, he is, for the moment, as he looks forward to a happy life with his people, a dormant one.

Numbers

What is the mood of the Bible? Its mood varies, of course; but with impressive frequency, it is one of irritability, denunciation, and angry complaint. "What makes God godlike?" we asked in Chapter 3, and our answer concentrated on God's lack of a history or a private life as the Bible opens. Answering the same question not about the protagonist of the Bible but about the referent of the noun/name *god/ God* in Western culture, we might begin a long list of adjectives on which *noble*, *serene*, *grave*, *solemn* would figure prominently but *whiny* would probably not come to mind. Western culture derives its image of the deity primarily from the Bible but secondarily from Greco-Roman antiquity. The gods of Greece and Rome had many shortcomings, but the distinctive irritability of the Lord God was not among them, and it may be classical influence that has muted this quality in the popular notion of God. Be that as it may, the profound originality of a divine-human pact in which both parties complain endlessly about each other has too rarely been acknowledged as such. If mankind is made in the image of God, if God's motive in sustaining creation is to make mankind more fully and perfectly his own image, can it be that this mutual irritability, of all possible reciprocities, is a step forward?

The answer is, as it were, a loud and disgruntled *yes!* God is not a stoic, does not teach stoicism, does not honor or encourage resignation or acceptance, and is, by and large, impossible to please. In each of these regards, Israel is made in his image. Which is not to say that God ever acknowledges Israel as a chip off the old denunciatory block. Nothing of the sort: He complains endlessly about their complaining. And yet, from the outside, a certain symmetry may be seen, never more clearly than in the Book of Numbers, as Israel complains about Moses, Moses complains about Israel, God complains about Israel, Israel complains about God, God complains about Moses, and Moses complains about God. That such a narrative should have been preserved and elevated to the status of sacred scripture and national classic was an act of the most profound literary and moral originality.

Literarily, the originality lies in the way the writers and editors of this text, by their incessant deprecation of complaining Israel as "stubborn" and "stiff-necked," force the (equally complaining) Lord God to the fore, making him the protagonist of the narrative that takes its own unprecedented character from him. Morally, the originality of the same ancient authors and editors lies in their refusal to "ennoble" either God or Israel by making their story merely one of estrangement and reconciliation rather than, as it is, one of continuous mutual complaint. Structurally, a simplification of that sort could easily have been managed. What would have changed would have been less the story line than the distinctive emotional tone—the spirit, in a word. By preserving the spirit of complaint—complaint against man in the name of God, and against God in his own name—on its first full-blown appearance, the ancient editors set something portentous in motion. What they began would sow the seeds of prophecy in the Bible and, more broadly, of moral reform as a perennial possibility in Western social history.

Historically speaking, it is quite possible that, though the Israelites were enslaved in Egypt, they were not, in fact, being worked to death, much less threatened by the (surely mythical) slaughter of their infant males. Their status as resident foreigners in Egypt may well have been approximately what the status of foreigners would later be in Israel: subjugation, to be sure, but not necessarily unbearable oppression. It is also possible, and indeed hinted at in the text of the Book of Exodus, that after long residence in Egypt the Israelites had largely forgotten the God of their fathers in whose name Moses ordered their emigration. Given this set of circumstances, they could easily have regretted their decision to follow Moses into the lethal harshness of the Sinai desert. Moses, too, could have felt that he had been undone by his very success in leading an entire captive nation to so fatefully imperiled a freedom.

The real history is unrecoverable; but if we could ever know it, it might provide context for the strikingly "Jewish" complaints heard on all sides in the Book of Numbers. "You're killing me," Moses complains to God, "so why haven't you killed me?" Similarly, the Israelites: "You're killing us, so why didn't you kill us?" And God: "Keep up this talk, and I'll kill you."

Moses to the Lord:

> Why have You dealt ill with Your servant, and why have I not enjoyed Your favor, that You have laid the burden of all this people upon me? Did I conceive all this people, did I bear them, that You should say to me, "Carry them in your bosom as a nurse carries an infant," to the land that You have promised on oath to their fathers? Where am I to get meat to give to all this people, when they whine before me and say, "Give us meat to eat!" I cannot carry all this people by myself, for it is too much for me. If You would deal thus with me, kill me rather, I beg You, and let me see no more of my wretchedness! (Num. 11:11–15)

The Israelites (after the first scouts report that Canaan is fortified and inhabited by giants) complaining to Moses and Aaron and lamenting among themselves:

> If only we had died in the land of Egypt, . . . or if only we might die in this wilderness! Why is the Lord taking us to that land to fall by the sword? Our wives and children will be carried off! It would be better for us to go back to Egypt! (14:2–3)

The Lord to Moses:

> "How long will this people spurn Me, and how long will they have no faith in Me despite all the signs that I have performed in their midst? I will strike them with pestilence and disown them, and I will make of you [meaning Moses individually, Moses as a potential new Abraham] a nation far more numerous than they!" But Moses said to the Lord, "When the Egyptians, from whose midst You brought up this people in Your might, hear the news, they will tell it to the inhabitants of that land. . . . If then You slay this people to a man, the nations who have heard Your fame will say, 'It must be because the Lord was powerless to bring that people into the land He had promised them on oath that He slaughtered them in the wilderness.' Therefore, I pray, let my Lord's forbearance be great, as You have declared, saying, 'The Lord! slow to anger. . . .' " (14:11–18)

The Lord relents. A determination on his part to impress the Egyptians was indeed a motive repeatedly mentioned in the Book of Exodus, and Moses is shrewd to bring it up. All the same, the Lord vindictively slays all the scouts but the two who brought back correct intelligence, and, even more vindictively, he vows that none of the current generation of Israelites, not even Moses himself, will actually enter the promised land. Their children will be the beneficiaries of the Lord's covenant fidelity. They themselves will not.

Not long after this exchange, a fresh rebellion of 250 Israelites breaks out against Moses and Aaron: "You have gone too far! For all the community are holy, all of them, and the Lord is in their midst. Why then do you raise yourselves above the Lord's congregation?" (16:3). This time, the Lord, not to be restrained, punishes the rebels spectacularly: The earth swallows them alive. The next day, further angered over these deaths, the Israelites attempt a wider revolt. This time, the Lord slays 14,700 of them before being placated by an atonement ritual.

One might expect this to cow Israel. Soon enough, however, other Israelites are wishing theatrically aloud that God had slain them too:

> The community was without water, and they joined against Moses and Aaron. The people quarreled with Moses, saying, "If only we

> had perished when our brothers perished at the instance of the Lord! Why have you brought the Lord's congregation into this wilderness for us and our beasts to die there?" (20:2–4)

In the Book of Deuteronomy the repeated complaints of Israel will be reviewed as a kind of cumulative, tacit proof of the fidelity of the Lord. But if they may bear that interpretation, they also serve as a characterization of the Lord God. Whatever else he may be able to command, he seems unable to command Israel's enthusiasm. The nation is nothing if not a grudging accomplice in his plan for them. The metaphor buried in the term *stiff-necked* is that of the yoking of oxen. An ox must relax his neck and lower his head slightly if the yoke is to be properly secured at the point where the neck joins the shoulders. Stiff-necked Israel repeatedly refuses to submit in this way to the Lord. Deuteronomy sees this as a statement about Israel, but it is inevitably also a statement about God. The Lord is a harsh character, to be blunt, and, reading our own emotional reaction to him, we are not surprised that Israel does not submit to him willingly.

If the Lord seems to have to impose himself on Israel by brute force, it is at least also true that his force on Israel's behalf is irresistible. The Israelites capture Heshbon and expel its inhabitants; they capture Bashan and exterminate its inhabitants (Num. 21). Balak, the king of Moab, seeks in vain to enlist divine power against the Israelites through the prophet Balaam (Num. 22–24). God turns Balaam's would-be curses to blessings. These victories have a scandalous sequel, however, as Israelite men join Moabite and Midianite women en masse in the orgiastic worship of the Baal of Peor. The shock value of this apostasy, like that of the golden calf, which comes just after the theophany at Sinai, is enhanced by its placement within the narrative.

And like the golden calf apostasy, this one is followed by a massive divine reprisal. After the golden calf episode, the Levites, at Moses' urging, slew three thousand Israelites, and the Lord, spurning Moses' plea for mercy, slew innumerable others. This time, the Lord sends a plague that kills 24,000 before Phinehas placates the Lord by impaling a copulating Israelite man and Midianite woman with one thrust of his spear (25:7–9). Afterward, Moses sends a punitive expedition against Midian. The Israelites, victorious, exterminate the Midianite men, but they bring the women and the rest of the booty to Moses, who is furious:

> Moses said to them, "You have spared every female! Yet they are the very ones who, at the bidding of Balaam, induced the Israelites to trespass against the Lord in the matter of Peor, so that the Lord's community was struck by the plague. Now, therefore, slay every male among the children, and slay also every woman who has known a man carnally; but spare every young woman who has not had carnal relations with a man." (31:15–18)

Moses is angry that the Israelites have been insufficiently ruthless with the Midianites, and he reduces their booty accordingly. They are allowed to keep only the virgin girls. The nonvirginal women, who would otherwise have been their possessions, and the boys, whom they had hoped to enslave, they must now slay. The number who perish in the ensuing slaughter is not given but may be measured by the number—32,000—of virgins who survive.

This is the last major military action before the crossing of the Jordan and the main attack on Canaan. The Lord allocates the land in advance to the tribes that will occupy it but, with the massacre of Midian still fresh in memory, the allocation includes a warning: "But if you do not dispossess the inhabitants of the land, those whom you allow to remain shall be stings in your eyes and thorns in your sides, and they shall harass you in the land in which you live; so that I will do to you what I planned to do to them" (33:55–56). Why is the Baal of Peor such a threat to the Lord God? In point of historical fact, Baal, during the six centuries that Israel will occupy and, to varying degrees, rule Canaan, will be the "strange god" who most appeals to the populace and most appalls the leadership. The appeal arises from the fact that, by becoming so warlike, stormy, and Baal-like at and after the time of the Exodus, the Lord has diminished the distance separating him from this one among his rivals. The Israelite leadership is perennially appalled, however, because though Baal is, like the Lord, a god of war whose manifestations included the sights and sounds of storm and volcano, he is also a fertility god whose cult involves ritual copulation. The Lord is, of course, also a fertility god of a sort. As we have seen, following his story from the creation through the covenant with Abraham and the consequences of that covenant in Egypt, he is a god obsessed with reproduction; and in the Book of Leviticus, though we have not examined the relevant passages, he is also a god obsessed with the physical manifestations of reproductive fertility: nocturnal emission, menstruation, and the variety of permitted and forbidden sexual couplings. It would be, as it were, logical for such a god to be himself sexual and to engage in sexual relations with other gods as well as with human beings. In that regard, Baal is what, logically, the Lord should be; and for that reason, as well as because of the attraction of sexual license itself, the cult of Baal will be a perennial temptation in Israel.

Baal-worship was the form of religious syncretism to which the Israelite leadership was most implacably opposed because, as we said in Chapter 3, it is precisely the Lord God's lack of history that makes him himself, and this ahistoricity, this crucial difference, cannot be maintained unless God is clearly understood to be sexually inactive, however masculine in demeanor. A god who fathers children is a god who will have been, earlier, a child himself, and who is thereby integrated into the natural processes of life. From all those processes the biblical authors intend to segregate God.

Though the authors of the Pentateuch knew the (lunar) calendar and were capable of reckoning years into the hundreds, their deeper sense of time was biological rather than astronomical. The RSV translation of Genesis 10–11, which reckons elapsed time from Noah to Abraham, begins, "These are the generations of the sons of Noah. . . ." Some more recent versions of these Hebrew words, *weʾeleh toledot bney noaḥ*, usually translate *toledot* as "descendants" or "lines," but the more literal translation has the advantage of suggesting a biological feel for time. Given this sense of what time is, God cannot stand apart from time unless he stands apart from biological generation: neither generating nor being generated. But precisely because our own experience not only of time but also of love comes to us in the sequence and network of generation (and because this was even more intensely the case in antiquity), God, by being removed from time and generation, is also somehow barred from love. And though it is hard to say quite how, this fact is surely connected with the mutual irritability that exists between him and Israel, an irritability unique in the annals of literature.

Total strangers do not complain about each other as Israel and the Lord do. Just how personal a relationship the Lord feels himself to have with Israel is suggested by the alternative relationship he proposed at Numbers 14:11–18: not some other nation instead of Israel but Moses instead of Israel. We are reminded by that suggestion that though he is now a volcanic god of war, he is still a personal god as well. The novelty is that now, when this personal god is disgruntled, thousands may die.

Deuteronomy

The titles of the books of the Tanakh that are used in English translations come from the titles assigned them in the first full translation ever made, a second-century B.C.E. translation into Greek, the Septuagint. *Deuteronomy* comes from the Greek *deuteronomion*, or "Second Law," so called because virtually everything in this last book of the Pentateuch has already been recounted or enjoined in the first four books.

Taking the form of a long, tripartite speech by Moses, his last words before his death, the Book of Deuteronomy is the first full-blown oratory in the Bible. The first two sections of the speech, in particular, bear fair comparison with the great speeches of Greek antiquity. Obviously, a great deal of dialogue has been heard in the first four books of the Bible, some of it vivid and impassioned. And in the Book of Leviticus, as noted, the Lord recites a detailed code of law. Before Deuteronomy, however, no one has spoken to the Israelites at anything like this length in anything like so personal and rhetorical a style about themselves, their God, and their destiny.

Within the history of the writing of the Bible, as distinct from the history that the Bible contains, the Book of Deuteronomy, written in the seventh century B.C.E., had enormous impact. Nothing like it had previously been written. Nothing written after it was not deeply affected by its rich, undulating cadences and its mood of soaring national pride balanced by a religiously motivated humility. But the Deuteronomist created not just a voice and a perspective but also an emotionally resonant character for Moses. He gave Moses the character of one who has suffered much at the hands of the nation he has led but now sees his own sufferings as well as theirs bathed in the radiance of a high calling.

Since the voice heard in the Book of Deuteronomy is Moses' rather than God's, its characterization of God is also Moses'. Deuteronomy offers an interpretation, in other words, as distinct from a divine self-presentation in word and deed. Moses' speech, following the broad outline of a treaty, begins with a review of the shared history of the two parties to the treaty, proceeds to the treaty's terms, and ends with the blessings and curses that sanction it. It is, therefore, not per se a discussion of God at all. At each stage, however, Moses gives uniquely clear and forceful expression to one aspect or another of God's personality. We have seen different aspects of that personality emerging through Genesis, Exodus, Leviticus, and Numbers. Moses brings them all into harmony with one another as never before.

At the end of his first speech (Deut. 1:1–4:40), having looked back to the beginning and forward to the end of Israelite history, Moses brings the character of God and the destiny of Israel into a single exultant vision:

> You have but to inquire about bygone ages that came before you, ever since God created man on earth, from one end of heaven to the other: has anything as grand as this ever happened, or has its like ever been known? Has any people heard the voice of a god speaking out of a fire, as you have, and survived? Or has any god ventured to go and take for himself one nation from the midst of another by prodigious acts, by signs and portents, by war, by a mighty and an outstretched arm and awesome power, as the Lord your God did for you in Egypt before your very eyes? It has been clearly demonstrated to you that the Lord alone is God; there is none beside Him. From the heavens He let you hear His voice to discipline you; on earth He let you see His great fire; and from amidst that fire you heard His words. And because He loved your fathers, He chose their heirs after them; He Himself, in His great might, led you out of Egypt, to drive from your path nations greater and more populous than you, to take you into their land and assign it to you as a heritage, as is still the case. Know therefore this day and keep in mind that the Lord alone is God in heaven above and on earth below; there is no other. Observe His laws and commandments, which I enjoin upon you this day, that it may go well with you and your children after you, and that you may long remain in the land that the Lord your God is assigning to you for all time. (4:32–40)

The "Lord your God" is the creator of the world. He is thus not merely Israel's national god in some world pantheon of such national gods but the God "of heaven above and earth beneath." However, he has—and just this is the wonder—chosen Israel "for himself." This creator is also a destroyer, a god of lethal fire, whom Israel has nonetheless miraculously survived. He is the god who "loved your fathers [and] chose their heirs after them"—a god, therefore, with a personal relationship with the fathers, personally renewed with the sons and with each subsequent generation. He is a warrior, the conqueror of Egypt and other mighty nations. Finally, he is a lawgiver whose laws, statutes, and commandments, if observed, guarantee Israel's long life and prosperity.

If God defined as the combination of just these elements and no others seems familiar, we have, in good measure, the Deuteronomist to thank. It was his gift to take the earlier materials whose disparate character we have stressed and to make them seem in combination, down to the phrase "the Lord our God" or "the Lord your God," not just plausible but inevitable, and not just inevitable but thrilling. If the various writers of the Bible were composers, the Deuteronomist would be Bach in his utter, majestic confidence. Obviously, this combination is not inevitable. Rather than the god of heaven and earth, God could have been the god of the sea. Rather than the god of law, he could have been the god of song. Rather than a god who chose your forefathers, he could *be* your forefather, the distant, mythical ancestor of a legendary king, or a divine couple, or a goddess. As Israel's apostasies at Sinai and Peor prove, the Israelites did not always find their own God inevitable for them. But the Deuteronomist tries to make that God *seem* inevitable; and his efforts, stunningly persuasive in the reading, have been definitive in their historical impact on how God is imagined. The God of Deuteronomy has remained God for Jews and Christians down to modern times. In the West, even atheism and agnosticism have tended to take this God as at least their imaginative referent. When the Western atheist says that he does not believe in God, it is, at the imaginative level, Deuteronomy's God whom he rejects.

Though the Book of Deuteronomy shows signs of editing, its inner unity greatly exceeds that of the first four books of the Pentateuch, sometimes called the Tetrateuch. The difference is that between editing and rewriting. The Tetrateuch is the edited and supplemented combination of earlier writings. Deuteronomy is a more personal, singular appropriation and restatement of earlier themes and a condensation of earlier narratives that, in the retelling, take on the aesthetic finality of art. The radically prospective, historyless character of the Lord God as the protagonist of the Tetrateuch and the resulting uncertain and uniquely anxious character of Tetrateuch narrative (never more apparent than in the Book of Numbers) yield in the Book of Deuteronomy to the clarity and serenity of a retrospective view. To the Deuteronomist, the desert wandering itself seems a triumphal march.

Moses' last speech, like one of the orations of Greco-Roman antiquity, comes as troops gather for battle. The generation that left

Egypt, the generation to which Moses himself belongs, will not cross the Jordan or enjoy the promised land. No matter: Moses is exhorting the younger men, summoning up for them the nobility of the history they are to continue. His address comes shortly after the great apostasy at Peor (it is, in fact, at Peor that the address is delivered) and shortly before, as it turns out, the great victory at Jericho. Moses thus brings Israel's history and his own life to a climax in a single, transcendent exhortation, and the exhortation accomplishes everything it was intended to accomplish.

In the history of such eve-of-battle orations, love is as frequent a motif as bravery, and the family at least as powerful an image as brotherhood in arms. In his own, utterly distinct way, Moses uses this image in a portion of his speech that has remained the single most sacred text of Judaism:

> Hear, O Israel! The Lord is our God, the Lord alone. You shall love the Lord your God with all your heart and with all your soul and with all your might. Take to heart these instructions with which I charge you this day. Impress them upon your children. Recite them when you stay at home and when you are away, when you lie down and when you get up. Bind them as a sign on your hand and let them serve as a symbol on your forehead; inscribe them on the doorposts of your house and on your gates. (6:4–9)

That passage is also, obviously, supremely relevant to the later history of Judaism as a religion based on sacred scripture. But our concern is with what God requires by what Moses calls *love.*

That he does not require love as we might ordinarily understand the word is clear from the passage that immediately precedes the one just quoted. In that passage the verb *fear*—translated *revere* in the JPS—functions almost exactly as the word *love* does in the one just quoted:

> And this is the Instruction—the laws and the rules—that the Lord your God has commanded [me] to impart to you, to be observed in the land that you are about to cross into and occupy, so that you, your children, and your children's children may revere [= fear] the Lord your God and follow, as long as you live, all His laws and commandments that I enjoin upon you, to the end that you may long endure. Obey [= hear], O Israel, willingly and faithfully, that it may go well with you and that you may increase

> greatly [in] a land flowing with milk and honey, as the Lord, the God of your fathers, spoke to you. (6:1–3)

What does the Lord require, then, love or fear? An easy answer is that he requires both, but in fact the two are alternative words for essentially the same attitude. Historical critical scholarship has made this point by stressing that the love in question is not a spontaneous, interpersonal emotion but covenant love. Loving the Lord your God "with all your heart and with all your soul and with all your might" merely means bending every effort to remain loyal to the terms of the covenant, and the difference between straining to keep a covenant and fearing to break one is slight. Just how remote *ḥesed*, "love" as the word is used in ancient Israelite texts, can stand from love in the usual modern sense of the word is clear somewhat later in the Tanakh, at Judges 1:24. There, Israelite spies preparing to attack Bethel see a man leaving the city and say to him: "Just show us how to get into the town, and we will treat you kindly"; literally, "do you *ḥesed.*" The message is scarcely more than "stick with us, and we'll stick with you": The man, cornered, cooperates, and when they take the city, they let him flee.

Leaving aside the difference, if any, between straining to keep a covenant and fearing to break one, has Israel done either? Obviously not: The attitude in evidence from the crossing of the Red Sea to the imminent crossing of the Jordan has been all obstinate complaint, skepticism, "stiff-necked" resentment of God's appointed leaders, and on two occasions desertion to another god. In that context, even supposing that the younger generation is different from the older, Moses has reason to call for a change. He does so with a remarkable metaphor:

> And now, Israel, what does the Lord your God require of you, but to fear the Lord your God, to walk in all his ways, to love him, to serve the Lord your God with all your heart and with all your soul, and to keep the commandments and statutes of the Lord, which I command you this day for your good? Behold, to the Lord your God belong heaven and the heaven of heavens, the earth with all that is in it; yet the Lord set his heart in love upon your fathers and chose their descendants after them, you above all peoples, as at this day. Circumcise therefore the foreskin of your heart, and be no longer stubborn. (RSV; Deut. 10:12–16)

Circumcise your heart! The metaphor is even more powerful in its barbaric vividness than the circumcision of the penis. The Bible never speaks of the brain. In the Tanakh, when the *lebab*, the heart, is referred to, we must understand the mind and the imagination. As we saw in the Book of Genesis, when Abraham surrendered a piece of his penis and, symbolically, his reproductive autonomy to God, he did so in silence. He submitted to it: no more. And submission is the most that the Israelites have mustered vis-à-vis the subsequent demands of the Lord God who, at Sinai and afterward, has quite literally forced them into covenant with himself. But mere submission, Moses is saying, will not do. The Lord requires ardor. A part of the mind—"the foreskin of your heart"—must be figuratively excised to signify the surrender of mental autonomy just as a part of the penis, the foreskin, was circumcised to signify the surrender of reproductive autonomy.

And what if "the foreskin of the heart" is withheld? The consequence is named throughout Moses' speech, but especially near its end, where formally announced blessings and curses complement and give specificity to the love/fear fusion we have already mentioned. The blessings consist of, in the first instance, plunder. As early as the verses immediately following the "Hear, O Israel" passage quoted earlier, Moses has said:

> When the Lord your God brings you into the land that He swore to your fathers, Abraham, Isaac, and Jacob, to assign to you—great and flourishing cities that you did not build, houses full of all good things that you did not fill, hewn cisterns that you did not hew, vineyards and olive groves that you did not plant—and you eat your fill, take heed that you do not forget the Lord who freed you from the land of Egypt, the house of bondage. (6:10–12)

The passage speaks for itself. Obviously, it is not simply the land that has been promised but the fruits of the labor of those who will be exterminated, enslaved, or expelled from the land. This will be spelled out in more detail in the Deuteronomic Code proper:

> When you approach a town to attack it, you shall offer it terms of peace. If it responds peaceably and lets you in, all the people present there shall serve you at forced labor. If it does not surrender to you, but would join battle with you, you shall lay siege to it; and when the Lord your God delivers it into your hand, you shall put

> all its males to the sword. You may, however, take as your booty the women, the children, the livestock, and everything in the town—all its spoil—and enjoy the use of the spoil of your enemy, which the Lord your God gives you.
>
> Thus you shall deal with all the towns that lie very far from you, towns that do not belong to nations hereabout. In the towns of the latter peoples, however, which the Lord your God is giving you as a heritage, you shall not let a soul remain alive. No, you must proscribe them—the Hittites and the Amorites, the Canaanites and the Perizzites, the Hivites and the Jebusites—as the Lord your God has commanded you, lest they lead you into doing all the abhorrent things that they have done for their gods and you stand guilty before the Lord your God. (20:10–18)

And the final stage in the blessing is simply the long life, prosperity, and security that militarily dominant Israel will enjoy forever after. It is this that is evoked in the formal blessings list at the beginning of chapter 28.

Grim as the fate of Israel's victims may seem, grimmer still is Moses' blood-chilling description of Israel's fate if it does not observe God's laws. The curses section in chapter 28 is four times as long as the blessings section and rises to an eloquence in the depiction of horror unmatched until Dante. In the latter half of the curses section, Moses imagines, in ghastly detail, an unfaithful Israel besieged by an implacable enemy:

> Because you would not serve the Lord your God in joy and gladness over the abundance of everything, you shall have to serve—in hunger and thirst, naked and lacking everything—the enemies whom the Lord will let loose against you. He will put an iron yoke upon your neck until He has wiped you out.
>
> The Lord will bring a nation against you from afar, from the end of the earth, which will swoop down like the eagle—a nation whose language you do not understand, a ruthless nation, that will show the old no regard and the young no mercy. It shall devour the offspring of your cattle and the produce of your soil, until you have been wiped out, leaving you nothing of new grain, wine, or oil, of the calving of your herds and the lambing of your flocks, until it has brought you to ruin. It shall shut you up in all your towns throughout your land until every mighty, towering wall in which you trust has come down. And when you are shut up in all your towns throughout your land that the Lord your God has assigned to you, you shall eat your own issue, the flesh of your

> sons and daughters that the Lord your God has assigned to you, because of the desperate straits to which your enemy shall reduce you. He who is most tender and fastidious among you shall be too mean to his brother and the wife of his bosom and the children he has spared to share with any of them the flesh of the children that he eats, because he has nothing else left as a result of the desperate straits to which your enemy shall reduce you in all your towns. And she who is most tender and dainty among you, so tender and dainty that she would never venture to set a foot on the ground, shall begrudge the husband of her bosom, and her son and her daughter, the afterbirth that issues from between her legs and the babies she bears; she shall eat them secretly, because of utter want, in the desperate straits to which your enemy shall reduce you in your towns. (28:47–57)

It is difficult to believe that this description does not build on some firsthand experience of an ancient city under siege by its enemies. The Babylonian siege and sack of Jerusalem in 587 B.C.E. is the most plausible candidate. The sickening image of a woman fighting with her husband and children over who will eat her afterbirth is just the kind of unimaginable detail that only actual experience can provide a writer.

The curses section goes on to imagine the revocation of God's promise to Abraham in the words of the promise itself: "You shall be left a scant few, after having been as numerous as the stars in the skies, because you did not heed the command of the Lord your God" (28:62). It concludes evoking the despair of an exile from which God will bring Israel back not to its own land but, very pointedly, to Egypt:

> In the morning you shall say, "If only it were evening!" and in the evening you shall say, "If only it were morning!"—because of what your heart shall dread and your eyes shall see. The Lord will send you back to Egypt in galleys, by a route which I told you you should not see again. There you shall offer yourselves for sale to your enemies as male and female slaves, but none will buy. (28:67–68)

Not even good enough for slavery! One stands in awe at the dark brilliance of this conclusion. And note well the opening words of the indictment: "Because you would not serve the Lord your God in joy and gladness." In other words, because you would not surrender the foreskin of your heart, because you were not ardent, because you merely submitted. But Deuteronomy 28, a warning to Israel, is also a terrifying revelation of the character of the Lord, Israel's God. In the savagery of its detail, this vision greatly exceeds the flood. Is the Lord God capable of this? Indeed he is.

Clearly then, the love of which Moses speaks in the Book of Deuteronomy is not a tender emotion, not love in our sense of the word. Yet despite the crushing sense of coercion that any objective reading of Moses' eloquence must leave, the word *love* is not simply misused. It would be wrong to translate the key passage "You shall be loyal to the Lord your God with all your heart," and so forth. Something more than loyalty underlies this relationship. For covenant love has been preceded by the more mysterious, gratuitous love that established the covenant in the first place. From the passage on circumcision of the heart that we quoted earlier: "Behold, to the Lord your God belong heaven and the heaven of heavens, the earth with all that is in it; yet the Lord set his heart in love upon your fathers. . . ." Why did he do that? Or who *is* he that he would do that? There is a rampant, furious side to his character. What keeps it in check? What makes him do the good that he does do?

Moses accepts the mystery of divine mercy gratefully without really attempting to solve it. He does, however, prescribe what is, in effect, its ritual enactment, and the ritual contains a clue of a sort. In chapter 27, he tells the Israelites that when they enter the promised land, they must proceed to Shechem, write the law on plastered stone tablets, offer sacrifice on an altar of unhewn stone, and then divide into two parties and ascend the two adjacent mountains, Ebal and Gerizim. Six tribes will recite the blessings from Gerizim, and the other six the curses from Ebal. This is quite clearly a covenant ratification ritual, but the place, Shechem, gives the ritual a deepened and allusive meaning. It was to Shechem that Abraham first came when the Lord summoned him from Ur, at Shechem that he offered his first sacrifice to the Lord. It was near Shechem that Joseph, God's favorite, was captured and sold into slavery by his brothers. Moses has brought Joseph's bones with him, and Joshua will bury them at Shechem. God, twice on the point of canceling his covenant with Israel, has renewed it for Moses' sake. And now Moses orders that the covenant be formally enacted at Shechem.

God's only announced motive, we have said, is the creation of mankind in his own image. But the quasi-divine power by which men and women create other men and women is sexual reproduction.

It is in this way that, if God is defined as the creator, mankind is most clearly in his image. But again, as we have seen, God was surprised at the outcome of his commandment to mankind to "be fertile and increase." The human increase on earth offended him, and he reacted first by destroying creation, then by establishing a covenant guaranteeing fertility and increase not to all but, this time, only to Abraham and his descendants and only at a price: the surrender of their reproductive autonomy. God's motive was not his desire to respond to some attraction he felt for Abraham, a response to some innate goodness he recognized in Abraham. Moses has reason to say, "Know, then, that it is not for any virtue of yours that the Lord your God is giving you this good land to possess" (9:6).

But if God was surprised by the consequences of his initial creative act and surprised again that his covenant with Abraham had the consequences it did, leading him into military action against Egypt and then down from heaven into a tent in Israel's encampment, he may also have been surprised to find his "steadfast love" going out personally to Joseph, surprised to find himself speaking to Moses as to a friend and acceding to Moses' bold request that God unveil his "glory" to Moses' gaze, and finally surprised, at this point in his own story, to hear Moses requiring of all Israel this "joy and gladness" toward God. If joy and gladness of heart are required of Israel toward God, are they required of God toward Israel? Moses, at the end of his life, is asking something in God's name that God himself has never before asked of anyone. Is Moses also asking it of God?

Moses' very last words are his blessing of the twelve tribes of Israel, echoing the blessing that Israel himself—Jacob, Moses' ancestor, who was so daring with God in his own way—spoke at the end of his life. The longest and by far the most heartfelt of Moses' blessings goes to Joseph, who was also Jacob's favorite. In this blessing, perhaps only hours from his own death, Moses alludes publicly for the first and only time to the most sacred and intimate moment in his life, the moment when "I Will Act" called to him from the burning bush:

And of Joseph he said:

> Blessed of the Lord be his land
> With the bounty of dew from heaven,
> And of the deep that couches below;
> With the bounteous yield of the sun,

And the bounteous crop of the moons;
With the best from the ancient mountains,
And the bounty of hills immemorial;
With the bounty of earth and its fullness,
And the favor of the Presence in the Bush.
May these rest on the head of Joseph,
On the crown of the elect of his brothers.
Like a firstling bull in his majesty,
He has thorns like the horns of the wild-ox;
With them he gores the peoples,
The ends of the earth one and all.
These are the myriads of Ephraim,
Those are the thousands of Manasseh.
(33:13–17)

Moses' blessing of the tribe of Joseph (Ephraim and Manasseh are Joseph's sons) is of a piece with all that he has said in his immortal exhortation to Israel, yet Moses himself cannot quite be contained by his own speech. Of Israel, Moses has demanded the foreskin of the heart for God. Of God, as Moses dies, he may wordlessly be seeking a comparable surrender.

5

Tribulation

The Lord's offer of a reproductive covenant with Abraham was, as earlier noted, coercive toward Abraham and aggressive toward the rest of mankind, however benevolent the Lord may have seemed when he "took [Abram] outside and said, 'Look toward heaven and count the stars, if you are able to count them' " (Gen. 15:5). That scene—a starry night, a childless man alone with his God—has nothing overtly coercive about it. But if from it we could have flashed forward to the curses of Deuteronomy 28, we might have found it easier to appreciate why Abram/Abraham was to resist God's offer and why Jacob, called Israel, Abraham's grandson, was to do so as well. If the special divine promise of, so to call it, astronomical fertility came linked to a divine threat of degradation worse than any death, why should one not choose to make do with no more than the general human hope of offspring?

In the end, as we have seen, Abraham and Israel abandoned their resistance, submitted to circumcision, and accepted God's promise. God has now kept the first part of his promise: Israel is grown to a mighty throng. The second part, the promise of land, is about to be kept. But will Israel meet the conditions that God has retroactively imposed?

This is the shadow that lies across the entire long narrative that runs from the conquest of Canaan at the beginning of the Book of Joshua to the fall of Jerusalem to the Babylonians at the end of II Kings. And throughout this narrative, the character of the Lord continues to be most broadly defined as liege to his Israelite vassals. At the start, they are generally faithful vassals, keeping the terms of his agreement with them, and he does his part, leading them successfully in battle. By the end, they have abandoned their agreement with him; as predicted, he abandons them to their enemies, and they suffer a catastrophic defeat. The events themselves are turbulent, but the Lord God's character from Joshua through II Kings is stable by comparison with what we have seen from Genesis through Deuteronomy. The synthesis achieved in Deuteronomy does not break down under the impact of subsequent events.

There are elements of divine self-discovery, however, within this broadly stable identity. The terms we attach to these are (1) conqueror, developing the earlier liberator; (2) father, developing the earlier friend of the family; and (3) arbiter, developing the earlier lawgiver.

1. *Conqueror.* In the Book of Joshua, the Lord does to the Canaanites no more than what he has already promised he would do at Exodus 23:27: "I will send forth My terror before you, and I will throw into panic all the people among whom you come, and I will make all your enemies turn tail before you." To make a promise is already to be in one's own eyes a character consistent with the promise made. When God promises conquest, he understands that, as to his character, he is already a conqueror. To that extent the Book of Joshua brings only incremental character development. The Lord sees more fully, by putting his words into action, what was entailed in his original, far less self-conscious promise to Abram.

When God promised superhuman fertility to Abram, he did not seem to foresee that the promise would require him to become a god of war and thereby liberate Abram's offspring from Egypt. However, once he was blooded in that first war, he does seem immediately to have realized that a second war would be required. The Israelites are not required to groan to him from the desert for a homeland: He anticipates their need; he appreciates that to keep his earlier promise of land, he must become a conqueror and take the promised land away from its natives. As an element in his identity, then, conqueror is closely linked to liberator, but there is one difference.

Pharaoh was oppressing the Israelites, and his humiliation is presented as more or less deserved. Moreover, the Lord is at pains to assure that Pharaoh understands by whom he has been defeated. By contrast, the Canaanites are not presented as guilty of any active offense against Israel. Their offense is passive and unintended: They are a temptation to Israel, the Lord believes, simply by being practitioners of their non-Israelite religions. And when they are expelled or exterminated, it is not important to him that they should appreciate, as Pharaoh did, that their fate is an exercise of his will. As allies in the conquest of Canaan, God and Israel are thus loyal to each other but otherwise brutal. This mood of brutality gradually darkens and by the end of the Book of Judges affects relations even among the twelve tribes of Israel.

2. *Father.* It is striking, then, that in the first chapters of I Samuel, just past the inter-Israelite savagery that concludes the Book of Judges, there comes an incident of great tenderness, ending with a touching prayer. In this prayer, God, though he is addressed as "Lord of Hosts," which is to say Lord of Armies, is also extolled, for the first time, as the friend of the oppressed against the might of the militarily powerful. As conqueror of Canaan, the Lord differs little from what he was as victor over Egypt. The military component in his identity remains dominant, but a subtheme of social concern begins to complicate that identity. That the plea to him comes from a woman and that the area of her concern is reproduction carries us back to the humbler, friendlier concerns of the Lord as "god of" in the Book of Genesis. But on those earlier occasions, he was not simultaneously a god of war. And no one who called on him on those earlier occasions ever spoke of him in any general way as the friend of the poor or the weak. On those occasions, he was, so to speak, an unarmed friend of one extended family; here he is a heavily armed friend of—at least by implication—all the oppressed.

Further development in the same direction occurs when God's elusively personal relationship with Joseph and his friendship with Moses are succeeded by God's first, rather tentative reference to himself as father. Responding to the ardor of David's devotion to him, God announces that he will adopt David's son, Solomon, as his own son (II Samuel 7). God's basic relationship to Israel remains that of liege to vassal, but within that relationship, a new relationship—and a developing aspect of God's character—emerges. Touching but fleeting in its first telling, this scene—expanded and nobly adorned—will achieve in its second telling in the Book of Chronicles a canonization of fatherhood as the deepest truth about God. In II Samuel, however, God is not yet wholeheartedly a father. He is only beginning to recognize himself in this role.

3. *Arbiter.* When he rescued Israel from Egypt, God did not seem to realize that he was revising the international order. By the end of II Kings, he has begun to take conscious possession of himself as not only Israel's liege but also the arbiter of relations among all nations. This world-judicial role is not included in his identity as lawgiver to Israel, but it builds on this identity.

The line of the Tanakh's plot from Joshua to II Kings begins with invasion and conquest and ends with defeat and exile; in Deuteronomic terms, it is the story of fidelity and blessings followed by apostasy and curses. In many of the events that make up these six books, God is not the central character. The very stabilization of his character that is achieved in the Book of Deuteronomy makes it possible for him to become, to a point, a part of the setting rather than one of the dramatis personae. The changes that do occur in his character are fateful not because of the immediate effect they have, for they have little, but because they are starting points for the recovery that God, no less than Israel, must attempt after he has carried out his curses against Israel to the full ghastly measure.

Conqueror

"And They Did Not Leave Any That Breathed"

JOSHUA, JUDGES

Historical critics believe, on good grounds, in the existence of a "Deuteronomistic History," a composite work beginning with the Book of Joshua and ending with II Kings, with the Book of Deuteronomy itself serving as extended prologue. Whether read as God's story or as mankind's, the Book of Deuteronomy functions as both an end and a beginning. If it did not exist, the narrative would move directly from the death of Moses (which would come at the end of the Book of Numbers rather than, as now, at the end of Deuteronomy) to the conquest of Canaan. That would make for a swifter exposition, but it would leave God far less vivid in our minds than he is in the Tanakh as we now read it. Deuteronomy pulls God together, bringing his self-presentation to a climax just before Joshua crosses the Jordan. Though it is Moses whom we hear speaking, and speaking indeed with the bounding confidence of a great orator, it is "the Lord our God" who ultimately makes the stronger impression on our imagination for his clarity of purpose, his overwhelming vitality, and his unique blend of ruthlessness and warmth.

As the action now begins that will fill Joshua, Judges, I and II Samuel, and I and II Kings, the books that are called in Jewish tradition "the former prophets," the question in the minds of the readers or hearers cannot be clearer than it is: Will Israel keep the covenant or not? If so, all will be well for Israel. If not, all will be extremely ill.

All goes well at the start. Under Joshua, Moses' lieutenant and now his successor, the Israelites inflict genocidal slaughter on some thirty-one Canaanite cities, only once, because of a rash promise by Joshua, merely enslaving the inhabitants of a set of related cities (Josh. 9). The thoroughness of the extermination is stressed by a variety of expressions. Thus, the slaughter of Makkedah includes "all the people in it . . . letting none escape" (10:30). The destruction of Hazor goes on until "they exterminated them; they did not spare a soul" (11:14); the RSV, more literal here and closer to the vividness of the Hebrew than the JPS, ends "and they did not leave any that breathed." Women as well as men are slain; only cattle and spoil escape destruction (8:26–27). The destruction of Ai, to give one example in some detail, begins when the Israelites set the town on fire. The inhabitants flee into the countryside, where the Israelites hunt them down and slay them. The conquerors then return to the city and kill the remaining inhabitants, saving the king for last:

> When Israel had killed all the inhabitants of Ai who had pursued them into the open wilderness, and all of them, to the last man, had fallen by the sword, all the Israelites turned back to Ai and put it to the sword.
>
> The total of those who fell that day, men and women, the entire population of Ai, came to twelve thousand.
>
> Joshua did not draw back the hand with which he held out his javelin until all the inhabitants of Ai had been exterminated. However, the Israelites took the cattle and the spoil of the city as their booty, in accordance with the instructions that the Lord had given to Joshua.
>
> Then Joshua burned down Ai, and turned it into a mound of ruins for all time, a desolation to this day. And the king of Ai was impaled on a stake until the evening. At sunset, Joshua had the corpse taken down from the stake and it was left lying at the entrance to the city gate. They raised a great heap of stones over it, which is there to this day. (8:24–29)

Israel is both unified and—but for one quickly corrected minor deviation—zealous under Joshua's command, and the Lord delivers the victories that he has promised.

The conquest narrative both begins and ends at historic Shechem, the town Abraham first visited when the Lord brought him to the land. The first plot of land that Jacob, Israel in person, bought was at Shechem. The Israelites' first approximation of a sacred genocide, a foreshadowing of the later conquest, occurred at Shechem after the rape of Dinah. When Joseph was kidnapped and sold into slavery in Egypt, he had set out first for Shechem. Moses gave instructions for a ritual reading of the blessings and curses at Shechem, instructions that Joshua duly carries out after entering the land and before beginning his attacks on the local population. And at the end of Joshua's own life, with the conquest spectacularly accomplished, the conqueror gives a memorable final speech at Shechem, to which the Israelites respond as one man at a pitch of enthusiasm never again reached:

> In reply, the people declared, "Far be it from us to forsake the Lord and serve other gods! For it was the Lord our God who brought us and our fathers up from the land of Egypt, the house of bondage, and who wrought those wondrous signs before our very eyes, and guarded us all along the way that we traveled and among all the peoples through whose midst we passed. And then the Lord drove out before us all the peoples—the Amorites—that inhabited the country. We too will serve the Lord for He is our God." (24:16–18)

Joshua warns the people that the Lord will not forgive their transgressions if they forsake him. But they are adamant: "No, we will serve the Lord."

> Thereupon Joshua said to the people, "You are witnesses against yourselves that you have by your own act chosen to serve the Lord." "Yes, we are!" they responded. "Then put away the alien gods that you have among you and direct your hearts to the Lord, the God of Israel." And the people declared to Joshua, "We will serve none but the Lord our God, and we will obey none but Him." (24:22–24)

Joshua dies and is buried shortly thereafter in the hill country of Ephraim, and the bones of Joseph, which Moses and Joshua brought from Egypt, are reinterred at Shechem, which also lies in the territory of Ephraim. Ephraim and his brother, Manasseh, Joseph's sons, constitute Israel par excellence, the chosen tribe within the chosen people. Joseph is home at last as the Lord's plan comes to what seems a perfect consummation.

Alas, the Israelites' bold words soon echo in judgment on their less bold deeds. Early in the Book of Judges, we read alongside a list of all twelve tribes a detailing of the Canaanite or other natives whom the respective tribes had failed to dispossess. Immediately following, the Lord appears in the form of an angel to deliver his fateful judgment:

> "I said, 'I will never break My covenant with you. And you, for your part, must make no covenant with the inhabitants of this land; you must tear down their altars.' But you have not obeyed Me—look what you have done! Therefore, I have resolved not to drive them out before you; they shall become your oppressors, and their gods shall be a snare to you." As the angel of the Lord spoke

these words to all the Israelites, the people broke into weeping. (Judg. 2:1–4)

Both the consequences that the Lord announces come to pass. First, the inhabitants of the land do become adversaries to Israel, and Israel is no longer invincible in combating them. The army of Joshua splinters into local guerrilla bands under various chieftains ("judges"). A state of apparently endless combat ensues. Second, beginning what will prove a long series of defections to the gods of Canaan, Israel's would-be first king, the renegade Abimelech, stages a coup at Shechem. Apostasy, a temptation from the very first moments of Israel's covenant with the Lord, now becomes ever more frequent. Gradually, the nation begins to change its religion.

Eventually recurrent local apostasies will accumulate to total, mass apostasy. At that point, Israel will be condemned to catastrophe. However, that point is only reached gradually. The mentioned charismatic local chieftains, various prophets, and a handful of exceptionally devout kings postpone it as they arise, call the nation to reform, and lead it again, for a while, to victory. The pattern, however, is inexorably downward and ends with the inflicting of the predicted, final curse of Deuteronomy 28: siege, conquest, and exile. At the end of II Kings, the last Israelite king is blinded, after witnessing the execution of his two sons, and what remains of the battered nation is carried into captivity in Babylon. The Deuteronomistic History is thus framed by genocide: the genocide Israel inflicts on its enemies at the start and the genocide its enemies inflict on Israel at the end. Both are the will and work of the Lord.

The downward spiral begins with a coup aimed at turning the league of tribes that Moses and Joshua set up into a monarchy. Abimelech slays his fellow heirs to their father, the chieftain Gideon, in a move connected somehow with the cult of a local god intriguingly called both Baal Berith ("Baal of Covenant") and El Berith ("El of Covenant"). The major resistance to Abimelech does not come from loyal Israelites, however, but from indigenous Shechemites, descendants of Shechem, son of the Hamor (the resistance invokes him by name) whom the sons of Jacob slew. Abimelech puts down the resistance and razes Shechem. When, shortly thereafter, he himself is slain, Israel's first monarchy and Shechem's religiopolitical ascendancy come to an end together. When next we hear of it, the ark of the covenant, on which the Lord is enthroned, has moved to Shiloh.

* * *

The razing of Shechem is a deeply shocking moment, but another, more shocking kind of violence comes in the last chapters of the Book of Judges. To be sure, horrendous violence is also inflicted on conquered Canaanite cities in the Book of Joshua, but the reports of it have a concise, schematic quality. With only a few exceptions, individual feats of military prowess either by or against Israel are not reported. During the Book of Judges, however, what was once a disciplined, unified, invading army has degenerated into guerrilla bands or, at best, militias. Though the successive chieftains who control the militias rule nominally over all Israel, they come from different tribes, and the actions reported of them are invariably localized. None of the chieftains speaks for the Lord as Moses or Joshua did. All are, if you will, zealous but not inspired, and only some of their zeal comes from the Lord. Thus, in Judges 18, near the end of the book, the tribe of Dan is quite clearly only in search of territorial aggrandizement when it leaves the area allotted to it and attacks Laish in the far north, "a people tranquil and unsuspecting, and they put them to the sword and burned down the town. There was none to come to the rescue, for it was distant from Sidon and they had no dealings with anyone" (Judg. 18:27). The Danites single out Laish for conquest on purely strategic grounds.

By far the worst incident of brutality reported in the Book of Judges comes in chapter 19 and pits the Israelites against one another. In this incident, a Levite (a religious functionary) from the tribe and territory of Ephraim, traveling through the adjacent territory of the tribe of Benjamin with his concubine, is received as a guest in the house of an Ephraimite living in the area. That night, the Benjaminites, repeating the offense of Sodom, demand sexual access to the visitor: "Bring out the man who has come into your house, so that we can be intimate with him." As on that previous occasion, the host offers the aggressors his daughter and his own concubine. The Benjaminites refuse the offer. The visitor then gives them his concubine, and the Benjaminites spend the night abusing her—raping her, in fact, to death:

> . . . and they raped her and abused her all night long until morning; and they let her go when dawn broke.
>
> Toward morning the woman came back; and as it was growing light, she collapsed at the entrance of the man's house where her

> husband was. When her husband arose in the morning, he opened the doors of the house and went out to continue his journey; and there was the woman, his concubine, lying at the entrance of the house, with her hands on the threshold. "Get up," he said to her, "let us go." But there was no reply. (19:25–28)

It is a brilliant move by the narrator to place the single most brutal line in the incident in the mouth of the woman's owner rather than in that of her attackers. But if the Levite is without pity, he is not beyond rage. His response to the murder is to cut his concubine's corpse into pieces and send one piece to each of the tribes of Israel except Benjamin. The tribes then muster and march against Benjamin, killing all the tribe's men, women, children, and animals and burning down all its towns. The only Benjaminite survivors are a remnant of the soldiers. Afterward, the other Israelites realize with regret that their vow—a part of their reprisal against Benjamin—not to permit any of their daughters to marry Benjaminites means that this tribe must now die out unless they come up with a solution. And they do: They notice that one Israelite town, Jabesh, has not mustered for the common action against Benjamin, and they send an army to kill all its inhabitants, including women and boys, sparing only virgin girls. These virgins they bring to the shrine at Shiloh, and the Benjaminite survivors are told that during the merrymaking at an upcoming religious feast, they may capture and rape the girls with impunity, thus preserving their tribe as one of the twelve.

Father

"O Absalom, My Son, My Son!"

I and II Samuel

The Book of Judges having concluded with a description of Israel as sunk in brutality, religious cynicism, and sexual degradation, the first Book of Samuel opens in a mood of wondrous dignity and calm. Some time has elapsed (perhaps a good deal), and we are in Shiloh again, the same shrine city where the Benjaminite men were allowed to rape with impunity. In the meanwhile the town has succeeded Shechem as the cult center of the twelve-tribe alliance, and the action begins with an Ephraimite very unlike the one who dismembered the corpse of his concubine.

Elkanah has two wives: Peninnah, who has children, and Hannah, whom he loves but who has no children. Peninnah resents the favor Hannah enjoys with Elkanah and mocks her childlessness:

> This happened year after year: Every time she went up to the House of the Lord, the other would taunt her, so that she wept and would not eat. Her husband Elkanah said to her, "Hannah, why are you crying and why aren't you eating? Why are you so sad? Am I not more devoted to you than ten sons?" (I Sam. 1:7–8)

"Am I not more devoted to you than ten sons?" In context, a context stretching back to Abraham and Sarah but most vividly including the Shiloh rapes we have just heard of and the rape-murder and dismemberment of the concubine, this line is breathtaking for its delicacy and gentleness. But more astonishing than this first-ever kind word by an Israelite man to an Israelite woman is the first recorded step backward from the tyranny of fertility. The step is a small one. In a polygamous society, a barren wife can function as a mistress. Elkanah has Peninnah for babies. All the same, his words count; for in the biblical narrative to this point, God and mankind alike have been obsessed with reproduction. Though love and love-preference are not altogether unknown (Rebekah for Jacob, Jacob for Rachel, Jacob for Joseph, et cetera), the inferiority of marital love to maternal fertility has been unmistakable. Not here: "Devoted" is a

JPS interpretation. What the line says literally is "Am I not more to you than ten sons?"

Whatever Elkanah has said, however, Hannah wants to be a mother. In the verses immediately following Elkanah's comforting words, we read:

> After they had eaten and drunk at Shiloh, Hannah rose. Now Eli the priest was sitting on the seat beside the doorpost of the temple of the Lord. In her wretchedness, she prayed to the Lord, weeping all the while. And she made this vow: "O Lord of Hosts, if You will look upon the suffering of Your maidservant and will remember me and not forget Your maidservant, and if You will grant Your maidservant a male child, I will dedicate him to the Lord for all the days of his life; and no razor shall ever touch his head." (1:9–11)

Hannah, vowing that her son will become what the Tanakh calls a "nazirite," a kind of monk or sanctuary minister, clearly feels that she has the right to bring her concern to the Lord.

But who is the Lord to whom she brings this concern? He is, in her prayer, "Lord of Hosts." The word *host* here is a synonym of *army*. She is praying to the Lord of Armies, a god of war, not a god of fertility. The name is in Hebrew *yahweh ṣebaʾot,* a phrase that consists morphologically of a verb, *yahweh*, and a noun, *ṣebaʾot,* though it functions syntactically as two nouns since the verbal element in it has long since begun to function as a name. Some scholars speculate that the original, full form of the name *yahweh ṣebaʾot,* "Lord of Hosts," may have been the sentence-name *ʾel yahweh ṣebaʾot,* "El Raises Armies." The full name of the god to whom Hannah prayed could also have been *baʿal yahweh ṣebaʾot,* "Baal Raises Armies." The subject of the sentence has been lost by abbreviation, as often happened, but we can tell from the object alone that the god the name refers to is a warrior.

But is it not an unusual warrior to whom a request like Hannah's can be brought? The Lord, the God of Israel, is a fusion of divine personalities. To one of them, the "god of," the friend of the family, hers would be an appropriate, humble request. Leah and Rachel made kindred requests in their day. To another, El, it would be appropriate if rather beneath the usual level of consideration. To a third, precisely the one to whom the prayer is addressed, it is inappropriate to the extent that the "Lord of Hosts" is in charge of warfare rather than fertility. But precisely in this moment of purest Israelite piety, we may see the beginning of a new kind of trouble.

Canaanite Baal, as we noted earlier, was both a furious god of war and an orgiastic god of fertility. By innumerable signals, we are given to understand that Hannah is the last Israelite who would ever turn to Baal-worship. But when she seeks a child from the Lord, Israel's liege and commander in battle, she is approaching him as a deity so similar in his functions to Baal that if she were to have confused him with Baal, we can imagine that her mistake might have been innocent. Similar, unrecognized confusions earlier in Israelite history played a role in the emergence of the Lord God as a character with several mingled personalities.

Past the Book of Deuteronomy, further confusions/fusions are prohibited. But the prohibition is widely disregarded: At all later moments some of the people—and at some later moments nearly all the people—continue their religious syncretism. To put it this way, of course, using the word *syncretism*, is to speak in the neutral language of the modern historian. The Deuteronomistic historian sees this syncretism as Israel's desertion of its covenant with the Lord. From a neutral, modern, historical perspective, Israel grows officially less tolerant of other gods as its leadership grows more self-conscious about the uniqueness of the Israelite religion. From the perspective of the Tanakh itself, the same change is, in effect, a change in the Lord God himself. Indifferent as regarded other gods at the time of his dealings with Adam, Noah, Abraham, Jacob, and Joseph, the Lord becomes, suddenly, "jealous," the very opposite of indifferent, starting with Moses. The narrative that runs from Joshua through II Kings enacts, again and again, this central conflict between newly jealous God and habitually promiscuous people.

To return to the story in I Samuel, the Lord hears Hannah's prayer, and she gives birth to a son, Samuel, who as priest and prophet will preside over the shrine at Shiloh and eventually crown Israel's first kings. All of this is in the future when Hannah speaks a prayer of gratitude in which, ecstatically, she praises the Lord as at once creator, warrior, friend of the forgotten and needy, custodian of life (fertility) and death (the underworld) alike, and international judge and arbiter. The middle third of the prayer reads:

> The bows of the mighty are broken,
> And the faltering are girded with strength.

Men once sated must hire out for bread;
  Men once hungry hunger no more.
While the barren woman bears seven,
  The mother of many is forlorn.
The Lord deals death and gives life,
  Casts down into Sheol and raises up.
The Lord makes poor and makes rich;
  He casts down, He also lifts high.
He raises the poor from the dust,
  Lifts up the needy from the dunghill,
Setting them with nobles,
  Granting them seats of honor.
For the pillars of the earth are the Lord's;
  He has set the world upon them. (2:4–8)

What is particularly interesting about Hannah's prayer, apart from its blending of divine character traits, is the first ever mention of concern on the Lord's part for the poor, the feeble, and the needy as well as the barren. Lowliness (to use that as a summary word) has not constituted, earlier in the Bible, any special claim on the Lord. When the Israelites groaned in bondage in Egypt, it was not principally because they were in bondage but principally because they were his covenant partner, that God noticed their groaning. And when Hannah speaks about the poor and needy, we are to understand the Israelite poor and needy. Nonetheless, there is a distinct new emphasis here; and when God accepts Hannah's thanks, he also accepts, tacitly, her characterization of him.

THROUGHOUT THE Deuteronomistic History, God remains a character in the drama with lines to speak and actions to perform, but entire scenes are enacted in which he is out of sight and, temporarily, out of mind. This is particularly true of the exceptionally dramatic narrative that runs from I Samuel 8 through II Samuel 1. These chapters recount the power struggle between Saul and David, Israel's first and second king, respectively, and crucially involve Jonathan, Saul's son and David's cherished friend. The Lord's favor, withdrawn from Saul and bestowed upon David, both times through Samuel's mediation, ultimately determines the outcome; but down to David's lament for the slain Saul and Jonathan in II Samuel 1, much of the action and even of the running commentary rests with the human actors. There is, strictly speaking, no tragedy in the Bible, no misfortune that comes about inevitably but innocently from human imperfection and from the unintentionally cruel course of events rather than from any angry divine intervention. There is, in other words, nothing in the Bible that "just happens." But the story of Saul comes close.

Saul's downfall comes about when he fails to execute properly the Lord's sworn judgment. At Exodus 17:14, many years before Saul's birth, the Lord said to Moses, in a passage we have already quoted: "Inscribe this in a document as a reminder, and read it aloud to Joshua: I will utterly blot out the memory of Amalek from under heaven!" Blotting out the remembrance, we noted when we first considered that incident, means extermination, and in I Samuel 15, it falls belatedly to Saul to wreak the Lord's bloody revenge. The Lord warns him not to show any mercy:

> I am exacting the penalty for what Amalek did to Israel, for the assault he made upon them on the road, on their way up from Egypt. Now go, attack Amalek, and proscribe all that belongs to him. Spare no one, but kill alike men and women, infants and sucklings, oxen and sheep, camels and asses! (15:2–3)

But when the moment comes, Saul invites the Kenites, a clan living with the Amalekites, to flee: "Come, withdraw at once from among the Amalekites, that I may not destroy you along with them; for you showed kindness to all the Israelites when they left Egypt" (15:6). True enough: Moses' wife and father-in-law were Kenites, and the tribe did assist the Israelites. But mercy for the Kenite sucklings was not among the Lord's instructions to Saul. Worse, Saul takes the Amalekite king captive rather than kill him, and, worst of all, he takes the best of the sheep and cattle as battle spoils rather than destroy them. For these actions, and greatly to the grief of Samuel, the Lord turns against Saul. Saul is not innocent, then, but the disproportion between his sin and his suffering is so extreme that he takes on some of the pathos of a Greek tragic hero, and his downfall produces in the reader or hearer something like the catharsis of Greek tragedy. By the same token, God's destructive power, by being linked so tenuously to ethical considerations, approaches the blind, autonomic character of Greek *ananke*.

As noted earlier, God takes no action in the Bible that does not have mankind as its referent, but the reverse is not the case: Some human actions do not have God as their constant referent. David's incomparable lament for Saul and Jonathan is a case very much in point, closing:

> How have the mighty fallen
> In the thick of battle—
> Jonathan, slain on your heights!
> I grieve for you,
> My brother Jonathan,
> You were most dear to me.
> Your love was wonderful to me
> More than the love of women.
>
> How have the mighty fallen,
> The weapons of war perished.
> (II Sam. 1:25–27)

Saul may have fallen because the Lord turned against him, but you would not learn this from David's lament: In a dozen verses he does not mention God once.

David may have good reasons, of course, reasons of tact and art as well as of religion, not to mention God in his lament. When word of the death of Saul and Jonathan comes to him, he is, after all, fighting *against* God by fighting for the Philistines against Israel. David spent years as the leader of a gang of bandits loyal to the Philistine Achish of Gath, who marveled at the savagery of David's raids against his own people (it was David's custom to exterminate all the inhabitants of any town he raided). Achish felt confident of David's loyalty because he doubted that such a traitor could return to his people even if he wanted to. Achish was wrong about that, but the narrative of David's rise is rife with incidents that seem to confirm the rule that there is no honor among thieves. In the narration of these incidents, though the Lord does indeed have a role, it is only a consultative one. David, who, whatever his faults, seems to have been a thoroughgoing Yahwist, untempted by Baalism, uses divination and the offices of a priest of Yahweh before all of his more important actions. Consultation, however, is a smaller role than the Lord has played before and will play after this point, in the books of Samuel and Kings.

The narrative of the Deuteronomistic History stands at a kind of midpoint between the myth and legend of the Book of Genesis, on the one hand, in which God utterly dominates, and such later Hebrew narratives as the Book of Ezra or the Book of Esther. Of the latter two, only Ezra can be considered history, but in both God is present more as the object of belief than as a purposeful subject. The distinctive character of the conquest-through-exile story, by contrast, including even the story of Saul and David, is the relatively matter-of-fact way in which it introduces God into a narrative combining genuine history with myth and legend. In the Deuteronomistic History, God becomes a historical character, and, conversely, history acquires the status of myth. Along the way folktales that have been caught up in this mix, pure fictions clearly created for their entertainment value, take on a mingled mythic and historical gravity. The argument over whether this narrative is really history, really myth, or really fiction is misbegotten. It is really a mixture of the three. The mixing is precisely what is distinctive about it as a form of literature.

The motives of those who produced this mixed form were not those of a modern historian or a modern novelist or a modern preacher. We may approach those motives, however, at the borders of the standard modern divisions; at the point, that is, where the historian's work "reads like a novel" or the novelist has immersed herself in the history of, for example, the Second World War just to "get it right" or the preacher tells pulpit stories that—never mind their morals—reduce the congregation to held-breath silence. The genre divisions are deeply entrenched in the culture of our day. We tend to be impatient as a result with a clergyman who wants too badly to entertain or a novelist who seems to be out to save the world. But the unique power of this classical Hebrew narrative is that it deliberately does just that which tends to make us impatient. Taking the Tanakh on its own terms, everything in it really happened (history), its outcome is of enormous personal consequence for each and every reader or hearer (religion), and, page by page and sometimes line by line, it has the unmistakable confidence and artistic panache of a living literature (fiction). There is no reversing the evolution of the modern mind. We shall never know this unity again. No historian, no preacher, no novelist can ever re-create it—can ever again, that is, be all three at once. But by an effort of the imagination, we can experience in this central text of our literary heritage the unity as it then was.

Much of the finest writing in the Bible is found in these six books. Were this a general literary introduction to the Bible rather than only a literary consideration of its protagonist, there is a great deal in them that would require full treatment. But our concern is with him; and so, after these digressions, we must turn to the second change in his character that, as suggested previously, permits his involvement with Israel to continue on a new basis. This change comes in II Samuel 7, at a point something less than halfway through the narrative, in connection with a development barely foreseen before it happens—namely, the transformation of the tribes of Israel into a monarchy.

MOSES WAS cautiously neutral about monarchy in the Book of Deuteronomy. He said: "If, after you have entered the land that the Lord your God has assigned to you, and taken possession of it and settled in it, you decide, 'I will set a king over me, as do all the nations about me,' you shall be free to set a king over yourself, one chosen by the Lord your God" (Deut. 17:14–15). Various restrictions follow, but they come down to one: The king is subject to the covenant no less than everyone else in Israel:

> When he is seated on his royal throne, he shall have a copy of this Teaching written for him on a scroll by the levitical priests. Let it remain with him and let him read in it all his life, so that he may learn to revere the Lord his God, to observe faithfully every word of this Teaching as well as these laws. Thus he will not act haughtily toward his fellows or deviate from the Instruction to the right or to the left, to the end that he and his descendants may reign long in the midst of Israel. (17:18–20)

Clearly, the change to monarchy, if it comes, will not change Israel's relationship to the Lord. For him, ruler and ruled alike are Israelites bound to observe the law.

Moreover, as the Deuteronomistic History begins, God has never characterized himself or been characterized by anyone else in his story as a king. This is true even at moments where the word might seem to come naturally to the speaker's lips. At Deuteronomy 4:39 we read, "The Lord alone is God in heaven above and on earth below." "King in heaven above and on earth below" seems a small, rhetorically inconsequential step, but it is never taken. When Israel is in the process of naming its first king, Samuel recalls the time when "the Lord your God [was] your King" (I Sam. 12:12). But he does not intend to say that the Lord was a king so much as that, with such a Lord, Israel had no need of a king, as if to say, "The Lord was all the king you needed." Other nations had kings, beginning with "Pharaoh, king of Egypt," and continuing through the Transjordanian Sihon, king of Heshbon, and Og, king of Bashan, down to the long list of Canaanite kings given in Joshua 12; but all were defeated by kingless Israel and its unroyal God. To the Israelites, early in their national life, monarchy was a foreign institution and a foreign category in thought and imagination. After and because of the establishment of the Israelite monarchy, this was to change; but straight through to the end of II Kings, the Lord God is never referred to as a king.

It is when the Lord speaks of himself not as king but as father that a fateful change in his self-understanding begins to occur. He does this for the first and, in this narrative, the only time just after a moment of high emotion tinged with eroticism. The ark of the covenant, on which the Lord is enthroned, has been brought to newly conquered Jerusalem, the city of David, crowning a triumphant series of Israelite military victories. The young ruler, exultant, dances wildly before the ark wearing only a linen *ephod*, at most a loincloth and perhaps as little as a small backless apron, a kind of fig leaf. After his dance, Michal, one of his wives, rebukes him:

> "Didn't the king of Israel do himself honor today—exposing himself today in the sight of the slavegirls of his subjects, as one of the riffraff might expose himself!" David answered Michal, "It was before the Lord who chose me instead of your father and appointed me ruler over the Lord's people Israel! I will dance before the Lord and dishonor myself even more, and be low in your esteem; but among the slavegirls that you speak of I will be honored." (II Sam. 6:20–22)

Just what it is that David expects the maids to honor him for he leaves playfully or brazenly ambiguous for Michal; but there is no doubt that he is genuinely dancing for the Lord, and there is no one before or after him in the Bible of whom an act of this exuberance and daring could be expected.

What now is its impact on God?

That night, in the quiet after the revelry, David experiences a sudden moment of shame, but not of the kind Michal had in mind. He says to Nathan the prophet:

> "Here I am dwelling in a house of cedar, while the Ark of the Lord abides in a tent!" Nathan said to the king, "Go and do whatever you have in mind, for the Lord is with you."
>
> But that same night the word of the Lord came to Nathan: "Go and say to My servant David: Thus said the Lord: Are you the one to build a house for Me to dwell in? From the day that I brought the people of Israel out of Egypt to this day I have not dwelt in a house, but have moved about in Tent and Tabernacle. As I moved about wherever the Israelites went, did I ever reproach any of the tribal leaders whom I appointed to care for My people Israel: Why have you not built Me a house of cedar?
>
> "Further, say thus to My servant David: Thus said the Lord of Hosts: I took you from the pasture, from following the flock, to be ruler of My people Israel, and I have been with you wherever you went, and have cut down all your enemies before you. Moreover, I will give you great renown like that of the greatest men on earth. I will establish a home for My people Israel and will plant them firm, so that they shall dwell secure and shall tremble no more. Evil men shall not oppress them any more as in the past, ever since I appointed chieftains over My people Israel. I will give you safety from all your enemies.
>
> "The Lord declares to you that He, the Lord, will establish a house for you. When your days are done and you lie with your fathers, I will raise up your offspring after you, one of your own issue, and I will establish his kingship. He shall build a house for My name, and I will establish his royal throne forever. *I will be a father to him, and he shall be a son to Me. When he does wrong, I will chastise him with the rod of men and the affliction of mortals; but I will never withdraw My favor from him as I withdrew it from Saul, whom I removed to make room for you. Your house and your kingship shall ever be secure before you; your throne shall be established forever.*"
>
> Nathan spoke to David in accordance with all these words and all this prophecy. (7:2–17, italics added)

Historical criticism identifies this passage as part of the "Court History" of the Davidic dynasty. The larger purpose of the passage, so read, is to provide propaganda for the dynasty. A smaller purpose is to provide an explanation for why it was that David's son Solomon rather than David himself built the temple in Jerusalem. And historians have postulated, as well, that this unconditional covenant with the Davidic dynasty was added editorially to the Deuteronomistic History after the fall of Jerusalem to provide the Jewish exiles with a theological rationale for their hope to return someday to their home.

All of this is true, or at least plausible, as far as it goes. But if we shift our attention from the Jewish community to the Lord, we may see that it matters somewhat less that an unconditional covenant has been announced than that the Lord, for the first time, has spoken of himself as a father, albeit as the father of a great king, and that he has done so just after David's high-spirited dance and his becoming moment of humility. The passage, by the way, contains a pun. The word *bayit*, in Hebrew, usually "house," can also mean either "dynasty" or "temple." So, David says he will build a *bayit* for the Lord, and the Lord says, no, that he will build a *bayit* for David. The exchange lightens an august moment with a touch of affectionate play. David, in a word, has endeared himself to the Lord.

Fatherhood is an absolute, not a conditional, state. The father of a son cannot, in the nature of things, cease to be such. If the father disinherits the son, he is the father of a disinherited son. If he slays him, he is the father of a slain son. If he denies him, he is the father of a denied son. Even if he aborts him, he is the father of an aborted son. Functionally, it is this about fatherhood that commended the image to the Lord and to the biblical writer. But once in the Lord's mouth, once on the page, fatherhood, one of the very richest natural symbols in human experience, inevitably begins to take on a life of its own. Unconditionality is just one among its innumerable possibilities.

There is an enormous difference between the God of our fathers and God our Father. To this point in the narrative and, effectively, for a good while after it as well, God is the God of our fathers and *not* God our Father. The Lord God—without a spouse—has created the world, but he has not fathered it forth. He spoke it into existence, and that mode of creation has rightly been seen as a deliberate repudiation of the sexual modalities otherwise so common in world mythology. One may say, of course, that, metaphorically or figuratively speaking, he fathered it. But to say this is to point up another, perhaps equally momentous change—namely, the change from literal to figurative language.

The biblical writers from the very start certainly understand the difference between the two. When Moses sings, "The Rock!—His deeds are perfect" (Deut. 32:4), we know—and we know that he knows—that he does not mean that the Lord is literally a rock. But if the biblical writers understand what it means to speak figuratively of God, they nonetheless do not often do so, or at least they are not speaking figuratively at many moments when a contemporary religious speaker would be. For them, the creation and destruction of the world are to be understood literally, and so are the parting of the Red Sea and the manna in the desert and the thunder and earthquake at Mount Sinai. Most of all, the covenant between the Lord and Abraham is a literal, not a figurative, agreement. If Israel follows God's genocidal instructions to the letter and, in addition, never flirts with strange gods, Israel will receive a literal land (though one only figuratively flowing with milk and honey). If Israel deviates from those military instructions and/or dallies with Baal or Chemosh or Dagon, then Israel will really, not figuratively, be subjected to genocide at God's hands.

Against this background, when the Lord promises David that he will be a father to Solomon and that Solomon will be a son to him, he is not simply employing a literary trope for its momentary effect as in "The Rock!—His deeds are perfect." He is announcing a real change in his own relationship to this one real human family, namely David's, and merely expressing the change metaphorically—that is, by a sustained comparison to something that is not itself. When, in the Book of Genesis, God says that mankind is his image, he does not intend that the word *image* should be a metaphor for the real relationship between himself and mankind. No, the original-to-copy relationship *is* their real relationship, a relationship as real as, though different from, the father-to-son relationship that two human beings might have. In ordinary conversation, we sometimes say, using a metaphor, that a son is the image of his father. Father/son names the real relationship; original/copy names the metaphorical one. In II Samuel 7, these two pairs are reversed. God says, using a metaphor, that a copy (Solomon) will become the son of its original (the Lord God). Solomon, who, like all men, is really the image of his original, will henceforth, metaphorically, be his original's son.

In the analysis this sounds more complex than it is in the doing. Metaphor is, in every case, an attempt to extend language. When none of the "right" ways of saying a thing is adequate, we choose a "wrong" way so as to have access to some deeper rightness that we desire. Death is, for Shakespeare's Hamlet, "that undiscover'd country from whose bourne/No traveler returns." Death is, of course, not really an undiscovered country: Death is not a country at all. But talking of it thus enables Hamlet to express as otherwise he could not his fear and wonder in the face of death. Fatherhood as a metaphor extends God's language about himself and enables him to escape from the dilemma in which his covenant with Israel has placed him. He cannot do otherwise than inflict the punishments he has sworn to inflict. But then what? Fatherhood is the beginning of an answer to that question. God cannot change the covenant, but he can change himself.

In this first attempt on the Lord's part to speak of his relationship to David's family as fatherly, he says: "When [Solomon] does wrong, I will chastise him with the rod of men and the affliction of mortals; but I will never withdraw my favor from him. . . ." The withdrawal of this favor—the rupture of the covenant, a final divorce—is just what God is obliged to bring about so long as he continues to understand his relationship to Israel exclusively as a covenant. But suddenly he says that for Solomon and David's later descendants he will not do that, not play the role of aggrieved divine covenant partner but assume instead a very different, quasi-human role as strict father. Whatever his strictness, a father knows that his son cannot cease to be his son. Agreements can be revoked, but there is no revoking fatherhood. Irrevocability is, to begin with, the aspect of fatherhood that the Lord requires.

But irrevocability is indeed only the beginning. In speaking about himself to the "latter prophets," those to whom we shall turn our attention in the next chapters, the Lord will discover a metaphorical mother in himself as well as the father he is discovering here. What we see here is a door not flung wide but only pushed open a crack, and the force doing the pushing is named David. Thus do plot and character interact in the Bible. David is not just a ruthless killer and a visionary leader; he is also a passionate lover, an ardent and loyal friend, and a poet and musician of melting tenderness and soaring lyricism. Why should God not fall in love with David? Everyone else does! But then why does God not adopt David rather than Solomon? Perhaps because the gift to the son is by way of being a victory over the very death of the father. When Nathan gives David the Lord's oracle, David rises in the night, enters the Lord's tent, and speaks to him in secret:

> What am I, O Lord God, and what is my family, that You have brought me thus far? Yet even this, O Lord God, has seemed too little to You; for You have spoken of Your servant's house also

> for the future. May that be the law for the people, O Lord God. What more can David say to You? You know Your servant, O Lord God. For Your word's sake and of Your own accord You have wrought this great thing and made it known to Your servant. (II Sam. 7:18–21)

David knows how to touch God, but God knows how to touch David as well.

SPEAKING OF himself as a father, God speaks metaphorically of himself for the first and only time in the Deuteronomistic History. But if we think of this passage as introducing, alongside the unconditionality of parenthood, an element of parental tenderness in God, then we may join to it one or two other moments in these six books. Of these the most directly relevant, as combining both the emotionality and the unconditionality of fatherhood, comes at II Samuel 18–19, when David receives word that his son Absalom is dead. Absalom has led a revolt against his father. Joab, David's commander and, repeatedly, his hatchet man, having killed the prince when he could easily have taken him captive, sends a foreign messenger, a Cushite, to bring the dire word to David:

> Just then the Cushite came up; and the Cushite said, "Let my lord the king be informed that the Lord has vindicated you today against all who rebelled against you!" The king asked the Cushite, "Is my boy Absalom safe?" And the Cushite replied, "May the enemies of my lord the king and all who rose against you to do you harm fare like that young man!" The king was shaken. He went up to the upper chamber of the gateway and wept, moaning these words as he went, "My son Absalom! O my son, my son Absalom! If only I had died instead of you! O Absalom, my son, my son!"
>
> Joab was told that the king was weeping and mourning over Absalom. And the victory that day was turned into mourning for all the troops, for that day the troops heard that the king was grieving over his son. The troops stole into town that day like troops ashamed after running away in battle. The king covered his face and the king kept crying aloud, "O my son Absalom! O Absalom, my son, my son!"
>
> Joab came to the king in his quarters and said, "Today you have humiliated all your followers, who this day saved your life, and the lives of your sons and daughters, and the lives of your

> wives and concubines, by showing love for those who hate you and hate for those who love you. For you have made clear today that the officers and men mean nothing to you. I am sure that if Absalom were alive today and the rest of us dead, you would have preferred it. Now arise, come out and placate your followers! For I swear by the Lord that if you do not come out, not a single man will remain with you overnight; and that would be a greater disaster for you than any disaster that has befallen you from your youth until now." So the king arose and sat down in the gateway; and when all the troops were told that the king was sitting in the gateway, all the troops presented themselves to the king. (18:31–19:8)

Joab is right, but is David wrong? Absalom has got only what he deserved, but can David not mourn? And what of the Lord when, by the terms of the covenant, rebellious Israel gets what it deserves? The Lord becomes a theologian of sorts when he speaks of himself analogically as a father, but to what is he drawing an analogy? The meaning of the analogy has to be drawn from fatherhood as it is known in Israelite life and above all in David's own life. In the Absalom story we see what it means to be a father when your son attacks you, and you destroy him, but he is still your son, and you are still his father. Can the Lord be such a father? At the very least, this possibility is held subconsciously in reserve.

Paternal tenderness and a concern for the defense of the weak against the strong join in another oracle of the prophet Nathan to King David at II Samuel 12, midway between Nathan's fatherhood oracle and Absalom's revolt. If David's courage, exuberance, and generosity moved God to think and speak of himself for the first time as a father, this time David's cowardice, adultery, blasphemy, treachery, and gluttony—a long list, but the Deuteronomist manages to indict David on every count—offend God.

Cowardice: The Israelite army is fighting the Ammonites, but David, so recently a military hero, has stayed behind in Jerusalem. Eventually, his men will ask that he do this for his own safety (21:17), but they have not done so yet. The king is safe at home in his cedar-paneled palace while his men risk their lives in battle.

Adultery: From the rooftop of his palace, David sees Bathsheba, the wife of one of his soldiers, bathing. The king "sent messengers to fetch her; she came to him and he lay with her." Did she resist? Did she consent? Had she arranged to be seen? The text is silent about all these matters, but under Israelite law her behavior would not in any event be regarded as mitigating his sin.

Blasphemy: It is an offense against the covenant for an Israelite to have sexual relations with a foreign woman, certainly with one taken as other than the spoils of war. Bathsheba, whose name is Canaanite and who is married to a Hittite, appears to be a convert to the worship of the Israelite God. Her bath is described as a bath of post-menstrual purification in conformity with Israelite law. But she remains a foreigner. Her conversion does not excuse David from observing the law.

Treachery: Uriah, Bathsheba's husband, has been fighting for David with the Israelite army. David sends word that Uriah should be sent on leave to Jerusalem, where the king attempts to induce him to sleep with Bathsheba. David's intent, obviously, is to provide a cover should Bathsheba become pregnant at a time when her husband could not have been the impregnator. But Uriah, though a Hittite, is more devout in observing the law than David is. He replies to David's suggestion: "The Ark and Israel and Judah are located at Succoth, and my master Joab [David's commander in chief] and Your Majesty's men are camped in the open; how can I go home and eat and drink and sleep with my wife? As you live, by your very life, I will not do this!" (11:10–11). Later, when Uriah returns to the front, David has him deliver a message, evidently a sealed message, to Joab: "Place Uriah in the front line where the fighting is fiercest; then fall back so that he may be killed" (11:15). Joab cynically complies, and the maneuver costs several lives besides Uriah's. The commander in chief sends a messenger to report on all these deaths to David, and David's cynicism more than matches his own. The king instructs the messenger how to convey his response to Joab: "Give Joab this message: 'Do not be distressed about the matter. The sword always takes its toll. Press your attack on the city and destroy it!' Encourage him!" (11:25).

Gluttony: The background for David's proxy murder of his loyal soldier and his theft of his victim's wife is that David already has many wives. The first seven of his wives are named Michal, Ahinoam, Abigail, Talmai, Haggith, Abital, and Eglah. Once David is installed in Jerusalem, however, the Deuteronomist stops counting and simply says (5:13) that at this point David took "more concubines and wives." To put it mildly, David does not need another wife, and it is on this aspect of David's abuse of his power that the Lord concentrates when he sends Nathan to deliver an oracle to David:

> And the Lord sent Nathan to David. He came to him and said, "There were two men in the same city, one rich and one poor. The rich man had very large flocks and herds, but the poor man had only one little ewe lamb that he had bought. He tended it and it grew up together with him and his children: it used to share his morsel of bread, drink from his cup, and nestle in his bosom; it was like a daughter to him. One day, a traveler came to the rich man, but he was loath to take anything from his own flocks or herds to prepare a meal for the guest who had come to him; so he took the poor man's lamb and prepared it for the man who had come to him."
>
> David flew into a rage against the man, and said to Nathan, "As the Lord lives, the man who did this deserves to die! He shall pay for the lamb four times over, because he did such a thing and showed no pity." And Nathan said to David, "That man is you! Thus said the Lord, the God of Israel: 'It was I who anointed you king over Israel and it was I who rescued you from the hand of Saul. I gave you your master's house and possession of your master's wives; and I gave you the House of Israel and Judah; and if that were not enough, I would give you twice as much more. Why then have you flouted the command of the Lord and done what displeases Him? You have put Uriah the Hittite to the sword; you took his wife and made her your wife and had him killed by the sword of the Ammonites. Therefore the sword shall never depart from your House—because you spurned Me by taking the wife of Uriah the Hittite and making her your wife.' " (12:1–10)

It would not have been at all necessary for the Lord to condemn David's sin in just the way he does. His choice of images and comparisons reveals that he has human family life, its intimacy, and the tenderness of its emotions on his mind.

To digress for just a moment, the story of the poor man with his ewe lamb, besides being indirectly a glimpse of an ancient Israelite at home, is perhaps the only time in the Bible when we hear of anyone having a pet. Perhaps this ewe lamb is one that, in due course, the poor man and his children will eat, but no American who has met the pig Wilbur in E. B. White's *Charlotte's Web* can doubt that stock animals can be genuinely, however temporarily, pets. The passage is revealing on another count in that it shows that the lamb was the animal that this pastoral society could most easily feed at the table, love as a child, and so on: "It used to share his morsel of bread, drink from his cup, and nestle in his bosom." In the long and endlessly rich history of the lamb as a Jewish and Christian religious symbol, this is an early and unexpectedly revealing moment.

The differences between the ewe lamb and Bathsheba remain large enough, of course, and David is easily misled. The Lord lays his trap well. David expects, perhaps, to be charged with adultery and murder. The Lord speaks instead of avarice and gluttony. His allegory, by turning Bathsheba into a ewe lamb, turns her into food and into wealth as well and turns David, the lecher, into a glutton and a miser. If we were attempting a historical reading of Nathan's oracle, we might see evidence of the shift from a nomadic society to a settled one, in which the ownership of land and the accumulation of wealth made possible abuses that nomads did not anticipate and that are barely alluded to in the Torah. So, historically, the change may have gone; but because it is God who is speaking, any new set of assumptions in an oracle from him becomes new data about him. Here, the Lord seems to take it for granted, as he never has before, that the poor and the weak have an a priori claim on his protection.

Arbiter

"You Are to Be King over Syria"

I AND II KINGS

This scarcely predictable affinity on the part of the Lord of Hosts, the Lord of Armies, for the weak and lowly may serve as a bridge to the prophet whose hold on the later Jewish and Christian religious imagination was rivaled only by that of Moses himself—namely, the prophet Elijah. Elijah and his successor, Elisha, were wonder-workers, champions of the poor, and implacable opponents of a corrupt religious and civil authority. To an extent they and their contemporary, the prophet Micaiah, fit squarely into the Deuteronomist's account of warnings unheeded en route to the Lord's destruction of Israel. To an extent, however, they point beyond it; and the story of Elijah does this to uniquely paradoxical effect.

Elijah's great opponent was a foreign queen married to an Israelite king, the infamous Jezebel, wife of King Ahab. In I Kings 21, Jezebel arranges the judicial murder of Naboth, whose vineyard she covets, and brings down on her head the wrath of the Lord, as conveyed by the prophet Elijah:

> Then the word of the Lord came to Elijah the Tishbite: "Go down and confront King Ahab of Israel who [resides] in Samaria. He is now in Naboth's vineyard; he has gone down there to take possession of it. Say to him, 'Thus said the Lord: Would you murder and take possession? Thus said the Lord: In the very place where the dogs lapped up Naboth's blood, the dogs will lap up your blood too.' " (I Kings 21:17–19)

The fact that Elijah so stresses this offense aligns him squarely with the subtheme of concern for the poor and weak that complicates the Deuteronomistic march to judgment at the national level.

But this is not ultimately what is most striking about Elijah. Jezebel, Sidonian by birth, is not just a worshiper of Baal but an active propagandist for Baal-worship and a persecutor of the followers of the Lord. Her abuse of her royal power against the innocent Naboth is, in a way, the least of the indictment against her. Elijah, resisting her as the ruthless missionary of a foreign religion, is involved in foreign relations of a sort. And it is in his career and that of Micaiah that we see a comparable development in God himself taking place. After God's new concern for the lowly and his new way of thinking of himself as a father, this is the third change in him that we shall consider.

Somewhat surprisingly, one of Elijah's actions is to anoint a new king in Aram to wage war against the sinful northern kingdom of Israel. (On the map ancient Aram coincides roughly with modern Syria, and the name *Syria* is used in the RSV verse placed as the epigraph to this section.) Before that particular Aramaean king comes to power, however, Jezebel's husband, Ahab, and Jehoshaphat, king of Judah, go to war against Aram and seek the counsel of prophets. Most of the prophets are sycophantic and predict glorious victory. One, Micaiah, declines to join the chorus. Summoned to the kings' presence, he sarcastically repeats what his fellows have said, but Ahab recognizes the sarcasm. He claims to want the truth:

> The king said to him, "How many times must I adjure you to tell me nothing but the truth in the name of the Lord?" Then he said, "I saw all Israel scattered over the hills like sheep without a shepherd; and the Lord said, 'These have no master; let everyone return to his home in safety.' " "Didn't I tell you," said the king of Israel to Jehoshaphat, "that he would not prophesy good fortune for me, but only misfortune?" But [Micaiah] said, "I call upon you to hear the word of the Lord! I saw the Lord seated upon His throne, with all the host of heaven standing in attendance to the right and to the left of Him. The Lord asked, 'Who will entice Ahab so that he will march and fall at Ramoth-gilead?' Then one said thus and another said thus, until a certain spirit came forward and stood before the Lord and said, 'I will entice him.' 'How?' the Lord asked him. And he replied, 'I will go out and be a lying spirit in the mouth of all his prophets.' Then He said, 'You will entice and you will prevail. Go out and do it.' So the Lord has put a lying spirit in the mouth of all these prophets of yours; for the Lord has decreed disaster upon you." (22:16–23)

We see here how the Deuteronomistic History's vision of punishment inflicted on Israel through the agency of other nations involves the Lord God in complex international manipulations of a sort not previously encountered. Called king of heaven, he is, on earth, more like an emperor, a kingmaker, a plenipotentiary international arbiter. But, again, we have to ask what it means for the Lord God if his manipulations succeed. Is the demonstration of his power not an extremely paradoxical, ultimately pointless one? Israel and Judah will have lost, but how will he himself have won?

The last quarter of the Deuteronomistic History stands in the shadow of a second theophany of the Lord God at Mount Sinai, also called Mount Horeb. This theophany is an appearance to Elijah recounted in I Kings 19. Everything that happens after it, including Micaiah's speech as just quoted and the final downfall of both Israelite kingdoms, is somehow different because of it. Elijah has bested, then slain, 450 prophets of Baal in a public contest, but he is now a marked man. Fleeing for his life, he comes by a roundabout, semimiraculous path to Horeb.

> Then the word of the Lord came to him. He said to him, {"Why are you here, Elijah?" He replied, "I am moved by zeal for the Lord, the God of Hosts, for the Israelites have forsaken Your covenant, torn down Your altars, and put Your prophets to the sword. I alone am left, and they are out to take my life."} "Come out," He called, "and stand on the mountain before the Lord."
>
> And lo, the Lord passed by. There was a great and mighty wind, splitting mountains and shattering rocks by the power of the Lord; but the Lord was not in the wind. After the wind—an earthquake; but the Lord was not in the earthquake. After the earthquake—fire; but the Lord was not in the fire. And after the fire—a soft murmuring sound. When Elijah heard it, he wrapped his mantle about his face and went out and stood at the entrance of the cave. Then a voice addressed him: {"Why are you here, Elijah?" He answered, "I am moved by zeal for the Lord, the God of Hosts; for the Israelites have forsaken Your covenant, torn down Your altars, and have put Your prophets to the sword. I alone am left, and they are out to take my life."
>
> The Lord said to him,}* "Go back by the way you came, [and] on to the wilderness of Damascus. When you get there, anoint Hazael as king of Aram. Also anoint Jehu son of Nimshi as king of Israel, and anoint Elisha son of Shaphat of Abel-meholah to succeed you as prophet. Whoever escapes the sword of Hazael shall be slain by Jehu, and whoever escapes the sword of Jehu shall be

* The words lying between the braces { . . . } are an example of the kind of copying error called dittography or double writing. Either the first or the second time, these words were introduced into the text by accident as the copyist's eyes landed on the wrong instance of the ubiquitous word *said*. The interpretation offered here would not be much affected by including both occurrences but will be based on a reading in which the first occurrence is ignored.

> slain by Elisha. I will leave in Israel only seven thousand—every knee that has not knelt to Baal and every mouth that has not kissed him." (19:9–18)

Though the memorable phrase from the King James Version "a still small voice" (translated here as "a soft murmuring sound") has taken on a life of its own, exegetes have often passed over this passage in virtual silence. In this and various other biographical details, it is clear that Elijah is presented as a second Moses, but what are we to make of the fact that all the features of the theophany to Moses—the wind, the earthquake, the fire—are mentioned and then rejected? It is out of the question that the "soft murmuring sound" is intended to signal gentleness, that it connects in any way with the moments of compassion or tenderness that we have been enumerating. Hazael of Aram will be a ferocious enemy to Israel; domestically, Jehu will perpetrate atrocity after atrocity; and Elisha, as Elijah predicts, will be a warrior as well as a prophet.

The challenge to Moses lies rather in the *outcome* of the actions that Elijah, at the Lord's order, sets in motion. Yes, Jehu will persecute the worshipers of Baal, but he will also continue to practice the idolatry of the golden calf, and he will fight against Hazael, though the two of them are supposedly fellow tools of the divine will. Elisha will be valiant in the Lord's service, but at the end of his life he too will be found straining to undo the effect of Hazael's victories, which are announced here as the Lord's work but will eventually fill Elisha with grief. In combination, the action of the three will reduce Israel to a divinely determined remnant of seven thousand, but can such an outcome pass muster as a proof of divine power?

It is at least possible that in a deliberately cryptic manner this passage expresses skepticism about the power of the Lord. Despite the greatness of Elijah, which continued to be recognized in later centuries, this passage is omitted from the later-written religiopolitically correct books of Chronicles. The divine power that was so spectacularly on display when Moses and the Israelites stood before the Lord at Sinai is brought into question here. That fearsome spectacle, Elijah is given to suspect, may not have been what it then seemed to be. What else may yet prove similarly illusory? Elijah veils his face at the "soft murmuring sound." What does his gesture mean? Is the stillness, the Lord's message to him, a revision? Is it a confession? In flight from Ahab and Jezebel, Elijah had asked to die:

" 'Enough!' he cried. 'Now, O Lord, take my life, for I am no better than my fathers' " (19:4). It was in response to this prayer that the Lord brought him to Mount Horeb (= Sinai), but is the theophany that he has now witnessed there a convincing reassurance? How fully does the Lord really control the course of events?

Historical scholarship believes that separate Elijah and Elisha "cycles" were combined in the books of Kings, and that this explains the anomaly that it is Elisha rather than Elijah who eventually commissions Hazael. So it may well be, but we may also note a continuity in pathos between the one scene and the other.

> Elisha arrived in Damascus at a time when King Ben-hadad of Aram was ill. The king was told, "The man of God is on his way here," and he said to Hazael, "Take a gift with you and go meet the man of God, and through him inquire of the Lord: Will I recover from this illness?" Hazael went to meet him, taking with him as a gift forty camel-loads of all the bounty of Damascus. He came and stood before him and said, "Your son [with exaggerated deference, Hazael refers to the king of Aram as the Israelite prophet's "son"], King Ben-hadad of Aram, has sent me to you to ask: Will I recover from this illness?" Elisha said to him, "Go and say to him, 'You will recover.' However, the Lord has revealed to me that he will die." The man of God kept his face expressionless for a long time; and then he wept. "Why does my lord weep?" asked Hazael. "Because I know," he replied, "what harm you will do to the Israelite people: you will set their fortresses on fire, put their young men to the sword, dash their little ones in pieces, and rip open their pregnant women." "But how," asked Hazael, "can your servant, who is a mere dog [Hazael refers, with feigned humility, to himself], perform such a mighty deed?" Elisha replied, "The Lord has shown me a vision of you as king of Aram." He left Elisha and returned to his master, who asked him, "What did Elisha say to you?" He replied, "He told me that you would recover." The next day, [Hazael] took a piece of netting, dipped it in water, and spread it over his face. So [Ben-hadad] died, and Hazael succeeded him as king. (II Kings 8:7–15)

Hazael, encouraged by Israel's God, has slain his master, but Elisha does not welcome Hazael's future attacks on Israel as the judgment of the Lord or even express a divided heart on that point. Through the Lord, Elisha knows the future, but he does not seem to recognize it as a future that the Lord controls and directs. On this point, the contrast between Moses and Joshua on the one hand and Elijah and Elisha on the other is striking.

The greatest leaders of the Israelite past before Elijah—Jacob, Moses, Joshua, and David—all delivered a final testament in stately verse and then were "gathered to their people" and buried with honor in a named place. It is strikingly different for Elijah:

> As they were crossing [the Jordan], Elijah said to Elisha, "Tell me, what can I do for you before I am taken from you?" Elisha answered, "Let a double portion of your spirit pass on to me." "You have asked a difficult thing," he said. "If you see me as I am being taken from you, this will be granted to you; if not, it will not." As they kept on walking and talking, a fiery chariot with fiery horses suddenly appeared and separated one from the other; and Elijah went up to heaven in a whirlwind. Elisha saw it, and he cried out, "Oh, father, father! Israel's chariots and horsemen!" When he could no longer see him, he grasped his garments and rent them in two. (2:9–12)

That Elijah was taken to heaven alive suggests that he had never died. The prophet Malachi predicted his return as a prelude to "the day of the Lord." The Gospels report speculation contemporary with Jesus that Elijah's return would herald the coming of the Messiah. A school of Jewish mysticism would arise around the *merkabah* or chariot in which Elijah rose into heaven. In different ways, all these developments testify to a kind of ecstatic ambiguity in this text. Elijah's being taken into heaven does not have about it the mood of quiet grandeur and peace that attends the other mentioned deaths. When Jacob, Moses, Joshua, and David die, the work that the Lord wished them to do is accomplished. No such mood attends Elijah's passing. His work is interrupted. His business is unfinished. The phrase "Israel's chariots and horsemen!" may have been a contemporary battle cry turned, here, into an anguished form of direct address to the dying—or at any rate departing—prophet: He was the last defender of the worship of the Lord God, the last champion of the covenant. After him, what remains but the terrifying judgment of the Lord God, the curses of Deuteronomy 28?

The same haunting phrase will be heard again as Elisha dies:

> Now when Elisha had fallen sick with the illness of which he was to die, Joash king of Israel went down to him, and wept before

> him, crying, "My father, my father! The chariots of Israel and its horsemen!" And Elisha said to him, "Take a bow and arrows"; so he took a bow and arrows. Then he said to the king of Israel, "Draw the bow"; and he drew it. And Elisha laid his hands upon the king's hands. And he said, "Open the window eastward"; and he opened it. Then Elisha said, "Shoot"; and he shot. And he said, "The Lord's arrow of victory, the arrow of victory over Syria [Aram]! For you shall fight the Syrians [Aramaeans] in Aphek until you have made an end of them." (RSV; 13:14–17)

Elisha dies, but Joash goes on to victory over Hazael. This is the scene that had made so powerful an impression on the English poet William Blake:

> Bring me my Bow of burning gold:
> Bring me my Arrows of desire:
> Bring me my Spear: O clouds unfold!
> Bring me my chariots of fire!

This, from his "Milton." Blake fuses the death scenes of Elijah and Elisha and takes other liberties, but his response is deep and true to the underlying sense in these two scenes of deep and desperate urgency, a kind of panic in the face of impending doom. Blake had just that sense about the England of his own day, and he is unerring in finding the moment in biblical history that best matches it.

Like fatherhood and the related motif of tenderness, this motif of doubt is raised but no more than raised. And before the end of the books of Kings, a rebuttal comes. At II Kings 19:23–25, the prophet Isaiah offers, in effect, a kind of rebuttal of Elijah's despair and Elisha's panic. Exuding confidence, he correctly predicts disaster at Jerusalem for the Assyrian invader Sennacherib (the Assyrian who "came down like a wolf on the fold" in Byron's poem). In the oracle that Isaiah speaks on that occasion, the Lord boasts that Sennacherib has done nothing but what the Lord has planned for him to do:

> Through your envoys you have blasphemed my Lord.
> Because you thought,
> "Thanks to my vast chariotry,
> It is I who have climbed the highest mountains,
> To the remotest parts of the Lebanon,
> And have cut down its loftiest cedars,
> Its choicest cypresses,

And have reached its remotest lodge,
Its densest forest.
It is I who have drawn and drunk the waters of strangers;
I have dried up with the soles of my feet
All the streams of Egypt."
Have you not heard? Of old
I planned that very thing,
I designed it long ago,
And now have fulfilled it.
And it has come to pass,
Laying waste fortified towns
In desolate heaps.

This philosophy or theology of history, overwhelmingly dominant in the Deuteronomistic History, will remain relatively dominant even after it. However, skepticism about it will steadily accumulate; and we may witness the faint dawn of this skepticism in the antitheophany that Elijah witnesses at Mount Horeb and the revelation there of events that then do not come to pass. What makes the skepticism, behind the coding, so bold is that it is the Lord, not Elijah, who expresses it. It is he who removes himself from the wind, the earthquake, and the fire and he who, in a soft murmuring sound, decrees a future that does not (that he knows will not?) come to pass.

Israel had quite clearly already evolved into two distinct realms —Israel proper, in the north, and Judah, in the south—when David succeeded in reversing the evolution and uniting the two at his newly conquered capital, Jerusalem. The memory of the shift is preserved in Psalm 78:67–68:

He rejected the clan of Joseph;
  He did not choose the tribe of Ephraim.
He did choose the tribe of Judah,
  Mount Zion, which He loved.

Psalm 78 also contains one of several allusions in the Tanakh to the destruction of Shiloh, an event not preserved explicitly in any narrative.

Broadly, the first four books of the Deuteronomistic History—Joshua, Judges, and I and II Samuel—chart the rise of Judah and a clear rise in material and political power of both kingdoms, despite their rivalry. The books of Kings, however, which begin after David's death, chart a decline from that high point into chaos and doom.

Solomon, one of David's sons, comes to the throne, builds and dedicates a temple to the Lord, and leads his nation to wealth and power that briefly surpass the standard his father had set. But Solomon also acquires a huge foreign harem, and his wives lead him into foreign worship. After his death, Jeroboam, son of Nebat, an Ephraimite, leads a revolt of northerners against the Judahite Davidic dynasty. The rebel cry (I Kings 12:16) is

> We have no portion in David,
> No share in Jesse's son!
> To your tents, O Israel!
> Now look to your own House, O David.

Solomon's heir, Rehoboam, attempts to rally north no less than south around himself, going to historic Shechem, the symbolic center of the north and the birthplace of the nation, to be proclaimed king, but in vain.

Through the remainder of the books of Kings, the idolatry and foreign worship that proliferated under Solomon continue to spread. Apostate kings in Israel, the north, are invariably compared with Jeroboam; in Judah, the south, invariably to Rehoboam. There are exceptions—notably, near the end of Judah's independent existence, Hezekiah and Josiah. They do attempt reforms, Josiah being linked by many historians to the later dominance, if not to the actual writing, of the Deuteronomistic History itself. And through all the corruption of the kings and the falsehoods of many false prophets, the voices of a handful of covenant loyalists such as Elijah, Elisha, and—near the very end—Isaiah continue to be raised in fierce, doomed protest. But the outcome has never been in doubt. The Assyrians take Samaria, capital of Israel (II Kings 17) in 722 B.C.E.; the Babylonians take Jerusalem, capital of Judah (II Kings 30) in 587 B.C.E.; and a divine effort that, by the Bible's reckoning, has lasted for more than a millennium ends in wreckage, slaughter, and the ignominy of exile.

6

INTERLUDE

Does God Fail?

If the rupture of the covenant and the resulting genocide are only too obviously a catastrophe in the life of Israel, what are they in the life of God? The reproductive covenant with Israel began, as we saw, as a kind of treaty *within* the divine character, a compromise between God's creative and his destructive impulses. He had repented of creation, then repented again of total destruction. The covenant with Abraham was a middle course: Within it, human fertility was implicitly restricted, divine destructiveness implicitly channeled and restrained. That covenant has now ended in failure. What does God do next?

Recall that God, as we noted at the first interlude, has no social life and no private life, no life among other gods, and no self-exploratory intellectual life. He is simply not that kind of being. His only way of knowing himself seems to be through mankind as an image of himself. What can his next move with mankind be, his centuries-long effort with the Abrahamic covenant having ended in apparent failure?

Is he to repent of one of his earlier repentances? That is, will he double back to the time before the flood, issue again his unconditional and universal command to mankind to "be fertile and increase" and resign himself to the consequences? Or will his destructive side triumph? Having failed with Israel, will he judge that he has failed with mankind as a whole? Twice he barely stopped short of destroying Israel and beginning afresh with Moses. Could he now destroy mankind as a whole and begin afresh with . . . ? But we cannot imagine with what or whom he could begin.

As it happens, the very terms of the covenant between Israel and the Lord end up involving the Lord in a new relationship with at least some other nations of the world. As we saw in the grisly detailing of curses in Deuteronomy 28, the Lord is sworn to do his worst against Israel not directly but through the agency of a nation or nations that will besiege and defeat his erstwhile covenant partner and carry it into a woeful exile. If Israel had not broken the covenant, the exercise of both God's creative and his destructive powers would have remained concentrated within his relationship with Israel. In other words, just as he has had no reproductive covenant with any nation but Israel, he would have had no military involvement. But once the armies of Assyria and Babylon become the instrument of his judgment on Israel, he does have at least that much of an involvement with them.

The result is that the overall scope of his activity increases: In order to punish his covenant partner, he must broaden the range of his international intervention. This is not to say that his instrumental relationship with Assyria or Babylon constitutes a new covenant. Once these nations have served their purpose, once Israel has received the punishment it deserves and the covenant is ruptured, there is, in principle, no reason for the Lord to have any further involvement with any human group. And if they go beyond his intentions, they themselves may incur his wrath. Yet to the extent that God's character is defined by his actions, even a temporary broadening of his involvement with the nations of the world as separate nations (rather than merely as mankind) entails a change in his definition-by-action: What he has done once, he might do again, one way or another.

When speaking of the Lord's victory over Pharaoh, we said that for Moses and the Israelites in the victory song of Exodus 15, it was as if El, a god of immense power but one unlikely to go to war on anyone's behalf, had turned up, astoundingly, on their side. Every nation had some kind of god on its side. At Judges 11:24, we hear a clear echo of this polytheistic view of the matter when an Israelite leader, hoping to avoid war with the king of Ammon, addresses the king in his own terms: "Do you not hold what Chemosh your god gives you to possess? So we will hold on to everything that the Lord our God has given us to possess." So, yes, every nation had some kind of divine support, but no nation had the support of the highest, most remote god until, or so it appeared to Israel, that god turned up fighting on the Israelite side. Quickly, however, the god that rescued Israel began to seem less like a militarized sky god/cosmic judge and more like the familiar and less exalted war god, Baal, though, by the unlikeliest turn of all, this newly appeared rescuer god combined Baal's lawlessly warlike functions with those of a lawgiver.

Taking that to be the Lord God's profile at the end of the Book of Exodus, we may fairly say that it remains very little changed through Leviticus, Numbers, Deuteronomy, Joshua, Judges, and I and II Samuel. Through all those books, Israel is led, in effect, by a war god who most resembles a desexualized Baal; and though Israel is not victorious in every engagement, there is at least a recovery and a return to victory after every defeat. The Baalistic element within the Lord God is dominant.

In the books of Kings, however, as the two fateful, final defeats approach, the fusion of the personalities of Baal and El subtly changes, and El returns to dominance. Thus, when the Lord goes into action with Joshua against Jericho (Josh. 6), he appears, Baal-like, in person. But when the time comes for the Lord to take punitive action against Israel, he directs the prophet Elijah to anoint a prophet and two kings, one of whom will rule over the foreign nation of Aram. If El, as the lord of all gods and men, were to become actively warlike, this is just how we might expect him to do it: to send one nation against another, to manipulate the pieces on a kind of world chessboard, rather than engage in combat himself.

Thus, as the covenant nears its final wreck, the close-up view that we have had of the Lord and Israel as covenant partners sojourning together in the desert or together crossing the Jordan to conquer Canaan is replaced by a longer view in which many nations are simultaneously seen, and the Lord has designs on at least several of them. The Lord does not become less warlike by this change, but his bellicosity is of a more "diplomatic" kind than it seemed in the most explosive moments with Moses on Mount Sinai. Indeed, the rupture of the covenant spreads the potential involvement of the Lord as warrior and shaper of national destinies beyond the covenant's narrow geographic scope—Egypt, the desert, Canaan—to those empires that, speaking historically, crushed Israel in their expansion. The militarization of the El-dimension in the Lord's character, though this does not in and of itself constitute a return to the mass destructiveness of the great flood, does spread the Lord's potentially destructive presence. His scope when he created the world was cosmic without being international, so to speak. Henceforth it will be international as well.

It is obviously possible to speak of these events in autonomous historical terms. For historical critical scholarship, the Tanakh is essentially just one source for the writing of a history of the religious beliefs of ancient Israel. But events that, to be sure, *can* be spoken of in autonomous historical terms *need* not be; and if the philosopher can see projection behind religious belief, the literary critic can also see the creativity of the projector behind the projection. What makes the Tanakh a work of literary art is precisely the way it turns the religious experience of a people into a character, the Lord God, and its historical experience into a plot. Such a transformation could never come about as a purely unconscious process, some kind of involuntary abreaction. It requires the exercise of an aggressively creative intelligence. It was a bold literary stroke to turn the historical victories of Assyria and Babylon into the actions of a protagonist, the Lord God, enforcing the terms of a prior agreement with his antagonist, Israel. It was a comparable literary move to permit the character of the protagonist to develop in and through these actions. In the Deuteronomistic History, the particular change just discussed is barely limned. It is in the oracles of the prophets, to which we turn in the next chapter, that this change receives its major elaboration. But even this foreshadowing of later developments in earlier ones is a matter of art rather than accident despite the fact that the process is accident prone and that no single artistic consciousness wholly controls it.

We have usually called the books of Joshua, Judges, I and II Samuel, and I and II Kings the Deuteronomistic History, less often the former prophets. But if stress is laid on the word *Deuteronomistic*, there is no difference between these two designations. Because Deuteronomy ends with an extended prophecy, the Deuteronomistic History unfolds as history encased in prophecy. Moses, the first and greatest of the prophets, the paradigmatic prophet, denounced Pharaoh, the king of Egypt, as later prophets would denounce the kings of Israel and Judah. Moses predicted God's action against Pharaoh if Pharaoh would not obey God. Pharaoh did not obey God, and spectacular divine action followed. But speaking again through Moses at the end of Moses' career, God promised comparably spectacular action against his own people if they failed to meet certain conditions. They failed to meet them, and he has now taken the action. Thus does Moses' prophetic shadow lie across Israel's entire national life, from its victory over Canaan to its defeat by Assyria and Babylon.

This interpretation is offered repeatedly and explicitly in the books of Kings, never more so than just after the fall of the northern kingdom to Assyria. The Deuteronomist writes:

> This happened because the Israelites sinned against the Lord their God, who had freed them from the land of Egypt, from the hand of Pharaoh king of Egypt. They worshiped other gods and followed the customs of the nations which the Lord had dispossessed before the Israelites and the customs which the kings of Israel had practiced. The Israelites committed against the Lord their God acts which were not right: They built for themselves shrines in all their settlements, from watchtowers to fortified cities; they set up pillars and sacred posts for themselves on every lofty hill and under every leafy tree; and they offered sacrifices there, at all the shrines, like the nations whom the Lord had driven into exile before them. They committed wicked acts to vex the Lord, and they worshiped fetishes concerning which the Lord had said to them, "You must not do this thing."
>
> The Lord warned Israel and Judah by every prophet [and] every seer, saying: "Turn back from your wicked ways, and observe My commandments and My laws, according to all the Teaching that I commanded your fathers and that I transmitted to you through My servants the prophets." But they did not obey; they stiffened their necks, like their fathers who did not have faith in the Lord their God; they spurned His laws and the covenant that He had made with their fathers, and the warnings He had given them. They went after delusion and were deluded; [they imitated] the nations that were about them, which the Lord had forbidden them to emulate. They rejected all the commandments of the Lord their God; they made molten idols for themselves—two calves—and they made a sacred post and they bowed down to all the host of heaven, and they worshiped Baal. They consigned their sons and daughters to the fire; they practiced augury and divination, and gave themselves over to what was displeasing to the Lord and vexed Him. The Lord was incensed at Israel and He banished them from His presence; none was left but the tribe of Judah alone.
>
> Nor did Judah keep the commandments of the Lord their God; they followed the customs that Israel had practiced. So the Lord

> spurned all the offspring of Israel, and He afflicted them and delivered them into the hands of plunderers, and finally He cast them out from His presence. (II Kings 17:7–20)

On the face of it, once Israel has clearly violated the covenant and once the condign punishment has been imposed upon Israel through the agency of Assyria and Babylon, nothing remains to be done. The story is over. The curtain comes down. But God cannot want the curtain to come down—on God. If it was some ancient writer's bold stroke to imagine the victories of Assyria and Babylon as divine actions, some other ancient writer had the challenge of writing a second act for a first act that seemed to permit no second. In the event, the path to a continuation of the action lies through the character of the protagonist. The Lord finds a way to continue his contact with Israel, and thereby his own unfolding life, by making a change in himself.

To an extent, this change and the survival of some kind of partnership between Israel and the Lord is foreseen in the Book of Deuteronomy itself. In one of those incandescent passages that explain, if anything can, the survival of the Jews over the millennia, Moses looks ahead to a day when the land of Israel will have been destroyed as completely and horrifyingly as Sodom was destroyed. What, he asks, is the generation *after* that destruction to do when it sees "the whole land brimstone and salt, and a burnt-out waste, unsown, and growing nothing, where no grass can sprout"? What is that generation to do when the nations ask "Why?" and the answer comes, crushingly, "Because they forsook the covenant of the Lord, the God of their fathers"? (Deut. 29:21–24, RSV)

> When all these things befall you—the blessing and the curse that I have set before you—and you take them to heart amidst the various nations to which the Lord your God has banished you, and you return to the Lord your God, and you and your children heed His command with all your heart and soul, just as I enjoin upon you this day, then the Lord your God will restore your fortunes and take you back in love. He will bring you together again from all the peoples where the Lord your God has scattered you. Even if your outcasts are at the ends of the world, from there the Lord your God will gather you, from there He will fetch you. And the Lord your God will bring you to the land that your fathers possessed, and you shall possess it; and He will make you more prosperous and more numerous than your fathers. . . .

> Surely, this Instruction which I enjoin upon you this day is not too baffling for you, nor is it beyond reach. It is not in the heavens, that you should say, "Who among us can go up to the heavens and get it for us and impart it to us, that we may observe it?" Neither is it beyond the sea, that you should say, "Who among us can cross to the other side of the sea and get it for us and impart it to us, that we may observe it?" No, the thing is very close to you, in your mouth and in your heart, to observe it.
>
> (Deut. 30:1–5, 11–14)

I say that "to an extent" survival is foreseen in this passage because the weight of Moses' book-long speech as well as the weight of a narrative in which God is thrice barely stopped from annihilating Israel falls heavily on the side of irreversible judgment. At the end of the last curse in Deuteronomy 28, when Moses says, "The Lord will send you back to Egypt in galleys. . . . There you shall offer yourselves for sale to your enemies as male and female slaves, but none will buy," he is naming what is unmistakably understood to be Israel's terminal condition. If the passage just quoted contradicts that finality, what are we to infer? That the Lord "didn't mean it," after all? Or that his sense of mercy will always master his sense of justice? If he can forgive Israel endlessly, then in what sense does he have a covenant with Israel? If he cancels his punishments but not his promises, does he not create for himself a unilateral, gratuitously assumed obligation to Israel? And is he not, then, in a sense, making a fool of himself?

The answers to the last two questions are "Yes, he does" and "Yes, he is," but the Lord will have to change before he can confront these questions. For now, as we find him at the end of II Kings, such possibilities are but dimly guessed at. Just before the passage in which Moses foresees disaster and then a divinely assisted recovery from disaster that, on the face of it, seems to make nonsense of everything else he has been saying, he says: "The secret things belong to the Lord our God; but the things that are revealed belong to us and to our children for ever, that we may do all the words of this law" (RSV; Deut. 29:29).

If there is a contradiction, in other words, between the hope of God's mercy and the demands of God's covenant, Moses wants Israel to base its behavior on the endlessly promulgated demands of the covenant and to treat the far more remote and mysterious promise of mercy as one of "the secret things [that] belong to the Lord." In context, the promise of a return from exile to the promised land is barely more than a wobble in the Lord's burningly clear resolve to blot Israel out if it fails to keep the terms of the covenant. The wobble cannot become a new direction unless God changes, and, as Moses says, there is no knowing or predicting that: Among the "secret things" of the Lord, the supreme secret is the Lord himself.

7

Transformation

If nothing in modern literature corresponds exactly to anything in the Bible, still, among all the biblical literary genres, nothing stands quite so clearly apart as prophecy. Prophecy combines preaching, politics, and poetry in a way that tends to baffle theological, historical, and literary commentary alike. Our own approach is literary, but its focus is not on language or literary effect per se but on character. We shall consider prophecy as characterization, the self-characterization of God in a nonnarrative form. The prophets are most often not speaking their own words. They are speaking the words or "the Word" (singular and quasi-personified, as they often describe it) of God. Taking their relationship to God as at least a truth of literature, we ought to find that this "Word" says as much about God as it does about any of them.

If the characterization of God through his message to the prophets is reasonable in principle, however, it is difficult in practice because there seem to be more messages than one and because, worse, the various messages contradict one another freely and frequently. Commentators typically circumvent this difficulty by tacitly dropping the fiction that God is the speaker here and, instead, treating each prophet as an autonomous religiopolitical commentator, an author in the modern sense, dividing the larger books into internally more consistent smaller books or even into individual oracles. To do that, however, whatever historical gains may be achieved, is to deny the major literary premise of the Bible itself—namely, that these seemingly contradictory messages all come from the same divine source.

The alternative path to coherence, not to minimize its difficulty, is to proceed on the assumption that these messages do all come from the same character but then to infer from the contradictions that the character must be in distress. In such a reading, the breach of the covenant, the fall of Jerusalem, and the exile of Israel to Babylon become a crisis in the life of God as well as in the life of the nation.

The biographer of God, turning from the Pentateuch and the Deuteronomistic History to the latter prophets, may be compared with the biographer of a general in some epochal, ancient war. Having relied on the major surviving history of the war, in which the general may be the central character but is far from the only one, the biographer, by a great stroke of luck, comes into possession of three large and twelve smaller troves of the general's personal correspondence—the fifteen books of prophecy. The letters are in a state of great disorder. Moreover, their recipients were a varied group of individuals, and the general clearly tried to fit his messages to their needs and abilities. Just as clearly, he himself was often under extreme stress as he did so. No simple sense can be made of his letters; and yet, they are a breathtaking discovery, a window into the mind of someone otherwise known only through his actions and through far briefer, ad hoc statements.

The relationship between divine protagonist and human antagonist in the Bible is a unique one. God makes mankind in his image, yet without this self-image God seems incapable of having any dealings, even with himself. In the present instance, without God as sender of his "Word," the prophets would have nothing to receive. And yet without them, he would have nothing to send. Moreover, what he does send them is—in the manner of a gifted correspondent—intimately shaped by who each of them is.

Time after time, in these "letters," the Lord both threatens and predicts the central disaster that was the loss of the land of Israel and the exile of the people in consequence of their breach of covenant with the Lord. Many, if not most, of these threats and predictions were made before the fact; and if, on internal grounds, historical criticism can demonstrate that some were made after the fact, what counts in our sequential reading of the Bible is that all are *read* after the fact. In this regard, their emotional impact may be compared, loosely, with that of post–World War II memoirs and collections of letters—like those of Montgomery, Churchill, Roosevelt, Speer, de Gaulle—as they were received by readers who already knew how the war had ended. When peace is restored and the war is over, there is leisure to consider its effect at the time on key individuals.

And what is the effect upon God of this epochal defeat of his covenant partner? In brief, it is poignant but powerfully engaging agitation. God—a god of parts, as we have already seen—draws on his own inner tensions in prophecy with a focused and creative resourcefulness, aiming to keep two lives, his own and Israel's, going. Like a gifted and resourceful warrior-statesman, he labors under extreme duress to produce something from within himself that may be relevant to a crushing external crisis. To accomplish that in the particular crisis he faces, the Lord must take possession of the disparate elements in his own personality and his own past and somehow make them yield a new version of the original-to-image relationship that drew him to create mankind in the first place and, after failing with mankind as a whole, led him to make a more restricted beginning with Abraham. He, who had no history at the start, now has a powerfully suggestive history. He must mine it aggressively, and he does.

In the books of Exodus and Deuteronomy, we saw the explosive, empire-defeating, nation-making potential of the several divine personalities that fused to make the character of the Lord God in the first place. In the books of prophecy, we begin to see that this fusion, though inherently unstable, is not *necessarily* explosive. Decay downward from explosive instability through fragmentation to the stability of inertness is also possible. We may say then that God is engaged in a life-or-death struggle to hold himself together in fusion that will still be dynamic or, changing the angle of vision, that the prophets are trying to put pressure on the elements of the original fusion so as to bring them once again to criticality. His character may need to explode again if it is to fuse again. Often unstable in person, the prophets are destabilizing in effect, but, without destabilization of some kind, the life of God threatens to come to a close.

Not to press any of these metaphors too far, God's conflicted personality and his checkered record do constitute the basic inventory of his developmental possibilities. To exploit that inventory, he calls on collaborators who are themselves conflicted personalities with checkered records. The three major prophets—Isaiah, Jeremiah, and Ezekiel—may be considered, respectively, the manic, the depressive, and the psychotic articulation of the prophetic message. As for calm, sane, moderate versions of prophecy, in effect there are none. Sanity and calmness make their home not in Israel's prophetic tradition but in its wisdom tradition. Wisdom accepts; prophecy rejects; and it requires a kind of madness to reject the basic givens of an entire society, all the more to suggest that history should begin again with a new creation of the world. The madness in question is not, to be sure, simple madness but the controlled madness that modern society sometimes honors in great artists. But neither is this madness so wholly unlike the other kind that the word *madness* cannot be used for it at all. There is a common holding between the two. The cliché that the madman thinks he is God is more nearly true for these mad prophets than for any other writers in all of world literature. The prophets "play" the old themes of Israelite history and theology in a crazed and driven new way. But at every point, as God tries on and sometimes immediately tosses aside each new idea, each new image, the underlying question in his mind, too terrifying for ordinary words, is *If this is true, if this works, then . . . can we begin again?*

Though the formal, continuous narrative of the Tanakh breaks off at the end of II Kings and does not resume until the Book of Ezra, twenty-five biblical books later, the oracles (prophetic speeches) of the three major prophets—Isaiah, Jeremiah, and Ezekiel—and two of the twelve minor prophets—Haggai and Zechariah—are framed by just enough narrative to provide a slender link between these two points. Particularly important in this regard is the Book of Jeremiah, in which the prophet's biography, alternating with his oracles, continues the narrative of II Kings long enough to show a tripartite division of the defeated Israelite people. In Jeremiah, the Israelites are often called *hayyehudim*, a word that can be translated "the Jews" but is usually translated "the Judeans" by the Jewish Publication Society. Of the twelve tribes of Israel, only the house of Judah will survive, but at this transitional point in its history it has not yet assumed the shape that it will henceforth have as the Jews, a nation living, uniquely, both in its homeland and abroad. Since the translation "the Jews" too automatically and anachronistically suggests that later identity, "the Judeans" is preferable at this point. After Persia defeated Babylon in 538 B.C.E., the diaspora became largely voluntary. From that point on, "the Jews" is usually the preferable designation, especially outside Judea itself.

A close reading of the last chapters of II Kings and the narrative chapters in Jeremiah, Ezekiel, Haggai, and Zechariah makes clear that the Babylonian conquest did not come at a single stroke. Nebuchadnezzar, king of Babylon, deported the religious and cultural elite of Judah to Babylon some decades before his final conquest of Jerusalem. The final conquest was savage, to be sure, and Jerusalem itself was ruined; and yet, as has often happened in the course of empire, the peasantry was left in place to work the land. The Babylonians did not pursue a scorched-earth policy through the whole of Judah, and in due course they installed a governor who ruled it from Samaria as part of one of the western provinces of the Babylonian empire. Jeremiah predicted that the Babylonian Exile would last seventy years; and if the calculation is made from 609 B.C.E., when the elite were deported, his prediction came true to the year in 538 B.C.E., when Cyrus, the king of Persia (Persia having, in the interim, conquered Babylon), sent a delegation of Judeans to rebuild the temple of the deity he called "the God of Heaven."

Many of the Judeans exiled to Babylon remained in Babylon, however, living on as a prosperous and influential minority while empires—Babylonian, Persian, Greek, Parthian, Sassanian, and so on—rose and fell. The modest national political life renewed in the Judean province of the Persian empire made Jerusalem once again the spiritual center of emerging world Jewry, but Babylon remained its cultural, intellectual, and financial center. Aramaic, the lingua franca of the Babylonian and Persian empires, became the language of Jewish learning. (Of two ancient editions of the Talmud, the more important was produced in Babylon.) More surprising, perhaps, the square-character Aramaic alphabet replaced the original Israelite cursive alphabet for the writing of Hebrew itself. In other ways, Babylonian influence was strong. The Judeans adopted the Babylonian names for the months of the calendar. The Judean creation myth—so strongly influenced, as we have already seen, by the Babylonian—may in fact have been written in Babylon. And Babylon was an influence even when its practices were rejected. The spectacle of Babylonian idolatry, like nothing the Judeans had seen among the Canaanites, sharpened their distinction between the Lord God and made-up gods, whether the making up was physical or not.

The strength of the large expatriate Jewish community in Babylon was of crucial importance six centuries later, when Jerusalem went down in flames again, this time as the result of two failed revolts (70 and 135 C.E.) against Roman rule. The mass deportations that resulted from those defeats vastly increased the Jews' Western Diaspora and profoundly disrupted the life of the western Jewish community, but in the East the life of Babylonian Jewry was not interrupted. Rather amazingly, the Talmudic academies at Sura and Nehardea in Babylonia were authoritative for Jews in the East and even in the West as late as the twelfth century of the common era.

There was, however, a third major Judean community. At the

time when Judean life was just beginning in Babylon, a revolt of unsubdued Judean military forces—this we also learn from Jeremiah—broke out against the Babylonian governor. The rebels were a kind of Judean resistance allied with a local non-Judean nation, the Ammonites. Though the rebels did assassinate the governor, their rebellion otherwise failed, and they themselves—against Jeremiah's fierce warnings—fled to Egypt. Symbolically, at least, this may be regarded as the beginning of the long postexilic history of dissident, militant Jewry in Egypt.

Egyptian Jewry would prove of unique importance in Jewish history because it was in Egypt, after Alexander the Great made it a part of the Hellenistic world, that a far-reaching attempt was made to reconcile Jewish religious thought with Greek philosophical thought. In Alexandria, for the first time, one may speak of Jewish theology in the strongest sense of the word. The master figure in this effort is the first-century Jewish religious philosopher Philo of Alexandria. Tragically, given the fact that the interest of the Jews and the (cultural) Greeks in each other's religious views was clearly mutual, civil strife between the two groups erupted in a doomed Jewish rebellion in 117 C.E. By that time, the Romans had replaced the Greeks as rulers, though language and culture remained Greek. Some scholars suspect that the powerful and confident Jewish community of Alexandria intended eventually to retake Jerusalem militarily, but this was not to be: The rebellion ended in crushing defeat and, as at Jerusalem, in mass deportations further enlarging the Jewish Western Diaspora. Some recent scholars say that though Alexandrian Jewish thought seems not to have influenced Judaism itself very much in the centuries immediately following the failure of the rebellion, Alexandrian Judaism may live on as Christianity. In other words, Jewish missionaries of the early Jesus movement, bringing to the Mediterranean Jewish diaspora what was still a form of Judaism, may have received their warmest welcome among culturally assimilated Jews influenced by Philonic, Alexandrian thought. Gnosticism was perhaps even more important as an intellectual destination for the train of thought set in motion by Philo.

Interesting as this history may be in its own right, however, our concern is not historical but literary, not with the evolution of ancient Israel into modern Jewry but with the character of the Lord God as presented in prophetic speeches interrupted by, at most, brief narrative interludes. Since this book is not a commentary on the Tanakh, a full examination of the speeches of all fifteen of the prophets is out of the question. Our compromise is to attempt a fairly extensive examination of one major and three minor prophets: Isaiah in this chapter; Haggai, Zechariah, and Malachi at the start of Chapter 9. A few of the other prophets will be mentioned in later chapters but only in passing.

We called Isaiah a moment ago a "manic" prophet. The fact that historical critics do not believe that all the prophecies in the Book of Isaiah are the work of one writer, sane or otherwise, does not really undercut that observation. Whatever the literary genealogy of the work and however many hands contributed to it, the literary effect of its rapid cutting, especially in the opening chapters, is that of a single mind bursting with concepts and images. The speaker—now the Lord, now Isaiah, now either or both—changes constantly. Typography may rationalize this by putting what appear to be God's words in quotation marks even when the text does not explicitly identify them as such, but the truth lies deeper than typography: Both minds—the Lord's and Isaiah's—are bursting and, for that reason, neither is at all tranquil. But by the same token, the almost painful fertility of the Book of Isaiah makes it a compendium of prophecy: Nearly every idea and very nearly every image that will appear in any of the other prophets appears at least briefly in Isaiah. With its wild plungings and veerings, its ravaged visions of universal destruction and ravished ecstasies of universal redemption, the Book of Isaiah is a kind of *Deus Agonistes*, a spectacle of struggle in which the Lord God strains every nerve.

It is not that Isaiah tells us, in so many words, that God is in a quandary. Everything the Lord says here he seems to say with as much confidence as we heard when he spoke to Moses or, if possible, with even greater confidence. But though his manner is proud, his matter is in a way humiliating, for the interpretations that the Lord gives of the fall of Jerusalem—none of them backed by anything less than total divine certainty—are in radical disagreement with each other and with the Deuteronomistic interpretation that we have just seen.

Two dominant interpretive options alternate and sometimes conflict:

1. Israel has sinned and received its well-merited punishment, and there God must let the matter rest. This is the Deuteronomistic interpretation repeated with rhetorical force.

2. Israel has been punished more than enough for its sins, and, one way or another, the Lord must now come to Israel's rescue.

Although, in the way just indicated, God speaks differently and so reveals a different aspect of himself to each of the prophets, in speaking to each he is nonetheless addressing the same set of events in his own life and the same set of questions. The events: Israel has been unfaithful to God; God has punished Israel. The questions: Can God and Israel begin again, and, if so, how? Will God's relationship to the other nations of the world now change, and, if so, how?

Jeremiah, rather than Isaiah, is the prophet who seems to have been most celebrated and cherished by the Judean elite that, working from Babylon, would reconstitute Judean national life. When they return, it is his prophecy that they say has come true. Unique among the prophets, he had urged those carried off to Babylon to marry, procreate, and prosper there until the Lord brought them home; by the same token, he had urged those left behind in devastated Judea not to leave for any other destination, such as Egypt. Vilified during his lifetime, Jeremiah became, after his death, something like the "official" prophet of the sacerdotal establishment.

But it is Isaiah, not Jeremiah, who brings out the eloquence in the Lord God. It is when the Lord is speaking to Isaiah that he goes most deeply and recklessly into himself, providing the most searching inventory of his own responses to the agony occasioned in his own life by the agony he has inflicted on his chosen people. To read these responses is to pass through this crisis in the life of God in the company of the God who is suffering it.

Executioner

"Lo, Swiftly, Speedily It Comes"

ISAIAH 1–39

It would be much easier for modern readers making their way through the Book of Isaiah if, within its pages, the Lord confessed himself dismayed to see his own punishment actually inflicted on Jerusalem and torn between the two positions—call them the justice position and the mercy position—just mentioned. But he does not do this.

To return once again to the personal-letter analogy, these "letters" from God are not the kind in which the writer confides his confusion but the kind in which, with different correspondents, he tries on radically different positions, pushing each one to the limit each time. Taken as a whole, the Book of Isaiah provides a repertory of at best partially compatible responses to this supreme crisis in the joined life of Israel and God.

In II Samuel 7, we saw how, speaking to David through the prophet Nathan, God tried out, tentatively and for the first time, a comparative, analogical way of talking about himself. "I am like a father," he said to David, to paraphrase very slightly. Here, he takes that comparison and develops it. But "like a father" proves just the beginning: He is also like a lover, a husband, a mother, a shepherd, a gardener, a king, and—categories never heard before—a redeemer and "the Holy One of Israel." Near the end of the Deuteronomistic History, we saw him backing into an involvement in, if scarcely a responsibility for, international relations. Here, that involvement mushrooms into a true responsibility and an attempt to ask how this new responsibility may be integrated with some still-to-be-defined new relationship with Israel. And yet, if all this amounts to what we might well call "the new Lord God," there are also moments—and many of them—when the massive synthesis of divine personalities that Moses enunciated with such commanding eloquence in the Book of Deuteronomy returns to silence all dissent and halt all further development.

Because some of the most famous lines in Isaiah have been set to music in G. F. Handel's *Messiah* oratorio, a reader may find snatches of that work coming to mind during the reading of Isaiah.

But at the level of composition, the Book of Isaiah is less like *Messiah* than it is like the second and third movements of Beethoven's Ninth Symphony. In those movements, theme interrupts theme and tempo breaks tempo. So it is in Isaiah. Even the culminating "choral" chapters (the work of the "Second Isaiah," as historical scholarship calls him), where all earlier themes and moods seem to come so splendidly together—even these chapters are shot through with more sudden halts, changes of gait, boltings forward, and veerings off than first meet the ear. The Ninth Symphony, as has often been remarked, is a composition almost uncomposed by its own sense of endless possibility. So it is here: The end of the only sustained relationship God has had and the looming end of Israel's history as a nation create a dizzying, sometimes grief-stricken sense of freedom. Intellectually speaking, very little is ruled completely out; and an almost reckless style reflects this unprecedented openness.

In the long opening vision of the book, Isaiah quotes the Lord to the kings of Judah, calling them, shockingly, "rulers of Sodom":

> Hear the word of the Lord,
> you rulers of Sodom!
> Give ear to the teaching of our God,
> you people of Gomorrah!
> "What to me is the multitude of your sacrifices?"
> says the Lord;
> "I have had enough of burnt offerings of rams
> and the fat of fed beasts;
> I do not delight in the blood of bulls,
> or of lambs, or of he-goats.
>
> "When you come to appear before me,
> who requires of you
> this trampling of my courts?"
> (RSV; Isa. 1:10–12)

The New Revised Standard Version translates the last verse

> When you come to appear before me,
> who asked this from your hand?
> Trample my courts no more.

The Jewish Publication Society version, very similar, reads:

That you come to appear before Me—
Who asked that of you?
Trample My courts
no more.

Taken literally, the question is astonishing. Any hearer who remembered Exodus or Leviticus could answer, "Who asked this? *You did!*" Questions beginning with the Hebrew *mi*, "who?" are sometimes more exclamations than questions, as in the American slang "Who needs it?" But that in no way mitigates the shock.

If the Lord does not want burnt offerings, what does he want?

Wash yourselves; make yourselves clean;
  remove the evil of your doings from before my eyes;
cease to do evil,
  learn to do good;
seek justice,
  correct oppression;
defend the fatherless,
  plead for the widow. (1:16–17; this and the remaining quotations from Isaiah are all from the RSV)

These words are included in a vision that Isaiah "saw concerning Judah and Jerusalem in the days of Uzziah, Jotham, Ahaz, and Hezekiah, kings of Judah" (1.1). But those four kings ruled, among them, for a century. In effect, the Lord is saying that this is what he always wanted, appearances to the contrary notwithstanding, and that he has been asking for it in vain for one hundred years. Elaborate animal sacrifices cannot be conducted in exile; but even in exile the fatherless may be defended, the widow pleaded for, and so on: Here is a new basis for establishing a covenant.

Punishment as such is not a new basis for a covenant, but perhaps the exile is not purely punishment:

Therefore the Lord says,
  the Lord of hosts,
  the Mighty One of Israel:
"Ah, I will vent my wrath on my enemies,
  and avenge myself on my foes.
I will turn my hand against you
  and will smelt away your dross as with lye
  and remove all your alloy.

And I will restore your judges as at the first,
  and your counselors as at the beginning.
Afterward you shall be called the city of righteousness.
the faithful city." (1:24–26)

"I will smelt away your dross": The Lord is now reconceiving his own action. When punishing the generation of Noah, he thought mankind as a whole incorrigible. There was no purifying them. And this has remained his view. With the exception of II Samuel 7, when the Lord said he would be a strict father to David's house but no more than that, punishment has not been understood as discipline at any earlier point in the Bible. Now it is.

And what of the other nations, the ones the Lord has been using to punish Israel?

It shall come to pass in the latter days
  that the mountain of the house of the Lord
shall be established as the highest of the mountains,
  and shall be raised above the hills;
and all the nations shall flow to it,
  and many peoples shall come, and say:
"Come, let us go up to the mountain of the Lord,
  to the house of the God of Jacob;
that he may teach us his ways
  and that we may walk in his paths."
For out of Zion shall go forth the law,
  and the word of the Lord from Jerusalem. (2:2–3)

The Lord can restore a covenant with Israel and yet continue a relationship of some sort with the other nations by making Israel the teacher—or at least the seat of instruction—and the other nations the students. The passage concludes with an oft-quoted vision of the "learning" of peace:

He shall judge between the nations,
  and shall decide for many peoples;
and they shall beat their swords into plowshares,
  and their spears into pruning hooks;
nation shall not lift up sword against nation,
  neither shall they learn war any more. (2:4)

"I ain't gonna study war no more," as the spiritual "Down by the Riverside" paraphrases this verse. The mountaintop is the home both of Baal (hilltops were endlessly denounced in the Deuteronomistic History as the sites of Baal-worship) and of Yahweh as a Baal-like god of war. Here, the same mountain is being turned into a place for instruction in peace.

But first there will be a "day of the Lord," on which the holy warrior will rage for one last, definitive time over all the earth. Only then will men "cast forth / their idols of silver and their idols of gold . . . to the moles and to the bats" (2:20). This too is a scarcely believable new departure. Even if it must be by warfare that the nations come to the Lord, the notion that they can come to him at all is radically new. The Deuteronomist warned Israel endlessly against worshiping the Canaanites' gods but never entertained the notion that the Canaanites would stop worshiping their own gods and start worshiping Israel's. The assumption that no such development was possible was precisely what justified genocide: Because conversion was impossible, extermination was necessary.

But if all mankind is a worshiper of the Lord, in what sense is Israel still the Lord's people? The Lord seems to be of two minds. At one moment, all Israel is still his covenanted people; at another, the ground begins to shift under the nation:

> The Lord enters into judgment
> with the elders and princes of his people:
> "It is you who have devoured the vineyard,
> the spoil of the poor is in your houses.
> What do you mean by crushing *my people,*
> by grinding the face of the poor?"
> says the Lord God of hosts. (3:14–15; emphasis added)

Is all Israel the Lord's people, or only Israel's poor? Or are the poor of all nations now his people? Though the law codes of the Pentateuch make moderate provision for widows, orphans, foreigners, slaves, and others in vulnerable categories, provision is not required because of any special relationship that the Lord has with such people. But if he is now inclined in that direction, then the list may easily be lengthened by one category: the defeated in war, not excluding defeated Israel. In short, another possible basis for a renewed covenant.

Having so often promised his chosen people wealth, the Lord has encouraged them to see wealth as a sign of his favor. But now, suddenly, this too is put in question. In Isaiah 3–5, the wealthy—and haughty, overindulged women in particular—are subjected to some of the most scathing language in the entire Bible. Isaiah 3:16–26 includes a kind of inventory of feminine luxuries—"the sashes, the perfume boxes, and the amulets," et cetera—and the bitter promise "The Lord will lay bare their secret parts." When the Babylonian conquerors come,

> Instead of perfume there will be rottenness;
>   and instead of a girdle, a rope;
> and instead of well-set hair, baldness;
>   and instead of a rich robe, a girding of sackcloth;
>   instead of beauty, shame. (3:24)

As to its language, this is not unlike a Deuteronomic curse; but the Lord's preoccupation with the abuses of wealth is new. Accumulation itself is condemned in one of the more directly anticapitalistic verses in the Bible:

> Woe to those who join house to house,
>   who add field to field,
> until there is no more room,
>   and you are made to dwell alone in the midst of the land.
> The Lord of hosts has sworn in my hearing:
> "Surely many houses shall be desolate,
>   large and beautiful houses, without inhabitant." (5:8–9)

Who is it who is offended by this behavior? As he announces his judgment, the Lord calls himself by a new name: "the Holy One of Israel." It is by this name that he is the friend of the poor, the bitterly sarcastic opponent of both the wealthy and the jaded corrupt:

> Woe to those who are wise in their own eyes,
>   and shrewd in their own sight!
> Woe to those who are heroes at drinking wine,
>   and valiant men in mixing strong drink
> who acquit the guilty for a bribe,
>   and deprive the innocent of his right! (5:21–23)

And it is the Holy One of Israel who sends Babylon as a kind of attack dog against Israel. In its hard, cruel beauty, Isaiah 5:26–30 is one of the finest brief war poems in any language:

He will raise a signal for a nation afar off,
  and whistle for it from the ends of the earth;
and lo, swiftly, speedily it comes!
None is weary, none stumbles,
  none slumbers or sleeps,
not a waistcloth is loose,
  not a sandal-thong broken;
their arrows are sharp,
  all their bows bent,
their horses' hoofs seem like flint,
  and their wheels like the whirlwind.
Their roaring is like a lion,
  like young lions they roar;
they growl and seize their prey,
  they carry it off, and none can rescue.
They will growl over it on that day,
  like the roaring of the sea.
And if one look to the land,
  behold, darkness and distress;
and the light is darkened by its clouds.

And who is this "Holy One of Israel," who whistles up the dogs of war? In the following chapter (Isa. 6), the prophet, in a vision, sees the Lord as he has never been seen before, seated on a lofty throne, his train filling the temple. He is attended by a host of six-winged "seraphs," who cover their genitals with one pair of wings, their faces with a second, and who fly with the third as they call out:

Holy, holy, holy is the Lord of hosts;
and the whole earth is full of his glory.

Isaiah cries out: "Woe is me! For I am lost; for I am a man of unclean lips, and I dwell in the midst of a people of unclean lips; for my eyes have seen the King, the Lord of hosts!"

The Lord God, as we saw before, has not hitherto been a king to Israel or to anyone else. Even in Micaiah's vision, discussed briefly earlier, he is a judge or international arbiter rather than a monarch. Now he is overwhelmingly, awesomely regal. But what is his wish? One of the seraphs (or "seraphim," to use the Hebrew plural, as the RSV does) places a burning coal on Isaiah's lips and says: "Behold, this has touched your lips; your guilt is taken away, and your sin forgiven." The Book of Leviticus makes elaborate provision for the removal of various kinds of guilt, but its measures are humanly enacted. Here the action is taken by the Lord himself. But why?

> And I heard the voice of the Lord saying, "Whom shall I send, and who will go for us?" Then I said, "Here am I! Send me." And he said, "Go, and say to this people:
>
> 'Hear and hear, but do not understand;
> see and see, but do not perceive.'
> Make the heart of this people fat,
> and their ears heavy,
> and shut their eyes;
> lest they see with their eyes,
> and hear with their ears,
> and understand with their hearts,
> and turn and be healed." (6:8–10)

"Here am I" was Moses' response to the voice that spoke to him from the burning bush, but there is another more unsettling similarity here. The Lord tells Isaiah to darken Israel's heart just as the Lord himself darkened (as well as hardened) Pharaoh's, making it impossible for Pharaoh to receive the message given him. As spoken, a line such as "see and see, but do not perceive" is ironic, but the irony is bitter. The Lord's instruction to Isaiah bespeaks his own now irreversible intention to destroy Israel. There is nothing ironic or equivocal about that. "How long?" Isaiah asks; that is, how long will ironic divine injunction to "not understand" be in effect? The answer: until the total destruction of the land. The land will be not merely felled like a tree but obliterated like a tree whose stump is burned out after it is felled:

> And though a tenth remain in it,
> it will be burned again,
> like a terebinth or an oak,
> whose stump remains standing
> when it is felled. (6:13)

The Holy One of Israel combines several elements, all of them new and none given more than a fleeting mention at this point. The Holy One is exalted, enthroned in heaven, yet his concern is with the lowly of the earth. He is a teacher, a revealer, sending Isaiah to proclaim his word. And yet with effortless control over all the nations of the world, he has deputed Assyria and Babylonia to destroy Israel, and he wills that Israel understand his message only *after* his punishment has been inflicted. It is no wonder that the Holy One is also described as unknowable.

The Book of Isaiah is, as we said earlier, full of jolting reversals. This divine decree of blindness is followed quite soon by its polar opposite:

> The people who walked in darkness
> have seen a great light;
> those who dwelt in a land of deep darkness,
> on them has light shined. . . .
> For to us a child is born,
> to us a son is given;
> and the government will be upon his shoulder,
> and his name will be called
> "Wonderful Counselor, Mighty God,
> Everlasting Father, Prince of Peace."
> Of the increase of his government and of peace
> there will be no end,
> upon the throne of David, and over his kingdom,
> to establish it, and to uphold it
> with justice and with righteousness
> from this time forth and for evermore.
> The zeal of the Lord of hosts will do this. (9:2, 6–7)

In its broadest terms, this prophecy recalls Nathan's prophecy to King David that his dynasty would be eternal, but Nathan foresaw nothing for any Davidic heir remotely comparable to the titles "Mighty God, Everlasting Father, Prince of Peace." True, Isaiah, even in naming his own children, was given to name play; and since Hebrew names are often either sentence-names or "theophoric" names (names that carry a god-name within them), his resources in this area are almost deceptively rich. If instead of saying "his name will be called . . . Prince of Peace," the translation read "his name will be called . . . Sarsalom," like Absalom, the fact that these names are finally *only* names would be unmistakable. All the same, the tradition of translating them rather than leaving them, like other names, in their transliterated Hebrew form is well justified. For when Isaiah says that "his name will be called . . . Elgibor (Mighty God)," he is not saying that a man of David's line will be divine; he is saying—precisely by his choice of that name—that he will be superhuman. Chapter 6 was a vision of King Yahweh on his heavenly throne. Chapter 9 parallels it with a vision of a future, exalted, messianic earthly king.

Historically speaking, this enlargement of the idea of kingship undoubtedly arose in Israel as a reaction to the emergence of the idea of a world state in Assyria. Though they were not the first empire of any kind and though they were not otherwise culturally original, the Assyrians were the first to consciously pursue an integrated, multinational empire, in which borders were eliminated, populations were forcibly exchanged among the tributary regions, and a single economy was administered from the royal capital. The Assyrians themselves were overthrown, but their imperial model survived in a Near Eastern ecumene ruled by, in succession, the Babylonians, the Persians, and the Greeks. More important, the *idea* of world empire, once born, never died. The Babylonians, being the nation that actually destroyed Jerusalem, loom larger in the Israelite imagination than the Assyrians, but the Assyrians, as the originators of this bold idea, are often mentioned; and a key mention comes, by a kind of psychological association, just now, as this messianic exaltation of Israelite kingship is receiving its first formulation. After the Lord has installed his messianic king on Mount Zion, he will punish the king of Assyria for saying:

> By the strength of my hand I have done it,
> and by my wisdom, for I have understanding;
> I have removed the boundaries of peoples,
> and have plundered their treasures;
> like a bull I have brought down those who sat on thrones.
> My hand has found like a nest the wealth of the peoples;
> and as men gather eggs that have been forsaken
> so I have gathered all the earth;
> and there was none that moved a wing,
> or opened the mouth, or chirped. (10:13–14)

Since the Lord has in fact simply used Assyria as his scourge, it clearly offends him that the Assyrian king does not realize the truth of the matter. He needs to be taught a lesson.

The new world empire that the Lord is planning, however, with Zion as its capital, is to be superior to Assyria in more than arms. In the passage immediately following, the earlier themes of the Lord's preferential concern for the poor and of Mount Zion as the world center of "knowledge of the Lord" converge with this theme of messianic kingship. The Lord's victories will be achieved as God's initial creation was achieved, by his word alone. In Isaiah's bold image, he will strike his enemies "with the rod of his mouth." But to all this is added yet another, very scantily integrated new idea: that of the coming world empire as a new creation.

The messianic kingdom/new creation will begin when there comes forth "a shoot from the stump of Jesse [David's father]"—new life, in other words, from that apparently burnt-out stump. This "shoot," the Lord's messianic prince,

> shall not judge by what his eyes see,
> or decide by what his ears hear;
> but with righteousness he shall judge the poor,
> and decide with equity for the meek of the earth;
> and he shall smite the earth with the rod of his mouth,
> and with the breath of his lips he shall slay the wicked. . . .

But this social transformation is just the beginning. It will be completed by a natural transformation:

> The wolf shall dwell with the lamb,
> and the leopard shall lie down with the kid,
> and the calf and the lion and the fatling together,
> and a little child shall lead them.
> The cow and the bear shall feed;
> their young shall lie down together;
> and the lion shall eat straw like the ox.
> The sucking child shall play over the hole of the asp,
> and the weaned child shall put his hand on the adder's den.
> They shall not hurt or destroy
> in all my holy mountain;
> for the earth shall be full of the knowledge of the Lord
> as the waters cover the sea. (11:3–4, 6–9)

This is the "peaceable kingdom" so endlessly portrayed in early American art.

In the synthesis of biblical conceptions of God that defines the word *God* and its equivalents in all the Western languages, a miraculous benignity of this sort may seem to have been eternally in place, but it was not: It has a beginning, and this is the point where it begins. Neither the God who circumcised Abraham nor the God who inspired Joseph's dream interpretations nor the war God who brought Israel out of Egypt nor the lawgiver who promulgated the covenant from Mount Sinai ever spoke of this kind of total transformation of social and natural reality. If the power to bring about such a change was presumptively his, an inference from his demonstrated power to create the existing world from nothingness, he found no occasion at those previous stages in his story to lay public claim to it. Now the occasion presents. In this crisis moment, the Lord ranges back over his own past, as we have been saying, to find what may make it possible for him to have a future. If Assyria needs to be matched and surpassed, if the establishment of a new covenant requires a whole new world, the means are not wanting. Speaking to Isaiah, the Lord "remembers" that, yes, he can do all this.

The Lord cannot avoid thinking of himself as an actor on the world stage now that Israel, its population scattered, has become world Jewry. His response to that scattering is to foresee, as the prelude to a new creation, a new kind of Exodus, not from one land but from the many lands to which the Judeans have been banished. On the day of the Lord, Isaiah says, "the Lord will extend his hand yet a second time to recover the remnant which is left of his people, from Assyria, from Egypt, from Pathros, from Ethiopia, from Elam, from Shinar, from Hamath, and from the coastlands of the sea" (11:11). The first time the Lord "extended his hand" was when he smote Egypt (see Exod. 7:5 among others). This time

> there will be a highway from Assyria
> for the remnant which is left of his people,
> as there was for Israel
> when they came up from the land of Egypt. (Isa. 11:16)

So far, so triumphant, but why only a remnant? We have heard the remnant mentioned as early as the Book of Deuteronomy; and yet, like the listing of the places of actual exile directly after the vision of the "peaceable kingdom," the word *remnant* strikes a jarring note of smallness in a context of mythic enlargement. And this is scarcely the only jarring note in the opening chapters of Isaiah, twelve chapters that, as we said earlier, constitute a kind of inventory of concepts that may be compatible but are far from integrated and remain collectively at odds with a much simpler concept—namely, that Israel has ended the covenant by sinning and provoking God's implacable wrath.

It is not clear at this point that God will go beyond his wrath, and wrath is all but the only subject of the next eleven chapters (Isa. 13–23). These chapters contain oracles predicting grim disaster for one nation after another. Individually monotonous, they are collectively remarkable simply because nothing like them has been seen before and because there is no real reason why anything of the sort should be seen now. Except when he has been using an Assyria or a Babylonia instrumentally, the Lord's relationship with the nations of the world has been bounded by the covenant with Noah, which forbade only murder and did not speak of sanctions. The nations other than Israel were not and are not at this point under any divine command to worship the Lord or to observe any legal or moral code imposed by him. For what then are they being punished?

Typically, little or no reason is given. Thus, against Arabia:

> The oracle concerning Arabia.
> In the thickets in Arabia you will lodge,
> O caravans of Dedanites.
> To the thirsty bring water,
> meet the fugitive with bread,
> O inhabitants of the land of Tema.
> For they have fled from the swords, from the drawn sword,
> from the bent bow, and from the press of battle. (21:13–15)

Not every oracle is as jejune as that one, but all are long on the wrath to be visited and short on just what provoked it. In the Book of Joshua, when the Israelites visited genocide upon Canaan in the name of the Lord, the Canaanites were similarly innocent. Perhaps these oracles, rather than images of divine judgment, are simply images of future Israelite victories, morally neutral in some sense, as those earlier victories were simply the enactment of a divine plan for the land, like clearing a field before planting. True, the Lord has been merciless against those who stood in his path, such as the Amalekites whom Saul failed to exterminate completely, but even then his ferocity was essentially not a moral judgment. Only in the case of Israel does physical annihilation follow unmistakable moral condemnation.

On the other hand, if other nations are now found worthy of moral condemnation, perhaps the Lord's view of them has changed. Paradoxically, the fact that those nations may now be truly punished rather than merely eliminated brings them a step nearer to moral equivalency with Israel. The older view may live on in some of these oracles, but a new view now competes with it. The premise of the older view was the impossibility—better put, the sheer unimaginability—of conversion. But midway in this series of classic prophecies of doom comes an astonishing prediction of conversion: "The Lord will make himself known to the Egyptians" and they will come to him.

> In that day there will be a highway from Egypt to Assyria, and the Assyrian will come into Egypt, and the Egyptian into Assyria, and the Egyptians will worship with the Assyrians. In that day Israel will be the third with Egypt and Assyria, a blessing in the midst of the earth, whom the Lord of hosts has blessed, saying, "Blessed be Egypt my people, and Assyria the work of my hands, and Israel my heritage." (19:23–24)

What are we to conclude? Does the Lord God want to defeat, humiliate, and punish the other nations of the world? Does he want to subordinate them to Israel in a new social order and a new creation? Or does he intend for them to join Israel as coequals in his service? Each of these sharply opposed views is expressed with equal, uncompromising rigor.

But God's mind is cloven even deeper than that. Monotheism's boast is that ultimate reality lives in its house and nowhere else. Monotheism's sorrow is that everything must be accommodated in that one house. In the second chapter of this book, discussing God's destruction of the entire world by flood, we noted that in ancient Mesopotamia there were two gods, a creator god and a destroyer god, who fought. In ancient Israel, by contrast, there was just one God, who both created and destroyed. The fight was within him. Just after the series of oracles against Israel's neighbors, interrupted by the just-quoted, wildly inconsistent vision of a glorious Assyrian-Egyptian-Israelite future, there comes welling up from the deep a return of God-the-Destroyer. This time, it is not Egypt or Assyria that is condemned but the whole world; and, once again, the crime is barely named, while the punishment is richly detailed:

> Terror, and the pit, and the snare
> are upon you, O inhabitant of the earth!
> He who flees at the sound of the terror
> shall fall into the pit;

and he who climbs out of the pit
  shall be caught in the snare.
For the windows of heaven are opened,
  and the foundations of the earth tremble.
The earth is utterly broken,
  the earth is rent asunder,
  the earth is violently shaken.
The earth staggers like a drunken man,
  it sways like a hut;
its transgression lies heavy upon it,
  and it falls, and will not rise again.
On that day the Lord will punish
  the host of heaven, in heaven,
  and the kings of the earth, on the earth.
They will be gathered together
  as prisoners in a pit;
they will be shut up in a prison,
  and after many days they will be punished.
Then the moon will be confounded,
  and the sun ashamed;
for the Lord of hosts will reign
  on Mount Zion and in Jerusalem
and before his elders he will manifest his glory.
(24:17–23)

This is the first apocalypse, or vision of final doom, in the Bible. Its eruption signals, as scarcely anything else could, that all the paths in the Lord's multiple personality have been broken open by the trauma of the breaking of the covenant and the fall of Jerusalem. The Lord's covenant with Abraham and all that followed from it was a compromise between the unqualified creativity of "be fertile and increase" (Gen. 1:22) and the unqualified destructivity of "everything on earth shall perish" (6:17). Now that that compromise has broken down, the original alternatives to it both come back into view. The peaceable kingdom vision is of unchecked creativity and benevolence; the vision just quoted is of unchecked destructivity and malevolence. Israel and its destiny are absent from this vision, which concludes with the attendants of the divine destroyer (*his* elders rather than Israel's) gathered round his mountain throne for no purpose other than to witness his glory amid the wreckage of the world.

One cannot allegorize every editorial accident in a collaborative, edited work like the Book of Isaiah. One cannot turn every move within it into a turn in the plot. The annotators of the Oxford Annotated Bible laconically advise, "Compare v. 19," at Isaiah 26:14, which reads:

> They are dead, they will not live;
> they are shades, they will not arise;
> to that end thou hast visited them with destruction
> and wiped out all remembrance of them.

Verse 26:19, five verses down in the same chapter, reads:

> Thy dead shall live, their bodies shall rise.
> O dwellers in the dust, awake and sing for joy!
> For thy dew is a dew of light,
> and on the land of the shades thou wilt let it fall.

The Oxford annotators have nothing to say other than what the juxtaposition says for itself—namely, that the text is inconsistent. Who can fault them?

At the same time, certain broader, slower moves deserve to be read as turns in the plot or developments of lasting consequence in the character of the protagonist, and it is appropriate to note these on their first appearance, just as we noted the first mention of divine fatherhood at II Samuel 7. Eschatology, speculation about the end of time and how its approach will be known, and apocalypticism, visions of that end as including unprecedented, world- or cosmoswide destruction, have played almost no part in the Bible since Genesis 6. From this point on, they will have a steadily growing role, not replacing all other views but emerging alongside them as a permanent option. The sine qua non for the emergence of eschatology and apocalypticism may have been, first, exposure to the Assyrian empire and the globalization of social thought that it represented and, second, the more personal experience of having one's own world, one's own society, utterly destroyed. But such influences might carry a writer in a variety of directions. They carried the biblical writers toward changes in the voice and character of the Lord God. God talks about the pretensions of Assyria and Babylon. He talks about the devastation of Israel. And he frames mutually inconsistent responses that reflect separate parts of his own character and his own past. Ultimately, by doing all this, he talks himself into being someone new. But the process is shot through with life-and-death contrasts.

In the "Little Apocalypse" of Isaiah, as it is sometimes called (Isa. 24–27), the vision of death previously quoted is succeeded, without quite being supplanted, by a vision of life. Verses 25:7–8, which will be quoted in Revelation, the last book in the Christian Bible, go extravagantly beyond the elimination of death to the elimination of grief and pain:

> And he will destroy on this mountain the covering that is cast over all peoples, the veil that is spread over all nations. He will swallow up death for ever, and the Lord God will wipe away tears from all faces, and the reproach of his people he will take away from all the earth; for the Lord has spoken.

Which vision comes from the mind of God? This one? Or "Terror, the pit, and the snare are upon you, O inhabitant of the earth"? Both do, and one can only infer that the mind that contains them both is by no means at peace with itself.

It can only have been a struggle for a king trying to hearken to oracles as varied as those we have just been reviewing. The Book of Isaiah is divided roughly in half by a prose interlude concerning Hezekiah, an almost-good king rescued from the Assyrians and healed of an illness that he thought was fatal. But after the recovered king injudiciously allows a visiting Babylonian delegation to view his treasure house, the prophet turns on him and prophesies eventual victory for Babylon, adding grimly that some of Hezekiah's sons will be made eunuchs for the Babylonian ruler. Hezekiah replies, and one can hear the weariness: " 'The word of the Lord which you have spoken is good.' For he thought, 'There will be peace and security in my days' " (39:8). An ancient Israelite version of *Après moi le déluge*? Perhaps, but the mix of good and bad news in Isaiah baffled his contemporaries no less than it does us.

Holy One

"To Whom Will You Liken Me?"

ISAIAH 40–66

Isaiah's baffling shifts begin to abate, and good news begins to predominate, in the last portion of the book, the part attributed to the writer whom historical criticism calls, as we shall, "Second Isaiah," *Second* because his style and distinctive synthesis clearly distinguish him from the writer or writers who produced Isaiah 1–39, *Isaiah* because so many of his images and concepts are developments of those we have just been reviewing. If the Book of Isaiah bears comparison to Beethoven's Ninth Symphony, then it is obviously in Second Isaiah that we hear the choral ode, with its mood of triumph, liberation, and, at least on first hearing, unity.

First Isaiah defies summary; Second Isaiah invites it; and the summary might run as follows:

> *Israel has sinned grievously and richly deserved punishment, but now the punishment received can be seen to be adequate and indeed much more than adequate. It is time for the Lord to comfort his people, and he is eager to do so. Their return across the desert from Babylon to Jerusalem shall be a triumphal march, eclipsing the glory of their trek through the desert from Egypt. The Lord of hosts has anointed Cyrus, king of the Persians, to defeat Babylon and reestablish Israel on the Lord's holy mountain at Jerusalem. There, through the "servant of the Lord," the Lord will gather a chosen people that includes, in principle, the entire human race. In establishing this new order, the Lord will be king as well as creator, and father as well as king. Above all, however, he will be "your redeemer, the Holy One of Israel"—invincible because he is the only God who actually exists and holy because he is exalted above all human knowing.*

In the vision of Second Isaiah, God may say little about either himself or Israel that is wholly new. However, he drastically transforms his own mood by strategic omissions, substitutions, and expansions and by the adoption of a tone of tender, almost maternal solicitude that is without precedent and is the more striking because joined to an equally new emphasis on his awesome uniqueness as the one and only god who is not a sheer fabrication.

Some particular changes:

1. God dispenses almost entirely with further oracles of destruction against either Israel or any other nation except, once, Babylon.

2. He refrains from condemning Israel for moral failings, abuse of the poor, graft, and so on, or for any other rupture of the Mosaic covenant. Moses is mentioned just once, and the law-related rhetoric of Deuteronomy is completely missing.

3. For the most part, rather than inveigh against Israel for past interest in Canaanite Baal, he mocks Babylonian idolatry without ever suggesting that the exiled Jews have shown any interest in it. Here, as in numbers 1 and 2, the assumption is that Israel, a sinner now forgiven, is well worthy of this glorious new relationship with the Lord.

4. Having established the utter nonreality of all competing gods as mere manufactured objects, he makes his own reliability and invincibility as redeemer seem the more overwhelming by drawing prodigally and eloquently on his entire history: creation, patriarchs, exodus, conquest, and a culminating personal and eternal covenant with royal David's line.

5. Without denying his own power, he insists in a new way on mystery rather than power as the source of his holiness. Holiness can only be defined dialectically. Holy is what is *other than* unholy or profane. The Lord is holy by being *other than* mankind. But in what regard? In Second Isaiah, the Lord insists that he knows mankind, but mankind does not and cannot know him, at least not on its own. This is how he and they differ. If the first, now broken covenant was based on the clarity of the law and its requirements, this new one is located in the mystery of the Lord's personality and his unknowable intentions.

The first and second of these changes are omissions that speak for themselves. The third through fifth, dealing with monotheism and the Lord's character, require more comment.

Between the prohibition of idolatry in the Decalogue and Second

Isaiah's polemic against Babylonian idolatry, there are surprisingly few mentions of idolatry in the Tanakh. The Deuteronomistic History only rarely brushes against the subject. Though the absoluteness of the initial prohibition is perhaps the most striking single feature of early Israelite religion, it must be noted that the Canaanite religion that was Yahwism's rival during the centuries before the Babylonian conquest was itself not notably idolatrous. Israelites who deserted the Lord and took up the worship of Baal did not thereby become idolaters, and idolatry is never the charge brought against them. The charge, one that admits a measure of reality to Baal, is typically covenant infidelity to the Lord by the offering of sacrifice to Baal. Canaanite Baal-worship employed a variety of sacred objects, including altars, sacred poles, trees, standing rocks, and more, but Israel had its own elaborate armamentarium of cult objects. The two traditions parted company not over idolatry but over sex. The cult of Baal was orgiastic; the cult of the Lord, an asexual God, was chaste. The "whoring after false gods" against which the Deuteronomist inveighs was literal enough: Cult prostitution was a standard feature of Baalism. And that practice was abhorrent to the Israelites. And yet, because Israel's Lord, like Baal, was a war god who was also, despite his own asexuality, intensely concerned with fertility, not excluding a direct concern with the penis, menstruation, the first fruits of the womb and the field, and so on, syncretism within Canaan may have been nearly inevitable and, for the syncretizers, may have involved a relatively minor culture shock.

Babylon delivered a larger shock. The image of the Babylonian god Marduk in his ziggurat temple, the famous "tower of Babel," was as close to literal divinity for the Babylonians as any icon in religious history ever has been. Five times, as the great capital was conquered and retaken by the several nations who held it at one period or another, the statue was either kidnapped and removed or recaptured and triumphantly returned. All this was deeply foreign and as ludicrous as it was repellent to the exiled Jews, even if Second Isaiah deliberately exaggerates for the sake of satire. If the Assyrian idea of a world state made a positive contribution to Jewish religious thought, the Babylonian idea of a divine statue made a negative one. It enabled the exiled Jews to sharpen as never before their understanding of just how literally their monotheism was to be taken. As this realization is placed in the mouth of God, it becomes a new insistence on his uniqueness and, thereby, his towering greatness.

The Deuteronomic confession "Hear, O Israel, the Lord is our

God, the Lord alone" did not mean at the start that the Lord was the only god as precisely and self-consciously as it would come to mean during this period and forever after. Once nonreality was, as we might well put it, smashingly predicated of the idolaters' gods, it was also predicated of all competing gods, whether idolatry was involved or not. And the result was a degree of awe vis-à-vis the Lord God, the Lord of hosts, the "Holy One of Israel," as Second Isaiah so loves to call him, that had not obtained when it was tacitly if unreflectively assumed that the Moabites would always have their Chemosh, the Philistines their Dagon, and so on, and that, all in all, they had some reason to have them.

This was, broadly, the way of the ancient world. Other nations did not deny the reality of the Lord as the Jews' national god. When Sennacherib threatens Hezekiah, he claims that the Lord, as Israel's national god, cannot defend Judah against him any better than the national gods of other now-defeated nations have managed to do. In fact, Sennacherib claims, the Lord has said to him: "Go up against that land and destroy it" (II Kings 18:25; Isa. 36:10). The Lord comes close in Deuteronomy to acknowledging a world of many nations and many more or less real gods, but in Isaiah he does so no longer. Henceforth, whether or not a nation has the Lord as its God, it has no slightest reason to have any other god. The choice he offers is, quite literally, worship me or worship nothing:

> To whom will you liken me and make me equal,
> and compare me, that we may be alike?
> Those who lavish gold from the purse,
> and weigh out silver in the scales,
> hire a goldsmith, and he makes it into a god;
> then they fall down and worship!
> They lift it upon their shoulders, they carry it,
> they set it in its place, and it stands there;
> it cannot move from its place.
> If one cries to it, it does not answer
> or save him from his trouble. (Isa. 46:5–7)

The Lord, the speaker of these verses, does not expect that any of his hearers will compare him with an idol. Implicitly, they stand with him every time he mocks the nothingness of the idolaters' gods. Rather does he expect that they will bring the rest of the world to him. Israel is no longer enough. In one of four passages in which

Israel is personified as a suffering servant whose long-hidden destiny is about to be revealed, the Lord says:

> It is too light a thing that you should be my servant
> to raise up the tribes of Jacob
> and to restore the preserved of Israel;
> I will give you as a light to the nations,
> that my salvation may reach to the end of the earth.
> (49:6)

The theme is one already raised in First Isaiah, but an outcome that there is still presented as a more or less military triumph is here presented as both the logical implication of Israelite monotheism and a spiritual achievement for Israel as a nation, the result as well as the reward of the national travail.

Uncompromising monotheism on mankind's side does suggest, almost inescapably, the possibility of uncompromising "monoanthropism" on God's side. It suggests, in other words, that a divine covenant with the entire human race—in effect, the Lord's covenant with Noah or a restoration of his implicit covenant with Adam—should be the only covenant, following the implicit proportion *many gods : many peoples :: one God : one people.* If, however, a single divine-human covenant is to come about by extension of the covenant with Abraham, rather than by its replacement, then that covenant must cease to be the fertility covenant it was when first announced. Obviously, a covenant promising disproportionate fertility to one nation cannot, in the nature of the promise, be extended to all nations. There is another alternative, however, and this is the one the Lord chooses. Rather than the rewards of the covenant, stated as fertility, he will extend its obligations. Unlike divinely enhanced fertility, a divinely authored law may be given to all nations without diminution, particularly if the law begins to be seen as a reward in itself, and this is just how he begins to see it. When first promulgated at Sinai, the law had a merely instrumental function: It stipulated the conditions that, if met, would result in disproportionate fertility and prosperity for Israel in the land of Canaan. But the Lord, reflecting on his own uniqueness, has clearly begun to think of his law as a good in itself and of Israel as his "light to the nations" by spreading knowledge of the law.

This resumes a theme we first saw at Isaiah 2:2–3, where the prophet imagines the nations saying:

"Come, let us go up to the mountain of the Lord,
to the house of the God of Jacob;
that he may teach us his ways
and that we may walk in his paths."
For out of Zion shall go forth the law,
and the word of the Lord from Jerusalem.

Israel's ascendancy, in this revision of the Lord's plan, comes about not principally by victory over an enemy but by the peaceful discharge of a universally acknowledged religious vocation:

Aliens shall stand and feed your flocks,
foreigners shall be your plowmen and vinedressers;
but you shall be called the priests of the Lord,
men shall speak of you as the ministers of our God;
you shall eat the wealth of the nations,
and in their riches you shall glory. (Isa. 61:5–6)

These foreign plowmen and vinedressers may be, as a much later era would put it, "second-class citizens," but the upward revision of their status is nonetheless breathtaking. Earlier, the Lord's plan for the inhabitants of the land that Joshua would conquer was extermination. And the reason was not just that they were worshipers of Baal who would constitute a temptation for the Israelites but also that the Lord required the fruits of their labor for Israel. Israel was to enjoy, as Moses put it, "great and flourishing cities that you did not build, houses full of all good things that you did not fill, hewn cisterns that you did not hew, vineyards and olive groves that you did not plant" (Deut. 6:10–11). Now the foreigners, in a passage that goes far beyond any mere injunction to be gentle with them, are made parties to the covenant and invited into the temple itself:

the foreigners who join themselves to the Lord,
to minister to him, to love the name of the Lord,
and to be his servants,
every one who keeps the sabbath, and does not profane it,
and holds fast to my covenant—
these I will bring to my holy mountain,
and make them joyful in my house of prayer;
their burnt offerings and their sacrifices
will be accepted on my altar;

for my house shall be called a house of prayer
  for all peoples.
Thus says the Lord God,
  who gathers the outcasts of Israel,
I will gather yet others to him
  besides those already gathered.
Come and gorge, all you wild beasts,
  all you beasts of the forest! (Isa. 56:6–9)

In all ethnic divisions, the temptation is constant to dehumanize the outsider. *Homo sapiens* is a single species, but pseudospeciation, as it is sometimes called, creates a powerful sense that the difference between one people and another, or between one people and all others, is the difference between human and nonhuman. In the last verse just quoted, the Lord seizes this sharpest of nettles, addressing the nations whom he admits to his covenant for the first time in language as prejudicial as any the Israelites would ever think of applying to them. They are beasts, but they are welcome.

If this represents a dramatic improvement in the nations' divinely ordained status, it represents no loss to Israel, even materially. By acknowledging the Lord as the only God, the nations also, indirectly, acknowledge the nation that provides the Lord's priests, teachers, and ministers. Though the wealth of the nations no longer comes to Israel by means of expropriation and extermination, wealth still comes, and from an incomparably wider circle of nations. With the rise of Cyrus, who has ordered that the temple be rebuilt, and with the impending defeat of Babylon, the nations seem on the threshold of disappearing as a threat to Israel. The threat arises, rather, from Israel's own fear and her doubt that all this will really come to pass. And yet the Lord is prepared even for this.

The Lord acknowledges that his defeated and exiled worshipers doubt his power, but he excuses the doubt as the result of—and here we return to the central novelty of the Lord's self-presentation in the entire Book of Isaiah—his own inherent unknowability.

Why do you say, O Jacob,
  and speak, O Israel,
"My way is hid from the Lord,
  and my right is disregarded by my God"?
Have you not known? Have you not heard?
  The Lord is the everlasting God,
  the Creator of the ends of the earth.

He does not faint or grow weary,
  his understanding is unsearchable. (40:27–28)

It is this inherent unknowability, rather than any culpable fault, that explains why the other nations are only now beginning to acknowledge the Lord:

Thus says the Lord:
"The wealth of Egypt and the merchandise of Ethiopia,
  and the Sabeans, men of stature,
shall come over to you and be yours,
  they shall follow you;
  they shall come over in chains and bow down to you.
They will make supplication to you, saying:
  'God is with you only, and there is no other,
  no god besides him.' "
Truly, thou art a God who hidest thyself,
  O God of Israel, the Savior. (45:14–15)

When Egypt acknowledges God, the acknowledgment will, to be sure, enrich Israel even as it did at the Exodus when the Egyptians showered gifts on the departing Israelites. But this prediction is much less a novelty than is the claim that God is a god who hides himself.

The notion that God is inscrutable, loftily mysterious, and beyond the comprehension of mere men, though standard in the received, popular notion of God, is all but absent from biblical presentations of him before Isaiah. First-time readers of the Book of Genesis who bring this notion with them are often surprised and charmed that the Lord God is so unaugust in his dealings with Adam and Eve, with the patriarchs, and in at least his quieter, face-to-face meetings with his "friend" Moses. The expectation that God will be remote and invisible, speaking from high heaven rather than walking in any garden or dwelling in any tent, is also biblical in origin, but an idea may be found somewhere in the Bible without being found everywhere in the Bible. This notion is not to be found in Genesis, is only alluded to perhaps once in Deuteronomy, and is absent from the Deuteronomistic History. It begins with Isaiah, in part, quite probably, as a way of escaping the eloquent but all-too-imprisoning clarity of Deuteronomy. Mystery opens the door to novelty: "Behold, I am doing a new thing" (43:19).

The inaugural text for divine augustness is Isaiah 6, an early chapter in First Isaiah, but the same theme grows steadily more frequent in Second Isaiah. To the God who spoke through Moses, what counted was not his unknowability but his superior power, as demonstrated in his mighty works. To the God who now speaks through Isaiah, power undeniably counts, but mystery counts for even more. Isaiah's God understands mankind, mankind does not understand Isaiah's God, and *that* is what divine miracles now serve to prove. Thus, at 29:13–14, we read:

> . . . their fear of me is a commandment of men learned by rote;
> therefore, behold, I will again do marvelous things with this people,
> wonderful and marvelous;
> and the wisdom of their wise men shall perish,
> and the discernment of their discerning men shall be hid.

Contrast this with Moses' insistence that the Lord's command was "not in the heavens, that you should say, 'Who among us can go up to the heavens and get it for us . . . ?' " (Deut. 30:12) as well as his insistence in Deuteronomy 6 on constant repetition and learning by heart. In pointed contrast, Isaiah compares the Word of the Lord to a text placed in the hand of an illiterate (29:12). Some of the time, the prophet blames Israel's obtuseness on a moral coarsening; much of the time, however, the cause is the Lord's intrinsic incomprehensibility.

THE LORD'S underlying question in all the prophets is, as noted earlier: *Can we begin again?* God's new mysteriousness is not itself an answer to that question, but it is the condition for an answer. God and Israel cannot begin again if, on clearly stated premises, with each side perfectly comprehensible and completely predictable to the other, the covenant between them has irremediably collapsed. But if one side, God's side, is so mysterious to the other that nothing can be predicted about it with total confidence, then novelty is again possible: History can begin again.

What raises the level of enthusiasm in Second Isaiah to an ecstatic, near manic level, however, is not this emergent mystery but a movement parallel to it—namely, the coincidence of the earlier mentioned new clarity about God's uniqueness with the announcement that, at God's bidding, Cyrus and the Persians are about to overthrow Babylon. Historically, the convergence of these two messages—that Israel's God was the one and only God and that he was *sending*

Cyrus—did not just "make" Second Isaiah but also remade Israel. It was this almost literally intoxicating convergence of ideas that brought the Jews back from the brink. In the prophetic text, the Lord himself seems intoxicated with the convergence and driven to ransack his own history for imagery equal to it. It will be a new creation, a new Exodus, a new covenant, a new monarchy. There is a kind of meltdown of imagery in the opening verses of the poem that runs from Isaiah 51:9 through 52:2. At 51:9–11, the prophet begins:

> Awake, awake, put on strength,
>   O arm of the Lord;
> awake, as in days of old,
>   the generations of long ago.
> Was it not thou that didst cut Rahab in pieces,
>   that didst pierce the dragon?
> Was it not thou that didst dry up the sea,
>   the waters of the great deep;
> that didst make the depths of the sea a way
>   for the redeemed to pass over?
> And the ransomed of the Lord shall return,
>   and come to Zion with singing;
> everlasting joy shall be upon their heads;
>   they shall obtain joy and gladness,
>   and sorrow and sighing shall flee away.

Rahab is a Hebrew name for the watery chaos-dragon whom in other Semitic creation myths the high god defeats to create order or the younger warrior god defeats to restore order. The dismemberment of that enemy of mankind at the start is linked here to the parting of the Red Sea at the Exodus and then further enlarged to include the "great deep," the Mediterranean. Under the pressure of defeat and exile, the personalities of the high god and of Israel's national god are fused as never before. But in the very next verse this fusion is also brought to a personal focus on Israel as never before:

> I, I am he that comforts you;
>   who are you that you are afraid of man who dies,
>   of the son of man who is made like grass,
> and have forgotten the Lord, your Maker,
>   who stretched out the heavens
>   and laid the foundations of the earth,

and fear continually all the day
  because of the fury of the oppressor,
when he sets himself to destroy?
  And where is the fury of the oppressor?
He who is bowed down shall speedily be released;
  he shall not die and go down to the Pit,
  neither shall his bread fail.
For I am the Lord your God. . . . (51:12–15)

Historically, once the Jews were reestablished as a community, they could and did go about reviving, albeit in a Persian vassal state, a semblance of their earlier life with its laws, its rituals, its rounded wholeness; and at that time prophecy died and this rhetoric subsided. But it was indispensable at the start. And it was not delusional even then. True, most of the marvels that Isaiah and the other prophets predicted for an Israel returned from exile never came to pass. The failure of prophecy, a fact of massive importance in the history of Israelite and then of Jewish religion, is a personal failure in the life of God. And yet the writer who first brought monotheism to full formulation and who so clearly felt that this idea was destined to sweep the world was, in point of historical fact, quite correct. The spread of this idea, principally through Christianity and Islam, has not been what he foresaw; and in the diffusion of the idea the Jews have been more often vilified than glorified. Yet Christianity and Islam do understand themselves to worship the same being that Israel first worshiped. And Jerusalem, to which Isaiah saw the converted nations paying spiritual and material homage, remains uniquely the sacred city of monotheism.

In the poem we have been citing, the speaker is Isaiah, quoting at length from words of the Lord to Israel, but the closing verse, directed to Israel in words that echo the opening words directed to the Lord, is one that either the Lord or the prophet could speak:

Awake, awake, put on your strength, O Zion;
put on your beautiful garments. . . .

God has "awakened" to his uniqueness as the one, true, living God, and this has awakened him to the meaning of his own past actions. But as he awakens, his people awaken as well, put on their own strength, and prepare to begin their history all over again, confident that the second time will be more glorious than the first.

AS THE LORD GOD comes to full consciousness of his literal uniqueness and thereby of his extraordinary power, we may say that the trauma of Israel's defeat and the crisis of the shattered covenant have shown him who he is. When we say such a thing of a human being, we mean that trauma and crisis have shown him who he has *come to be*—that is, what his history and his personality have combined to make of him. And so it is, to an extent, of the Lord God. He began without a history, but he has now acquired a tumultuous history; and he knows himself better as a result of it. However, just as God's history has not proceeded through the usual human stages of birth, childhood, youth, and the rest, so his self-discovery does not proceed through those stages. Because God was not generated and does not generate, he can experience only an analogous version of human sexual identity, sexual desire, sexual latency, sexual intimacy, sexual inhibition or frustration, and so on. And since he does not age, even these analogous experiences are not bound to the stages of any physical maturation. There is, for example, something grandfatherly about the Lord's manner with Abraham, yet in his experience this stage comes first, as in the life of a man it could not.

Accordingly, though we have now come somewhere near to the middle of God's story, we need not be surprised if we do not find him at what would be a typical midpoint in human psychosexual development. Our nearest approach to him may be through human beings whose own psychosexual development has been forced out of the usual order. A little boy whose mother has been widowed may be told, for example, that he is now the man of the family and may experience, ahead of the normal schedule, some version of an adult male relationship with a woman. Even a little girl whose mother has been widowed may find herself filling some of the space in her mother's life left by her father's death. But now imagine a being *all* of whose experiences are of this sort—imitations, borrowings, analogues of the real thing, occurring in a biologically uncoupled, idiosyncratic order. This is the Lord God, a parentless, childless being, a cosmic orphan, literally the only one of his kind. Such a one has no alternative but to borrow, yet nothing that he borrows will ever quite fit. Herein lies the deep psychological peculiarity, the uncanniness, the elusive weirdness of the Lord God. Wherever his character originated, it is difficult to believe that it is the simple projection of a human character. The human character whose projection it would be can scarcely ever have existed.

Some readers may feel uncomfortable with talk of development in God. Religious readers may object that the categories of human psychosexual development are blasphemous when applied to him: God is eternal, unchanging, beyond all human knowing; don't try to shrink him to the size of a therapist's couch! And even secular readers may wonder whether the categories of literary character analysis are not strained past the breaking point when they are applied to him. Perhaps he is more suitably discussed as a personification—of life force or society or order or some blend of such personifications—rather than, as in the analysis this book attempts, as a true fusion of personalities.

To the religious objection the reply must be a counterquestion: How do you know that God is unknowable? Who told you so? If your answer comes from outside the Bible, your objection is undercut because it is only the God of the Bible that we are considering. If your answer does invoke the Bible, it is fair to point out to you that through all the books of the Bible down to the point we have now reached (a point, by the way, that comes much later when the Tanakh is read in the Christian order as the Old Testament), the opposite assumption from yours is made. From Genesis through II Kings, no one doubts, ever, that God is knowable. Then, in the Book of Isaiah, God's unknowability begins to be asserted. It is as if God *becomes* unknowable at that point, and one can only ask why. And if you will not concede that he becomes unknowable only at that point, then you must find some other way to explain why assumptions in this regard differ before and after a given point in the text.

The reply to secular readers is a partial concession. Yes, a being who has been defined out of the human condition cannot properly be discussed in categories that are defined by that condition. But such a being can be improperly—which is to say analogously—discussed in those categories, for there is one decisive regard in which his condition and the human condition are identical—namely, the temporality of experience. Things happen to God one at a time. He acts, then reacts to what he has done, or to what others have done in reaction to him. He makes plans and adjusts them when they don't quite work out. He repents, starts over, looks ahead, looks back. As a result of all this, he learns, and learning is the minimum necessary condition for a discussion of any character.

Parenthetically, it might be noted that God begins in the Book of Isaiah to claim a past-and-future simultaneity of knowledge that, as it were, edges toward omniscience. Thus at 41:4 he says:

> Who has performed and done this,
> calling the generations from the beginning?
> I, the Lord, the first,
> and with the last; I am He.

But the paradox is that this superhuman mental ability seems to be something he has *learned* about himself, not something that, as would be the case with true omniscience, he has always known.

Does God find himself strange? At the start, he most certainly does not. In the opening verses of the Book of Genesis, God has the blind self-confidence of a sleepwalker. He does what he does. He does not know what he is doing or why. Only afterward, as he collides with obstacles, does he discover what his intentions may have been or must now become. This impression may be muted for long stretches. Certainly, the Lord who speaks the entire, meticulously detailed Book of Leviticus to Moses knows what he is doing in one sense or other of that phrase. And yet, as late as the end of II Kings, the Lord has still not become in any significant way a question for himself.

In the Book of Isaiah, he does begin to become a question for himself. This is the self-perception that lies behind his talk of his own unknowability. And even though it is to mankind rather than to himself that he claims to be unknowable, the change is a momentous one. Hitherto, even for mankind, it has been the unequivocal clarity of God's law rather than obscurity of any kind that has been insisted on. Now, for the first time, the Lord seems to recognize how bafflingly *different* he is. He is different from the nongods put forward as his rivals because he is real and they are not. The spectacle of idolatry teaches him this. But he is also different from human beings because they love and he—through the whole of his history to this point—has not loved. Now, in the Second Isaiah, as he crosses into love, what he says of himself is not just "How I love you!" but "How mysterious I am!"

There is undeniably something eerie and mysterious about the opening lines of Isaiah 40, lines spoken in a voice for which nothing in the Bible to this point has quite prepared us:

> Comfort, comfort my people,
> says your God.
> Speak tenderly to Jerusalem,
> and cry to her
> that her warfare is ended,
> that her iniquity is pardoned,
> that she has received from the Lord's hand
> double for all her sins. (40:1–2)

Comfort? *Comfort?* It can scarcely be overstressed that the Lord God has never spoken of comfort before. The concept of recovery after disaster may be less than a total novelty, but the voice of the one who employs the concept, noticing and vicariously experiencing human pain, is not just utterly new but also shocking in its juxtaposition of comfort to overwhelming divine power. A few verses further along we read:

> Who has measured the waters in the hollow of his hand
> and marked off the heavens with a span,
> enclosed the dust of the earth in a measure
> and weighed the mountains in scales
> and the hills in a balance?
> Who has directed the Spirit of the Lord,
> or as his counselor has instructed him? (40:12–13)

Rhetorical questions like these will be strung together later when the Lord rebukes Job, and they lend themselves well enough to rebuke, for they bespeak sheer power. Here, however, they serve to underline the fact that the tender opening words have this improbable power behind them.

And just there, in that incongruity, is the deepest ground for the Lord's claim that he is mysterious, hidden, beyond comprehension. In other words, it is not just that God is a secret that men cannot know but that God knows all human secrets. We have already quoted the following verses from the opening speech of Second Isaiah:

> Why do you say, O Jacob,
> and speak, O Israel,

"My way is hid from the Lord,
  and my right is disregarded by my God"?
Have you not known? Have you not heard?
  The Lord is the everlasting God,
  the Creator of the ends of the earth.
He does not faint or grow weary,
  his understanding is unsearchable.

But that passage goes on to explain what the unknowable Lord does with his new awareness of human pain, especially Israel's:

He gives power to the faint,
  and to him who has no might he increases strength.
Even youths shall faint and be weary,
  and young men shall fall exhausted;
but they who wait for the Lord shall renew their strength,
  they shall mount up with wings like eagles,
they shall run and not be weary,
  they shall walk and not faint. (40:29–31)

Just as incomprehensibility is a feature introduced into the received idea of God at a particular time and under a particular set of circumstances, so with the related notion that though we do not know God, he does know us and knows us intimately and individually without our telling him about us. In the passage just quoted, the Lord knows, without being told, that Israel is assailed by doubt. Earlier, he would have had to be told, as Moses had to tell him of his fears at the burning bush or Hannah of her needs at the door to the temple in Shiloh.

There was, we saw at the Exodus, something exhilarating in the notion that the sky god, El, could be simultaneously Israel's national God, the warrior *yahweh*, and Moses' personal friend. Isaiah takes those already incongruous elements and sharpens each of them, insisting, on the one hand, on the Lord's immediate, intimate access to the experienced sorrow of Israel (making him, implicitly, every Judean's personal God); insisting, on the other hand, on the Lord's cosmic, world-creating power. The result is an ecstatic mood both in the prophet and, at those many moments when the Lord is the speaker, in the Lord himself. But the ecstasy does not gainsay the mystery. In this, the Book of Isaiah, to repeat, contrasts sharply with the Book of Deuteronomy, where God is, on the one hand, crystal clear in his demands and promises and, on the other hand, without evident prior interest in the suffering or the interior life of even Moses himself.

The combination of these two elements—divine access to the human heart and divine omnipotence and mystery—has remained the defining incongruity at the core of the word *God* as it is understood in the vernacular languages of the West, and Isaiah's role in creating this incongruity can scarcely be exaggerated. The human heart with which the Lord is intimate is, most especially, the heart of the oppressed:

> Do not fear, you worm Jacob,
> you insect Israel!
> I will help you,

the Lord says at 41:14 in the NRSV translation. (The JPS Tanakh proposes "maggot" for "insect.") There has been little or no indication before now that even as a personal god, a "god of," the Lord had the ability or, more especially, the inclination to eavesdrop on the human heart; to note fears, sorrows, confusions, and so on; to be the soul's omniscient companion. Much of the time, even the Lord's most apparently personal relationships—with Abraham, Jacob, Joseph, Moses, and David—have seemed to stand in function of his collective relationship with the nation-to-be, Israel. Even at the rare moments when the personal appeared to take precedence over the collective, God has seemed to deal only from the outside with those whom he chose. His concern has been with the foreskin, not with the imagination.

If, therefore, starting at Isaiah 40, the Lord begins suddenly to show an intense, intimate, and prior awareness of Israel's fears and sorrows, doubts and assumptions, the novelty is, in and of itself, ground for the claim that the Lord is somewhat mysterious: By ceasing to be what for so long he seemed to be, he has *become* mysterious. But because this new awareness is joined to an equally unprecedented tenderness, it leads to the further compelling question of why the Lord has been so complete a stranger to the tender emotions.

8

INTERLUDE

Does God Love?

The Hebrew verb *yd*ᶜ, "to know," when it refers to personal acquaintance, can imply love somewhat more easily than the English verb *to know* can. In the vision of the peaceable kingdom at Isaiah 11, the concluding vision—"for the earth shall be full of the knowledge of the Lord / as the waters cover the sea"—refers to a flood of personal knowledge, not theological scholarship. On occasion, *yd*ᶜ can even refer to sexual intimacy. A similar emotive force inheres in other Hebrew verbs of perception: *zkr*, "remember"; *šm*ᶜ, "hear"; and others. Accordingly, even without any reference to the Lord's tenderness toward Israel, the sudden intensification of his personal knowledge of Israel could imply something of an emotional transformation as well.

That much conceded to a distinct ancient psychology, it must be said plainly that, until this point in his history, the Lord God has never loved. Love has never been predicated of him either as an action or as a motive. It is not that he has had no emotional life of any sort. He has been wrathful, vengeful, and remorseful. But he has not been loving. It was not for love that he made man. It was not for love that he made his covenant with Abraham. It was not for love that he brought the Israelites out of Egypt or drove out the Canaanites before them. The "steadfast love" of the Mosaic covenant was, as we saw, rather a fierce mutual loyalty binding liege and vassal than any gentler emotion.

God has been strikingly purposeful and fully faithful to his covenant responsibilities. But these attitudes fall well short of love. Even when he performs a kind deed for an individual, as when he hears Hannah's prayer and she bears a son, Samuel, he never makes, nor does anyone ever make of him, any reference to his having kind feelings. Consider Exodus 2:23–24:

> A long time after that, the king of Egypt died. The Israelites were groaning under the bondage and cried out; and their cry for help from the bondage rose up to God. God heard their moaning, and God remembered His covenant with Abraham and Isaac and Jacob. God looked upon the Israelites, and God took notice of them.

God is not moved by their condition. He does not grieve for their condition. He merely knows their condition. The text does not say ". . . his covenant with Abraham and Isaac and Jacob, *whom he loved*," as so easily it might. The verbs of the passage, repeated when God commissions Moses, are verbs of perception only: "heard . . . remembered . . . looked upon . . . took notice of." And even fully allowing for the emotive force that the corresponding Hebrew verbs can carry, the sense of abstention from emotion is inescapable here. Classical Hebrew has abundant resources for the expression of emotion, and this passage declines to draw on them. It is no exaggeration to say that, to judge from the entire text of the Bible from Genesis 1 through Isaiah 39, the Lord does not know what love is.

Equally striking, if not more so, God takes no pleasure in anything or anybody. Against this sweeping statement, we may note, to be sure, a few counterinstances. At Genesis 8:21, when the floodwaters recede, Noah offers a burnt sacrifice to the Lord; and "The Lord smelled the pleasing odor, and the Lord said to himself, 'I will never again curse the ground because of man . . . ,' " at least implying that he had taken pleasure in the odor. Near the end of the curses detailed in Deuteronomy 28, Moses warns: "And as the Lord took delight in doing you good and multiplying you, so the Lord will take delight in bringing ruin upon you and destroying you" (Deut. 28:63; a similar sentiment is expressed at 30:9). And when Solomon asks the Lord for wisdom, "it pleased the Lord that Solomon had asked this" (I Kings 3:10). But these few, meager allusions to divine delight or pleasure are the very opposite of representative: They are virtually the *only* passages of the sort. In their paucity, they serve only to highlight the otherwise total silence of the Bible, from Genesis through II Kings, about divine joy, happiness, or pleasure.

Men and women express their joy in God. In fact, the Israelites are required to do so: In the Book of Deuteronomy, Moses repeatedly orders Israel to "rejoice before the Lord" and warns: "Because you did not serve the Lord your God with joyfulness and gladness of heart . . . , therefore you shall serve your enemies . . ." (28:47). But Moses never describes the Lord as glad at this gladness. God takes no joy in their joy. Even in moments of peak religious exultation, as when Moses and the Israelites sing to him after he saves them from Pharaoh's army or when Deborah and Barak sing to him after he saves them from the Canaanites (Judg. 5), the Lord never evinces any answering exultation of his own.

Once this pattern is recognized, even the description of God at the close of each day of creation—"And God saw that it was good"—takes on a weirdly anhedonic quality. The text does not read, as so obviously it might: "And God rejoiced, for it was good." God does not rejoice. He never rejoices. He takes no pleasure even in himself. The Tanakh's abstention from attributing to him any satisfaction with his creative work begins, in effect, a long and remarkably consistent series of such abstentions. On innumerable occasions between the creation of the world and the fall of Jerusalem, the Lord God might have given evidence of joy or pleasure. For all Israel's stubbornness, the victories have been many, the occasions not wanting. But with a few exceptions, he has not taken the occasions.

In the earlier chapters of this book, we have deliberately sought to highlight those exceptions. There may be no direct reference to joy or pleasure in the Lord's response to David at II Samuel 7, the oracle that Nathan delivers after David has danced before the tabernacle and spontaneously declared his wish to build the Lord a temple, but one may hear an unwonted note of personal warmth in the Lord's first-ever reference to himself as a father. Earlier, Exodus 33 notes, with understated wonderment, that the Lord and Moses converse as two human friends might; and on the strength of that friendship, the Lord checks his wrath against Israel and takes up residence in a tent in Israel's camp. Still earlier, Joseph is said to enjoy the "steadfast love" or the "kindness and faithfulness" of God without reference to his being in any way the vehicle for the creation of a covenanted nation. But these are mere flickers of possibility. In the main, God's character is, page after page, book after book, one of imperious impassivity, frequently interrupted by rage.

Is this character inhuman or merely inhumane? Or inhumane because inhuman? The ancient Israelite genius who first thought of a god who would be personal but not sexual cannot have simply stumbled upon this idea or patched it together from earlier ideas. It is simply not that *kind* of idea. A great many ideas about the Lord God are indeed patched together from earlier ideas, and this book has never concealed the patchwork, but this idea is different. Nothing like it was known, anywhere in the civilization where it emerged, at any time before it emerged. A genius original enough to have had this idea in the first place may well have been original enough to put measures in place to protect it—that is, to begin a literary tradition of portraying the personal, asexual God in such a way that he would not, by degrees, be sexualized.

The text of the Tanakh from Genesis through II Kings is rather freely anthropomorphic: We hear of the arm, hand, finger, and face of God, among other physical references; and the angels of God, indistinguishable from God himself, have male bodies including (one can infer) genitalia. But perhaps because, even in everyday life, human language uses the parts and functions of the human body in endlessly metaphorical ways, these anthropomorphisms never seem to derogate in the slightest from the godlikeness of God. The writer's judgment that this was a liberty that could be taken is confirmed by centuries of readers who have known without being told that the arm that God extended against Egypt was not an ordinary human arm.

But, perhaps with equally good reason, the same writer may have concluded that certain bodily feelings would indeed derogate from the godlikeness of God by derogating from the perfection of his power. The most obvious instance of this is sexual desire, which we rightly recognize as a passion rather than an action, using a word cognate in our language with the word *passive*. Pleasure is not a feat. Lust is something to which one yields, not something one does. And someone in the grip of lust surrenders a degree of power to whatever or whoever has aroused the lust. The same is true, if less obviously, of the other tender emotions. Grief is the wreckage of desire: The loved person or thing is gone, but the desire for him, her, or it remains. True joy is always a surprise and, to that extent, an infringement on one's privacy and autonomy. Compassion, as the very word shows, is a variety of passion. One feels with the object of one's compassion whatever he or she is feeling; and to the extent that the compassionate or piteous feelings are involuntary, they derogate from the perfection of one's self-control. There is so great a degree of bodily interaction and bodily interdependence in all this that it is, so to speak, perilous to predicate it of a being whose power as well as whose asexuality one wishes to insist on. The diffuse, visceral physicality in the sentence "The Lord was moved to pity" vastly exceeds in its sexualizing, corporalizing potential the sentence "The Lord extended his arm." Perhaps this is why the writers who produced the Pentateuch and the former prophets were willing to write endless variations of the latter sentence but never came close to the former.

As for the untender emotions that these writers do feel free to predicate of God, perhaps we can say that they are, yes, emotions but not passions. At Genesis 6:6–7, we read:

> And the Lord regretted that He had made man on earth, and His heart was saddened. The Lord said, "I will blot out from the earth the men whom I created—men together with beasts, creeping things, and birds of the sky; for I regret that I made them."

The words *regretted* and *saddened* are used, of course, but as the action to be taken indicates, this regret and sadness flow not from an attachment but from the sundering of an attachment. Anger and displeasure (and, as we have seen, the Lord is endlessly angry and displeased) have the same sundering effect. Far from creating any vulnerability in the Lord via some physical sympathy or other link between him and a human being, they restore a separateness and invulnerability, especially because God's anger is always perfectly controlled: The Lord God, except perhaps at Sinai, never comes close to losing his temper. Usually, the only negative consequence of God's anger for God himself is the discontinuance of his covenant with Israel or, in the extreme case foreseen in Deuteronomy 28, the genocidal termination of his relationship with Israel. So it was also when, in the verse just quoted, he repented of the creation of all animal life. If Noah and his ark had not mitigated that action, and all animal life on earth had ended, in what condition would God be? He would be the God he was at the end of the fourth day of creation, before birds, reptiles, mammals, or human beings were created, and when has he ever been more godlike than that?

Although, from the point of view of the writer who characterized him for the first time, God may well have had to be made inhumane because he had first been made inhuman, we certainly cannot rule out the possibility that this same writer was inspired by human beings who had sought to seem godlike by seeming inhuman. Though the human character of whom the Lord God would be the simple projection can indeed have scarcely ever lived, surely many a power-hungry warlord has sought to portray himself as without pity, beyond need, and above passion, intimidating in his unpredictable anger, and imperious for no discernible motive. Is not the mask of power ever thus? No matter that it can never be more than a mask. No matter that no human being is ever truly beyond need or above passion or that anger aimed at intimidation eventually becomes predictable or that undiscernible motives are still motives. If the mask is well made, it can still terrify. And the compelling power of the Lord God as the Tanakh first portrays him is that the terrifying mask on his face is his face itself.

But then his face changes. Something happens to bring him from his condition of fierce and protracted affective latency to the lyric ardor that bursts upon us in Second Isaiah. In ordinary human experience, is any spirit more broken than that of an older woman deserted by her husband, a grass widow, a widow by abandonment? Of the innumerable possible moments in a love history, this is the point at which the Lord God, who never goes through the usual steps in the usual order, seems to take his most decisive step:

> Fear not, for you will not be ashamed;
> be not confounded, for you will not be put to shame;
> for you will forget the shame of your youth,
> and the reproach of your widowhood you will remember no more.
> For your Maker is your husband,
> the Lord of hosts is his name;
> and the Holy One of Israel is your Redeemer,
> the God of the whole earth he is called.
> For the Lord has called you
> like a wife forsaken and grieved in spirit,
> like a wife of youth when she is cast off,
> says your God.
> For a brief moment I forsook you,
> but with great compassion I will gather you.
> In overflowing wrath for a moment
> I hid my face from you,

> but with everlasting love I will have compassion on you,
>   says the Lord, your Redeemer. (54:4–8)

One of the greatest novels ever written about the learning of love is Gustave Flaubert's ironic *L'Education sentimentale*. Its moral, to put it in one line, is Before you can have a love, you must have an unrequited love. The Lord God is no Frédéric Moreau, no shallow romantic in love with himself as Flaubert's protagonist is. The aspirations of the two are clearly different, and their failures are also different. But failure is indeed what the Lord God and Frédéric have in common. What each learns about love comes at the end of a failed affair that neither, while it is in progress, deigns to think of as truly a love affair at all.

God is in the condition of a man who has beaten his wife and thrown her out of their house. She had turned herself into little more than a common whore, humiliating herself as well as him, consorting with the most repugnant of their neighbors. He was endlessly patient with her, sending one intermediary after another to remonstrate with her and warn her, but to no avail: She was sunk in her vice. And so, at length, he threw her out: Let the neighbors do what they want with her; he is finished with her.

Or so he thinks. An action that ought not to have brought any surprises in its train, given that it had been foreseen, repeatedly predicted, and understood by both of them from the beginning as the inevitable consequence of this kind of behavior, does bring a surprise, a huge surprise. He discovers, for the first time, what it means to love her. He discovers that he had never truly loved her before. He takes her back; and whether or not she has changed when he does so, he has unmistakably changed. There is an utterly new tone in his voice.

The noun for "love" in the Hebrew phrase translated previously by "everlasting love" is *ḥesed*, and *ḥesed*, we said earlier, the "steadfast love" or "kindness and faithfulness" of the covenant, is the loyalty that binds liege and vassal rather than any more tender or personal feeling. Lest there be any doubt, reference is made to the covenant and its permanence in the verses immediately following those quoted above:

> For the mountains may depart
>   and the hills be removed,

but my steadfast love shall not depart from you,
and my covenant of peace shall not be removed. (54:10)

This is undeniably covenant love, but the covenant relationship, always potentially more than contractual, is just as undeniably reaching a new intensity. And marital reconciliation is, at such a moment, the perfect metaphor. Many a marriage in the course of human history has been begun without feelings of love. The contracting spouses, when they promise "to love and to cherish," are not necessarily insincere. Particularly in an arranged marriage, and the marriage of Israel to God was an arranged marriage (Israel had no choice about it), what the couple promise is, in effect, the degree of lovelike behavior required to meet the other, more external obligations of the contract. Many a marriage continues on this basis until death parts the spouses, and if Israel had remained faithful to God, the metaphorical marriage between God and Israel could have remained indefinitely on a comparable basis, the basis set out by the Deuteronomic covenant. But Israel did not remain faithful. By the massive testimony of the prophets, the nation actually changed its religion. And the breaking of the initial covenant, the violent termination of the marriage, now leads, improbably enough, to a new relationship established on—for God and, implicitly, for Israel—a drastically different emotional basis.

The novelty for God is greater than the novelty for Israel. God has never been loved by his mother or father: He has no mother or father. He has had no friend except Moses. One way or another, his entire emotional life has occurred within the bounds of one singular, collective relationship. David, to name just one Israelite, when he loves Jonathan, Saul, Bathsheba, Abigail, or Absalom does not do so in function of his relationship with God, but God has had no affective relationship that is not part of his collective relationship with Israel. Any change in that relationship, therefore, is proportionately, if paradoxically, of much greater affective importance for him than for any individual Israelite or even for Israel as a whole.

It would be wrong to say that, at this point in his story, God falls in love with Israel, or falls in love with mankind for the first time. What he feels is more accurately described as loving pity. At 62:5, looking forward to his happy future with Israel, he says: "As the bridegroom rejoices over the bride, / so shall your God rejoice over you," which sounds like love. Certainly rejoicing and delight are predicated of God after Isaiah 40 as they never have been before. And yet, as fuller quotation shows, the context is of pity:

> You shall no more be termed Forsaken,
>   and your land shall no more be termed Desolate;
> but you shall be called My delight is in her,
>   and your land Married;
> for the Lord delights in you,
>   and your land shall be married.
> For as a young man marries a virgin,
>   so shall your sons marry you,
> and as the bridegroom rejoices over the bride,
>   so shall your God rejoice over you. (62:4–5)

Is it possible to marry, or to remarry, out of pity? Of course it is. The Lord's remarriage to Israel is not motivated purely by pity, but we must at least speak of a pitying love or a loving pity. But to say this takes nothing away from the fact that, looking on the consequences of his own action, God has been surprised into a new sense of himself.

AND WITHIN this surprise, there is another surprise of even greater moment. In the rough hierarchy of emotions that most modern Western men and women carry, love seems a step closer to maturity than does pity. Someone capable of pity but incapable of love—well, what could such a person be? But in the emotional evolution of the creator of the world, pity may be of far greater eventual consequence than love, for it involves a radical revision of the meaning of suffering. In the mental life of the Lord God as we saw it from Genesis through II Kings, there was no need for pity. The wicked did not deserve it when they were punished. The good did not need it, for they were rewarded. True, the actions of God were never entirely bounded by considerations of human good and evil; that is, the possibility of purely arbitrary action was never denied. However, particularly after the Book of Deuteronomy, God's actions were almost always seen as the enactment of reward or punishment, and, by clear implication, he never made a mistake.

By equally clear implication, as God allows himself to feel pity, the feeling carries within it the suspicion of mistake. At 40:2, the Lord tells Isaiah to cry to Jerusalem

that her warfare is ended,
  that her iniquity is pardoned,
that she has received from the Lord's hand
  double for all her sins.

At 51:22–23, again speaking to Jerusalem, the Lord says:

Behold, I have taken from your hand
  the cup of staggering;
the bowl of my wrath
  you shall drink no more;
and I will put it into the hand of your tormentors. . . .

The first quotation is a half admission that the Lord's punishment has gone too far, the second that the nations which were allegedly inflicting no more than the Lord's ordained punishment on Israel have gone further than he intended and now themselves deserve punishment. In that case, events are less than perfectly under his control; but either way, the result is unmerited suffering for Jerusalem.

One kind of response to this perception on the Lord's part is simply the promise to make it up to Israel. In Isaiah 54, continuing his address to Israel as his reclaimed wife, the Lord says:

O afflicted one, storm-tossed, and not comforted,
  behold, I will set your stones in antimony,
  and lay your foundations with sapphires.
I will make your pinnacles of agate,
  your gates of carbuncles,
  and all your wall of precious stones. (54:11–12)

Three verses later, as if to admit at least in principle that not all of Israel's misfortunes have come as punishment from his hand, he says:

If any one stirs up strife,
  it is not from me;
whoever stirs up strife with you
  shall fall because of you.
Behold, I have created the smith
  who blows the fire of coals,
  and produces a weapon for its purpose.
I have also created the ravager to destroy;

> no weapon that is fashioned against you shall prosper,
> and you shall confute every tongue
> that rises against you in judgment. (54:15–17)

The very last lines insist on the Lord's sovereignty in detail over all those who might bring or have brought destruction on Israel, but the first lines move in a different direction. And that direction is confirmed by the Lord's promise to change a city built of stone into one built of jewels: He is making amends.

This response, by a simple correction, restores the mental universe in which God has operated from the beginning: The good are rewarded, the evil punished; and if the accounts are out of balance, God will bring them into balance, *though it may take a little while.* A little while is all that, most of the time, Isaiah expects will be necessary, but he has taken one of the basic options in coping with the problem of evil, as it has come to be called. When the innocent are seen to suffer and the evil to prosper, what do we infer? There seem to be only a few possibilities:

1. Yes, the innocent do suffer and the wicked prosper. The world is immoral—in effect, ruled by a fiend.

2. No, the innocent suffer and the wicked prosper only some of the time. Sometimes the innocent prosper and the wicked suffer. The world is amoral and meaningless—in effect, ruled by nobody or by chance.

3. Yes, the innocent do sometimes suffer here and now, and the wicked do sometimes prosper here and now. But our world of time and space is only a part of the real world. Later or elsewhere, the innocent will receive their just reward and the wicked their just punishment. The world, if you see it whole, is moral—in effect, ruled by a just judge.

4. The prosperity of the wicked need imply only mercy in a world judge. As for the suffering of the innocent, it is not simply evil (option 1) or simply meaningless (option 2) or simply to be compensated for (option 3). It may, instead of any of these, be *meritorious* by serving as a tool by which the just judge ultimately brings justice to all. The innocent who suffer will ultimately be rewarded beyond the innocent who do not suffer. The world is moral; in effect, it is ruled by a mysteriously just judge who sometimes requires human suffering to achieve his ends.

Options 3 and 4 are clearly related. In effect, where option 3 foresees another place or time, heaven or the future, option 4 discerns another dimension. Most often, the Lord speaks of option 3 (the future, rather than heaven), turning Israel's punishment to reward by an enlargement of the context. But in the last of several poems that speak of a servant who seems to be, simultaneously, Israel personified and some real person, quite possibly the prophet himself, option 4 is given its first articulation. The suffering referred to in this extraordinary poem is never denied: It is an extreme, appalling, heartrending sorrow. However, the Lord is unwilling either to regard the suffering as meaningless or, in the manner of the later Book of Job, to make it the occasion for exalting himself beyond good and evil. The Lord gives no indication that he believes in any such transcendentally amoral universe. His servant has suffered, his servant will be rewarded; but en route from suffering to reward, his servant will have brought redemption to many:

> Behold, my servant shall prosper,
> he shall be exalted and lifted up,
> and shall be very high.
> As many were astonished at him—
> his appearance was so marred, beyond human semblance,
> and his form beyond that of the sons of men—
> so shall he startle many nations;
> kings shall shut their mouths because of him;
> for that which has not been told them they shall see,
> and that which they have not heard they shall understand.
>
> Who has believed what we have heard?
> And to whom has the arm of the Lord been revealed?
> For he grew up before him like a young plant,
> and like a root out of dry ground;
> he had no form or comeliness that we should look at him,
> and no beauty that we should desire him.
> He was despised and rejected by men;
> a man of sorrows, and acquainted with grief;
> and as one from whom men hide their faces
> he was despised, and we esteemed him not.
>
> Surely he has borne our griefs
> and carried our sorrows;
> yet we esteemed him stricken,
> smitten by God, and afflicted.

But he was wounded for our transgressions,
he was bruised for our iniquities;
upon him was the chastisement that made us whole,
and with his stripes we are healed.
All we like sheep have gone astray;
we have turned every one to his own way;
and the Lord has laid on him
the iniquity of us all.

He was oppressed, and he was afflicted,
yet he opened not his mouth;
like a lamb that is led to the slaughter,
and like a sheep that before its shearers is dumb,
so he opened not his mouth.
By oppression and judgment he was taken away;
and as for his generation, who considered
that he was cut off out of the land of the living,
stricken for the transgression of my people?
And they made his grave with the wicked
and with a rich man in his death,
although he had done no violence,
and there was no deceit in his mouth.

Yet it was the will of the Lord to bruise him;
he has put him to grief;
when he makes himself an offering for sin,
he shall see his offspring, he shall prolong his days;
the will of the Lord shall prosper in his hand;
he shall see the fruit of the travail of his soul and be satisfied;
by his knowledge shall the righteous one, my servant,
make many to be accounted righteous;
and he shall bear their iniquities.
Therefore I will divide him a portion with the great,
and he shall divide the spoil with the strong;
because he poured out his soul to death,
and was numbered with the transgressors;
yet he bore the sin of many,
and made intercession for the transgressors. (52:13–53:12)

What has happened to God that he is speaking this way? His life has surprised him. When he punished Israel, he did not anticipate that her sorrow would lead him toward love. Even less did he anticipate that the interaction of her sorrow and his love would have, as its precipitate, this radically revised notion of what sorrow actually is—or can be. Not all of the poem, of course, is spoken by God. The middle verses may be spoken by Isaiah. They may also be spoken by God quoting the unidentified group of people ("we . . . us") who look upon his servant in horror, in awe, and eventually in gratitude. Is that group Israel? Then why is it not called by that name? Unlike some later biblical writers, Second Isaiah is not given to code: He almost always names names. We don't know the answer. But one way or another, framed as it is by God's words in its opening and closing verses, this haunting poem represents a change in God's mind that is even more important than his crossing, or his near crossing, to love.

And the change has come about, just as every previous change has come about, by the unmistakable subversion of his ostensible intentions. Accident is a part, but usually only a part, of all human experience. Perhaps because God has no life other than the one he lives through mankind, because, in other words, there is no purely divine experience from which he might benefit, nearly all his key experiences seem to subvert his intentions. After each of his major actions, he discovers that he has not done quite what he thought he was doing, or has done something he never intended to do. He did not realize when he told mankind to "be fertile and increase" that he was creating an image of himself that was also a rival creator. He did not realize when he destroyed his rival that he would regret the destruction of his image. He did not realize that his covenant with Abraham, the reconciliation of such contrary urges within his own character, would require him, precisely because he had so effectively made Abraham into a great nation, to go to war with Egypt. He did not realize when he went to war with Egypt that his victory would leave him with an entire people on his hands and would require him to become a lawgiver for them and conquer a land for them to live in. He did not realize when he gave them the law that where there is law, there can be transgression, and that, therefore, he himself had turned an implicitly unbreakable covenant into an explicitly breakable one. He did not realize when he began to withdraw from his alliance with Israel, after Israel's first, minor infidelities, that the aftermath would be the rise of a king, David, whose charisma would draw the Lord almost despite himself into a quasi-parental relationship with his semiabandoned ally. He did not realize when his erstwhile ally deserted him wholesale and he made Assyria and Babylonia the tools of his vengeance that he was creating a new international role for himself. He did not realize that once they had inflicted his punishment for him, his feelings, rather than only those of a vindicated suzerain, would also be those of a grieving husband for a battered wife. He did not realize as he contemplated her suffering that he would find a meaning in human suffering unlike any he had ever seen before.

The inference that one might make looking at the entire course of his history to this point from the outside is that God is only very imperfectly self-conscious and very slightly in control of the consequences of his words and actions. Even from inside that history, his own inferences come one at a time, often gropingly after the fact. Here is how he puts it in Second Isaiah:

> For my thoughts are not your thoughts,
> neither are your ways my ways, says the Lord.
> For as the heavens are higher than the earth,
> so are my ways higher than your ways
> and my thoughts than your thoughts.
> For as the rain and the snow come down from heaven,
> and return not thither but water the earth,
> making it bring forth and sprout,
> giving seed to the sower and bread to the eater,
> so shall my word be that goes forth from my mouth;
> it shall not return to me empty,
> but it shall accomplish that which I purpose,
> and prosper in the thing for which I sent it. (55:8–11)

On the surface, he is boasting of the power of his word; beneath the surface, he is admitting that his word is as poorly under his control as rain that has already fallen from the sky and that his thoughts must strain to be equal to his experience. "Behold, I do a new thing." Yes, and behold, you think a new thought, one whose implications you will be sorting out for a long while to come. Though drastically unlike mankind in some ways, God is like his creatures in that he too lives his life one stage at a time and, his protestations to the contrary notwithstanding, he is painfully unable to foresee his end in his beginning.

9

Restoration

As dramatists well know, a character may be characterized in and sometimes even by his absence. A peculiar power accrues to a character who is known but missing or whose appearance is delayed. In Shakespeare's *Macbeth*, the title character does not appear until the third of the seven scenes in Act One; and as the first two scenes end without him, his hold on the audience grows perceptibly. The mechanism is psychologically primitive and easily enough grasped. Who has not seen someone arrive deliberately late at a party so as to "make an entrance"? We may know exactly what is happening, but our knowing it has little power to reduce an almost automatic effect. Can we imagine a character for whom the other characters wait indefinitely, who never makes his entrance and so is characterized entirely by what they say of him? Is such a character not an impossibility?

If it were, then Samuel Beckett's play *Waiting for Godot* would be a dramatic failure, for it is a play whose title character never arrives, a play whose action consists of endless waiting. And yet, as anyone who has seen it or performed in it can testify, it is one of the most reliably audience-holding, actor-friendly plays in the modern repertory. By its deep connection with just that primitive and infallible mechanism, it retains its suspense until its very last line—and, in fact, past it. The offstage power of Godot in Beckett's play is a comic transformation of the presence of God's absence in modern life. The very name *Godot* is a compound of the English name *God* and the French diminutive ending *-ot*, the equivalent of *-ie* in English. Charlie Chaplin was Charlot to the French. Beckett, an Irishman whose first language was English but who wrote in French, presented the human condition as a tragicomic waiting for "Goddie" to show up.

The Tanakh obviously does not work like *Waiting for Godot* at the start. God speaks its first line, after all; and indeed the uncanny, artless power that Genesis 1:1 exerts over readers derives in some measure from our sense that nothing in it is being said or done merely for its effect on an audience. God makes no contrived entrance: He raises his own curtain. From that moment to the one at which we now arrive, God has never been offstage, and what he says about himself has loomed larger in our understanding of him than what anyone else says about him. But with the Book of Psalms, one of whose stock phrases is "How long, O Lord?" a brave and patient waiting for God begins. God has promised, through the prophets, restoration as well as judgment. He has promised a new creation on "the day of the Lord." But when will the day of the Lord come? The Psalmist knows not but only waits. There is that much of a literary link between God and Godot.

No clear and clean rule determines when a character is merely absent and when he is an absent presence. But if the absent character is constantly being addressed by others who are present, as the Lord is addressed in the Book of Psalms, or if others speak for him and predict his action, as is the case, at least residually, in the books of Haggai, Zechariah, and Malachi, then he tends to be an absent presence rather than merely an absence. We may perhaps distinguish a spectrum: presence, absent presence, present absence, absence. Very roughly, presence is what a man senses when he is in a room with a woman and directly aware of her. Absent presence is what he senses when she has just left but the sound of her voice, the scent of her body, still linger in the air. Present absence is what he senses when she is gone, quite gone, but he misses her. Absence is what he senses when he must struggle to recall if he ever knew her.

The Lord God is an absent presence in the Book of Isaiah. He is en route from absent presence to present absence in Haggai, Zechariah, and Malachi. He is a present absence in the Book of Psalms. He is perhaps en route (one is left wondering) from present absence to simple absence in the Book of Proverbs. He is an absence in Song of Songs and, above all, in Esther, which we shall consider in Chapter 12.

Let us stipulate that the ordering of the Tanakh is partially intentional and partially accidental. Thus, it is clearly by intent that II Samuel follows I Samuel and probably by accident that Job follows Proverbs. The artistic question that remains is What is the aesthetic effect of the combination? We should "hear" the alternation of the two as we would hear the alternation of music composed in the ordinary way with aleatory music. To many, aleatory music is mere noise. To some, however, even noise can be music of a sort if you stop and listen to it. We engage in an analogous stopping and listening when we ask after the aesthetic effect of unintended parts of the ordering of the books of the Tanakh.

To read the sequence of six books considered in this chapter and the next—Haggai, Zechariah, Malachi (the three postexilic prophets); Psalms; Proverbs; and Job—is, analogously, to hear music mixed with noise. One is not, however, listening past the noise to the music but listening for the effect produced by the combination. In the first three books, there is still a good deal of hope and intercommunicative vitality between God and Israel. These books play, if you will, an old familiar tune. But in the Book of Psalms what others say to and about God replaces what God says about himself or reveals by his action. In the Book of Proverbs there comes an apparently irrelevant kind of talk that, as regards the character of God, might seem mere noise. Finally, in the Book of Job, there is the sound of divine silence.

If all these works are attentively heard, and heard in order, each can be made to yield a quantum of understanding about the Lord God; and the sequence, though it does not have the kind of plot that history or fiction has, will have the suspense of a set of bold musical variations or, to change the metaphor, the suspense of testimony delivered in a courtroom by a series of strikingly different witnesses. As each witness leaves the stand, you think the last word must surely have been spoken. And then the next witness takes the stand. The question What will *happen* next? is by no means the only intellectual species of What next? that can seize and hold the human mind. What will we *hear* next? also works. And because, through all the "page time" that the testimony occupies, God is, by implication, *listening* to what his creatures are saying about him, their testimony becomes a distinctly felt period in his life despite the fact that it is not located in any narrative sequence.

Before turning to that testimony about God, however, we must hear the last speeches that God himself gives before mankind begins its Psalms-Proverbs-Job reply. These divine speeches come in the books of Haggai, Zechariah, and Malachi, the last three of the twelve minor prophets. When the Psalmist opens his mouth to speak, the words of these three prophets are ringing (or rather hanging) in the air.

Wife

"A Day of Small Beginnings"

HAGGAI, ZECHARIAH, MALACHI

Earlier we compared the oracles of the prophets to collections of letters published after a great war. The prophets are, we then said, a kind of commentary on the narrative that has preceded them, the narrative that runs from Joshua through II Kings. In point of fact, however, that characterization can apply only to the three major prophets and to the first nine of the twelve minor prophets. The last three of the minor prophets, the ones we now consider, are a commentary on events that have not yet been narrated. The events in question, partly narrated nearer the end of the Tanakh, in the books of Ezra and Nehemiah, are the return of a group of Judeans from Babylon and the reestablishment of Israel as a province now called Yehud, meaning Judah or Judea, in the Persian empire.

By rights, then, Haggai, Zechariah, and Malachi ought to be incomprehensible, like an overheard conversation all of whose references escape the hearer. In fact, however, Haggai and Zechariah are so carefully dated and contain so many short, context-setting prose interludes that despite the lack of a preceding formal narrative, the basic situation in which God speaks through these two prophets, and through the undated Malachi, is quite clear. Thus, in Haggai 1:1, the word of the Lord comes to the prophet "in the second year of King Darius." We are not told of what Darius is king, but in Haggai 2:2, the prophet is ordered to speak to "Zerubbabel son of Shealtiel, the *governor* of Judah" (italics added). Darius is, in fact, king of Persia; but even though Haggai never so labels him, he makes clear by the foreignness of the name *Darius* and the use of the word *governor* that the Judeans have returned to their home and are subject there to a foreign potentate of some kind. God's promise of restoration has, we infer, been kept in some form. But in what form? And how does God feel about it?

The material specificity of some of God's demands becomes a surprising answer to both questions, enough of an answer to provide a new setting—or, if not quite a setting, then at least a suggestive backdrop—for Psalms, Proverbs, and Job. Through Haggai, God upbraids the Judeans for rebuilding their own homes but not rebuilding the temple, his house:

> Is it a time for you to dwell in your paneled houses, while this House is lying in ruins? Now thus said the Lord of Hosts: Consider how you have been faring! You have sowed much and brought in little; you eat without being satisfied; you drink without getting your fill; you clothe yourselves, but no one gets warm; and he who earns anything earns it for a leaky purse. (Hag. 1:4–6)

Indirectly, the Lord tells us that the return of the Judeans to Jerusalem has not been a glorious return. They are barely getting by. This is not nearly what had been promised them. But the reason adduced for the shabbiness of their new national life is surprising: They have not built their God a temple.

This is surprising because at II Samuel 7, the Lord was magnificently indifferent to human architecture. It did not trouble him that, as David was abashed to say, "Here I am dwelling in a house of cedar, while the Ark of the Lord abides in a tent!" (II Sam. 7:2). Through the prophet Nathan, the Lord asked David, rhetorically: "As I moved about wherever the Israelites went, did I ever reproach any of the tribal leaders whom I appointed to care for My people Israel: Why have you not built Me a house of cedar?" (7:7). Eventually Solomon builds the temple, having turned the remaining non-Israelite population of the land into a slave-labor force for the building (I Kings 9:15). And the Lord accepts Solomon's gift. At the conclusion of the king's long dedicatory prayer, the Lord says: "I have heard the prayer and the supplication which you have offered to Me. I consecrate this House which you have built and I set My name there forever. My eyes and My heart shall ever be there" (9:3).

The Lord's loyalty to the "house," the dynasty, he has built for David is unconditional, but not so his commitment to the temple. There is a condition on its permanency:

> [But] if you and your descendants turn away from Me and do not keep the commandments [and] the laws which I have set before you, and go and serve other gods and worship them . . . this House shall become a ruin; everyone passing by it shall be appalled and shall hiss. And when they ask, "Why did the Lord do thus to the

> land and to this House?" they shall be told, "It is because they forsook the Lord their God. . . ." (I Kings 9:6, 8–9)

If there is now no temple in the land, therefore, it is because the Lord willed the destruction of the temple Solomon built for him. He needed no temple in the first place, by his own clear statement. Now he wants one. Whatever the reason for the change, this is clearly a change.

A change in Judea's circumstances as well as a change in the Lord's attitude can be seen in what the Lord says after the temple is built (as in short order it is). He says to the governor, the high priest, and the rest (RSV: "the remnant") of the people:

> Who is there left among you who saw this House in its former splendor? How does it look to you now? It must seem like nothing to you. But be strong, O Zerubbabel—says the Lord—be strong, O high priest Joshua son of Jehozadak; be strong, all you people of the land—says the Lord—and act! For I am with you—says the Lord of Hosts. . . . The glory of this latter House shall be greater than that of the former one, said the Lord of Hosts; and in this place I will grant prosperity—declares the Lord of Hosts. (Hag. 2:3–4, 9)

God's claim in his first statement through Haggai was that because no temple had been built,

> the skies above you have withheld [their] moisture and the earth has withheld its yield, and I have summoned fierce heat upon the land—upon the hills, upon the new grain and wine and oil, upon all that the ground produces, upon man and beast, and upon all the fruits of labor. (1:10–11)

Now that the temple has been built, God will again send rain, prosperity will return, and all will eventually be better than ever. Still, the glory has clearly been postponed: The Lord admits—preemptively, as it were—that the new temple is nothing compared with the old one.

And what of the new ruler? The temple was, of course, intimately connected with the Israelite monarchy. There, as nowhere else, the glory of God and the glory of the king commingled; God's house (temple) and David's house (dynasty) were celebrated as one. The Lord sends Haggai to the Persian-appointed governor, Zerubbabel, a descendant of David, to tell him that he is the messiah, the "servant of the Lord" celebrated anonymously in the mystical poems of Isaiah. It is he who will usher in the new age:

> Speak to Zerubbabel the governor of Judah: I am going to shake the heavens and the earth. And I will overturn the thrones of kingdoms and destroy the might of the kingdoms of the nations. I will overturn chariots and their drivers. Horses and their riders shall fall, each by the sword of his fellow. On that day—declares the Lord of Hosts—I will take you, O My servant Zerubbabel son of Shealtiel—declares the Lord—and make you as a signet; for I have chosen you—declares the Lord of Hosts. (2:21–23)

The rhetoric is tired, derivative, and altogether too grandiose for a man whom even God, apparently, cannot bring himself to address as king but only as governor. Speaking through Zechariah, Haggai's contemporary, the Lord links Zerubbabel, who presided over the building of the disparaged new temple, with the glory promised for its future, as if to suggest that the one future will be as glorious as the other:

> Zerubbabel's hands have founded this House and Zerubbabel's hands shall complete it. Then you shall know that it was the Lord of Hosts who sent me to you. Does anyone scorn a day of small beginnings? When they see the plummet in the hand of Zerubbabel, they shall rejoice. (Zech. 4:9–10)

Yet, having sent a dozen coded signals that Zerubbabel and the high priest, Joshua, are to be corulers of a sort, the Lord instructs Zechariah to crown Joshua rather than Zerubbabel. All the Davidic-heir language is transferred to Joshua, who, though already a priest, is to rule "with a priest on his right." Historical critics believe that the text has been altered and the name *Joshua* substituted for the name *Zerubbabel*. Why was the change made? Did the Persians halt as rank sedition this scheme to restore an heir of David to some semblance of a throne? Did the people turn against Zerubbabel for some reason? Did the high priest stage some kind of coup? Historians know only what any close reader of the text cannot fail to notice—namely, that the messiah Zerubbabel is never heard of again and that the silence that swallows him swallows the Davidic line as well.

God hailing a Persian appointee as messiah begins to seem like

Don Quixote hailing the peasant maid Aldonza Lorenzo as his noble mistress Dulcinea del Toboso. God acknowledges that the new temple he insisted on was greeted with some scoffing. Did the Jews also scoff at Zerubbabel? Though the Tanakh is capable of humor, the humor is never at God's expense. The kind of incongruity that Cervantes portrays as comic, though touched with poignancy, here appears as exclusively poignant and only just touched with unintentional comedy, as in the Lord's last words to Zechariah: "In those days, ten men from nations of every tongue will take hold—they will take hold of every Jew by a corner of his cloak and say, 'Let us go with you, for we have heard that God is with you' " (8:23).

The Jews to whom God makes this promise are descended from the Judeans to whom he promised that their return from Babylon would be a triumphant march across the desert: a new exodus and a new creation that would bring all nations streaming to Zion to worship the one God and enrich the nation that would be his priestly attendant. That promise was thrilling, but its refutation is staring it in the face. Why send ten gentiles per Jewish sleeve to a Jewish colony that, by God's own testimony, is on the verge of starvation?

GOD HIMSELF seems to be hungry, figuratively speaking, in the last of the three postexilic prophets, Malachi. Israelite religion never went through any charade of feeding its God. The priests and Levites ate the food that was sacrificed to God. This was their right, and everyone knew what they were doing. Nonetheless, three chapters from the end of the little book that ends all prophecy, God gives voice to a complaint about the poor quality of the animals sacrificed to him, a complaint that could scarcely contrast more sharply with his usual lordly sarcasm on this subject. "What to me is the multitude of your sacrifices?" the Lord said to Isaiah;

> I have had enough of burnt offerings of rams
> and the fat of fed beasts;
> I do not delight in the blood of bulls,
> or of lambs, or of he-goats." (Isa. 1:11)

This sentiment has been repeated to the point of cliché through all the major and minor prophets to this point. But speaking to Malachi, God stands that cliché on its head:

> A son honors his father, and a servant his master. If then I am a father, where is my honor? And if I am a master, where is my fear? says the Lord of hosts to you, O priests, who despise my name. You say, "How have we despised thy name?" By offering polluted food upon my altar. And you say, "How have we polluted it?" By thinking that the Lord's table may be despised. When you offer blind animals in sacrifice, is that no evil? And when you offer those that are lame or sick, is that no evil? Present that to your governor; will he be pleased with you or show you favor? says the Lord of hosts. (RSV; Mal. 1:6–8)

At the start, it should be remembered, God did not ask or expect worship from mankind. The first account of creation contained only the positive injunctions to be fruitful and multiply and to exercise dominion over the created world. There were no prohibitions. The second account added one prohibition, on eating the fruit of the tree of the knowledge of good and evil. But of worship, of honor of any kind to the name of the Lord, not a word. And not a word on that subject was spoken to Abraham, Isaac, Jacob, or Joseph. Worship and indeed exclusive worship was required of the Israelites starting with Moses; but even then it was clear from the Lord's hair-trigger readiness to abrogate the covenant that he did not need what he was demanding. The covenant with Abraham was a fertility covenant; and as the nation descended from Abraham grew in numbers, it was necessary to police aggressively the borders that divided that nation from others whose fertility was not divinely fostered and guaranteed. Worship was a part of that policing; it was covenant-functional; it helped to keep Israel as a nation apart. But God did not require it in any more personal way. Now, somehow, he does appear to require it.

That he requires it seems to place him and Israel in a comparably needy condition. Neither appears to enjoy the power that was once enjoyed. And as God harangues Israel in the manner of a preacher complaining about the collection, we sense that both are hard up:

> Will man rob God? Yet you are robbing me. But you say, "How are we robbing thee?" In your tithes and offerings. You are cursed with a curse, for you are robbing me; the whole nation of you. Bring the full tithes into the storehouse, that there may be food in my house; and thereby put me to the test, says the Lord of hosts, if I will not open the windows of heaven [send rain] for you and pour down for you an overflowing blessing. (RSV; 3:8–10)

Very strikingly, it is amid these complaints that we hear God's first completely unequivocal and unmistakable reference to himself as female:

> And this again you do. You cover the Lord's altar with tears, with weeping and groaning because he no longer regards the offering or accepts it with favor at your hand. You ask, "Why does he not?" Because the Lord was witness to the covenant between you and the wife of your youth, to whom you have been faithless, though she is your companion and your wife by covenant. Has not the one God made and sustained for us the spirit of life? And what does he desire? Godly offspring. So take heed to yourselves, and let none be faithless to the wife of his youth. "For I hate divorce, says the Lord the God of Israel, and covering one's garment with violence, says the Lord of hosts. So take heed to yourselves and do not be faithless." (RSV; 2:13–16)

In Isaiah, God was the husband and Israel the wife of his youth, rejected but then taken back with merciful tenderness. Now, God is the wife, and Israel is the husband.

This passage, very nearly the last word that the Lord will speak through a prophet, forces as no previous passage has done the question of whether among the personalities that fuse in the character of God we must recognize a goddess. But before taking up that question, we should note the uniformly subordinate and disparaged character of women in ancient Israelite society. In announcing his judgment against sinful Israel, a judgment brought to a particular focus on the haughty and materialistic daughters of Zion, the Lord predicts a punitive anarchy recognizable by the fact that women will have taken power:

> My people—children are their oppressors,
> and women rule over them.
> O my people, your leaders mislead you,
> and confuse the course of your paths. (Isa. 3:12)

Much earlier, when a woman in the besieged town of Thebez fatally wounded the rebel king Abimelech by dropping a millstone on him from the town wall, Abimelech called his armor-bearer and said: "Draw your sword and kill me, lest men say of me, 'A woman killed him' " (RSV; Judg. 9:54). God's and Abimelech's attitudes toward women are one and the same. A woman ruler, a woman warrior—either is an insult and a disgrace.

Not all women are disparaged, of course. Jael the Kenite is praised in the Song of Deborah and Barak (Judg. 5) for driving a tent peg through the skull of the sleeping Canaanite general Sisera, Israel's enemy and her own erstwhile ally. And in plotting successfully to take the throne of Israel away from David's eldest son, Adonijah, and secure it for her own son, Solomon, Bathsheba is, at least by implication, judged quite positively. The same, of course, would go for Rebekah when she plots with Jacob to defraud Esau. Whatever a modern reader might judge of these actions (their masculine equivalents can, of course, easily be adduced), the Tanakh does not condemn them. They serve rather to demonstrate that women were at least sometimes powerful actors in ancient Israelite society. And wholly benign minor examples are not wanting, such as Hannah, praying for a son and then thanking the Lord with touching eloquence, or Abigail, trusting in the Lord and in David at once.

The deeper question is not about whether women ever held power in Israelite society but whether, so to put it, there is a goddess inside Israel's God. Is God female as well as male, a mother as well as a father, a matriarch as well as a patriarch, a wife as well as a husband, and so forth?

Historical criticism has drawn attention to the fact that the ancient Canaanite god El, the sky god whose personality was taken up into that of the Lord God, had a consort, Asherah, who bore monsters to battle El's younger rival, Baal, but was also, very generally, a goddess of fertility and motherhood. By identification with El, Israel's God could, so to speak, have inherited Asherah; and a few verses (a very few, to be sure) survive in which Israel's God seems to be described as male and female in successive lines—thus, by possible implication, as a divine couple. Deuteronomy 32:18, a verse in the Song of Moses, is often cited:

> You were unmindful of the Rock that begot you,
> and you forgot the God who gave you birth. (RSV)

The verse may originally have ended "and you forgot the *tree* who gave you birth," rock and tree or stone altar and wooden pole standing for the divine couple El (Yahweh) and Asherah. If Yahweh and Asherah were once a couple, however, they seem to be a couple no longer. Yahweh, the Lord, is without spouse, and the text of the

Tanakh invariably links Asherah with Baal rather than with him. Speaking rather loosely, Yahweh may once have shared Asherah with El; but if so, then when Yahweh became a celibate, the bereft Asherah ended up with Baal.

But just as a divorced man will have a different inner relationship to women than a man who has never married, the Lord's relationship to Asherah and to femininity may not be at an end simply because she is no longer his consort. The natural object most often associated with Asherah is the tree or its representation the sacred post. Thus, Jeremiah 17:1–2 (italics added):

> The guilt of Judah is inscribed
> With a stylus of iron,
> Engraved with an adamant point
> On the tablet of their hearts,
> And on the horns of their altars,
> While their children remember
> Their altars and sacred posts [ʾ*ašerim*]
> *By verdant trees,*
> Upon lofty hills.

The Hebrew common noun ʾ*ašerah* (plural, ʾ*ašerim*), meaning "sacred post," in this passage is also the goddess's name.

Stone and wood, as paired representations of god and goddess, are standard in Canaanite religion and are mocked as a pair at Jeremiah 2:27:

> They said to wood, "You are my father,"
> To stone, "You gave birth to me."

In fact, Israelites gone culturally Canaanite would probably have said to the stone, "You are my father," and to the tree, "You gave me birth." The reversal may be intentional mockery. It is noteworthy, however, that in the cult of the Lord God, stone, the masculine element, was fully acceptable in the form of the stone altar. Wood, in the form of the pole or asherah, was unacceptable; yet the text makes it clear that, endless denunciations notwithstanding, the asherah remained in use as a piece of cult furniture set alongside the Lord's stone altar.

As a comment on the character of God, what does this state of affairs suggest? It suggests that at whatever point the Lord

God became asexual (or ceased to be sexual), he did not—at least not immediately—fuse with his erstwhile consort, becoming in the process equally male and female, an ambisexual being, but rather divorced his consort and attempted to exclude the feminine from his own character. The exclusion of Asherah must not be seen as, on the Lord's own part, anything less than a violently emotional revulsion. In the Lord's eyes, Israel's worst crime, the crime that finally provokes him to destroy Jerusalem and then to blot out even the remnant of Judah, is King Manasseh's horrifying decision to place a sculpted image of Asherah in the Lord's own temple:

> The sculpted image of Asherah that [Manasseh] made he placed in the House concerning which the Lord had said to David and to his son Solomon, "In this House and in Jerusalem, which I chose out of all the tribes of Israel, I will establish My name forever." . . . Therefore the Lord spoke through His servants the prophets: "Because King Manasseh of Judah has done these abhorrent things—he has outdone the wickedness all that the Amorites did before his time—and because he led Judah to sin with his fetishes, assuredly, thus said the Lord, the God of Israel: I am going to bring such a disaster on Jerusalem and Judah that both ears of everyone who hears about it will tingle. I will apply to Jerusalem the measuring line of [the already conquered and destroyed] Samaria and the weights of the [already annihilated] House of Ahab. I will wipe Jeusalem clean as one wipes a dish and turns it upside down. And I will cast off the remnant of My own people and deliver them into the hands of their enemies." (II Kings 21:7–14)

And Yet despite the Lord's overwhelming revulsion at the thought that a goddess should be permitted to cohabit his House with him, he remains the creator who said "Let *us* make man in *our* image, after *our* likeness" and who then proceeded to create a female as well as a male. What may be for historical criticism no more than a fossilized scrap of mythological language is for literary criticism an inexpungable characterological fact. The human male alone is not the image of God, only the male and the female together. And this duality in the image must somehow be matched by a duality in the original. It is this fact that requires us to speak of the exclusion rather than the mere absence of the feminine from God's character. And it is that exclusion which lends pathos to the asherah as a liturgical fossil, an opaque object with an all-but-forgotten goddess's name, symbolizing his worshipers' memory of what he once was or yet might be.

The asherah underscores the reason why *asexual*, though useful and probably unavoidable, is an inaccurate word for the Lord. The Lord is not a neuter or neutered being, much less an abstract or impersonal principle, a world soul or vital force. He is an otherwise male being who has no parents, wife, or children and no sexual relations of any kind. A destroyer as well as a creator, a warmonger as well as a lawgiver, a remote ruler as well as an intimate friend, he comes into being by addition or combination, as the precipitate of several earlier divine personalities. But subtraction also plays a role in the formation of the Lord's character. His identity is crucially defined by what is denied or taken from him. The question just now is *Has femininity been subtracted from him?*

The best answer seems to be *Yes, but not entirely*, and, by yet another unforeseen reversal in his history, his denied femininity will be reasserted. The Lord God with the asherah standing beside his altar is rather like an extremely virile man carrying a woman's purse. Whatever the rest of his seeming character, the object is sufficient to raise a question.

This much conceded in advance, it would nonetheless be a mistake, notwithstanding all the tenderness in many passages of prophecy, to say that at this point in his story God is both mother and father, both female and male. The maternal imagery in a verse such as Isaiah 66:12–13 is transparent:

> Behold, I will extend prosperity to [Jerusalem] like a river,
> and the wealth of the nations like an overflowing stream;
> and you shall suck, you shall be carried upon her hip,
> and dandled upon her knees.
> As one whom his mother comforts,
> so I will comfort you;
> you shall be comforted in Jerusalem.

But it is only imagery. On balance, it is altogether less noteworthy that God occasionally uses maternal imagery when speaking of himself to the prophets than that for so very long he avoided paternal as well as maternal imagery. With the single, salient exception of II Samuel 7, both kinds of parental imagery are all but entirely absent from Genesis through II Kings. Starting with Isaiah, God begins to speak of himself fairly freely as both a mother and a father, but rather than see the return of the feminine at this point, we should recall that this freedom of expression comes amid a veritable explosion of metaphorical language in which he speaks of himself as husband, lover, shepherd, redeemer (metaphorically, a ransomer from slavery), and much else. The thrust is undeniably toward tenderness and gentleness; but particularly since Near Eastern goddesses are so often utterly ferocious, that thrust does not in and of itself bespeak feminization.

The Lord God, we said earlier, is only analogously a father. When he begins to speak of himself as a mother, he is also only analogously a mother. The metaphor he chooses to use of himself at any given point will always reflect what he wants to say of himself at that point, and different metaphors may follow rapidly on one another. Thus, in Malachi 2, just before God speaks of himself as Israel's wife, Malachi speaks of God as Israel's father: "Have we not all one Father? Did not one God create us?" (2:10).

To say this is not to say that everything God says of himself is an analogy. On the understanding of the Tanakh, God is really, not analogously, a creator, and his covenant with Israel is really an agreement. Moreover, in a characterological rather than genital sense, he has been really male and not really female. Since he presents himself sometimes in human form and then always in male form, he may even be said to have male genitalia; but in him they are without genital function. Peculiar as all this may seem, it has been definitive of his identity and his character.

And yet even this will change. In the aftermath of the Judeans' return from their Babylonian captivity, God will become gradually more androgynous. The analogous femininity implicit in his characterization of himself as abandoned wife—a femininity, obviously, of weakness—is not unconnected with the deeper change to come. It is a condition for and prelude to it. For now, however, God is neither female nor androgynous. He may best be described as a chastened and shaken male, even when he compares himself to an ill-supported wife, and the answer to the question *Is there a goddess inside this God?* rather than *No* is *Not yet.*

Earlier in this chapter, we said that a discussion of Haggai, Zechariah, and Malachi would set the stage for mankind's extended reply to God in Psalms, Proverbs, and Job. And to that purpose we have highlighted a set of passages that bring these postexilic prophets into sharp contrast with the preexilic and exilic prophets, passages that leave a clear suggestion of disappointment and dejection among the Judeans and, in God, an unwonted narrowness of perspective and shrillness of tone. The promises God made through Isaiah and the earlier prophets have clearly not been kept. A semblance of national life has been reconstituted, but to those with clear memories, it is no more than a semblance. The Judeans and their God both find themselves with identities sharply modified by history. There are other passages in these three prophets that read somewhat more hopefully than the ones we have quoted and still others, particularly in Zechariah 9–14, in which hope takes the very particular shape of apocalypse. About this a further word needs to be said.

AN APOCALYPSE is a cryptic revelation of imminent destruction to be followed by a definitive divine intervention at the end of time. Historically, apocalypticism is a kind of weed sprung up in Judea from the charred earth of failed prophecy. Its predictions are coded and otherwise elaborately mysterious in part to mislead the Judeans' and later the Jews' foreign oppressors, in part to renew the nation's own belief in God's power and its national uniqueness when all the evidence seems to point the other way. It is global in its reach, reflecting a now well-developed awareness that Judea's future and the future of the other nations of the world are inseparable. It is, in general, vaster but also vaguer in its promises than prophecy. Even as God's specific demands (for a temple, tithes, top-quality sacrificial animals, and so on) grow more petty, his promises and threats grow more grandiose. But the fact that the "day of the Lord" which apocalypticism predicts is always nigh but never exactly dated preserves it from the kind of refutation by event that prophecy suffers in the Judean restoration.

The apocalyptic or protoapocalyptic moments in Zechariah are not the only ones in the biblical prophets. There are apocalyptic passages in the last chapters of Isaiah, in Ezekiel, and elsewhere. But it is noteworthy that the intensity of the apocalyptic tendency—the tendency to encode and to postpone—does not abate at all with the restoration of the Judeans to their homeland. That it does not do so bespeaks their profound discontent with the character of the restoration, a discontent for which, as we have seen, there is much other evidence in Haggai, Zechariah, and Malachi.

As a statement about God, apocalypticism seems to say that he is progressively more preoccupied with a destruction soon to come and progressively more inclined to encode what he has to say about it. As an encoded prediction of destruction, we may consider the following long passage from Zechariah:

> Thus said the Lord my God: "Become shepherd of the flock doomed to slaughter. Those who buy them slay them and go unpunished; and those who sell them say, 'Blessed be the Lord, I have become rich'; and their own shepherds have no pity on them. For I will no longer have pity on the inhabitants of this land, says the Lord. Lo, I will cause men to fall each into the hand of his shepherd, and each into the hand of his king; and they shall crush the earth, and I will deliver none from their hand."
>
> So I became the shepherd of the flock doomed to be slain for those who trafficked in the sheep. And I took two staffs; one I named Grace, the other I named Union. And I tended the sheep. In one month I destroyed the three shepherds. But I became impatient with them, and they also detested me. So I said, "I will not be your shepherd. What is to die, let it die; what is to be destroyed, let it be destroyed; and let those that are left devour the flesh of one another." And I took my staff Grace, and I broke it, annulling the covenant which I had made with all the peoples. So it was annulled on that day, and the traffickers in the sheep, who were watching me, knew that it was the word of the Lord. Then I said to them, "If it seems right to you, give me my wages; but if not, keep them." And they weighed out as my wages thirty shekels of silver [the price of a slave]. Then the Lord said to me, "Cast it into the treasury"—the lordly price at which I was paid off by them. So I took the thirty shekels of silver and cast them into the treasury in the house of the Lord. Then I broke my second staff Union, annulling the brotherhood between Judah and Israel.
>
> Then the Lord said to me, "Take once more the implements of a worthless shepherd. For lo, I am raising up in the land a shepherd who does not care for the perishing, or seek the wandering, or heal the maimed, or nourish the sound, but devours the flesh of the fat ones, tearing off even their hoofs.
>
> Woe to my worthless shepherd,
>   who deserts the flock!
> May the sword smite his arm
>   and his right eye!
> Let his arm be wholly withered,
>   his right eye utterly blinded!" (RSV; Zech. 11:4–17)

Who is the shepherd? Who are the buyers and sellers? Why are the staffs named Grace and Union? What is the annulled covenant?

What is the meaning of the wages and the allusion to the price of a slave? Who is the predatory shepherd predicted in the last verses? And when will all this happen, or is it already happening? The passage is an allegory that may well have been only somewhat less opaque when first written than it is now. Real-world references may be fit to each of its elements, but in earlier prophecy those references would have been included rather than implied or encoded.

Speaking to and through the earlier prophets, God used metaphor freely but allegory only sparingly. Allegory is a form well suited to equivocation, but God had no desire to equivocate. He did not seem concerned, as he does here, to reveal and conceal at the same time. When the prophet told the allegory of the ewe lamb in order to shame David after the murder of Uriah, the Lord required that he explain the allegory immediately. In Isaiah 5:1, the prophet speaks of "my beloved" and his "vineyard" but immediately (5:7) decodes it:

> For the vineyard of the Lord of hosts
>   is the house of Israel,
> and the men of Judah
>   are his pleasant planting;
> and he looked for justice,
>   but behold, bloodshed;
> for righteousness,
>   but behold, a cry!

No comparable decoding is to be found in the allegory of the evil shepherds in Zechariah, and the reason is plain to see: The Lord is hiding. And Israel, aware that he is hiding, is growing hostile to the very institution of prophecy.

Zechariah 13, in the most extraordinary way, puts prophecy with idolatry and uncleanness on a short list of practices that will be blotted out on "the day of the Lord":

> And on that day, says the Lord of hosts, I will cut off the names of the idols from the land, so that they shall be remembered no more; and also I will remove from the land the prophets and the unclean spirit. And if any one again appears as a prophet, his father and mother who bore him will say to him, "You shall not live, for you speak lies in the name of the Lord"; and his father and mother who bore him shall pierce him through when he prophesies. On that day every prophet will be ashamed of his vision

> when he prophesies; he will not put on a hairy mantle in order to deceive, but he will say, "I am no prophet, I am a tiller of the soil; for the land has been my possession since my youth." (RSV; Zech. 13:2–5)

Prophecy is a mistake the Lord will not make twice.

Of equal importance, however, alongside God's tendency to conceal his intentions is his tendency to linger over the destructive rather than the restorative aspects of the great events to come. The archetypal destruction of the world—the only one that was not just predicted but actually occurred—is the world-destroying flood of Genesis 6–8. That action, we saw, was the work of God the destroyer, a distinct personality profoundly at odds with the personality of the creator. The covenant with Abraham, which some of the earlier prophets dreamed of extending in some form to all mankind, was at the outset the resolution of a conflict within God. When Israel broke the covenant, that resolution was in principle undermined. By promising to restore Israel to the promised land, God was also promising to reconstitute his own inner compromise. But if he has failed to accomplish what he set out to do, if the returning Judeans find the restoration a disappointment and he finds their treatment of him niggardly, then the covenant is tacitly called into question again, and his dark side is again free to assert itself. In Zechariah's allegory, when the prophet accepts the role of shepherd of the doomed flock, is he acting, allegorically, for God? Whose voice do we really hear in the line "What is to die, let it die; what is to be destroyed, let it be destroyed; and let those that are left devour the flesh of one another"? The vagueness of the reference is extremely ominous, and equally ominous is the fact that the passage as a whole lingers about destruction as a criminal might linger about a gun shop.

In discussing Israel's Exodus from Egypt and the Lord God's triumph over Pharaoh, we said that if the entire Bible could be summarized in one word, that word would be *victory*. That statement remains valid even at this riven and contradictory moment in the life of God. Zechariah 14, the last chapter in the book, moves past a description of apocalyptic battles to a vision of miraculous peace as the survivors from all nations stream to Jerusalem to worship. The very bells of the horses, the Lord promises, will be inscribed "Holy to the Lord." Promise, even after the failure of promise, lives on and outweighs threat; but as his silence begins, God is as disappointed in his people as they are in him.

Counselor

"How Precious to Me Are Thy Thoughts, O God!"

PSALMS

The 150 prayers that make up the Psalter or Book of Psalms constitute a kind of recapitulation of much, though decidedly not everything, that precedes them in the Bible. Many of the events and issues raised in the first twenty-six books of the Tanakh (the five books of the Pentateuch, the six of the Deuteronomistic History, and the fifteen of the prophets) recur in the Psalms by allusion. Many of the Psalms are explicitly attributed to King David, and a few of them are further specified to a given moment in David's career. Others, by their content, give other clues to when they were first spoken or, more likely, sung.

Such diversity in content and occasion makes it difficult to specify what the Psalms collectively say about God, much less to make that something a step forward in the biography of God. But three factors greatly mitigate that difficulty. First, the Psalms are all spoken in the present tense. Though the moment in which a given Psalm was written may in fact lie in the past, the fact that the Psalm has been preserved and collected constitutes an implicit claim that its thought or sentiment is still valid. When a Psalm is very specifically located in the past, the implication is that that past moment and the sentiment then expressed are worth recalling and in some way still valid. Thus Psalm 59 is one that David spoke "when Saul sent men to watch his house in order to put him to death," but the sentiment in its opening verses transfers easily to other situations:

> Save me from my enemies, O my God;
> secure me against my assailants.
> Save me from evildoers;
> deliver me from murderers. (Ps. 59:2–3)

The second mitigating factor for a synthetic reading of the Psalms is the fact that a great many of them are altogether without specification as to time or place.

The third mitigating factor is that though the Psalms may have been written at very different historical moments, we are reading them all at the same literary moment. We may say of the Psalms something analogous to what we said of the prophets when we compared them to the correspondence of a great general read after the war was over. His character, as the letters reveal it, will have been his character even during the war; but because we only discover after the war what the letters say about his character, it is as if for us his character changes after the war. Rather than correspondence with the great, the Psalms often read like interviews with the obscure: anonymous foot soldiers and taxpayers who testify to the character of their leader most convincingly not by what they say about him but by what they say to him. Notably, they all do seem to have all spoken to him on one occasion or another, great or small, public or private.

What is the moment in which these interviews are conducted? It is the moment characterized at the start of this chapter by our reading of the three postexilic prophets. Israel changed its religion and abandoned God. Then God, enforcing the terms of his covenant with Israel, punished Israel and sent her into exile. But he had promised that he would take pity on her and bring her back in triumph, a triumph that would lead the whole world to pay homage to the two of them, God and Israel together. Now Israel, in the person of the exiled Judeans, has returned to her capital city and resumed a national life, but that national life has proven parlous and dreary. We should imagine the Psalms spoken or sung in the temple that the returned exiles built in Jerusalem. They were slow to build it, so pressing were their practical needs, and after it was built it struck many of them as decidedly unimpressive.

As we come upon the congregation praying to him in just this building, what do we hear that surprises us? They are living at peace. The Jews in fact did live more or less peacefully as a province of the Persian empire for two centuries before Alexander the Great, sweeping in from the West, ushered in another period of extreme violence in their history. Let us imagine them about halfway through the Persian period. Malachi, the last prophet, has died a century ago. Alexander, undreamt of, is still a century in the future. Quite clearly God and Israel have come to terms with each other, but what are the terms?

What should strike anyone who reads the Psalter after reading straight through the prophets is that whereas the prophets speak of wicked Israel, the Psalmists speak of the wicked *in* Israel. The prophets did speak some of the time about a faithful remnant, which they contrasted with the apostate majority, but from the Exodus to the Babylonian captivity, the more frequent contrast was between Israel and the other nations of the world. Individual differences were all but eliminated in this religiously collectivized worldview. If King Manasseh led Judah into idolatry and child sacrifice, no effort was made to find or deal separately with those of his subjects who may not have joined him in his sin. Guilt and innocence were shared.

This seems clearly to have changed. One of the most touching of the Psalms is the briefest, Psalm 131:

> O Lord, my heart is not proud
> nor my look haughty;
> I do not aspire to great things
> or to what is beyond me;
> but I have taught myself to be contented
> like a weaned child with its mother;
> like a weaned child am I in my mind.
> O Israel, wait for the Lord
> now and forever.

In the imposed peace of the Persian empire, Israel has ceased to be even a minor actor on the international scene. Centuries have passed since Israel's God last went to war. His victories over Pharaoh, over the thirty-one Canaanite kings who fell to Joshua, over the Philistines whom David routed, are a distant memory. What loom larger for a nation thus confined within its own borders are personal victories and defeats, joys and sorrows, and—most important, it seems—personal innocence and guilt. Enemies are referred to in perhaps one-third of all the Psalms, and the attack that they have launched against the Psalmist, the attack that prompts his prayer, is far more often than not an accusation of wrongdoing.

It is possible if not, indeed, all but certain that many of these Psalms of individual entreaty to God make reference to an ancient courtroom and that the vindication prayed for is legal relief. Even if this is not true or is only metaphorically true in some cases, the effect of the preoccupation is to make God seem less an invincible warrior and more a powerful magistrate whose "steadfast love" for the defendant will protect the defendant from the plaintiff and the plaintiff's powerful and unscrupulous allies.

It is noteworthy that the Psalmists, though they be as humble as the author of the Psalm just quoted, never apologize for addressing

God directly and never fear to do so. They may doubt their own innocence. They may worry about his inattention or severity. But they do not fear to approach him in the first place as the Israelites rightly feared to approach the all but out-of-control, volcanic deity who gave the law on Mount Sinai. Even the guilty may come to him if, as in the following famous example, they arrive pleading for mercy:

> Out of the depths I call You, O Lord.
> O Lord, listen to my cry;
>   let Your ears be attentive
>   to my plea for mercy.
> If You keep account of sins, O Lord,
>   Lord, who will survive?
> Yours is the power to forgive
>   so that You may be held in awe.
>
> I look to the Lord;
>   I look to Him;
>   I await His word.
> I am more eager for the Lord
>   than watchmen for the morning,
>   watchmen for the morning.
>
> O Israel, wait for the Lord;
>   for with the Lord is steadfast love
>   and great power to redeem.
> It is He who will redeem Israel from all their iniquities.
> (Ps. 130)

The Psalter contains a number of Psalms that read as war songs. One is Psalm 144:

> Blessed is the Lord, my rock,
>   who trains my hands for battle,
>   my fingers for warfare;
>   my faithful one, my fortress,
>   my haven and my deliverer,
>   my shield, in whom I take shelter,
>   who makes peoples subject to me. (144:1–2)

And the signal victories of the past are ceremoniously recalled again and again: Their martial spirit is familiar, even—by this point—classic. A different spirit, however, shapes the group of thirty or forty Psalms that make no reference to war or to any national enemy, past or present. A good many, as noted, refer to personal enemies, but others simply call on God in distress for relief or even in the absence of distress for favor and support. And the universal assumption, which we noted first in Second Isaiah, is that God is a friend intimately acquainted with the supplicant. In the Psalms, any Jew may pray to God for deliverance as Jacob prayed to the personal God of his father Abraham or as David prayed to his invincible ally.

In Psalm 56, identified as "of David, when the Philistines seized him in Gath," David imagines, in a vivid metaphor, that God will capture and save the young captive's every tear:

> You keep count of my wanderings;
> put my tears into Your flask,
> into Your record. (56:9)

Comparable claims in less dramatic settings are everywhere in the Psalter. One of the most eloquent comes at the opening of Psalm 139:

> O Lord, You have examined me and know me.
> When I sit down or stand up You know it;
> You discern my thoughts from afar.
> You observe my walking and reclining,
> and are familiar with all my ways.
> There is not a word on my tongue
> but that You, O Lord, know it well.
> You hedge me before and behind;
> You lay Your hand upon me.
> It is beyond my knowledge;
> it is a mystery; I cannot fathom it. (139:1–6)

The subtle but pervasive change that separates this passage from comparable passages about the unknowability of the Lord in Second Isaiah is that here the focus is on the individual human knower—not on Israel as a whole—and that, quite clearly, the Psalmist regards knowledge of the Lord as, in and of itself, a prize beyond compare. Later in Psalm 139, the Psalmist exclaims:

> How weighty Your thoughts seem to me, O God,
> how great their number!

I count them—they exceed the grains of sand;
I end—but am still with You. (139:17–18)

The RSV translates: "How precious to me are thy thoughts, O God!" The Hebrew word can bear either meaning. The echo in the next line is, of course, of the Lord's promise of innumerable offspring to Abraham. Now it is God's thoughts rather than Israel's offspring that are beyond number. But how has the Psalmist come to know the thoughts of God? At various points earlier, we have noted that God seems to have not only no private life but also no private thoughts. He speaks no long, thoughtful soliloquies and in fact says nothing that does not have mankind or, more often, Israel as direct referent. The words God speaks in creating the world are a soliloquy of a sort, as are the words he speaks when announcing the world's watery destruction, but otherwise all his words, including all his legislation, are spoken to mankind. This is true even about the Torah, which is not imposed upon Israel at Sinai as a way to open to the nation the weighty or precious thoughts of its God but as a way to establish a covenant. And the covenant itself is imposed not as its own reward but as a means to rewards that for both sides were extrinsic. Israel would receive a land and the supernatural fertility promised to Abraham. God, tacitly, would accomplish the restriction of his initial gift of fertility to this one nation alone.

All that conceded, the law remains a uniquely extended externalization of the mind of God. However merely instrumental it may have been when first revealed, it is susceptible of a second kind of appreciation as what the Psalmist calls the "precious thoughts" of God. And this appreciation, the main theme of a number of Psalms sometimes called the "Torah Psalms," is the background theme of literally dozens of others. In effect, whenever the Psalmist claims righteousness as his ideal or celebrates righteousness in God, whenever he mentions "steadfast love" or speaks the rhythmic and lapidary Hebrew phrase *ki leʿolam ḥasdo*, "for his steadfast love is forever," he is reclaiming the covenant and extolling the law.

Each of the Psalms after the first two carries a heading indicating, variously, its author, the occasion on which it was spoken, the melody to which it was to be sung, the instrumental accompaniment it was to have, or any of a variety of other now scarcely decipherable matters. The first two Psalms, lacking any such heading, are almost certainly to be taken as themselves headings for the collection. And

Psalm 1 establishes the new centrality of the law as meditation and delight, the vehicle by which the individual Jew establishes a personal relationship with God:

> Happy is the man who has not followed the counsel of the wicked,
> or taken the path of sinners,
> or joined the company of the insolent;
> rather, the teaching of the Lord is his delight,
> and he studies that teaching day and night.
> He is like a tree planted beside streams of water,
> which yields its fruit in season,
> whose foliage never fades,
> and whatever it produces thrives.
>
> Not so the wicked;
> rather, they are like chaff that wind blows away.
> Therefore the wicked will not survive judgment,
> nor will sinners, in the assembly of the righteous.
> For the Lord cherishes the way of the righteous,
> but the way of the wicked is doomed.

When the Psalmist says "studies," we should almost certainly understand private and public recitation rather than silent contemplation; yet "studies" is not a mistaken translation: This was and, in some synagogues, still is a distinct form of study, an intimate, sensuous communing with the text through its sound, though not to the exclusion—because a total exclusion would be impossible even if sought—of its meaning.

Why does the Psalmist not delight in the prophecy as well as in the teaching of the Lord? Why does he not study day and night Isaiah, Jeremiah, Ezekiel, Hosea? These too are the weighty thoughts of God, but they are passed over in total silence in the Psalter. The very words *prophet, prophets,* and *prophecy* occur, among them, perhaps five times in the entire 150-Psalm collection. The reason why prophecy is passed over in silence is almost surely also the reason why it died out and why the prophet Zechariah himself looked forward to its dying out—namely, that what the prophets prophesied had, in very large measure, not come true. The statutes and ordinances of the law as such, not being predictions, could not be invalidated by mere history as the prophecies could be and had been. There were, of course, promises and threats to Moses in the

Pentateuch, but the Mosaic promises and the threats, both the blessings and the curses, had come true, the one at the beginning, the other at the end of the preexilic period. It was the prophesied great restoration—the promises made through Isaiah, Jeremiah, and Ezekiel—that had not come to pass.

The silence of the Psalms about the prophets extends even to those matters in which, as regards the law, the prophets may seem to have anticipated the Psalms. Thus circumcision, whether of the penis or of the heart, is never mentioned in the Psalms. When God spoke to Jeremiah about circumcision of the heart, he took up again an image that he had used when speaking through Moses and one that might have seemed to commend itself to the Psalmists. Through Jeremiah he said "to the men of Judah and to the inhabitants of Jerusalem":

> Circumcise yourselves to the Lord,
> remove the foreskin of your hearts,
> O men of Judah and inhabitants of Jerusalem;
> lest my wrath go forth like fire,
> and burn with none to quench it,
> because of the evil of your doings. (RSV; Jer. 4:4)

The injunction given through Moses in the Book of Deuteronomy was Jeremiah's model: "Circumcise therefore the foreskin of your heart, and be no longer stubborn" (RSV; Deut. 10:16). In both cases, the image is intended to suggest sincerity, the mind being scarred inwardly as a sign of fidelity to the covenant just as the penis is scarred outwardly. And in both cases, as well, the reason for fidelity is inseparable from the consequences of infidelity: The Lord will reward the one and punish the other. This is true even when, through Moses, the Lord tells Israel to think about his words:

> Therefore impress these My words upon your very heart: bind them as a sign on your hand and let them serve as a symbol on your forehead, and teach them to your children—reciting them when you stay at home and when you are away, when you lie down and when you get up; and inscribe them on the doorposts of your house and on your gates—*to the end that you and your children may endure, in the land that the Lord swore to your fathers to assign to them, as long as there is a heaven over the earth.* (Deut. 11:18–21, italics added)

And yet by this insistence on inward obedience a path was laid for an inwardness that would be of delight as well as of obedience. This is the "delight in the law of the Lord" that opens the Book of Psalms.

If the spirit of the Psalter is a spirit looking away from battle and grand predictions and toward private life and the law, one would not know it from Psalm 2, the second of the two Psalms that together are an extended superscription for the collection. This Psalm envisions nothing less than a world empire for the Lord and the anointed king of Israel, the Lord's messiah. What is foreseen is notably *not* the conversion of the nations, as spoken of in the prophets, but outright military domination of the sort that was promised to the tribes of Israel when they conquered Canaan:

> Why do nations assemble,
> and peoples plot vain things;
> kings of the earth take their stand,
> and regents intrigue together
> against the Lord and against His anointed?
> "Let us break the cords of their yoke,
> shake off their ropes from us!"
>
> He who is enthroned in heaven laughs;
> the Lord mocks at them.
> Then He speaks to them in anger,
> terrifying them in His rage,
> "But I have installed my king
> on Zion, My holy mountain!"
> Let me tell of the decree:
> the Lord said to me
> "You are My son,
> I have fathered you this day.
> Ask it of Me,
> and I will make the nations your domain;
> your estate, the limits of the earth.
> You can smash them with an iron mace,
> shatter them like potter's ware." (Ps. 2:1–9)

Were it not for its placement, this Psalm might be regarded, in the manner indicated earlier, as one carried forward from the nation's past, more a celebration of past glory than a program for current action. Because of its placement, it should be regarded as stating the ideal relationship between Israel and the other nations. In that regard, the two Psalms state a kind of double ideal: Israel at home and Israel abroad. To judge from the rest of the Psalter, however, Psalm 1 states an ideal that is being pursued, Psalm 2 a dream that has not been abandoned. It is not that there are no other moments in which the Psalmist speaks to the Lord as to a warrior. The second most famous Psalm (after Psalm 23) is Psalm 137:

> By the rivers of Babylon,
> there we sat,
>   sat and wept,
>   as we thought of Zion.
> There on the poplars
>   we hung up our lyres,
>   for our captors asked us there for songs,
>   our tormentors, for amusement,
> "Sing us one of the songs of Zion." (137:1–3)

But this plaintive beginning soon yields to a thirst for revenge:

> Fair Babylon, you predator,
>   a blessing on him who repays you in kind
>   what you have inflicted on us;
>   a blessing on him who seizes your babies
>   and dashes them against the rocks! (137:8–9)

Nothing that once appears in God's personality ever quite disappears. Anything that disappears for a time may always stage a return. In principle, God will never not be a destroyer and never not be a warrior.

And yet, on balance, the dominant mood of the Psalter is one of gentle trust in God, ardent or urgent in times of strife, in the personal laments and entreaties that so crowd the opening pages of the Psalter, grateful and lyrical in times of peace, as in the best-known Psalm in the Psalter and perhaps the best-known poem in Western literature after the Lord's Prayer:

> The Lord is my shepherd, I shall not want;
>   he makes me lie down in green pastures.
> He leads me beside still waters;
>   he restores my soul.
> He leads me in paths of righteousness
>   for his name's sake.

Even though I walk through the valley
  of the shadow of death,
  I fear no evil;
for thou art with me;
  thy rod and thy staff,
  they comfort me.

Thou preparest a table before me
  in the presence of my enemies;
thou anointest my head with oil,
  my cup overflows.
Surely goodness and mercy shall follow me
  all the days of my life;
and I shall dwell in the house of the Lord
  for ever. (RSV; Ps. 23)

The difference in mood between this Psalm and

a blessing on him who seizes your babies
and dashes them against the rocks!

is breathtaking; and in the long run any discussion of the character of the Lord God must simply admit that both moods are native to him. Neither Psalmist is mistaken about him. And it should be noted that even Psalm 23, so often printed in illustrated versions for children, includes the prayer that the Lord will make it possible for the Psalmist to flaunt his good fortune before his enemies:

Thou preparest a table before me
in the presence of my enemies.

The God of the Psalms is never too tender for vindication.

And yet, to return to the central assertion, what is new in the Psalter, what seems to represent a distinct and pervasive change of emphasis in it, is the shift of attention from national to personal and familial welfare and from aggressive public and political themes to the quiet study of the law. The militaristic Psalm 2 is, in point of fact, not the prelude to a series of Psalms praying for the destruction of individual nations, matching the oracles in which the prophets predicted such destruction, nation by nation. And the context—probably the historical context and certainly the literary context—

in which Psalm 2 is spoken is the virtual erasure of prophecy by David's last heir, the failed messiah Zerubbabel.

The king of Israel was at one point a king with peoples subject to him, bound in the bonds that Psalm 2:1 alludes to. In Psalm 2, is the Psalmist thinking of God as an imperialist in his own time? We should probably say, rather, that he is *remembering* the imperialist of the past. Dreams can arise from memories, and subsequent, grandiose, ultimately suicidal adventures in secular messianism may well have fed on certain of the Psalms. On the other hand, memories may also remain memories. Staying at the literary level, and noting the ambivalence and implicit conflict, one may also reasonably concede a greater force to that in the anthology which is not just vigorous but also new. In the Book of Psalms, what is vigorous and also new is the romance of law.

Sometimes by direct statement, more often by implication, the Psalmist opposes the great man to the good man, and it is the good man with whom he and his God are in love:

> Come, my sons, listen to me;
>   I will teach you what it is to fear the Lord.
> Who is the man who is eager for life,
>   who desires years of good fortune?
> Guard your tongue from evil,
>   your lips from deceitful speech.
> Shun evil and do good,
>   seek amity and pursue it.
> The eyes of the Lord are on the righteous,
>   His ears attentive to their cry.
> The face of the Lord is set against evildoers,
>   to erase their names from the earth.
> They cry out, and the Lord hears,
>   and saves them from all their troubles.
> The Lord is close to the brokenhearted;
>   those crushed in spirit He delivers. (34:12–19)

The opposition is not between Israel and the nations but between the righteous and the evildoers, either within Israel or simply without regard to nationality. Law, longevity, and stability are linked motifs in this vision. In Psalm 1, the righteous man is like a tree planted near water, growing, maturing, bearing fruit over many years, while the wicked is chaff carried by the wind. Torah, the religious teaching of Israel, and wisdom, the common secular heritage of the ancient Near East, are near a fusion in this vision, a fusion that, as we shall see, grows more complete in Proverbs. And the rewards of Torah/wisdom are all on an emphatically human scale. No Psalmist ever promises that the righteous will have offspring as numerous as the stars of heaven or the territory of a long list of neighboring peoples. The rewards are rather those of a reasonably prosperous family life. Thus do the romance of the law and the romance of the family become a single romance:

> Happy are all who fear the Lord,
>   who follow His ways.
> You shall enjoy the fruit of your labors;
>   you shall be happy and you shall prosper.
> Your wife shall be like a fruitful vine within your house;
>   your sons, like olive saplings around your table.
> So shall the man who fears the Lord be blessed.
>
> May the Lord bless you from Zion;
>   may you share the prosperity of Jerusalem
>   all the days of your life,
>   and live to see your children's children.
> May all be well with Israel! (Ps. 128)

In the presence of the truly great, the good always seem small. In the presence of the truly good, the great always seem vain. The competing visions of the Jewish people, as we have them in the Psalms, have held the imagination of so many other peoples over so many centuries because they contain such an extraordinary range of human possibilities. Imagine a meeting between two Jews. The first is the man addressed by the Psalmist here, the man at the head of his table, or, perhaps better, one of the olive shoots around his table, a boy of, say, eighteen years. The second is that other young Jew of whom Isaiah dreamed:

> For to us a child is born,
>   to us a son is given;
> and the government will be upon his shoulder,
>   and his name will be called
> "Wonderful Counselor, Mighty God,
>   Everlasting Father, Prince of Peace." (Isa. 9:6)

Whatever the logical or theological contradiction between the two visions, there is a night-and-day emotional difference between them. But how irresistible each is on its own terms! Which boy do you choose?

And the deeper, biographical question, of course: Which boy does God choose? In Psalms, on balance, God chooses the olive shoot over the branch of Jesse, the symbol of the Davidic, messianic line. The holy king is dead; long live the pious commoner:

> Better the little that the righteous man has
> than the great abundance of the wicked.
> For the arms of the wicked shall be broken,
> but the Lord is the support of the righteous. . . .
> I have been young and am now old,
> but I have never seen a righteous man abandoned,
> or his children seeking bread.
> He is always generous, and lends,
> and his children are held blessed. (Ps. 37:16–17, 25–26)

If the question God asks through the prophets, and essentially of himself, is Can we begin again? the question the Jews ask in the Psalms, after the failure of prophecy, is Can we again begin again? They answer their question in the affirmative by circling back not, as God himself did when speaking through the prophets, to cosmic and historic victories of yore, but to the law as a good in itself—indeed as God himself. When the Lord gave the law at Sinai, he himself did not become lawful by giving it. Power, not lawfulness, was his defining feature. But now, to speak plainly, the Lord has been defeated. He has only the memory of victory. And by a paradoxical move, the Jews are taking the law imposed on them and imposing it on him by their very delight in it, by their very celebration of it as his precious thoughts. The idea of morality as an end rather than a means, as a good in itself rather than an instrument to achieve some other good, is an idea even at this point still in the making. A happy family life is, after all, no mean reward. And by, as it were, retrojecting God's projection of himself, his law, back into him, by personalizing it and inserting their acceptance of it into a personal relationship with him, the Jews who collected the Psalms, dividing them into five books, mirroring the five books of Torah, moved that idea an enormous step toward accomplishment.

God has been continually surprised by what ensued from his initial creation of an image of himself. And the change in him—the taming, we might almost call it—that occurs in Psalms is scarcely the least of these surprises. We all know the trick of forcing a performer offstage by applause. The Psalms do nothing so crude as that, but their praise certainly goes disproportionately to *ṣedeq* and *ḥesed*, God's righteousness and his steadfast love, rather than to his prowess in battle or his bounty. But if God is surprised, so are the Jews, for they owe this new relationship with God to the gentiles via the accommodation made for the gentiles by the prophets. Tacitly, this much of prophecy does find its way into the Psalms.

As monotheism came to final formulation in Second Isaiah, it became apparent that the gentiles would have to be accommodated in some way in Israel's covenant with the Lord. But in the end, the place made for them became a place occupied as well by the Jews. The Noachian covenant, until the prophets the only formal covenant in the Tanakh that did not distinguish Israelites from gentiles, did not in fact require worship of anyone. By its meager terms, human beings, plant eaters in the garden of Eden, were permitted to kill and eat animals, so long as they did not eat them alive (this is the meaning of the command at Genesis 9:4, "you must not eat flesh with its life-blood in it") but forbidden to kill their own kind. Nothing else was required of them. God, for his part, agreed to refrain from destroying the whole world again; he promised nothing more. To a much later generation of anthropologists, the Noachic covenant might be fascinating as a dim memory of the transition of the human species from pure gatherers to hunter-gatherers and from hunters eating the kill immediately, as simple predators, to hunters eating the corpse of the kill after a delay at least long enough for it to bleed to death. But abstention from devouring a live kill or murdering a fellow human amounts to exceedingly little as the acknowledgment of God, much less as the expression of a relationship with God, and in speaking to the prophets of his new relationship with the gentiles, the Lord never mentions Noah.

The covenant within which the Lord intends—or once intended—to accommodate the gentiles is the Mosaic covenant. To cite again two passages cited earlier,

> The foreigners who join themselves to the Lord,
> to minister to him, to love the name of the Lord,
> and to be his servants,

every one who keeps the sabbath, and does not profane it,
  and holds fast to my covenant—
these I will bring to my holy mountain,
  and make them joyful in my house of prayer;
their burnt offerings and their sacrifices
  will be accepted on my altar;
for my house shall be called a house of prayer
  for all peoples. (Isa. 56:6–7)

But this development, the Lord assures Israel, will only enrich his original covenant partner:

Aliens shall stand and feed your flocks,
  foreigners shall be your plowmen and vinedressers;
but you shall be called the priests of the Lord,
  men shall speak of you as the ministers of our God;
you shall eat the wealth of the nations,
  and in their riches you shall glory. (61:5–6)

In other words, the gentiles will be included in the obligations of the covenant, and this is clearly regarded as a boon and a privilege for them, but only Israel will be materially enriched by the covenant. In the event, of course, the gentiles did not volunteer to accept the covenant or come to make burnt offerings and sacrifices in Jerusalem. But it may well have been through a consideration of the religious situation of the gentiles that the idea of Torah as boon and delight, quite apart from the blessings and curses of Deuteronomy 28, first came to the fore. And after the failure of prophecy, which is to say the failure of God to restore Israel to autonomy and even hegemony as he had said he would, the Jews were faced with the choice of Torah as a good in itself or no Torah at all. They chose the former and celebrated their choice in the Psalms.

To say this is to present, as coolly as if it were a move in chess, a change that was surely attended by inner as well as outer agony. When, under Hezekiah, Jerusalem succeeded in turning back the army of the Assyrian Sennacherib, Judah seems to have made the tragically false inference that its fortress capital was impregnable. As the truth began to dawn on them and the fall of Jerusalem began to seem not just possible but inevitable, a ghastly panic took hold. The Jerusalem Bible translates Jeremiah 30:5–7, from the eve of disaster, as follows:

We have heard a cry of panic,
of terror, not of peace.
Now ask and see:
can a man bear children?
Then why do I see each man
with his hands on his loins like a woman in labor?
Why has every face grown pale?
Disaster! This is the great day,
no other like it:
a time of distress for Jacob,
though he will be saved from it.

It seemed, in other words, almost contrary to nature itself that Jerusalem should fall. And though this was a disaster that would also overtake the guilty, it was nonetheless distressing that short of that point the guilty seemed to prosper. Jeremiah again, this time in the Jewish Publication Society translation:

You will win, O Lord, if I make claim against You,
Yet I shall present charges against You:
Why does the way of the wicked prosper?
Why are the workers of treachery at ease?
You have planted them, and they have taken root,
They spread, they even bear fruit.
You are present in their mouths,
But far from their thoughts.
Yet You, Lord, have noted and observed me;
You have tested my heart, and found it with You.
Drive them out like sheep to the slaughter,
Prepare them for the day of slaying! (Jer. 12:1–3)

The defeat itself was such as to all but drive the nation mad. Almost equally mind-rending was the scandal that the innocent, those who knew in their hearts that they had indeed kept the covenant, were punished along with the guilty. This view receives extended, explicit, and, in context, shocking formulation in Psalm 44, which rehearses God's past victories as many another Psalm does, and humbly concedes that it was

not by their sword that they took the land,
their arm did not give them victory,
but Your right hand, Your arm,

> and Your goodwill,
> for You favored them. (Ps. 44:4)

But to this bright past the Psalmist contrasts the dark present, in which

> You sell Your people for no fortune,
> You set no high price on them (44:13),

and then proceeds to the core of the indictment:

> All this has come upon us,
> yet we have not forgotten You,
> or been false to Your covenant.
> Our hearts have not gone astray,
> nor have our feet swerved from Your path,
> though You cast us, crushed, to where the sea monster is,
> and covered us over with deepest darkness.
> If we forgot the name of our God
> and spread forth our hands to a foreign god,
> God would surely search it out,
> for He knows the secrets of the heart.
> It is for Your sake that we are slain all day long,
> that we are regarded as sheep to be slaughtered.
> Rouse Yourself; why do You sleep, O Lord?
> Awaken, do not reject us forever!
> Why do You hide Your face,
> ignoring our affliction and distress? (44:18–25)

The language—"Rouse Yourself" and so on—echoes Second Isaiah; but that prophet, when promising that the Lord would rouse himself and awake, conceded that the punishment inflicted on Israel had been deserved even if, ultimately, it had gone too far. No such concession is made here. Some historical critics believe that Psalm 44 must have been written in response to some later defeat, and so it may have been; but by its placement, it can only refer backward to the defeat by Babylon and to the condition of the restored nation as a byword and a laughingstock among its neighbors. The mention of the sea monster recalls the flood and alludes to the deepest, most unspeakable fear of the demonic persona still latent in the God of precious thoughts.

Guarantor

"In the Markets She Raises Her Voice"

PROVERBS

The new centrality of the law as a defining reality in the life of God creates a new vulnerability in him, a vulnerability not, as before, to rival gods but to rival laws or law equivalents. This is the drama hidden in one of the least read books in the Tanakh, the Book of Proverbs. God's law, which in the Psalms is regarded as his most important and most abiding self-expression, yields much of its space in Proverbs to a larger, anonymous, and impersonal tradition of secular wisdom, and this alternative to the law is "preached" by a completely unexpected alternative to the prophets—namely, Lady Wisdom, a mysteriously allegorical combination of goddess, prophetess, and angel.

The subtle emergence of Lady Wisdom as God's rival as well as his handmaiden or consort is accompanied by a paradoxical reversal of the role that the Psalms assign to God. In the Psalms, God is the guarantor of justice in a world of karma without samsara—a world, that is, in which the good are rewarded and the evil punished within their own lifetimes or, at most, in the persons of their children or grandchildren. Not quite so in Proverbs, where God appears for the first time as the mysterious being to whom reference must be made and from whom recourse must be had when just the opposite occurs—that is, when the good are seen to be punished and the wicked rewarded. God continues to be honored as the creator, through Wisdom, of a world which enjoys in general an immanent moral order—a world, in other words, in which reward for the good and punishment for the wicked is on the whole a natural and therefore automatic outcome. God is not expected to ensure the functioning of this moral order by intervening ad hoc with rewards and punishments. These come about as the intrinsic result of mankind's cultivation, or otherwise, of human wisdom, a pursuit sometimes characterized as devotion to Lady Wisdom. God created the world through her, Proverbs says, and the world's normal and normally benign functioning is in her custody. God takes or is presumed to have taken a direct hand only in counterintuitive, unpredicted, unwelcome limit cases.

In brief, when things go right, as Proverbs expects they will, God is honored as the creator of a world in which things go right, while when things go wrong, God is acknowledged as the source as well as the explanation of exceptions to the rule. God is marginal as a picture frame is marginal. He is not often in the picture, but the picture requires him.

This quasi-negative but necessary framing function for God is the meaning of a proverb—"The beginning of wisdom is the fear of the Lord"—that is repeated almost as a mantra three times in Proverbs (1:7, 9:10, and 15:33), at least once in the Psalms (111:10), and elsewhere in these books with minor variations. Its meaning, in a secular formulation, might be "The first thing a man of understanding must understand is that there is much that he will never understand." Mankind will ever strive to bring life under control, and Proverbs commends that effort. But a man who does not recognize how much inevitably will escape his control is doomed to frustration and despair. Common sense is, so to speak, never more than a clearing in the forest, and it is best to be prepared for this at the outset. Proverbs 16 gives this view, central as it is to the marriage of Torah and Wisdom, an extended gloss:

> A man may arrange his thoughts,
> But what he says depends on the Lord.
> All the ways of a man seem right to him,
> But the Lord probes motives.
> Entrust your affairs to the Lord,
> And your plans will succeed.
> The Lord made everything for a purpose,
> Even the wicked for an evil day. (Prov. 16:1–4)

There is no easy transposition of this last line into a secular key since, now as then, it is at just this point that secular wisdom reaches its limit. But we must recognize, all the same, that Proverbs 16:4 is an answer of a new and most untraditional kind to the entreaty in literally scores of Psalms that the Lord put the petitioner's wicked enemies in their place, give them what they deserve, and give the righteous petitioner his own due. "No," the Lord is here imagined to respond, "I have my purpose for them, and [by clear implication] you must endure them."

This is both a drastic restriction and a drastic revision of God's role as protagonist of the Bible. In a sense, mankind now becomes the protagonist, and God the antagonist. The happier outcomes are assigned to human effort, and God is assigned ultimate, personal responsibility for those times when the opposition, human and circumstantial, proves insuperable. He is made, in a remarkable way, the personification of all that; and as such, he becomes, if not the explanation of it, then at least a name for it. Instead of saying, in other words, "There is no figuring it out," Proverbs says, "There is no figuring *him* out."

Secular, contemporary reformulations tend to make impersonal what Proverbs makes personal. Thus, for example, "Into each life some rain must fall" or such uglier, more recent versions as "Life's a bitch, and then you die" or "Shit happens." But these actually fall short as reformulations of Proverbs 16:4 because they are in no way confessions that life exceeds the speaker's understanding. On the contrary, they are smug in their confidence that all relevant evidence has been examined, and this is the bitter result. In order to avoid claiming omniscience, they would have to admit mystery in some way and thereby cease to be as terminally secular as they wish to be.

The verse "The Lord made everything for a purpose, / Even the wicked for an evil day" may have been most comforting to those who wrote and preserved it because of its assumption that the Lord was good, but the same verse has a liberating potential even if nothing is assumed other than that the Lord is mysterious or, at a further reduction, that life itself is a mystery and not just a mess. Better a humble but at least potentially merciful uncertainty, in short, than a proud and inevitably masochistic certainty. This is perhaps Pascal's wager two millennia before Pascal. And yet it is scarcely a triumphant moment for God himself. Now that the world is up and running, God is to be summoned only when things are at their worst, so he is all but forced to be always and only his own worst self. "Comfort, comfort my people" is a line he no longer gets much chance to speak. In most troubles, mankind comforts itself or has itself to blame. There is no scope at all for God's newfound tenderness. Rather than a comforting person, he here seems to be a semicomforting assumption at best and the old destroyer at worst.

Reading Proverbs after reading Psalms is rather like leaving the steamy murmur of a crowded church where hidden agonies and immoderate hopes have all been on sometimes painful display and stepping into the busy briskness of the marketplace outside the church door—close enough, to be sure, but still outside. The stakes out here in the daylight may be much lower, the only eloquence a rough-

and-ready tartness of repartee, yet there is something bracing about the change. Everyone still believes in God, indeed casually refers to him in every other sentence, but everyone also seems to have other business than his in hand and to be relying on mother wit, as we might well put it, rather than on father or grandfather God, for the Lord God is indeed beginning to seem an elderly relative still nominally the head of the house but no longer very active as a manager.

In Proverbs' marriage of Torah and Wisdom, Torah—or at least the Lord whom Torah honors as its author—deepens Wisdom. But Wisdom also broadens and brightens Torah by discussing such matters as character formation and prudence, parts of human moral experience about which Torah is generally silent. The most surprising feature of this new synthesis, however, is that in it prophecy, about which Psalms maintains such a pained silence, is revived, after a fashion, as Lady Wisdom preaching on a street corner. But what kind of prophecy does she preach? Dispensing with impassioned indictments, intoxicated visions, all mention of foreign countries, and any prediction of apocalyptic doom, she has the mannerisms of a prophetess but a message that scarcely goes beyond "If you make a fool of yourself, don't say I didn't warn you." Her revival of prophecy is, in a way, its burial:

> Wisdom cries aloud in the streets,
> Raises her voice in the squares.
> At the head of the busy streets she calls;
> At the entrance of the gates, in the city, she speaks out:
> "How long will you simple ones love simplicity,
> You scoffers be eager to scoff,
> You dullards hate knowledge?
> You are indifferent to my rebuke;
> I will now speak my mind to you,
> And let you know my thoughts.
> Since you refused me when I called,
> And paid no heed when I extended my hand,
> You spurned all my advice,
> And would not hear my rebuke,
> I will laugh at your calamity,
> And mock when terror comes upon you,
> When terror comes like a disaster,
> And calamity arrives like a whirlwind,
> When trouble and distress come upon you.
> Then they shall call me but I will not answer;

They shall seek me but not find me.
Because they hated knowledge,
And did not choose fear of the Lord;
They refused my advice,
And disdained all my rebukes,
They shall eat the fruit of their ways,
And have their fill of their own counsels.
The tranquillity of the simple will kill them,
And the complacency of dullards will destroy them.
But he who listens to me will dwell in safety,
Untroubled by the terror of misfortune."
(1:20–33, italics added)

In prophecy as we have hitherto seen it, the events mentioned in the italicized lines would have been presented as punishment rather than, as here, mere comeuppance. Here the only punishment is self-inflicted; it is simply the predictable, built-in consequence of foolish behavior.

Is it surprising that this clearest, largest eruption of the feminine into the relationship of mankind and God should turn out to speak with the voice of common sense? That will depend, obviously, on what you understand by "the feminine" and also on what you expect of a mother or a wife. Historical criticism has paid little attention to the possibility that Wisdom may be either mankind's mother or God's wife, but this is largely because historical criticism has generally taken her to be a personification of the wisdom of the male God and therefore, notwithstanding the feminine grammatical endings, ultimately male herself. She has been seen as a figure of speech loosely akin to the Word of the Lord in the endlessly repeated figure of speech "Then the Word of the Lord came to. . . ."

In fact, however, her identity is a good bit more complicated than that, for Lady Wisdom speaks not just *for* God but also in her own name *about* God and about her relationship with him. The word *goddess* probably does misrepresent her; but even taking her as allegorical rather than mythological, she should almost certainly be seen as the personification of human wisdom in the newly autonomous sense of which we were just speaking rather than as the personification of unfathomable divine wisdom. As such she may well be spoken of, metaphorically, both as God's partner, even God's wife (mankind cooperating with God), and as mankind's mother (mankind caring for its own). And as both wife and mother, Wisdom wakes the echoes of Asherah.

Wisdom speaks of her double relationship with God and mankind at Proverbs 8:22–9:6:

"The Lord created me at the beginning of His course
As the first of His works of old.
In the distant past I was fashioned,
At the beginning, at the origin of earth.
There was still no deep when I was brought forth,
No springs rich in water;
Before [the foundations of] the mountains were sunk,
Before the hills I was born.
He had not yet made earth and fields,
Or the world's first clumps of clay.
I was there when He set the heavens into place;
When He fixed the horizon upon the deep;
When He made the heavens above firm,
And the fountains of the deep gushed forth;
When He assigned the sea its limits,
So that its waters never transgress His command;
When He fixed the foundations of the earth,
I was with Him as a confidant,
A source of delight every day,
Rejoicing before Him at all times,
Rejoicing in His inhabited world,
Finding delight with mankind.
Now, sons, listen to me;
Happy are they who keep my ways.
Heed discipline and become wise;
Do not spurn it.
Happy is the man who listens to me,
Coming early to my gates each day,
Waiting outside my doors.
For he who finds me finds life
And obtains favor from the Lord.
But he who misses me destroys himself;
All who hate me love death."

Wisdom has built her house,
She has hewn her seven pillars.
She has prepared the feast,
Mixed the wine,

And also set the table.
She has sent out her maids to announce
On the heights of the town,
"Let the simple enter here";
To those devoid of sense she says,
"Come, eat my food
And drink the wine that I have mixed;
Give up simpleness and live,
Walk in the way of understanding."

At the point in this speech where Wisdom says to mankind, "Now, sons, listen to me," the burden of proof might seem to shift to those who would deny that she is in any way a mother not just because of the use of the word *banim*, "sons" or "children," but also because of the clearly parental manner. But in what sense, if any, can the speaker be a wife? True, the fact that God has created her by no means rules out this possibility. As his wife, in any ancient Near Eastern context, she would not need to be his uncreated equal. Nothing would prevent him from creating her as his consort after or—as she insists—before creating mankind. No, the difficulty in naming Wisdom as God's consort appears to lie rather in the fact that, despite his delight in her, she seems as much assistant as companion. She is a builder, a butcher, a baker, a vintner, as well as a teacher and a "confidant." But does all this taken together make her a wife?

Obviously, one must first ask: What is a wife? In the entire Bible, there is only one description of the wife, and it comes, as it happens, in just this book, at Proverbs 31:10–31, which opens:

What a rare find is a capable wife!
Her worth is far beyond that of rubies.
Her husband puts his confidence in her,
And lacks no good thing.
She is good to him, never bad,
All the days of her life.
She looks for wool and flax,
And sets her hand to them with a will.
She is like a merchant fleet,
Bringing her food from afar.
She rises while it is still night,
And supplies provisions for her household,
The daily fare of her maids.

> She sets her mind on an estate and acquires it;
> She plants a vineyard by her own labors.
> She girds herself with strength
> And performs her tasks with vigor. (31:10–17)

In the ancient Near East, wives were both a form and a source of wealth for their husbands. Like Lady Wisdom, the good wife in this description combines delight with good management. By the same token, then, if we find this combination in Lady Wisdom, we may infer that she is to be considered, at least metaphorically, as God's wife. She and God do not have even an analogous genital relationship. There is not the slightest hint of that in the text. But she is genuinely female in the same characterological way that he has always been genuinely male, and their partnership to that extent is a connubium. And if in addition she represents mankind as a whole, where is the difficulty? In the prophets, God has repeatedly and ardently called himself Israel's husband. Here, he would be mankind's husband in a relationship in which mankind is an unusually vigorous and self-reliant wife.

It need come as no surprise that as the Tanakh shifts its attention to practical skills, its attention to women should grow. Before as well as after the exile, several of Israel's larger neighbors enjoyed a noticeably higher level of material development than Israel did as well as a deeper integration into world commerce. The skilled workmen who built David's palace and Solomon's temple were brought in from Phoenicia. Certainly before and probably after the exile, foreign wives were a major channel by which non-Israelite material culture entered Israelite life. Despite the severe strictures placed on intermarriage in Torah, Moses, David, and, most notoriously, Solomon (not to speak of Abraham, Judah, and Joseph) all are reported to have had foreign wives. Solomon's many wives are blamed in I Kings for the introduction of foreign religion into Israel, but doubtless they also brought foreign crafts, languages, music, food, and so on—in short, all the foreign forms of industry and wealth—and doubtless taught what they brought with them to their Israelite sisters. Thus was the good wife "like a merchant fleet"; and thus over time, the sense may well have grown in Israel that women, especially foreign women, were the repository of much of the material expertise of the world.

If this is the case, then we should not assume that every time Proverbs begins one of its anonymous speeches "My son," a father is to be imagined as the speaker. The New Revised Standard Version's "inclusive language," substituting "My child" for "My son" throughout, is at odds with the content of a good many speeches that seem explicitly aimed at young men; but if it is rarely easy to imagine a young woman as the hearer, it is often quite easy to imagine an older woman as the speaker. Not that Proverbs is a feminist text: By contemporary standards, it is serenely sexist, inveighing repeatedly, for example, against the loose woman with nary a word about the loose man. But often a closer look exposes an interesting ambiguity, especially where sexual morality is concerned.

Who is speaking in Proverbs 7, a long speech against the loose woman that is barely begun before it turns to an eyewitness account of seduction as seen through a latticed window? A man might, of course, watch a seduction through a latticed window, but this is just the vantage from which, in a Near Eastern society accustomed to female enclosure, a respectable woman would be most likely to witness such a scene. It is easy to imagine, as a result, that "my son" is being warned against the loose woman by his mother. Daringly, the speaker imagines a woman of her own social class, a woman married to a man of some means, betraying her husband in his absence by seducing a young stranger. Who but a mother could imagine so well what a woman of a certain age might say to an innocent like her boy?

From the window of my house,
Through my lattice, I looked out
And saw among the simple,
Noticed among the youths,
A lad devoid of sense.
He was crossing the street near her corner,
Walking toward her house
In the dusk of evening,
In the dark hours of night.
A woman comes toward him
Dressed like a harlot, with set purpose.
She is bustling and restive;
She is never at home.
Now in the street, now in the square,
She lurks at every corner.
She lays hold of him and kisses him;
Brazenly she says to him,

"I had to make a sacrifice of well-being;
Today I fulfilled my vows.
Therefore I have come out to you,
Seeking you, and have found you.
I have decked my couch with covers
Of dyed Egyptian linen;
I have sprinkled my bed
With myrrh, aloes, and cinnamon.
Let us drink our fill of love till morning;
Let us delight in amorous embrace.
For the man of the house is away;
He is off on a distant journey.
He took his bag of money with him
And will return only at mid-month." (7:6–20)

Feminine authorship seems plausible for this passage on another ground besides the lattice window. Though obviously full of resentment and censure, the writer is quite without the kind of visceral revulsion that the prophets so often seem to feel at the very thought of a woman in a state of sexual arousal. The writer sees the loose woman as, with all her faults, a fellow human being and not, as a Jeremiah would see her, as a beast in heat:

a wild ass, used to wilderness,
in her heat sniffing the wind!
Who can restrain her lust?
None who seek her need weary themselves;
in her month they will find her.
(RSV; Jer. 2:24)

Metaphorical prostitution and literal prostitution, male as well as female, are inseparable for the prophets, and with reason. When Jeremiah begins this indictment of Israel for Baal-worship by saying, "On every high hill and under every green tree you have sprawled and played the whore" (2:20), he is referring to the sacralized sexual relations that were a part of the fertility cult of Baal and Asherah. But what is it that appalls him more, apostasy or fornication? For Proverbs, a whore at her most brazen is not to be compared to an unclean animal in heat.

Proverbs may have occasional sharp words about sexual misconduct, but much of the time its writers simply show a lively interest in the subject. Whom do we imagine, what kind of man or woman, juxtaposing the following two bons mots?

> Three things are too wonderful for me;
> four I do not understand:
> the way of an eagle in the sky,
> the way of a serpent on a rock,
> the way of a ship on the high seas,
> and the way of a man with a maiden.
>
> This is the way of an adulteress:
> she eats, and wipes her mouth,
> and says, "I have done no wrong."
> (RSV; Prov. 30:18–20)

This is, as the saying goes, splitting the arrow, a bull's-eye followed by another bull's-eye, eloquence about the wonder of sexual love followed by superb bluntness about what it can sometimes become. There is no reason whatsoever why "my son" might not have seen both arrows shot by his mother.

So might he also have heard from her the wry and pungent lesson offered at 6:6–11:

> Lazybones, go to the ant;
> Study its ways and learn.
> Without leaders, officers, or rulers,
> It lays up its stores during the summer,
> Gathers in its food at the harvest.
> How long will you lie there, lazybones;
> When will you wake from your sleep?
> A bit more sleep, a bit more slumber,
> A bit more hugging yourself in bed,
> And poverty will come calling upon you,
> And want, like a man with a shield.

Surely it is beyond argument that, time out of mind, Jewish parents, like all parents, have found themselves urging industry upon their children. And yet until Proverbs such sentiments do not receive even the most modest formal accommodation in Israelite, Judean, or Jewish religious experience. No book of the Tanakh before Proverbs contains anything comparable to "Go to the ant." The Decalogue contains no commandment "Thou shalt work." And on innumerable occasions God has stressed in speaking to his people that it was on his power rather than their own that they should rely. We have referred more than once to what is perhaps the most striking example of this—namely, Deuteronomy 6:10–12:

> When the Lord your God brings you into the land that He swore to your fathers, Abraham, Isaac, and Jacob, to assign to you—great and flourishing cities that you did not build, houses full of all good things that you did not fill, hewn cisterns that you did not hew, vineyards and olive groves that you did not plant—and you eat your fill, take heed that you do not forget the Lord who freed you from the land of Egypt, the house of bondage.

Moses is not licensing laziness per se, but his aggressive deemphasis of the importance of human effort in Israelite achievement began a tradition that continues unbroken to the point we have now reached—not, we may be sure, in the unwritten life of the nation but very definitely in its written literature.

Sigmund Freud defined happiness, famously, as *"Lieben und Arbeiten,"* "love and work." Lady Wisdom, as we have just seen, is frank about sex and frankly interested in sex, a hard worker and an advocate of hard work. She is not Asherah redux, but she does take Asherah's ancient symbol as her own:

> She [Wisdom] is a tree of life to those who grasp her,
> And whoever holds on to her is happy. (Prov. 3:18)

We may recall that the tree of life was the tree whose fruit the Lord God feared Adam and Eve would "take also . . . and eat, and live forever!" (Gen. 3:22). This tree was the second for which the Lord God was concerned. The first, the object of his direct prohibition, was the one called "the tree of the knowledge of good and evil." After Adam and Eve ate from that tree, the Lord God said: "Now . . . the man has become like one of us, knowing good and evil." However, for Adam and Eve themselves, that first tree seems to have been not very unlike the spreading green tree of Asherah, for when they tasted its fruit, they knew desire for the first time: "Then . . . they perceived that they were naked."

When Lady Wisdom insists on her earliness, when she places herself in the primal scene of creation, close to God in a relationship of delight, and when we find her represented by the tree of life, a tree standing not just for sexual fertility but for all the practical skills that support life, we hear many echoes of Asherah. But it would be mistaken to say that Wisdom now feminizes God's character by being absorbed into it. She remains distinct from him by representing, instead, collective humanity, God's image and God's antagonist. God's full command to his image at Genesis 1:28 was "Be fertile and increase, fill the earth and master it; and rule the fish of the sea, the birds of the sky, and all the living things that creep on earth." If the first half of that command was a command to beget and bear children, the second half was a command to use wisdom—the created, human strengths of mind and body—to provide all that children would require. God's relationship with Adam and Eve, though the word *covenant* is never used of it, was implicitly a covenant that, minimally, he would not prevent what he had commanded.

But then, at the flood, he did prevent it; and after the flood his covenant with Abraham compromised it. Lady Wisdom personifies mankind, by a roundabout path indeed, obeying God's initial command and reclaiming God's initial promise. But was God, even supposing his intentions to be the purest and stablest, ever able to keep his promise? This is the question that Proverbs leaves unanswered by assigning to God the role it does. And this is just the question that is taken up with a vengeance in the Book of Job: Can God be trusted?

10

Confrontation

Among the books of the Bible, the Book of Job has long been a favorite in literary circles. In the United States and in the twentieth century alone, poets Hart Crane, Robert Frost, Archibald MacLeish, W. S. Merwin, and John Ashbery, not to speak of comic playwright Neil Simon, have all based important work on it. Ranging further afield in space and time, one could easily assemble a much longer list, for the spectacle of a truly innocent man in unmerited agony—the central scene in this book—touches the deepest of philosophical and psychological chords. Secular exegetes have often enough seen the Book of Job as the self-refutation of the entire Judeo-Christian tradition. In Frost's "A Masque of Reason," God calls Job "the Emancipator of your God" and thanks him for helping

> To stultify the Deuteronomist
> And change the tenor of religious thought.

Political commentator William Safire entitled his book on Job *The First Dissident*. Even the most orthodox exegetes, however, have been quick to concede that Job's agonized demand that God explain why his righteous servant must suffer calls the existence and character of God into question with unique urgency. For the purposes of this book, what counts most is that God's destructive or demonic side, already presented in the Tanakh, is here brought to full consciousness in his mind as well as ours, thanks to a climactic confrontation with an individual human being. The remaining books of the Tanakh, though interesting and moving in ways that we shall briefly consider, never quite erase the admittedly disturbing impression of God that this confrontation leaves behind.

That much stated clearly at the start, it must be noted that if Job is a dissident, he is by no means the first dissident in the Bible, and that the Job-writer only rather indirectly stultifies the Deuteronomist. Though the eloquence of the Job-writer's poetry is beyond compare, neither his statement nor his solution of the problem of innocent suffering is without previous parallel in the Bible. As a statement of the problem of innocent suffering, the Book of Job does not go beyond Psalm 44:

> All this has come upon us,
> yet we have not forgotten You,
> or been false to Your covenant.
> Our hearts have not gone astray,
> nor have our feet swerved from Your path,
> though You cast us, crushed, to where the sea monster is,
> and covered us over with deepest darkness. (Ps. 44:18–20)

And as a solution to that problem, the Book of Job does not go beyond Proverbs 16:4, a verse already repeatedly quoted:

> The Lord made everything for a purpose,
> Even the wicked for an evil day.

Extrabiblical parallels to the Book of Job are often cited; but it is more important to note that nothing subversive in this book—certainly nothing in the speeches of Job himself—has not been posed in one form or another in one of the books that precede Job in a straight-through reading of the Bible. True, some important and relevant ideas about the providential function of suffering from earlier in the Bible, such as Second Isaiah's theology of suffering, are ignored in this book. But as a presentation of doubts about God or those dark intuitions about the destructive, inimical side of God that we have already so often glimpsed, the Book of Job comes as a culmination rather than an inauguration.

As regards the Deuteronomist in particular, it must be noted against Frost that, since Job is not an Israelite, his sufferings do not constitute any violation of the Deuteronomic covenant. Job has never heard of Moses. Nor does anything about the structure of the Book of Job suggest that it is to be taken as an allegory for the sufferings of Israel during or after the Babylonian exile. Neither Job nor God nor Satan nor any of Job's accusers ever so much as alludes to the history of Israel. The only covenant Job knows is the covenant of Eden, so to call it, and he does not know this by knowing the Israelite creation myth as such. He merely believes that God is the creator and good and that a good God would not create a world in which an innocent man like himself would be made to suffer for no good reason. His cosmology is, in effect, that of the just-concluded Book of Proverbs minus the Jewish or Torah-derived escape clause.

The Book of Job poses a profound new challenge, but it does so, as it were, by recombination. Having adopted the generally reassuring worldview of Proverbs, it then recurs by implication to the most disturbing moment in Genesis. In effect, the Job-writer does not take on all comers. He takes on one comer in a way that has spectacularly wide implications. To appreciate this, it is necessary to think somewhat less about Job and his plight and somewhat more about God and what we might call his embarrassment. The worldview that the Job-writer intends to challenge is the sunny folk wisdom whose influence on the Book of Proverbs we have just reviewed. According to that tradition, the world God has created is one in which the righteous are usually rewarded and the wicked punished. But within Proverbs, the Torah of the Jews has already provided a crucial correction to this otherwise not particularly Jewish view. "The beginning of wisdom is the fear of the Lord"; in other words, the righteous are rewarded and the wicked punished *except when the Lord, for mysterious reasons of his own, decrees otherwise.* At the start of the Book of Job, neither Job nor his friends have learned this corrected or, as we may quite properly call it, this Jewish version of wisdom. But they have all learned it by the end of the book, after the Lord has responded to Job not by giving reasons for Job's suffering but only by rebuking Job for imagining that a human being may dare to call God to account and, crucially, after Job has withstood this rebuke and been rewarded for doing so.

During the long central section of the Book of Job, as Job and his interlocutors debate his moral condition, they refer to the divinity as *ʾelohim*, "God," using a common noun that is routinely used in Hebrew for the God of Israel but may be used for other gods as well. The divinity who rebukes Job, speaking out of a whirlwind at the end of the book, is *yahweh*, "the Lord," a divinity generally known by that name only to Israel, though the gentile Job also calls him by that name in the opening fable. What difference does the nomenclature make? Two kinds of difference.

First of all, the impact on any Jew reading or hearing the conclusion of the book in Hebrew would be analogous to the impact on a contemporary European or American audience of the sudden intrusion of the phrase "Our Lord" on a long public discussion of Jesus. "Jesus" is a name available to all. "Our Lord" is only used by Christians among themselves. The Book of Job is, analogously, a story in which "Our Lord" is the protagonist in a story that very quickly yields to an extended philosophical dialogue about "Jesus," which dialogue then yields, in turn, to the continuation of the story when "Our Lord" himself intervenes in the discussion about "Jesus."

The second difference is the difference we last saw in the creation and flood narratives that begin the Bible. The world as created by God, *ʾelohim*, was almost wholly positive; nothing in it was forbidden to mankind, whom God commanded only to be fertile, to increase, and to have dominion. By contrast, the world as created by the Lord, *yahweh*, was shot through with a kind of danger; there was indeed a prohibition in it, and when the prohibition was not observed, massive and largely inexplicable punishment followed swiftly. A similar difference obtained at the second beginning, after the flood. God, *ʾelohim*, then called on mankind again to be fertile and increase. The Lord, *yahweh*, merely promised never again to "destroy every living being, as I have done." The angry, imperious, and literally stormy (speaking from the whirlwind) Lord *(yahweh)* who confronts Job at the climax of the Book of Job is no stranger to Israel: Since the Exodus and the exultant cry "the Lord is a warrior," his personality has been by far the dominant one in the fusion character of the Lord God. But Job seems initially baffled by God in this guise, God as destroyer and creator at once. In the closing theophany of the Book of Job, he meets him for the first time and is struck almost dumb.

The Job-writer does more, however, than just confront a righteous but naive man with the full ambivalence of the Lord God. He goes a large and subversive step further. We have said that, whether as God or Lord, the deity has within him a submerged demon, a serpent, a chaos monster, a dragon goddess of destruction. The Job-writer externalizes that inner conflict by presenting God as prey to temptation by an actual demon, Satan, who is more clearly separate from God in the Book of Job than Wisdom is separate from him in the Book of Proverbs.

And this new actor is introduced to make a point. On the view taken in Proverbs, the world is generally just, but when it isn't, the Lord is presumed to have his reasons. The Job-writer accepts this view as a starting point but then speculates, in effect, "Very well, what might those reasons be?" He answers his own question by telling a profoundly blasphemous story about the Lord God. The subversive originality of the Book of Job is to be found in that blasphemy no less than in the anguished eloquence of the title character's speeches.

Fiend

"I Shudder with Sorrow for Mortal Clay"

JOB

> One day the divine beings presented themselves before the Lord, and the Adversary came along with them. The Lord said to the Adversary, "Where have you been?" The Adversary answered the Lord, "I have been roaming all over the earth." The Lord said to the Adversary, "Have you noticed My servant Job? There is no one like him on earth, a blameless and upright man who fears God and shuns evil!" The Adversary answered the Lord, "Does Job not have good reason to fear God? Why, it is You who have fenced him round, him and his household and all that he has. You have blessed his efforts so that his possessions spread out in the land. But lay Your hand upon all that he has and he will surely blaspheme You to Your face." The Lord replied to the Adversary, "See, all that he has is in your power; only do not lay a hand on him." The Adversary departed from the presence of the Lord. (Job 1:6–12)

"As flies to wanton boys, are we to the gods," the pagan King Lear put it: "They kill us for their sport." Gambling is sport, and the Lord has been tempted into making a wager with the enemy of mankind. The word that the Jewish Publication Society translates as "the Adversary" is the Hebrew *satan*, occurring here with the definite article, "the *satan*," suggesting that it is to be read as a common noun rather than a proper name. Some other translations have "Satan" at this point. For our purposes, it is quite enough that the Lord is susceptible to the suggestions of a celestial being hostile to a human being. Just this much links these opening chapters of the Book of Job with all the earlier moments in the Tanakh when the Lord God has placed or found himself in an adversarial position vis-à-vis his human creature.

As part of the game, the devil (as we may legitimately call him) is permitted to slay all Job's sons, daughters, and servants. Job does not curse God, however, and God thinks he has won the wager. But no, the devil toys with him further:

> "Skin for skin—all that a man has he will give up for his life. But lay a hand on his bones and his flesh, and he will surely blaspheme

> You to Your face." So the Lord said to the Adversary, "See, he is in your power; only spare his life." The Adversary departed from the presence of the Lord and inflicted a severe inflammation on Job from the sole of his foot to the crown of his head. He took a potsherd to scratch himself as he sat in ashes. (2:4–8)

Three of Job's friends now come "to console and comfort him" (2:11). For seven days, the four of them sit together unable to do more than weep and rend their garments. Only then does Job speak his immortal opening line. In Stephen Mitchell's translation:

> God damn the day I was born
> and the night that forced me from the womb. (3:2)

"THE WORLD in which we live can be understood as a result of muddle and accident," Bertrand Russell once wrote, "but if it is the outcome of a deliberate purpose, the purpose must have been that of a fiend." Though the Job-writer stops short of espousing the view that God is a fiend, he is certainly able to entertain an equivalent view. The world in which he imagines Job to be suffering is one ruled by a God who plays games with a fiend and is manipulated and controlled by a fiend. The never-absent demonic side of the Lord God has suddenly a demonic ally. Satan in the Book of Job is a mirror image of Wisdom in Proverbs. Just as Wisdom assumes many of the Lord's benign responsibilities, so the Adversary is seen here to have a hand in those cruel and unexplained reversals that Proverbs attributes uniquely to the Lord. Proverbs is willing to regard these as mysteries, and potentially benevolent ones at that; the Job-writer is prepared to regard them as horrors.

Many interpretations of the Book of Job see it as somehow pitting the quid-pro-quo morality of Deuteronomy or the cause-and-effect morality of Proverbs against a higher morality in which virtue is its own reward. So it may be, but it should be noted that it is the devil who introduces this higher morality and that he does so in the course of tempting the Lord into abusing Job. It is the devil who insinuates that unless practiced "for nought," virtue is not true virtue. This hard standard is definitely Satan's own coinage. In all the Bible to this point, it has never occurred to God that mankind should serve him "for nought," that is, for no reward. On the contrary, it seemed at first not to occur to God that mankind should serve him at all.

The God of Adam, the God of Noah, the God of Abraham, never sought worship and sought obedience only minimally. The God of Moses did seek both worship and obedience, but even he took it for granted that rewards should be forthcoming for such service and never suggested that he would have the right to the service if the rewards were denied, much less if they were replaced by gratuitously inflicted punishment. But the Lord, his thinking now changed on this point by the devil, withdraws reward and inflicts punishment for no reason other than to prove to the devil that Job will indeed "fear God for nought."

Obviously, one cannot take the frame story, the fable, of the Book of Job as seriously as we are taking it without giving full weight to its conclusion. After speaking his last words, Job is restored to his fortunes, and, mysteriously indeed, the Lord says that Job has spoken rightly of him, while Job's friends, who insisted on God's justice, have not done so. In so saying, the Lord seems to admit that he has indeed not been as just as Job's friends claimed he was; and strikingly enough, in his furious speech to Job, the Lord never directly claims to be just, only to be almighty. But even if the Lord is not righteous or at least not required to defend or explain his righteousness to a mere human being, he may yet, for reasons of his own, choose to be as lavish with Job on Tuesday as he was savage with him on Monday.

But then again he may not, or he may do it the other way around. Proverbs is confirmed in some abstract sense; its system holds up functionally if not morally. Job, now initiated into Jewish wisdom, knows a God who does not play by rules that human beings can wholly understand, who truly does defy understanding. But in the implicit contract joining God and mankind, God's unknowability now seems perilously close to an escape clause into which not just the entire contract but one of the contracting parties may disappear. When God himself turns out to be a gambler, all human bets are off.

Two millennia after the Job-writer wrote, the French thinker René Descartes introduced what he called "hyperbolical doubt" into his philosophy by asking whether it was not possible that a *malin génie*, an "evil genius" or fiend, had systematically distorted all human perceptions so that nothing was what it seemed to be. Though this was a possibility that Descartes entertained only theoretically, he found no way to resolve it other than by defending the thesis that God was God and would not be God if he were a deceiver or subject to deceit. If the opposite should seem to be true of God at the end of the Book of Job, then everything that precedes and follows that book would be in principle invalidated. If the devil should seem to be determining God's actions and the welfare or otherwise of those who serve God, then, looking backward through God's biography to this point, any or all of God's actions could actually have been the devil's (or a devil's). According to Exodus 31:18, the tablets of the covenant were "inscribed with the finger of God," but, really, whose finger was it? Similarly, looking forward through the remainder of God's story, nothing God might henceforth do or say would deserve to be taken at face value. Is God's idle slaughter of Job's entire family an isolated instance of such behavior in him? Why may it not be typical? How could we know? At the point where the subject of even a quasi biography or mythobiography turns out to be not himself but only a pawn for another subject about whom otherwise nothing is known, the biography must be abandoned: It simply cannot be written.

Thus, even though the Book of Job was not written to stultify the Deuteronomist or Isaiah or the Psalmist or Saint Paul but only to bring smug and schematic Near Eastern wisdom to its knees before the unpredictable Lord of the Jews, this book of the Bible achieves potentially a far broader subversion. Intuitively, the writers who have been drawn to Job as to a yawning abyss have been right. However, the subversion need not take place or, at least, may be radically contained if (1) Job can be seen not to have repented and, instead, to have withstood the Lord's speech from the whirlwind, and if (2) the Lord's restoration of Job's fortunes can be seen as his own repentance and his own break with the devil. On such a reading, Job's naive confidence in the day-by-day fairness of the world is still sharply chastened, but the Job-writer has destroyed only his intended target and not God himself. God is stronger than the devil, or, if you will, God's bright side is stronger than his dark side.

Of the Lord's wager with the devil, the crucial observation is that the Lord does not win it, he simply drops it. The first stage in the frame fable, as we have just seen, is the Lord's consenting to the devil's attack on everything except Job's body. The second stage is the Lord's consent to the torture of Job; the devil is barred only from killing the man. The third stage (fables often have three parts) should resume the heavenly debate and the Lord should say something akin to what he said after Job withstood the devil's first attack. He should boast that Job "still keeps his integrity, so you have incited me against him [a second time] for no good reason." Thus, as the Lord won the wager, would the tale end. The fable would conclude with a scene like the one in Zechariah 3:1–5, in which Joshua, the high priest, stands accused by the Adversary (here, the JPS translates as "the Accuser") but is defended by an angel and finally vindicated by the Lord himself.

In fact, the devil receives no such formal rebuke in the Book of Job. After Job gives his speeches challenging the Lord, the devil simply vanishes from the story, like the Fool from *King Lear*, and the Lord, by implication, dispenses with the wager or the trial by ordeal in light of what Job has said.

Does the Lord also regret what he did? If the Lord has nothing to apologize for, and that is certainly his contention when he rebukes Job from the whirlwind, he would also have no reason to give Job "twice what he had before" (Job 42:10). But as we saw in Second Isaiah, when the Lord promises double compensation, he implies that his own actions have gone too far. The Lord's action here, if not explicit repentance, is unmistakable atonement and implicit repentance. If there were no offense on the Lord's part, and/or if there were even a small offense on Job's part, then Job could have been restored, sadder but wiser, to the kind of modest good fortune that Proverbs favors:

> Better is a little with righteousness
> Than a large income with injustice. (Prov. 16:8)

But, the objection will come, Job is guilty of no injustice! To this, the response shouted back from nearly every line of the Bible would ordinarily be "No one is guilty of no injustice!" The Hebrew scriptures, as a national literature, are utterly remarkable in the way they cut their greatest figures down to sinful, mortal size. King David, the very type of the messiah, a man who more than any other single figure embodies the nation in its beauty and its glory, is exposed and exposed and exposed again. To the rage and despair of a Nietzsche, the national literature of the Jews is a literature without supermen, so the true and proper response of Jewish wisdom to the challenge of the Job-writer could always have been a simple denial of his major premise: There *is* no just man; we are all sinners. This is, of course, just what Job's "comforters" do say, but it is the premise of the story that Job is the exception to the rule, the impossibility incarnate, a man wholly without sin, explicitly (and uniquely) declared so by God himself.

And because of this premise, the Lord has no exit from the impasse he has created for himself. If Job does not repent, then the Lord must.

And just at this point we encounter the deepest conundrum in the traditional interpretation of the Book of Job. Job, in all his pain and grief, has (1) insisted on his own righteousness, (2) demanded that God explain why his servant must suffer, and (3) consistently expressed his trust that God would ultimately vindicate him, more than once evoking a court scene like the one in Zechariah 3, but then, according to the most common interpretation, (4) *repented of what he said.* When the Lord says that Job has spoken rightly of him, does he refer to the repentance or to the speeches? He cannot coherently refer to both if the repentance repudiates the speeches. In his second speech to Job, the Lord makes this very point with blunt clarity:

> Would you impugn My justice?
> Would you condemn Me that you may be right?
> Have you an arm like God's?
> Can you thunder with a voice like His? (Job 40:8–9)

The last word about the Book of Job will never be spoken, but a strong case can be made that Job, to his very last word, denies that the preceding questions are all the same question. He does not concede that if the answer to the second two is no, then the answer to the first two cannot be yes. Job refuses to accept mere physical power as the criterion of moral integrity.

To prove this point, we must depart (for the first and only time) from the usual method of this book. A biography of God is not a true commentary on the Bible; and in general we have neither engaged the text line by line, as a commentary must, nor debated with previous commentators and quarreled with the adequacy of their translations. If the reading of the Bible that has so far resulted has been at times a novel one, this has never been because of eccentric readings of individual lines, much less outright emendations or excisions of the Hebrew text. As regards history, we have sought only to avoid making surreptitious historical claims in the name of literary criticism. To the extent that there is a consensus view of the history of ancient Israel, we accept it. The reading offered here attempts a consciously postcritical or postmodern reintegration of mythic, fictional, and historical elements in the Bible so as to allow the character of God to stand forth more clearly from the work of which he is the protagonist.

But the pivotal importance of Job's response to the Lord dictates that an exception to this procedure be made here. The Lord's two-part speech to Job is his testament, his last words. He will not speak again in the Tanakh; yet everything, as regards the meaning of this speech, depends on how Job receives it. Unfortunately, a tradition of interpretation based on a silent correction of the Hebrew text (see below) has managed to change into repentance a reply that should properly be heard as irony responding to sarcasm. That tradition has turned a rhetorical standoff between the Lord and Job into a lopsided victory for the Lord. But since the victory is won by the Lord at his worst, the Lord as the devil's gaming partner, the victory becomes a paradoxical defeat for the Lord, and the pious intentions of the interpreters end in blasphemy. Careful reading can restore the original irony but not without an argument of occasionally tedious linguistic detail (though its most technical parts have been placed in an endnote).

FEW SPEECHES in all of literature can more properly be called overpowering than the Lord's speeches to Job from the whirlwind (Job 38–41). Were they to be set to music, nothing but Igor Stravinsky's *Rite of Spring* would come close to their surging, crashing power. But therein lies all their difficulty. The Lord refers to absolutely nothing about himself *except* his power. In fact, in one astonishing passage, following immediately on the last verse quoted earlier, he explicitly subsumes his justice to his power. Might makes right, he thunders at Job. Only if and when the wretch scraping his sores with a potsherd can unleash a demonstration of power comparable to the Lord's own will the Lord take the wretch's objections seriously:

> Deck yourself now with grandeur and eminence;
> Clothe yourself in glory and majesty.
> Scatter wide your raging anger;
> See every proud man and bring him low.
> See every proud man and humble him,
> And bring them down where they stand.
> Bury them all in the earth;
> Hide their faces in obscurity.

Then even I would praise you
For the triumph your right hand won you. (40:10–14)

The Lord presents himself, with withering sarcasm and towering bravado, as an amoral, irresistible force. But Job has never called the Lord's power into question. It is his justice of which Job has demanded an accounting. For Job and for the tradition he defends, it is the simultaneity of justice and power that makes God God. Absent either one, God is not God. At no point in the Bible, either before or after these speeches from the whirlwind, does the Lord God speak of himself as a sheer amoral power. Why then does he do so here? Why does he not rebuke Job in language like that of Psalm 36:6–7:

My faithfulness reaches to heaven,
My steadfastness to the sky;
My beneficence is like the high mountains;
My justice like the great deep.

Why does he not claim that his justice is beyond Job's understanding rather than that there is no such thing as justice? Job would be, after all, equally rebuked.

In the Psalms, the Lord's greatness as creator and master of the physical universe is always implicitly and often explicitly just a prelude to his true greatness as judge and guarantor of justice. Thus, Psalm 98:

Let the sea and all within it thunder,
   the world and its inhabitants;
   let the rivers clap their hands,
   the mountains sing joyously together
   at the presence of the Lord,
   for He is coming to rule the earth;
   He will rule the world justly,
   and its peoples with equity. (Ps. 98:7–9)

Why, this time, does the Lord stop with the prelude? He does so because he is in a bind. On this occasion, thanks to the ingenuity of the Job-fabulist, the Lord's inscrutable ways have been made all too scrutable. The deity has something to hide, to be blunt, and he hides it by rising to his full majestic stature, drawing the robes of creation around him, and regally changing the subject. Though it is most unlike the Lord God to omit his justice when contrasting himself with mankind, he has no choice. He has subjected a just man to torture on a whim. The question then becomes, as the creature lies naked in his agony, listening to his creator boast of his power to tame whales: *Will Job be taken in?*

The pathos of Job's plight is intensified, and with it the suspense of the closing pages of the book, by the fact that though the Job-writer identifies for us the voice speaking out of the whirlwind as the Lord, he does not do so for Job himself. The voice from the burning bush identified itself to Moses in the words "I am the God of your father. . . ." No comparable identifying statement comes to Job from the whirlwind, only sarcastic rhetorical questions *suggesting*, to be sure, that the voice is the voice of God but (to use the language of a much later corruption) preserving deniability. Without addressing the justice or injustice of Job's plight, without deigning to claim that he is a just God, without condescending to so much as identify himself as God, the voice from the whirlwind fairly dares Job to call his bluff:

> Shall one who should be disciplined complain against Shaddai?
> He who arraigns God must respond. (Job 40:2)

Job has repeatedly demanded that God answer Job's questions about justice. Now the owner of this voice, rather than identify himself (even the reference to *šadday*, commonly translated "the almighty," is equivocal) and answer those questions, tries to turn the tables and require that Job answer questions not about justice but about power.

If the Lord is accurately presenting himself in these speeches, then he has erased the whole of his more recent history, everything from Exodus through Psalms, and recurred to what he was at the moment of the flood, when considerations of morality barely existed for him. He has, in fact, taken an ugly step past even that point, for even as world destroyer he did not stoop to wanton personal torture. However, the Lord, as he delivers these speeches, may already have dropped his wager with the devil. He may be deliberately misrepresenting himself in the vain hope of inducing Job to recant and so letting the Lord off this most unexpected hook. For that desperation move, what better device than the unanswerable rhetorical question? The Lord's speeches to Job may be, in short, Job's last trial, a test by calculated deception in a book that, taken as a whole, is a gigantic test by calculated deception.

Everything, in the end, hangs by the thread of Job's response to these speeches of the Lord, and a thread it is: seven short verses, in two brief statements, responding to 123 verses from the Lord. But brief and heart-stunned as they are, these verses bristle with ironic double entendres and with mock-deferential quotations of the very divine words that are supposed to intimidate Job.

Consider Job's first reply:

> See, I am of small worth; what can I answer You?
> I clap my hand to my mouth.
> I have spoken once, and will not reply;
> Twice, and will do so no more. (40:4–5)

So much and no more. Job concedes nothing. "What can I answer You?" is an evasion. "I am of small worth" may be true, but when has he claimed otherwise? "I have spoken once, and will not reply; / Twice, and will do so no more" are words that defy the thunderer's demand that Job comment on his thunder.

A refusal to speak can be wondrously inscrutable. Moshe Greenberg, in his essay on Job in *The Literary Guide to the Bible*, cites Saadya Gaon writing in the tenth century: "When one interlocutor says to his partner, 'I can't answer you,' it may mean that he acquiesces in the other's position, equivalent to 'I can't gainsay the truth'; or it may mean he feels overborne by his partner, equivalent to 'How can I answer you when you have the upper hand?' " Job is in the second position, acknowledging the Lord's power and stopping there. Silence can be defiant as well as deferential. The Jerusalem Bible translates Job's reply:

> My words have been frivolous: what can I reply?
>   I had better lay my hand over my mouth.
> I have spoken once, I shall not speak again,
>   I have spoken twice, I have nothing more to say.

But following the text more literally, we may translate with a note of recalcitrance:

> Look, I am of no account. What can I tell you?
>   My hand is on my mouth.
> I have already spoken once: I will not harp.
>   Why go on? I have nothing to add.

Structurally, the Job-writer has created symmetry in the form of two demands and two refusals. Job speaks at length about justice and demands that God respond. God refuses. God speaks at length about power and demands that Job respond. Job refuses. Sheer silence on Job's part would be, for dramatic purposes, a bit too ambiguous. It is important that Job respond just enough to let us know that he is refusing to respond, enough to answer in the negative our question Will he be taken in? Both of Job's responses to the Lord are refusals to respond. Thus does he prove that he has not been taken in. Thus does he clear the way for the Lord's atonement and for the joy and reconciliation of the conclusion.

We have already considered Job's first refusal to reply. About this, Job 40:4–5, there is little exegetical dispute. The second refusal, however, is quite another matter. The Septuagint of the third and second centuries B.C.E. reads Job 42:2–6 not as a refusal to reply but as an outright recantation, beginning an exegetical tradition essentially unbroken to our own day. Strikingly enough, however, even Stephen Mitchell and Edwin M. Good, very recent commentators who do break with the view that Job repents, seem unable to forgo the satisfaction of seeing a decisive final transformation of *some* kind taking place within the title character of this book. Our own view is that, in the final stage of his struggle with the Lord, making no change is precisely Job's triumph. He, who has spoken so eloquently, speaks in the end most eloquently by resting his case. The Lord, by his silence, tortured Job. Job, by his near-silence, leaves the Lord in another kind of agony. Job's first speech, in which he announces his silence unmistakably, is the best gloss on his less transparent second speech, to which we now turn.

We may begin our interpretation of it by drawing attention to two verses which quote earlier speeches by God and by Elihu, Job's last human interlocutor. Many translations—including the New English Bible and the Jerusalem Bible—reword these quotations, obscuring the fact that they are quotations. The more conservative Revised Standard Version gives them verbatim and frames them with quotation marks. In that version Job's final speech reads:

> 2"I know that thou canst do all things,
> and that no purpose of thine can be thwarted.
> 'Who is this that hides counsel
> without knowledge?'

> 3Therefore I have uttered what I did not understand,
> things too wonderful for me, which I did not know.
> 4"Hear, and I will speak;
> I will question you, and you declare to me.'
> 5I had heard of thee by the hearing of the ear,
> but now my eye sees thee;
> 6therefore I despise myself,
> and repent in dust and ashes."

The first verse in this speech, as the RSV translates it, acknowledges nothing more than superior power. Old Testament confessions, as supremely in the Psalms, are typically acknowledgments of power and justice at once. Job's acknowledgment stops carefully at what has been claimed. But Job's recalcitrance becomes bolder if we read the text as *written* in the Hebrew and not as conventionally pronounced (and therefore translated) over the centuries. The annotations to the Masoretic or standard Hebrew text of the Tanakh include what are called *ketib* and *qere* indications. The former word means "written," the latter means "read" (the imperative), in Aramaic, which succeeded Hebrew as the spoken language of Jews living in Palestine and became the language of these annotations. For reasons of sense but also, on occasion, for reasons of reverence, the synagogue reader was instructed by these marginal notations to read another word than the one he found written in the text. In Job 42:2 he was instructed to change the word *yadaᶜta*, "thou knowest," to *yadaᶜtiy*, "I know." Change verse 42:2 in the RSV translation by just that much—from "I know that thou canst do all things" to "Thou knowest that thou canst do all things"—and its air of confession and submission immediately becomes ambiguous and potentially ironic.

Twice, in the remainder of this short speech, Job first quotes something that God has said and then comments on it. In ordinary human discourse this is a faintly insulting thing to do. If, after hearing your long tirade against me, I calmly quote your very first words verbatim into your teeth, I serve notice quite effectively that I have kept my cool, that what you have said has not bowled me over. This is precisely what Job does. The first verse that he quotes is the flung gauntlet of God's initial speech: "Who is this that hides counsel without knowledge?" Do we know that by quoting these words Job really means to take up the flung gauntlet? Yes, because he continues with the Hebrew word *laken*, "therefore." A question, "Who is this . . . ?" does not establish a premise from which a conclusion can be drawn. But we need only supply some form of the implied words "You say" before God's question, now in Job's mouth, and it instantly becomes a premise: "You say, 'Who is this that hides counsel without knowledge?' Therefore [i.e., because you have said this] I say. . . ." The words "You say" need not even be added as such. Quotation may be suggested by intonation alone. Informally, the pairing is

> "Do you say . . . ?"
> "Well, then. . . ."

But what does Job infer from the premise that the quotation provides? What does it tell him? His next words are a calculated double entendre. In the RSV:

> Therefore I have uttered what I did not understand,
> things too wonderful for me, which I did not know.

The words translated "too wonderful" are the ones where the irony lodges. They may be a confession. They may also be just the opposite, an ironic counterboast. Comparisons in any language have this potential. In Italian, for example, if I say to you, *"Fa caldo, no?"* "It's hot, isn't it?" you may reply *"No,"* meaning that, unlike me, you think it is actually cool, or you may say *"Anzi,"* meaning that, unlike me, you think it is sweltering and thus altogether too hot for the plain word *caldo*. The now slightly old-fashioned British usage *Rather!* functions in a similar way. If I say, "That chap is a bit cheeky, wouldn't you agree?" you may respond noncommittally "Rather" and mean only that, yes, now that I mention it, he is a bit on the cheeky side, or you may respond more emphatically "Rather!" and mean that, rather than merely cheeky, he is an insufferable boor. "Too wonderful" in Job 42:3 is ambiguous in just this way. In short, this doublet of quoted verse and commentary can be coherently translated as follows:

> "Do you say, 'Who is this that hides counsel without knowledge'?
> Well, then, I said more than I knew, wonders quite beyond me."

Job may be saying that, having now heard the Lord's overpowering speech, he knows that he was mistaken in his own speeches. He may also be saying that, having now heard the Lord's bombastic speech, he concludes that he spoke a truth beyond what he could have guessed at the time.

We must remember when reading Job's comments on God's quoted words that Job's repeated demand has been that God should stand forth and reveal himself as just either by vindicating Job's innocence or by convicting Job of sin. The implication in all those speeches was inescapable: If God failed to do the one or the other, then it would be he who would be convicted—of injustice. Given all that, when God finally does speak and when, instead of meeting either of Job's demands, he replies ad hominem, "Who is this that hides counsel without knowledge?" he may be said at that moment to have exceeded Job's worst fears. Like a cornered political candidate, the Lord tries to make his opponent the issue. But his opponent is dismayed rather than angered. This reading is plausible whether or not Job believes that the voice from the whirlwind is God's. The refrain in Archibald MacLeish's play *J.B.* is

> I heard it in a yellow wood.
> If God is God He is not good.
> If God is good He is not God.

Whether the Voice speaking to Job is not good or not God is all the same to Job. Either way, he is forced to conclude sadly that he spoke more than he knew when he challenged the divine judge.

Job never addresses the voice from the whirlwind by name. In all speech by a social inferior to a social superior, it is the inferior who is obligated to soften his direct statements with honorifics. Not "yes" and "no" but "yes, sir" and "no, sir." The Tanakh rarely if ever dispenses with these forms when a human being is addressing the Lord, often adding a further mollifying phrase of some sort, on the order of "My Lord, if I have found favor in your sight," and so on. Strikingly, in his two closing speeches, Job never addresses his interlocutor as God or Lord or anything in particular and never otherwise speaks of him as divine.

The voice from the whirlwind declines to identify itself. Job declines to supply what the voice has omitted. Whatever he wonders privately, Job leaves his statements "unaddressed." And this may be precisely what the Lord wants him to do. The devil, one recalls, is a character in this book, one into whose hands the Lord has delivered Job's body, delivering himself at the same time into the devil's moral clutches. By speaking to Job as if he, God, were the devil, God—

deliberately or not—tests Job just as God tested Abraham. That is, he tempts him by speaking to him in the tones of merciless power. Job passes the test precisely as Abraham did. Abraham, we must never forget, did *not* sacrifice Isaac and never said that he was willing to do so. If God had not intervened to end the masquerade, it is not at all clear what Abraham would have done. Quite possibly, God called his own bluff rather than force Abraham to call it by a final act of disobedience. Abraham, who, as we have seen, did not welcome God's covenant, complied with God's wishes up to and (pace Kierkegaard) only up to the point past which he would have been paying homage to the devil. So it is here: Job is not gratuitously defiant. He concedes what must be conceded—namely, that his interlocutor is somehow a being of enormous power. But at the same time, Job successfully withholds everything that can be withheld.

Before considering the next verse in Job's closing speech, we need to remind ourselves that Job has not heard the Lord's speech alone. His friends have also heard it, and they are listening to his responses. By ignoring ethical matters and disdaining to convict Job on any charge other than that of asking for an explanation, the Voice has confounded their expectations just as much as Job's. But having now taken a blow from either side, Job himself can only feel beleaguered. No one, human or divine, sees things as he does. If he agrees with the Voice that might makes right, he contradicts his human friends; if he agrees with them and defends the Lord as just, he claims for the Voice what the Voice has not claimed for itself. What is he to do?

As Edwin M. Good suggests in *In Terms of Tempest: A Reading of Job*, the opening half of 42:4 in Job's final speech echoes words that Elihu, one of Job's interlocutors, speaks at 33:31. Job, by his choice of quotations, turns in implicit exasperation from God to man and back to God. And his next couplet clearly contrasts their words about him with his testimony about himself. In the RSV:

> I had heard of thee by the hearing of the ear [he refers to his friends' pious lectures to him],
> but now my eye sees thee [he hears the Lord's speeches from the whirlwind].

Good believes that, though nothing more visible than a whirlwind is mentioned, Job is looking upon the Lord as he says this.

This is a possible interpretation; but Isaiah 2:1 speaks of "The word which Isaiah the son of Amoz *saw* concerning Judah and Jerusalem" (italics added). A seen word is a word received firsthand rather than secondhand. The RSV is wise in this verse to remain literal.

We come now to the linchpin of the traditional interpretation, the cryptic closing verse of Job's speech, which is linked by a logical connector to the two verses we have just now been examining; in the RSV translation:

> therefore I despise myself,
> and repent in dust and ashes.

This is the filament from which hangs the thread from which hangs the entire traditional reading of Job's last words as a recantation. If the first four verses in the speech have usually been translated to read as a recantation, it is because they have all been interpreted in the light of this closing verse. In the Hebrew, however, this verse is ambiguous, and in the RSV's resolution of the ambiguity no word has less support from the original than the word *myself.* This last word, supplied in the Greek of the Septuagint and, one way or another, in nearly every translation since then, might be described as the thin air to which is anchored the filament from which hangs the thread by which the traditional interpretation dangles. Against the traditional interpretation, it is likely that though Job is in the grip of profoundly changed and negative feelings about *something* at this point, the something is not himself.

Good and Mitchell blame the dominance of the repentance interpretation of 42:6 on Christianity. Good writes that the RSV committee members, "all but one being Christian, were affected by the long Christian tradition of contrition, which calls for the sinner's awareness of sinfulness. They were certainly affected by it in 'repent in dust and ashes.' " Mitchell writes:

> The King James and most other versions present us with a Job who, in his last words, "abhor[s] [him]self / and repent[s] in dust and ashes." They do this on the shakiest of philological grounds; though understandably, because they are thinking with orthodox Christian ideas and *expecting* to find penitence and self-abasement as the appropriate response to the righteous, ill-tempered god they expect to find.

Both he and Good ignore the fact that the repentance tradition, as it affects this verse, is as old as the Septuagint, a Jewish translation centuries older than Christianity, and deeply established as well in the *ketib/qere* annotations of the Masoretic text of the Book of Job, to which Christians made no contribution. Repentance itself is a thoroughly Jewish notion, merely taken over by Christianity.

Whatever the source of the error, however, Mitchell and Good are right to recognize it as such. "He may well slay me; I may have no hope; / Yet I will argue my case before Him," Job said at 13:15, in a line notoriously bowdlerized by the *qere* to "Though he slay me, yet will I trust him." The Lord is now on the point of slaying Job, and Job indeed continues to argue his case before him. If death at God's hands was Job's worst fear, the Lord has now all but realized it: Physically, Job is more dead than alive. The richness of his earlier speeches is such, however, that it is all too easy to imagine him nude, heroic, and ecstatic, as William Blake drew him, rather than, as would be more appropriate, in the wretched guise of a terminal AIDS case.

A more modest approach to a verse on which so very much admittedly hinges is to demand as little novelty of it as possible but only a final restatement of views Job has held from the start and indeed clung to with the force of irony right through the verses immediately preceding this one. In everything he has said in his closing speeches down to this last line, Job has responded by refusing to respond. Absent strong evidence to the contrary, we should assume that his intransigence is not reversed in the last dozen words he speaks. Were it otherwise, a man of his linguistic resources would not be so brief. Throughout all of his longer, earlier speeches to his human interlocutors, Job has insisted on his innocence. The Lord has said nothing to change Job's mind on that point. If there is only one questionable verse to suggest that Job's mind has in fact changed, we should assume that his conviction continues.

Job was concerned, of course, about the implications for his fellow men should God prove to be what he seemed to be for Job. Reading "dust and ashes" as an expression of this concern, as a reference to mankind in its mortal frailty, reading the verbs that the RSV translates "despise myself, / and repent" as transitive, with "dust and ashes" or (more idiomatically) "mortal man" as their common object, we may translate the closing words

Now that my eyes have seen you,
I shudder with sorrow for mortal clay.

In its entirety, the climactic speech would then read:

Then Job answered the Lord:
"You know you can do anything.
  Nothing can stop you.
You ask, 'Who is this ignorant muddler?'
Well, I said more than I knew, wonders quite beyond me.
'You listen, and I'll talk,' you say,
  'I'll question you, and you tell me.'
Word of you had reached my ears,
  but now that my eyes have seen you,
I shudder with sorrow for mortal clay."

Mitchell and Good, despite their philosophical differences, see Job first admitting, one way or another, that his moral concerns are petty and then being raised or released to some nobler vision of human mortality and divine or natural greatness. But are Job's concerns any pettier than the Lord's opening wager? And can Job be breaking through at the end to any acceptance of mortality greater than the resignation he expressed with such serenity at the very start: "Naked came I out of my mother's womb, and naked shall I return there; the Lord has given, and the Lord has taken away; blessed be the name of the Lord" (1:21)? One can easily imagine an editor moving that line to the end of the book, making it Job's climactic breakthrough. Cathartic as such a placement might be, however, the text as we have it begins, it does not end, with those words. Their placement powerfully suggests that when Job says at 13:15 that he will call for justice with his dying breath, he knows exactly what he is saying.

Brevity at the end from a man of such passionate fluency indicates a defeat, all right, but the defeat is purely physical. Morally, Job has held out to the very end, treating the Lord's speeches from the whirlwind as his last trial. And thus, to return to the original puzzle, when the Lord praises Job at the end of the book, he is praising both Job's earlier stubbornness with his human interlocutors and his final, utterly consistent, stiff-necked recalcitrance before the Lord himself. Job has won. The Lord has lost. But the loss, paradoxically, has preserved the Lord from demonization or irrelevance. By his recalcitrance, Job has withstood the Lord's overpoweringly eloquent presentation of a form of impiety condemned again and again in the Tanakh, perhaps with particular clarity at Zephaniah 1:12:

> At that time I will search Jerusalem with lamps;
> And I will punish the men
> Who rest untroubled upon their lees,
> Who say to themselves,
> "The Lord will do nothing, good or bad."

This last view is not altogether absent from the Tanakh. We shall hear a dejected but intermittently eloquent presentation of it in Ecclesiastes, but before Ecclesiastes this is the view consistently attributed to those whom Psalms calls "scoffers," Proverbs calls "fools," and the prophets call "false prophets" and "adulterers." Obviously, through the Job-writer, this clearly substantial group in Israel has spoken to an extent in its own voice—but only to an extent: The Book of Job, after all, ends with the restoration of Job's fortunes, confirming the orthodox view of retribution, which never claimed, in fact, that justice was perfectly implemented at each and every moment. Changing the orthodoxy into full-blown heterodoxy in the mind of Job himself is possible only by grievously overloading with novelty the last verse of Job's last speech.

Earlier we said that in Psalms, Proverbs, and Job, the Lord God would be characterized principally by what human beings would have to say about him rather than by his own words or deeds. In the Book of Job, this has been, of course, only partially true. In agreeing to a savagely cruel wager with the devil, the Lord has characterized himself by his own action. What he expected was a swift victory in the wager. He expected that Job, having blessed rather than cursed God after the first round of satanically inflicted agony, would simply bless him again after the second. Instead, though Job explicitly refuses his wife's invitation to curse God, he goes on, past either blessing or curse, to a third alternative that neither God nor the devil has anticipated: He harangues God, countercharacterizing him relentlessly as not the kind of God who would do what we the readers know he has just done. Without realizing that he does so, Job changes the subject, making God's righteousness rather than his own the question on the reader's mind. And ultimately on God's own mind as well, for in the end, Job wins: The Lord bows, in a way, to Job's characterization of God, abandons his wager with the devil, and after a vain attempt to shout Job down, atones for his wrongdoing by doubling Job's initial fortune.

Job may, therefore, have saved the Lord from himself, yet God can never seem to Job after this episode quite what he seemed before it. More to the point, the Lord can never seem quite the same to himself. The devil is now a permanent part of his reality; and though at the eleventh hour he has broken free from the Adversary, he has done so through a deeper humiliation at the hands of a terrestrial adversary, Job himself. To be sure, Job has brought his own all too simpleminded trust in God into accord with a far more nuanced and mature Jewish wisdom—into accord, in other words, with a realistic vision of the world in which justice is both guaranteed by the good God and occasionally threatened by the bad God. But the God who is seen in this vision is new not just for Job but also for God himself.

The vision with which the Book of Job ends recognizes no principle operating independently of God, to which both divinity and humanity must submit. There is, in other words, no higher, impersonal synthesis beyond personal good and personal evil. The Lord God himself is ultimate in this vision, and therefore evil and good must be found simultaneously and personally in him if they are found anywhere. If Zephaniah rejects, as error, the claim "The Lord will do nothing, good or bad," the counterclaim, the scandalous truth that the Book of Job places in evidence, is not "The Lord will do only good"; it is "The Lord will do good, and he will do ill." Within so hyperpersonalized a vision of ultimate reality as ancient Israel had, "the slings and arrows of outrageous fortune," as Hamlet calls them, are slung and shot by Shaddai himself.

WHAT IS IT that makes God godlike? What is it that makes the protagonist of the Bible so weirdly compelling, so repellent and so attractive at once? We have asked this question before, but we may answer it more fully now. God maintains his peculiar power as a literary character because in him—around and through whatever fusion of ancient Semitic divinities he represents—that which is most radically, unanswerably terrifying in human existence is endowed with voice and intention as well as with caprice and silence. In the confrontation between Job and the Voice from the Whirlwind, the process by which that inescapable condition becomes this overpowering character comes to a climax.

The climax is a climax for God himself and not just for Job or for the reader. After Job, God knows his own ambiguity as he has never known it before. He now knows that, though he is not Bertrand Russell's fiend, he has a fiend-susceptible side and that mankind's conscience can be finer than his. With Job's assistance, his just, kind self has won out over his cruel, capricious self just as it did after the flood. But the victory has come at an enormous price. Job will father a new family, but the family he lost during the wager will not be brought back from the dead; neither will the servants whom the devil slew. And neither will God's own innocence. The world still seems more just than unjust, and God still seems more good than bad; yet the pervasive mood, as this extraordinary work ends, is one not of redemption but of reprieve.

11

Occultation

A view common to nearly all commentators on the Book of Job is that, one way or another, the Lord has reduced Job to virtual silence. Unnoticed is the fact that from the end of the Book of Job to the end of the Tanakh, God never speaks again. His speech from the whirlwind is, in effect, his last will and testament. Job has reduced the Lord to silence. The books of Chronicles will repeat speeches the Lord made earlier, usually quoting them verbatim from the books of Samuel and Kings. Miraculous feats and escapes will be attributed to him in Daniel, where, remote and silent, he will be seen for the last time, seated on a throne, and referred to as the "Ancient of Days." Though not so much as mentioned in Song of Songs and Esther, he will be frequently enough referred to in Lamentations and Ecclesiastes and even fervently prayed to in Nehemiah. But he will never speak again.

In the last chapter of Job, the Lord, without telling Job that he intends to end his agony, says to Eliphaz: "I am incensed at you and your two friends, for you have not spoken the truth about Me as did My servant Job" (42:7). And then, amazingly, the Lord requires that Job *pray* for his three friends, for, as the Lord continues to Eliphaz, "to him I will show favor and [therefore] not treat you vilely." Job complies, and the friends who so relentlessly accused him of wrongdoing are spared. Only then does the Lord restore Job's health and fortune.

Can we imagine how Job's prayer would have gone? Or how he would have conducted himself in that pregnant moment after the prayer and before his fortunes were restored? And what, after restoring his fortunes, might the Lord have said to him? Would he have told Job about the wager? Is all well that ends well? Even released from pain, how would Job have felt about the pain earlier inflicted on him? The Book of Job has forty-two chapters. Robert Frost's "A Masque of Reason," in which the Lord and Job have a ruminative reunion, has as its last line *"Here endeth chapter forty-three of Job."* Frost gives unusually rich and reflective scope to an impulse to continue and complete the Book of Job that many thousands have felt. The Book of Job is an outstanding example of what John Keats called "negative capability" in a writer or a work. A poet of negative capability, Keats wrote, is one "capable of being in uncertainties, Mysteries, doubts, without any irritable reaching after fact & reason." Keats thought William Shakespeare the supreme example of negative capability for his unmatched ability to defer to his own characters. The characters in a Shakespeare play go their several ways, and the playwright has the negative capability to let them take his play with them as they go. He imposes upon it no more coherence than they will allow.

The author of the Book of Job lets Job and the Lord take the Book of Job with them as they go, but what they make of it is, to a very considerable extent, what the Tanakh finally makes of itself. Job, as we have seen, remains himself to the very end, but so, despite all we have said, does the Lord. The Lord suspends his wager with Satan, lauds Job after Job's recalcitrance, and makes atonement to Job, but the Lord remains beyond predicting and, despite everything the Psalmist says, seems to hold himself above the law. The Lord may exalt the righteous and humble the wicked, but, then again, he may not. Nothing he says or does need imply more than "I Am Who I Am."

The Job-writer scarcely seems the aesthete that Keats was. His passions are moral rather than aesthetic. Yet such is the separate and contending beauty of Job's and God's speeches that each acquires a commanding power. Lift your eyes to the whirlwind and the sky, to the vision of all reality in which, in Stephen Mitchell's memorable phrase, "death is a pin," and Job's complaints seem earthbound and trivial. Lower your eyes to Job's sores and the ash heap, and the Lord's boasts ring gruesomely hollow. In the way of great art, each voice for its moment is all-silencing; and the Job-writer's negative capability is such that, particularly as we move past the Book of Job into the rest of the Tanakh, it is all but impossible to say who has had the last word. If we infer from God's silence from the end of the Book of Job through to the end of the Tanakh that Job has reduced

God to silence, is that a victory for Job? Perhaps, but Job has always wanted God to speak, after all; particularly after his fortunes are restored, would he not continue in this wish? Certainly Israel does not want God to remain silent.

Israel. The very name falls, at this point, with a certain strangeness on the ear. God's spouse and principal human antagonist has stood silent in the background for some time now as her Lord contended with this gentile. And yet the Book of Job, for all its seeming isolation from the rest of the Tanakh, may be linked to it and to Israel if it is read as what Jewish tradition would later know as haggadic midrash—legend in lieu of discursive commentary—on a strange passage in the Book of Ezekiel.

In Ezekiel 20, a group of "elders of Israel" comes to question the Lord, and, as in the Book of Job, the Lord refuses to answer. Speaking to the man whom we earlier called the psychotic among the prophets, the Lord says:

> O mortal, speak to the elders of Israel and say to them: Thus said the Lord God: Have you come to inquire of Me? As I live, I will not respond to your inquiry—declares the Lord God.
>
> Arraign, arraign them, O mortal! Declare to them the abhorrent deeds of their fathers. (Ezek. 20:3–4)

In the ensuing indictment, the Lord accuses Israel of disobeying "My laws and . . . My rules, by the pursuit of which a man shall live." The phrase "by the pursuit of which a man shall live" is repeated later in the indictment, but then there comes a strange reversal:

> I swore to them in the wilderness that I would scatter them among the nations and disperse them through the lands, because they did not obey My rules, but rejected My laws, profaned My sabbaths, and looked with longing to the fetishes of their fathers. Moreover, I gave them laws that were not good and rules by which they could not live. When they set aside every first issue of the womb, I defiled them by their very gifts—that I might render them desolate, that they might know that I am the Lord. (20:25–26)

Laws that were *not* good? Rules by which they could *not* live? Is this how he demonstrates "that I am the Lord"?

What the Lord alludes to in the phrases the "first issue of the womb" and "I defiled them by their very gifts" is child sacrifice.

The practice of burning children alive as a propitiatory sacrifice to Moloch, though condemned at Leviticus 18:21 with specific reference to this Canaanite deity, was well-known in ancient Israel. References to it in II Kings are frequent. It was one of the familiar forms by which apostasy from the received religion was expressed.

Because the elders of Israel continue to engage in this abomination, the Lord now refuses to speak to them:

> . . . if to this very day you defile yourselves in the presentation of your gifts by making your children pass through the fire to all your fetishes, shall I respond to your inquiry, O House of Israel? As I live—declares the Lord God—I will not respond to you. (20:31)

But if the historical mind is satisfied once Ezekiel 20 has been situated in the Yahwist polemic against Moloch-worship, the philosophical or theological mind is not. Are the Israelites killing their children to appease Moloch or, as the Lord's earlier words seem to indicate, to please the Lord? And if it is the Lord who requires this of them, is he God or the devil? This is, of course, just the possibility that Soren Kierkegaard took so seriously in discussing Genesis 22, where God calls for Abraham to sacrifice Isaac.

The philosophical questions are undeniably interesting. If God occasionally becomes a demon, then on those occasions ethical mankind is his superior and must disobey him. If God is capable of testing mankind by masquerading as a demon, then paradoxically mankind can only please God and pass the test by defying God. For literary criticism, however, what counts most is neither the historical struggle between the Yahwists and the Molochists nor the speculative problem of deceit by God but simply God's character as such. In Ezekiel 20, the Lord characterizes himself alternately as benevolent and malevolent, a god of life and a god of death. If one is interested not in what he means but in who he is, both sides of his character must be acknowledged.

The Jerusalem Bible strains in a highly interpretive translation of Ezekiel 20:25–26 to integrate the two:

> I even gave them laws that were not good and observances by which they could never live, and I polluted them with their own offerings, making them sacrifice all their first-born, which was to punish them, so that they would learn that I am Yahweh.

In a note, it adds:

> Primitive theology ascribed customs and practices to Yahweh for which men themselves were responsible. Here Ezekiel seems to have in mind the commandment to offer the newly born [Exod. 22:28–29], often so grossly misconstrued by the Israelites.

But the text does not say that Ezekiel has this in mind. It says that the Lord himself has this in mind. Ezekiel is not characterizing the Lord, the Lord is characterizing himself. If in the most ordinary, literary way, the Lord is allowed to be the Bible's protagonist, then the demonic strand in his character, though never finally dominant, can never be excised from it.

The Book of Ezekiel raises, though it does not develop, the possibility that the historical sufferings of Israel are the crime of God. The writer is willing to imagine, however fleetingly, that God seduced Israel into the very sins that he then punished—all to prove "that I am Yahweh," which is to say, to reveal his character, to put himself on display.

But to whom? The victim of his seduction, deceived Israel herself, cannot easily be the target of the demonstration. At least so long as the deception lasts, the Lord's action virtually requires another witness for whose benefit Israel may be demonstratively abused. It is this scandal or this conundrum that the Book of Job may address, for Job is indeed a just man abused by his creator for the sake of argument.

As a literary character, Job has an abstract and impossible perfection, and his suffering, as a result, seems to stand outside history. Ezekiel and the suffering nation the Lord addresses through him stand squarely within history. The question on the far side of the Book of Job is: How, if at all, will the Lord—as we now know him to be, as he now knows himself to be—return to action in the life of Israel? That question eventually receives its answer, but the answer does not come at all quickly.

SLEEPER

"Do Not Wake or Rouse Love"

SONG OF SONGS

The Song of Songs, a cycle of poems about young lovers, might almost be compared to a Greek satyr play following the tragedy of Job. The Book of Job, with its happy ending, is formally more comedy than tragedy. But the mood that lingers after it is dark and heavy with questions. It comes therefore as a surprise and a relief when something so sensual, so playful, so free from pain and even effort as the Song of Songs rings through the air. The young lovers arrive on the scene almost as children and force the adults to change the subject just as children will. Whatever Job and the Lord were arguing about is no concern of theirs:

> Oh, give me of the kisses of your mouth,
> For your love is more delightful than wine.
> Your ointments yield a sweet fragrance,
> Your name is like finest oil—
> Therefore do maidens love you. (Song of Songs 1:2–3)

Who are the boy and the girl and the group of girls also so frequently spoken of? The cycle contains a poem for King Solomon's wedding, alludes to Solomon, and opens with the words "The Song of Songs, by Solomon." And yet the boy, most of the time, does not seem to be a prince, nor does the girl seem to be a princess.

> I am a rose of Sharon,
> A lily of the valleys.
>
> Like a lily among thorns,
> So is my darling among the maidens.
>
> Like an apple tree among trees of the forest,
> So is my beloved among the youths.
> I delight to sit in his shade,
> And his fruit is sweet to my mouth. (2:1–3)

These poems break the mood of the Book of Job and establish their own mood more effectively by being about everyman and everywoman in love than ever they could by being about a king and queen.

The Song of Songs never mentions God and never seems to allude in any other way to the religious traditions of Israel or, for that matter, to religious traditions of any kind. For this reason, there were those who argued in antiquity that it did not belong in the Bible. They lost the argument to others who noted the mentions of the great Solomon and further maintained that the poems were an allegory of the love between the Lord and Israel. Contemporary historical critics are all but unanimous in regarding the Song of Songs as secular love poetry—lyrics about human love and not an allegory for divine love. Yet when these poems are read as part of a reading of the Tanakh, they cannot fail to remind us of the only previous love lyrics in the collection—namely, the ardent, if wounded, reconciliation scenes imagined in Isaiah and Hosea:

> The Lord has called you
>   like a wife forsaken and grieved in spirit,
> like a wife of youth when she is cast off,
>   says your God.
> For a brief moment I forsook you,
>   but with great compassion I will gather you.
> In overflowing wrath for a moment
>   I hid my face from you,
> but with everlasting love I will have compassion on you,
>   says the Lord, your Redeemer. (RSV; Isa. 54:6–8)
>
> Therefore, behold, I will allure her,
>   and bring her into the wilderness,
>   and speak tenderly to her.
> And there I will give her her vineyards,
>   and make the Valley of Achor [pain] a door of hope.
> And there she shall answer as in the days of her youth,
>   as at the time when she came out of the land of Egypt.
> (RSV; Hos. 2:14–15)

Both Isaiah and Hosea compare Israel and the Lord not to young lovers but to a grievously estranged older couple finding their way back to the love of their youth. This is a far cry from the love evoked in the Song of Songs, yet nothing in all the poetry of the Tanakh comes closer to the Song of Songs than these lyrics of reconciliation do. A reader who has noted the emergence of tenderness in the character of the Lord and then seen that quality forgotten or abandoned in the postexilic prophets, as well as in Psalms, Proverbs, and Job, cannot fail to be reminded of it by the Song of Songs. Is an old couple not naturally reminded of love by a young couple?

Hosea was ordered by the Lord to marry a prostitute so that the children she would have would not be unmistakably his. She bore him three children, all of whom are given symbolic names, the third being "Lo-ammi [not-my-people], for you are not My people and I will not be your God" (Hos. 1:9). But in the imagined reconciliation scene, God accepts Lo-ammi as his child (as quite probably Hosea accepted the prostitute's child in real life):

> And I will say to Lo-ammi, "You are My people,"
> And he will respond, "[You are] my God." (2:25)

If this scene were set to music, it would call for a composer like the Arnold Schoenberg of "Transfigured Night," a composition that translates into music a poem by the minor German poet Richard Dehmel. In Dehmel's poem, a distraught woman confesses to her lover that she is pregnant by another man and he responds:

> The child you are to bear
> Let it cause your soul no care.
> Ah look! The glistening universe how clear!
> The brilliance of the whole is gathered here.
> You will traverse with me an icy sea,
> But warmed by a glow, our own,
> to me from you, to you from me,
> We will transform the stranger's child. Yours
> But you will bear it now of me, for me. Ours
> For the splendor that you wake in me
> And for the child that you create in me.
>
> He embraces her strong loins,
> In the air their breathing joins,
> Two humans walk through high, bright night.

The moment in Schoenberg's composition when these words are "spoken," when power yields to tenderness and agitation to calm in a few bars of music, is one of the artistic high points of the twentieth century, and such a transfiguring moment seemed to have been reached in Second Isaiah and Hosea. In the postexilic prophets, however, that moment seems to be forgotten. Or does something in Psalms, Proverbs, or Job substitute for it?

By a strange via negativa or mysticism by subtraction, the Book of Job does become a book about love between Job and God. The word *love* does not occur in this book. But the devil, by luring the Lord into requiring gratuitous service from Job, by forcing Job to prove that he will indeed "fear God for nought," strips down the relationship between God and a man to its pure form. Unless in some sense Job values God in and for himself, how can he say, when he has lost everything and his own wife tells him to curse God and die, "You talk as any shameless woman might talk! Should we accept only good from God and not accept evil?" (2:10). And unless God also values Job in and for himself and not just as a trophy to show off to the devil, why may he not simply dispense with Job when the inconvenient harangues begin?

We compared the Lord in Second Isaiah to the grieving husband of an abused and abandoned wife. The Lord in the Book of Job is more like the husband of a wife who, while protesting her devotion and his virtue, nonetheless recites a bill of particulars that any jury would regard as grounds for divorce. And by his reply to the Voice from the Whirlwind, Job does divorce the Lord: Forced to choose between justice and God, he chooses justice, a choice that the Lord eventually concedes was the correct one. The concluding reconciliation of the Book of Job reverses the initial via negativa, the process of stripping away: Job is provided, again, with many extrinsic reasons to fear/love the Lord. But if in this strange way the Book of Job can be read as a comedy, a love story with its own variety of happy ending, it is certainly not a love story with much tenderness or pleasure. It does not step into the dropped traces of Hosea and Isaiah or summon their language or rich promise back into the mind.

The Song of Songs does all that. Granting to modern exegetes that this is secular love poetry, it is nonetheless easy to imagine how an ancient editor might have wanted it to be more than that and might have included it in default of any more genuinely religious love poetry. But if such is the hope, Song of Songs can only disappoint it. A cycle of secular love poems of some sort might be pressed into service as a way of expressing the Lord's love relationship with Israel allegorically, but this cycle is not of the right sort. On any possible reading of it, the relationship between God and Israel carries forward a great deal of pain on both sides. Love poetry can accommodate pain, but the Song of Songs has no need to. Pain may come someday to the young lovers who speak these poems, but it has not yet arrived. And the one and only verse that, by dint of being a bit cryptic and several times repeated, might seem to invite symbolic reading is almost comically wrong for allegorical use:

> I adjure you, O maidens of Jerusalem,
> By gazelles or by hinds of the field:
> Do not wake or rouse
> Love until it please! (Song of Songs 2:7 and passim)

The standard biblical image for Israel's fear that the Lord has deserted her or, for whatever reason, will not support her is the image of sleep: "Rouse Yourself; why do You sleep, O Lord?" (Ps. 44:24). And, conversely, the standard language for consolation and new beginnings, especially in Second Isaiah, is "Awake! Awake!" Song of Songs is not written in conformity with those conventions but cannot quite escape them either. A part of the charm of the book, to be sure, is that it is bathed not just in love but in luxury and in the safety of, as it were, a great secret garden, and what greater, deeper security can there be than the security of protected, lovingly guarded sleep? But the glimpses we have had of the newly established Jewish community in Jerusalem have given us clear enough evidence of just the opposite: want, incipient bitterness, and endlessly vigilant anxiety. If the maid is Zion and the youth is God, she cannot, just at this moment, want him to sleep on. Song of Songs, accordingly, is not and cannot be an allegory.

At the same time, if God is now absent from the Tanakh, it is not because he has made any clear exit. No terms of retirement have been announced. He has not departed for heaven with a last blessing for Israel. If his speech from the whirlwind is de facto his last will and testament, we can only know this with certainty after more literary time passes. He did not indicate that it was a final speech when he gave it. His silence, even at this early point, begins to weigh on us. The charm of the verses can distract us from this background preoccupation, but the preoccupation also distracts us from the charm: *Where is he? What has happened?*

Bystander
"Returned to Her People and Her Gods"
RUTH

What follows the Song of Songs in the Jewish canon is another book about love and marriage, the Book of Ruth. This book, though it alludes piously enough to the Lord at several points, attributing both good and ill to his intervention, makes an oblique but shocking comment on how intensely or otherwise his presence is felt when, for the first and only time in the Tanakh, an honest Israelite innocently suggests the worship of a false god. The context, to be sure, is more than enough to make the suggestion primarily prudent and only secondarily blasphemous, yet what is assumed rather than stated when the suggestion is made is still of great note—namely, that there is no need to stop and ask whether the Lord will take offense at such advice. The matter is up to the human beings involved.

The suggestion of foreign worship is made by the Israelite Naomi to her widowed Moabite daughter-in-law Ruth. Naomi is herself a widow, both of whose sons have recently died. Her family had been driven by famine in Israel to settle in Moab, where her sons both married Moabite women, Orpah and Ruth. The famine has now abated in Israel, and Naomi is preparing to return to her home in Bethlehem. She urges her daughters-in-law to stay behind and find husbands for themselves in Moab: "Turn back, each of you to her mother's house." Weeping, they insist that they will return to her country with her, but Naomi repeats her counsel, and at length Orpah agrees to stay behind. It is at this point that Naomi says to Ruth: "See, your sister-in-law has returned to her people and her gods. Go follow your sister-in-law" (Ruth 1:15). In context, the suggestion is not shocking, but that is only another way of stating that the context has drastically changed. The Book of Ruth is nominally set "in the days when the chieftains [judges] ruled," an era of bloody warfare between Moab and Israel, when it would have been unthinkable for any Israelite to urge the worship of Chemosh, the Moabite god, on anyone already worshiping the Lord. But the action of Ruth is only nominally set in that remote era. By its placement in the canon, its literary time, Ruth comes much later, after the rise and fall of the monarchy, after the exile and the return. In effect, the

Book of Ruth is about relations between Jews and Moabites after the reestablishment of a Jewish community in Jerusalem.

The Moabites were non-Jews, possibly Hebrew-speaking, correctly understood by the Jews to be a closely related people. The author of the Book of Ruth implies (and implies approval of) mutually tolerant and even supportive relations between the two nations. But the Lord has never revoked his implacable opposition to just that sort of tolerance and mingling. Necessarily, then, the author of Ruth implies that the Lord is so inactive at this point that, at the very least, no reprisal need be feared from him when his wishes are disregarded.

Having returned to Bethlehem with Ruth, Naomi instructs her daughter-in-law to attempt a kind of benign seduction of Boaz, a wealthy male relative of Naomi's late husband. On a night after the harvest is in and Boaz has been drinking in celebration, Ruth is to go secretly to the threshing floor, where he will be sleeping, and uncover "his feet," a euphemism for his genitals. She does so, he awakens, and she asks him to "spread your robe over your handmaid," meaning that he should take pity on her and marry her. The writer artfully slows the story at this point, but eventually Boaz and Ruth do marry, and among their descendants, we are told, is King David (for whose partially Moabite descent there is other evidence). The story is told with great affection and delicacy and ends with the women of Bethlehem attributing its happy ending to the Lord, but with more than a nod to Ruth herself:

> And the women said to Naomi [after Ruth had borne a child by Boaz], "Blessed be the Lord, who has not withheld a redeemer from you today! May his name be perpetuated in Israel! He will renew your life and sustain your old age; for he is born of your daughter-in-law, who loves you and is better to you than seven sons." (4:14–15)

The Book of Ruth makes a piquant contrast with the Song of Songs. If the difficulties of marriage that the Song of Songs passes over in blithe silence include, among others, poverty, infertility, bereavement, and the in-laws, then Ruth can clearly enough be read as a book about the difficulties of marriage. But in this writer's hands, those difficulties are all met and overcome: Love among women, crossing generations and national lines, triumphs over all. The pure devotion in Ruth's statement to Naomi "Do not urge me to leave you, to turn back and not follow you. For wherever you go, I will go; wherever you lodge, I will lodge; your people shall be my people, and your God my God" (1:16) is justly famous and utterly convincing as delivered. Yet the Book of Ruth also has the same, distinctly feminine brand of realism that we saw at points in Proverbs, a pungent shrewdness about men and what they can and cannot be relied on to do. As scarcely any other narrative in the Bible, this one is a tale of resourceful women and their relationships among themselves. Women have all the major roles and initiate all the major actions. Boaz, a supporting actor in the story, is a good man, but he needs to be helped to do the right thing, and Naomi—sending Ruth in the dark of night—knows just what kind of help will do the trick. What men mostly do in the Book of Ruth is die, leaving the women to cope for themselves; and the acclamation of Ruth as a daughter-in-law "better than seven sons" (an echo of Elkanah's line to Hannah in I Sam. 1:8) is more than merely rhetorical. The shoe fits, and the women wear it with a certain flourish.

As for the Lord, however, or rather for his traditional sensitivities, if the Book of Ruth can be said to characterize them at all, it can only be to suggest a change in them. The change would be implicit in an allusion the book makes to the anonymous woman who was the mother of all the Moabites. In the destruction of Sodom, only Lot, his wife, and their two daughters were spared. With all the men of Sodom dead, there was no one left for Lot's daughters to marry. The two young women ply their father with wine, sleep with him, and

> thus the two daughters of Lot came to be with child by their father. The older one bore a son and named him Moab; he is the father of the Moabites of today. And the younger also bore a son, and she called him Ben-ammi; he is the father of the Ammonites of today. (Gen. 19:36–38)

Boaz is not Ruth's father, merely a relative of Ruth's father-in-law. She does not get him drunk; she simply goes to him after he has been drinking. And, taking the story as it is written, he does not sleep with her that night, after she bares his genitals, but only does so after their marriage, a marriage he contracts only after several proprieties have been duly attended to. But this honorable version of the seduction of Lot by the mother of all Moabites only serves the more effectively to turn a story celebrating the dignity, mutual devotion, and initiative of women in general into one rehabilitating Moabite women in particular.

In discussing Proverbs, we noted that foreign women were almost inevitably the channel through which most of foreign culture came to Israel. It would have been so inevitably for other peoples as well, given a culture of war that treated the women of a defeated nation as property and exterminated the defeated men. Women were the carriers of culture across national lines simply because they survived to be such. Women would, of course, very often have adopted the culture into which they married, but how convincing could they ever be in that role? After the seduction of Lot, the other bit of Israelite history or legend featuring Moabite women was the infamous orgy involving the Baal of Peor, when Phinehas won the Lord's favor by impaling an Israelite man copulating with a Moabite priestess-prostitute with a single thrust of his spear (Num. 25). This, in general, is the image of the Moabite woman: idolater, prostitute, debaucher of older men.

The almost certainly female and possibly Moabite author of the Book of Ruth responds to all this by celebrating Ruth's chaste love for her mother-in-law and fervent loyalty to Israel's Lord and by suggesting, finally, that not all love between an older man and a younger woman is debauchery. But what does God think? Jews and Moabites, both subject to Persia after the fall of Babylon, would not have been in a position to exterminate each other but would certainly have been able to intermarry. The author of the Book of Ruth is clearly not opposed to such intermarriage. However, the Lord, speaking through Malachi, the last of the prophets, made clear his disagreement with her view when he said:

> Judah has broken faith; abhorrent things have been done in Israel and in Jerusalem. For Judah has profaned what is holy to the Lord—what He desires—and espoused daughters of alien gods. May the Lord leave to him who does this no descendants dwelling in the tents of Jacob and presenting offerings to the Lord of Hosts. (Mal. 2:11–12)

In Ruth the people of Bethlehem invoke the Lord against the Lord and compare the Moabite with the greatest names in Israelite womanhood when they say to Boaz on his wedding day:

> May the Lord make the woman who is coming into your house like Rachel and Leah, both of whom built up the House of Israel! Prosper in Ephrathah and perpetuate your name in Bethlehem! And may your house be like the house of Perez whom Tamar bore to Judah—through the offspring which the Lord will give you by this young woman. (Ruth 4:11–12)

They allude publicly and boldly to another widowed non-Israelite woman, Tamar, who seduced her father-in-law, Judah, rather than remain childless.

Conceivably, we could take as a new stage in the developing character of the Lord the implicit characterization of him here as a God who endorses intermarriage. What would make this a moment of characterological change for him as well as, so to put it, of disciplinary change for Israel is that it would return him to the universal benignity toward human fertility that his opening "Be fertile and increase" bespoke. If that benignity has returned, then the creator would seem to have won a round against the destroyer in his character. But such a reading would overuse a legitimate technique. A character can, to be sure, be characterized in his absence by others who interact with him. But the Book of Ruth lacks the copious characterization of the Lord that we find in Psalms or in the long, impassioned speeches of Job. Even in Proverbs, the text, for all its frequent secularity and remoteness from concerns special to Israel, has a clear and identifiably new role for the Lord to assume.

The Book of Ruth, however, pays only very modest attention to the Lord God. It is far more concerned with a change in the dignity and mutual respect of women. The underlying polemic over the decency and orthodoxy of foreign wives translates with some difficulty into a statement that God himself has grown more tolerant of them. Whether the Lord God is tolerant or intolerant, he is, with respect to the action of this story, almost otiose. In the cast of characters of the Book of Ruth, he is a bystander. Happy and unhappy outcomes are routinely attributed to him, good wishes are delivered with reference to him, but the references, the pronouncements, seem purely pro forma. The Lord God says nothing, as already noted; and, for all practical purposes, he also does nothing.

RECLUSE

"You Have Screened Yourself Off with a Cloud"

LAMENTATIONS

Many, perhaps most, newspaper reporters have had the experience of attending a press conference at which the news maker—the president, shall we say—never arrives. The concentration and dissipation of energy before and after such a nonevent are instructive to witness. At just what point does the great man begin to not-arrive? At what point is his nonarrival fully accomplished? At the start, an observer senses gathered attention, a presence to the absence, an emotional and physical focus on the spotlit, camera-watched position the president will occupy. And then . . . the ungathering of that same energy, the mounting restlessness and slight physical disarray of the crowd, heads turning, someone half-rising or perhaps waving, then voices rising above the initial respectful murmur, and at length a trickle turning to a flood of departures as the absent presence becomes a present absence.

A transitional mood of this sort affects the six books that follow the Book of Job in the Jewish canon: Song of Songs, Ruth, Lamentations, Ecclesiastes, Esther, and Daniel. Figuratively speaking, the Song of Songs is a pair of reporters who are in love with each other and oblivious to all the goings-on; Ruth is a wonderful story that one nicely dressed, rather dark-complexioned woman still in the seats is telling to another woman while keeping an idle eye on the door just in case the president comes after all; Ecclesiastes is an older columnist who fancies himself the "dean" of his profession and takes the occasion to hold forth a bit too loudly in a vein that he intends to be cynical but that strikes many as merely confused; Esther is a slightly truculent print reporter who cares more about putting the television people in their place than about anything the president has ever said or will say; Daniel is a troubled young radical who is rumored to have had private contact with the president.

All quite interesting. You could write a book about any one of these reporters. And yet, what about the president? And what about the people who still care about what the president might have to say, who still think that what the president will or won't do is of immense importance?

Imagine Lamentations as a somber-faced reporter in the front row, clipboard on his lap, voice-activated minirecorder in his vest pocket, far more sad at the president's absence than irritated over it or inclined to hasten on to other matters. *How can you all take this so lightly?* he thinks to himself about his nonchalant colleagues; *the country is falling apart!*

Lamentations is a mini-Psalter, just five chapters long, consisting of laments over the destruction of Jerusalem. The challenging tone that occasionally is heard in the Book of Psalms and that becomes a kind of war between God and a man in the Book of Job is nowhere to be heard here. The author, whom we may call the Elegist, pleads guilty on Israel's behalf. The Lord warned Israel repeatedly, he insists, that this would be the result of a national apostasy. The nation apostatized anyway. The Lord was as good as his word:

> The Lord has done what He purposed,
> Has carried out the decree
> That He ordained long ago;
> He has torn down without pity.
> He has let the foe rejoice over you,
> Has exalted the might of your enemies. (Lam. 2:17)

Lamentations draws the imagery of the Suffering Servant of Second Isaiah together with complaint-language redolent of Job. The opening line of Lamentations 3 recalls Isaiah's "man of suffering" just as a bit later the reference to the wearing away of the writer's flesh and skin recalls Job:

> I am the man who has known affliction
> Under the rod of His wrath;
> Me He drove on and on
> In unrelieved darkness;
> On none but me He brings down His hand
> Again and again, without cease.
> He has worn away my flesh and skin;
> He has shattered my bones.
> All around me He has built
> Misery and hardship;
> He has made me dwell in darkness,
> Like those long dead.
> He has walled me in and I cannot break out;

He has weighed me down with chains.
And when I cry and plead,
He shuts out my prayer;
He has walled in my ways with hewn blocks,
He has made my paths a maze. (3:1–9)

But the middle verses of the same long poem, which proceeds in Hebrew alphabetic order, with a verse for each letter, offer a clear if stern explanation of what has happened and why; even for the suffering individual, it is all part of the Lord's plan:

It is good to wait patiently
Till rescue comes from the Lord.
It is good for a man, when young,
To bear a yoke;
Let him sit alone and be patient,
When He has laid it upon him.
Let him put his mouth to the dust—
There may yet be hope.
Let him offer his cheek to the smiter;
Let him be surfeited with mockery.
For the Lord does not
Reject forever,
But first afflicts, then pardons
In His abundant kindness. (3:26–32)

Lamentations is remarkable for its juxtaposition of an excruciating sense of loss with an unflinching admission that the loss was merited and with, finally, a desperately trusting plea for vindication against those who have inflicted the deserved punishment:

Give them, O Lord, their deserts
According to their deeds.
Give them anguish of heart;
Your curse be upon them!
Oh, pursue them in wrath and destroy them
From under the heavens of the Lord! (3:64–66)

Though God made their sin his instrument, it is still sin.

Psychologically, the Elegist is still fully present to the Lord, still deeply engaged in the traditional problematic of Israel's sin and reconciliation, and still, through all the pain, refusing to despair of major divine intervention. There is integrity as well as pathos in this position. The writer refuses just to suffer: He insists on suffering as a Jew. What is happening is not merely happening: It is all part of an unseen transaction. To make it that, he must make it the result of his own and the nation's sins. Having done so, he can then believe that the Lord can and will end it, even though, as he puts it:

> You have clothed Yourself in anger and pursued us,
> You have slain without pity.
> You have screened Yourself off with a cloud,
> That no prayer may pass through. (3:43–44)

Unfortunately, there is another kind of pathos for the reader coming to Lamentations at this point in the Tanakh. The Book of Lamentations, through the painfully vivid, firsthand impression its descriptions convey, announces itself as spoken after the fall of Jerusalem and before the restoration. At the time of its imagined writing, in other words, the Elegist faces the full impact of the destruction of the city and the cruel onset of national captivity and oppression. But horrible as that time was, it was brightened by the hope of a great restoration. Now the restoration has taken place, and, sadly, much of what the Elegist lamented continues, including, by the testimony of the postexilic prophets, subservience, want, and a painful sense of loss. The reader knows, as the Elegist seems not to know, that even after the restoration, Jerusalem could still say:

> Slaves are ruling over us,
> With none to rescue us from them.
> We get our bread at the peril of our lives,
> Because of the heat of the wilderness.
> Our skin glows like an oven,
> With the fever of famine. (5:8–10)

That knowledge forces the question of the Lord's silence back to the fore and would disrupt the new synthesis that seemed all but accomplished in the Book of Psalms even if the Book of Job had not disrupted it in another way.

In Psalms, language like the Elegist's about the sad state of the nation, though not absent, was rare. The Lord of the beauteous heavens and the wondrous law had become the intimate of the soul and the sturdy foundation of family welfare. The backdrop for the contemplation of Torah/Wisdom was increasingly the splendor of nature rather than the glory of Israelite history. And against that backdrop personal and familial concerns seemed largely to have replaced the earlier hope for a true, massive national vindication. By implication, conditions of Jewish life on the near side of any such major change were bearable. To the Elegist, however, they seem quite unbearable. And whoever is right, the Lord continues silent: No further answer, no better answer, seems at all imminent. To return to our mundane comparison, in the room where the presidential news conference was to have taken place, they are now folding the chairs and taking down the bunting, almost afraid to disturb the last, earnest reporter still in his seat, the one sitting so quiet and so straight, with his clipboard on his lap and his pencil at the ready, refusing to give up his hope, refusing to hear the silence.

PUZZLE

"Who Can Straighten What He Has Twisted?"

ECCLESIASTES

The word *ekklesiastes* in Greek, translating *qohelet* in Hebrew, means something like "assemblyman" or "assembler" and may refer either to assembled human beings or to sayings assembled into a book. Like the Book of Proverbs, the Book of Ecclesiastes contains both longer speeches and brief sayings; and, like Proverbs, Ecclesiastes offers sayings on both sides of any number of issues. Folk wisdom is typically unsystematic and self-contradictory in this way. For every "Look before you leap," there is a "Hesitate and you are lost." Thus, at 3:19–21, Ecclesiastes says:

> In respect of the fate of man and the fate of beast, they have one and the same fate: as the one dies so dies the other, and both have the same lifebreath; man has no superiority over beast, since both amount to nothing. Both go to the same place; both came from dust and both return to dust. Who knows if a man's lifebreath does rise upward and if a beast's breath does sink down into the earth?

But at 12:7, he says, concluding a melancholy poem on the ravages of old age:

> And the dust returns to the ground
> As it was,
> And the lifebreath returns to God
> Who bestowed it.

As for practical counsel concerning how life should be lived, Ecclesiastes is equally divided. The first preceding quotation comes to the practical conclusion

> I saw that there is nothing better for man than to enjoy his possessions, since that is his portion. For who can enable him to see what will happen afterward? (Eccles. 3:22)

And yet at another point, speaking of his attempt to enjoy his own possessions, he says:

> Then my thoughts turned to all the fortune my hands had built up, to the wealth I had acquired and won—and oh, it was all futile and pursuit of wind; there was no real value under the sun! For what will the man be like who will succeed me, and who is to rule over what was built up long ago? (2:11–12)

Ecclesiastes is more than a cracker-barrel philosopher, however. His inconsistency is not simply the inconsistency of folk wisdom, which is always ad hoc and in need of completion by the particular situation to which one of its offerings is applied. He is more accurately a protophilosopher, a seeker after wisdom who has looked with skepticism on many of the ordinary pursuits of mankind and has begun to look with skepticism on traditional wisdom itself, not excluding the special kind of wisdom that tries to cope with skepticism by a retreat to the would-be subphilosophic business of just living a life. There is a quiet and appealing resignation in some of Ecclesiastes' speeches, but his judgment on his own speeches is that they are futile, and one believes that he is not feigning his rather frequently expressed loathing of life (2:17).

As regards God, though Ecclesiastes may be described as, here too, on both sides of every question, he has clearly begun challenging what might be called the hidden premises of Jewish monotheism. The notion of reward as in any way the consequence of human action—whether as covenant reward or simply as the reward of diligence—is seriously undercut by the quasi-Platonic notion of total divine foreknowledge of an endlessly recurring cycle of events:

> I realized, too, that whatever God has brought to pass will recur evermore:
>
> Nothing can be added to it
> And nothing taken from it—
>
> and God has brought to pass that men revere Him.
>
> What is occurring occurred long since,
> And what is to occur occurred long since:
>
> and God seeks the pursued. And, indeed, I have observed under the sun:

> Alongside justice there is wickedness,
> Alongside righteousness there is wickedness.
>
> I mused: "God will doom both righteous and wicked, for he has set a time for every experience and for every happening." (3:14–17)

If this has a fatalistic sound, it must be noted that fatalism has its consolations. At 9:7, Ecclesiastes writes: "Go, eat your bread in gladness, and drink your wine in joy; for your action was long ago approved by God." (The King James Version translates: "Go thy way, eat thy bread with joy, and drink thy wine with a merry heart," catching the avuncular gentleness of the verse.)

If the nonrecurrence of time is one presupposition of the Tanakh's belief in God, the interconnectedness of generations is another. Abundant offspring constitute a reward in the eyes of the Deuteronomist, and other rewards—as well as punishments—when visited upon the offspring count for all the older writers as if visited upon the self. Ecclesiastes has a far more modern and individualistic, not to say somewhat jaundiced, view of these matters: You can't take it with you, and if you must leave it behind, what good does it do you?

> There is an evil I have observed under the sun, and a grave one it is for man: that God sometimes grants a man riches, property, and wealth, so that he does not want for anything his appetite may crave, but God does not permit him to enjoy it; instead, a stranger will enjoy it. That is futility and a grievous ill. Even if a man should beget a hundred children and live many years—no matter how many the days of his years may come to, if his gullet is not sated through his wealth, I say: The stillbirth, though it was not even accorded a burial, is more fortunate than he. (6:1–3)

In this connection, Ecclesiastes' vision makes a striking comparison with Job's, echoing Job's language at the start but then veering off in his own distinctive direction:

> Another grave ill is this: He must depart just as he came. As he came out of his mother's womb, so must he depart at last, naked as he came. He can take nothing of his wealth to carry with him. So what is the good of his toiling for the wind? (5:14–15)

Job's "Naked came I . . ." ended with "Blessed is the name of the Lord." The equivalent from Ecclesiastes does not.

Ecclesiastes neither curses nor blesses God but only finds him incomprehensible and does his best to hedge all his bets, including any bet on wisdom or righteousness:

> Consider God's doing! Who can straighten what He has twisted? So in a time of good fortune enjoy the good fortune; and in a time of misfortune, reflect: The one no less than the other was God's doing; consequently, man may find no fault with Him.
>
> In my own brief span of life, I have seen both these things: sometimes a good man perishes in spite of his goodness, and sometimes a wicked one endures in spite of his wickedness. So don't overdo goodness and don't act the wise man to excess, or you may be dumfounded. Don't overdo wickedness and don't be a fool, or you may die before your time. It is best that you grasp the one without letting go of the other, for one who fears God will do his duty by both. (7:13–18)

Here, too, Ecclesiastes makes an instructive comparison with Job, who said to his wife, "Should we accept only good from God and not accept evil?" (Job 2:10) but certainly went on to "find fault with Him." The scandalous notion that God is both friend and foe, creator and destroyer, is offered casually here, as little more than theological common sense, at least if we translate as the Jewish Publication Society does, following the medieval commentator Rashi. The Hebrew is opaque. The words translated "consequently, man may find no fault with Him" are translated in the Jerusalem Bible "so that we should take nothing for granted" and in the New Revised Standard Version "so that mortals may not find out anything that will come after them." Rashi's reading is simultaneously more pious and more daring than either of these more modern ones.

Ecclesiastes' advice—be good but not *too* good, be clever but not *too* clever—is the ethical common sense that he derives from his theological common sense. Ecclesiastes, by the widest consensus among exegetes, is the ringer in the canon, the book that by rights shouldn't have got in. Even more than Job, it is a kind of inversion of all that has gone before. Yet a passage like this one is probably closer to what parents have been teaching their children, not excluding Jewish and Christian parents walking with their children to synagogue or church, for millennia. Ecclesiastes is the Polonius of the Bible.

But what if anything does God have to say of this world-weary skepticism regarding his justice and his control over the course of events? Will the sky darken with another whirlwind and that thunderous voice be heard again:

> Who is this who darkens counsel,
> Speaking without knowledge? (Job 38:1)

No, God lets Ecclesiastes pass in silence, just as Ecclesiastes generally lets God pass in silence. The most famous lines in Ecclesiastes are among the most famous in the entire Bible; in the King James Version:

> I returned, and saw under the sun that the race is not to the swift, nor the battle to the strong, neither yet bread to the wise, nor yet riches to men of understanding, nor yet favour to men of skill; but time and chance happeneth to them all. For man also knoweth not his time: as the fishes that are taken in an evil net, and as the birds that are caught in the snare, even so are the sons of men snared in an evil time, when it falleth suddenly upon them. (Eccles. 9:11–12)

These lines present as thoroughly secular a worldview as can be imagined. That the race is not to the swift is a kind of low-stakes, inframoral version of the Jewish complaint in Psalms that the righteous suffer and the wicked are rewarded. What Ecclesiastes overturns with his somber eloquence is not the covenant between Israel and God but the vision, in Proverbs, that effort (at least typically) brings reward ("Go to the ant . . ."). And the verse immediately following—in which death is seen not as the common lot at the end of life but as a sudden cruel entrapment in the midst of life—is, again, no attack on religious belief. Ecclesiastes, like the Job-writer, has the common holding of Near Eastern wisdom rather than the particular traditions of Israel as his target. He differs noticeably from the Job-writer, however, for he does not regard God as even a topic of overriding importance. And if God disagrees, he isn't saying so.

12

Incorporation

At what point does a sense of pause yield to the sense of an ending? The Book of Job is the climax of the Tanakh and the climactic moment in the biography of God. The books that then follow—Song of Songs, Ruth, Lamentations, and Ecclesiastes—are, in effect, a denouement. The French word *dénouement* means, literally, untangling. In drama, after the conflict that the dramatist has created has been essentially resolved, there always remains a further loosening and untangling, a final sorting out, before the play can come to a satisfying close. If nothing else, a little time must pass for the impact of the climax to be assimilated.

It is in this last sense that the four books we considered in Chapter 11 function as a denouement. There are, yes, occasional points of contact between them and the Book of Job: the anguished tone of Lamentations, the resignation of Ecclesiastes, and a few others. But these links do not make them a final sorting out of the tangle of Job and God. They become a denouement principally by interposing a pause between the Book of Job and the books that end the Tanakh. They change the subject. They mark time. They lull.

And then their sense of pause yields to something different, an elusive but eventually pervasive sense of movement and culmination. The biography of God, as we saw earlier, has several beginnings. God, *ʾelohim*, creates the world in one way; the Lord, *yahweh*, in another. But if there had been no creation story, the Tanakh could have begun with Noah; if there had been no flood story, it could have begun with Abraham; if no patriarchal covenant, then with Moses. In the books to which we now turn, the Tanakh, with its several beginnings, comes to several endings. In each of these endings, God's life comes to a close, but in none of them does he die.

We may say, keeping our focus tightly on him, that he subsides; but widening the focus somewhat, we may say that he is incorporated in the Jewish nation. The act by which God became man as Jesus Christ is referred to in Christian theology as the incarnation—from the Latin word *carnis*, "flesh": The spirit of God became flesh in the person of Jesus. *Incorporation*—from the Latin *corpus*, "body"—is a similar concept but one that carries no such theological freight: Judaism does not claim even for the Jewish nation as a whole the relationship with God that Christianity claims for Jesus.

Nonetheless, leaving theological speculation aside, it does seem that in the books of Esther, Daniel, Ezra, Nehemiah, and Chronicles, a pragmatic transfer of functions and expectations occurs. Actions that once God would have taken on behalf of the Jews, statements that he would have made to them, they now take and make for themselves. God is still God and the only God. They are still no more than human beings. And yet in a strange way, he and they exchange roles.

ABSENCE

"He Explained to Them That He Was a Jew"

ESTHER

The evolution of the religion of ancient Israel into Judaism and of the nation of Israel into world Jewry is not the subject of this book, and in any event only the very first stages in that process are recorded at all in the Bible. The books of Esther and Daniel, neither of which contains any record of historical events, are both nonetheless of interest to historians as evidence of a changing national consciousness. They tell, respectively, the story of a woman and of a man rising to distinction at the imperial court of an empire in which the Jews are just one among many peoples. Esther, who becomes queen of the Persian empire, uses her power to arm the Jews for action against their foes. Daniel, who becomes courtier, counselor, and "chief magician" to the king of Babylon, also achieves a violent, if narrower, triumph over his foes and goes on to have a series of apocalyptic visions in which Babylon and succeeding empires are destroyed and Daniel's own nation triumphs.

Though the attitude taken in Esther toward the Persian empire is far more benign than that taken in Daniel toward the Babylonian, Persian, and Greek empires, both books take empires for granted. And in both books, a pattern that will be replicated innumerable times in 2,500 years of Jewish history is already operative. In this pattern, the Jews are an identifiable, vulnerable minority, hated by some but thriving by dint of talent (Esther's beauty, Daniel's brilliance) and integrity. Their survival depends on their willingness to take risks for one another, on their skill in winning protection from the very top, and on their ability to determine in a timely manner the likely course of events—especially dangerous events. Fidelity to the Jewish religion need not always be an element in either Jewish identity or Jewish self-defense.

The Book of Esther—scarcely less remarkable for its inclusion in the Bible than the Book of Ecclesiastes—marks something of an extreme in the separation of Jewish destiny from Jewish religion. God is not mentioned in this book, nor, when the Jews are spoken of as a distinct minority within the Persian empire, is their religion mentioned as even a secondary feature of their identity. They are merely an ethnic group, and the Book of Esther is the story of a triumphant episode in their history. The queen of Persia has offended her husband, and the king has decided to take a new wife. The most beautiful maidens of the realm are brought to Shushan, his capital city. Esther, an orphan adopted by her cousin Mordecai, pleases him most and becomes his queen. That her Jewish identity is a handicap is suggested by the fact that she conceals it from Ahasuerus, the king, but she has no compunction about marrying a Persian and apparently makes no effort to practice her religion, even secretly. Meanwhile, in the book's second plot, Mordecai declines to kneel or bow low to Haman, who has recently been promoted to prime minister and enjoys this homage by royal edict. The courtiers importune Mordecai—who has recently saved the king from assassination by alerting Queen Esther—to comply, but he "explained to them that he was a Jew," and this book comes no nearer than that to a religious commitment or allusion to God.

Haman then says to Ahasuerus:

> There is a certain people, scattered and dispersed ["a certain unassimilated nation scattered," as the Jerusalem Bible translates] among the other peoples in all the provinces of your realm, whose laws are different from those of any other people and who do not obey the king's laws; and it is not in Your Majesty's interest to tolerate them. If it please Your Majesty, let an edict be drawn for their destruction, and I will pay ten thousand talents of silver to the stewards for deposit in the royal treasury. (Esther 3:8–9)

Haman will presumably get this silver by plundering the Jews who will be slain. The reaction to this edict among the Jews is remarkable:

> When Mordecai learned all that had happened, Mordecai tore his clothes and put on sackcloth and ashes. . . . Also, in every province that the king's command and decree reached, there was great mourning among the Jews, with fasting, weeping, and wailing, and everybody lay in sackcloth and ashes. (4:1, 3)

Fasting, sackcloth, and ashes were sometimes signs of repentance in ancient Israel, but Mordecai mentions no sin, does not summon the Jews to repentance, and does not speak of the king's decree as an act of God. Fasting, sackcloth, and ashes were also signs of mourning, and they seem to be no more than that in this case. They could also, finally, be employed in conjunction with prayer at the time of a personal or, especially, a great national crisis. But, in an extremely striking omission, neither Mordecai nor any of the Jews now in peril for their lives calls on the Lord in prayer.

The omission is stunning because this decree of extermination so closely resembles that earlier decree of Pharaoh against the male infants of the Israelites. Whether or not, when they cried out, the Israelites in Egypt were consciously crying to their God, "their cry for help rose up to God," and he heard it and came to their rescue. The cry of the Jews in Persia does not rise up to God, God takes no action on their behalf, and they give no indication whatsoever that they expect him to do so.

On the contrary, they rescue themselves from this peril by their own courage and resourcefulness. When Esther fears to enter the king's presence unsummoned, a capital offense against the rules of the court, Mordecai urges her on:

> Do not imagine that you, of all the Jews, will escape with your life by being in the king's palace. On the contrary, if you keep silent in this crisis, relief and deliverance will come to the Jews from another quarter, while you and your father's house will perish. And who knows, perhaps you have attained to royal position for just such a crisis. (4:12–14)

Mordecai's advice to Esther is forceful but worldly in the way that Ecclesiastes' more general advice on the same point is worldly:

> Two are better off than one, in that they have greater hope for their earnings. For should they fall, one can raise the other; but woe betide him who is alone and falls with no companion to raise him! Further, when two lie together they are warm; but how can he who is alone get warm? Also, if one attacks, two can stand up to him. A three-fold cord is not readily broken! (Eccles. 4:9–12)

Ecclesiastes, as we have noted, refers often, if casually, to God; Esther never refers to him. But we can imagine that in circumstances like those described in the Book of Esther, Ecclesiastes would conduct himself more or less as Esther and Mordecai do. He too would spend little time talking to or of God. Parts of Ecclesiastes read, indeed, like slightly jaded advice to a courtier:

> Don't revile a king even among your intimates.
> Don't revile a rich man even in your bedchamber;
> For a bird of the air may carry the utterance,
> And a winged creature may report the word. (10:20)

A little bird told me . . . , as the saying still goes. The Book of Esther, to a point, is the Book of Ecclesiastes put into practice.

Esther takes the risk Mordecai urges on her and wins big. The king, still smitten with her, offers her half his kingdom. Instead, she alerts him to the fact that Haman is planning the public execution of Mordecai, who, as the king has fortuitously discovered in palace archives, once tipped him off to a planned assassination. Esther further explains to her husband Haman's plan to exterminate the Jews, who are, she now reveals, her ancestral people. Outraged, the king gives Haman's fortune to Mordecai, executes Haman on the very gibbet Haman had prepared for Mordecai, and officially decrees a one-day immunity for the Jews to wreak revenge on any and all of their enemies:

> If any people or province attacks them, they may destroy, massacre, and exterminate its armed force together with women and children, and plunder their possessions—on a single day in all the provinces of King Ahasuerus, namely, on the thirteenth day of the twelfth month, that is, the month of Adar. (Esther 8:11–12)

Esther asks for a second such day, and the king grants her request. The Jews slay 75,000, and otherwise "wreak their will on their enemies" (9:5). Later, in memory of their deliverance and of this revenge, they create the two-day feast of Purim, named for the *pur* or lot that Haman had cast to select Adar as the month when the Jews would die, "the fourteenth and fifteenth days of Adar, every year—the same days on which the Jews enjoyed relief from their foes and the same month which had been transformed for them from one of grief and mourning to one of festive joy" (9:21–22).

The absence of even a passing reference to God in the Book of Esther has suggested deliberate exclusion to many commentators. The Purim holiday, a late addition to the Jewish calendar quite probably borrowed from the Babylonians before the Book of Esther was written, became a kind of Jewish bacchanalia, and perhaps for that reason it may have been judged best to keep the divine name clear of association with it and possible desecration through it. On this reading, the Book of Esther is conscious historical fiction, written for entertainment, and its violence is no more (if no less) unedifying than the violence of an American-style "action adventure" film in which the hero mows down hundreds of generic bad guys with his machine gun. The Septuagint translation of Esther, however, does refer to God and, in fact, includes prayers by Mordecai and Esther among its several substantial additions to the text. Though some of these references and additions, whose effect is to make the story more appropriate, prima facie, for inclusion in the Tanakh, may have been supplied by the Greek-speaking Jews of the Western Diaspora, others may go back to an uncorrected Hebrew original; that is, to a time before all references to God were purged from the story. All of this lies in the realm of historical speculation. What remains is the actively rather than passively secular effect of the Hebrew text as placed in the Jewish canon.

The Tanakh is a collection of books dealing in the main with the relationship between God and Israel. The supreme crisis in that relationship was Israel's mass apostasy from God and God's devastating punishment of Israel by defeat and exile. Their covenant, which had begun when he liberated them from slavery and imminent genocide in Egypt, seemed effectively to end as the land he had so long ago given them became the possession of foreign invaders. It is at that point that the formal narrative of the relationship between God and Israel, running from Exodus through II Kings, breaks off. To be sure, much can be inferred about divine and human hopes for a new beginning, even in the absence of narrative, from the preexilic and exilic prophets, and a good deal can be inferred about the actual new beginning from the postexilic prophets. Yet through all the prophets and writings from Isaiah through Ecclesiastes, no formal narrative dealing with the further life of the nation as a whole has been encountered. After the last prophet (Malachi), moreover, the drift has been decidedly toward individual rather than collective concerns.

For all these reasons, the resumption of the narrative in Esther and the fact that the narrative resumed do indeed deal with the collective destiny of the nation in its diaspora lend this book an undeniable impact. Of all the occurrences of the words *Jew* and *the Jews* in the Tanakh, the great majority are found in this one book. In the earlier books of the Tanakh, the corresponding words are *Israelite* and *Israel*, the name of the nation (and its eponymous ancestor) referring collectively to all who belonged to it. Israel was a twelve-tribe union, within which the Jews, the sons of Judah, were one tribe. Reference was rarely made to the sons of Judah as Judahites, Judeans, or Jews, however. The collective word for them was *Judah*, and they were rarely referred to in any other way. That the resumption of the narrative of national history should coincide with this crucial change in self-designation only makes Esther, the book in which the resumption occurs, that much more important. Israel is back, as we might put it, now calling itself "the Jews," still speaking Hebrew, still beyond confusion with any other nation, but, amazingly, without its God.

This last inference would not be required if the Book of Esther took any other shape than the one it does—if, in other words, it were not a story of genocide averted, mimicking the very foundation myth of the nation. The power of the Exodus memory as a paradigm of divine redemption from genocide is such that when the threat that led to the Exodus is so nearly duplicated, God cannot be merely and neutrally absent from the story. If he does not intervene to save his people or, at the very minimum, if they do not so much as call upon him in their hour of peril, then he seems aggressively dismissed from their story. Whatever the intent of the Book of Esther, this is the effect. There are certain households in which certain words may not be spoken. Years may go by in which no discussion is permitted of why they may not be spoken, but the silence continues and is "heard" at every moment. Whatever the intent of the silence about God in the Book of Esther, this is its effect. Esther and Mordecai are not God incarnate. To call them that, one would need at least to speak the word *God*. But they are very nearly God's redemptive action incarnate. They do for the Jews under Ahasuerus what the Lord did for Israel under Pharaoh. They do what the Lord's anointed was once expected to do again for a restored Israel. It may go without saying that the Lord's anointed, the Messiah, is not mentioned in Esther, and the very word *Israel* never crosses the protagonists' lips.

Literarily, the Book of Esther is sometimes joined to the books of Judith and Tobit, works originally written in Hebrew or Aramaic but preserved only in Greek translation in the Septuagint. All three are edifying historical fiction about Jews living under foreign rule. But in that characterization of them, the key word is *edifying*, for one man's edification can always be another man's scandal. Judith and Tobit are far more pious than Esther. In both, alongside the valor of the human protagonist, help continues to come in the name of the Lord, but neither of them is included in the Jewish canon, and Esther is. To speculate at any length about why this is so would be to stray too far into the history of Diaspora Jewry, but, as a bare minimum, one cannot rule out that Esther was included precisely because it does *not* wait on the Lord for redemption. Somebody back there may have liked it for just that reason. And it is quite striking to link its self-reliance with the self-reliance of Nehemiah, another Persian Jew who takes defense of the Jews as his responsibility rather than God's. Historians rightly read Esther as fiction and Nehemiah as history, but there is an important spiritual link between the two.

But even if nobody back there liked Esther for any such reason (and from the beginning, there have been both Jewish and Christian objections to it), even if the literary effect of its placement is purely accidental, the effect remains. When, in the Book of Esther, wicked men plot against the Jews of Shushan and when the Jews do not cry out to God for relief from this injustice as the Psalmist does, something changes. Though the Jews are grief-stricken and almost panic-stricken over the threat to their lives, their sense of grievance stops with the human beings involved, and their sense of panic does not prevent them from taking decisive, autonomous action. This too changes something. "From India to Nubia," the extent of Ahasuerus's empire according to the Book of Esther, the Jews have become, as it were, God's ex-wife now responsible for her own debts only, God's former client now representing herself, God's grown-up child moved out of the house. The Jews' world is sometimes hostile, but with talent, courage, and a little luck, they are making a go of it. As for God, he is, to all seeming, no longer any concern of theirs.

Ancient of Days
"Seal the Book Until the Time of the End"
DANIEL

Though there is something terminal about the Book of Esther, it is not the last book in the Tanakh, and its last word, or studied silence, about God is not final either. In the Book of Daniel, God and Israel at least through intermediaries are together again. Daniel, like Esther, is a Jew at an imperial court, but God is also present in the Book of Daniel as the acknowledged source of success as he is not in any corresponding way in the Book of Esther. Esther is a single, continuous narrative, whereas Daniel consists of a set of tales from the hero's life at the Babylonian court (Dan. 1–6) followed by a set of visions (Dan. 7–12). But at least the first half of Daniel may be considered a kind of religious version of Esther.

Perhaps the clearest single contrast between Esther and Daniel, in this regard, is that between two episodes in which particularly devious enemies of the Jews are hoist by their own petard. In Esther 5–7, Haman ends up impaled on the fifty-cubit stake he had raised for the execution of Mordecai. In Daniel 6, Daniel's persecutors die in the lions' den that they had prepared for his execution. Mordecai's offense scarcely exceeded, if it exceeded at all, personal disrespect for Haman, whereas Daniel's offense was the specifically religious one of defying a decree—issued to entrap him—that for thirty days all prayer should be offered only to the king. Mordecai's vindication, by the same token, is a purely personal (or personal and national) triumph, whereas Daniel's redounds to God's worldwide credit. The king in Daniel writes "to all the peoples and nations of every language that inhabit the earth":

> May your well-being abound! I have hereby given an order that throughout my royal domain men must tremble in fear before the God of Daniel, for He is the living God who endures forever; His kingdom is indestructible, and His dominion is to the end of time; He delivers and saves, and performs signs and wonders in heaven and on earth, for He delivered Daniel from the power of the lions. (6:26–28)

The Book of Daniel opens with the protagonist and three other young Jews—Hananiah, Mishael, and Azariah—at the court of Nebuchadnezzar, king of Babylon, brought there as captives after Nebuchadnezzar's sack of Jerusalem. These opening chapters are akin in mood to the closing chapters of the Book of Genesis, in which Joseph, brought to Egypt as a captive, rises to power at the court of Pharaoh. Like Joseph in his day, Daniel and his friends are more astute than the other attendants at the royal court: "Whenever the king put a question to them requiring wisdom and understanding, he found them to be ten times better than all the magicians and exorcists throughout his realm" (1:20).

Daniel's special expertise, like Joseph's, is in divination by dream interpretation, but there are differences. When Joseph interpreted Pharaoh's dream of seven fat cows and seven lean cows and so on, God assisted him in reading a course of events that was not itself the result of a divine plan. The God who was assisting Joseph was not so great a god as that: great enough to know what was going on but not great enough to determine what would go on. He was, as we said in discussing Joseph, a personal god with a limited mandate. And though Joseph enjoyed God's steadfast love and acknowledged God's help, he did not speak to God either in petition or in thanksgiving. By contrast, Daniel extravagantly thanks the "God of Heaven," who is also the "God of my fathers," for revealing the meaning of Nebuchadnezzar's dream to him in a night vision; and as he does so, he honors this God as the cause of the very events whose course he has now revealed:

> Let the name of God be blessed forever and ever,
> For wisdom and power are His.
> He changes times and seasons,
> Removes kings and installs kings;
> He gives the wise their wisdom
> And knowledge to those who know.
> He reveals deep and hidden things,
> Knows what is in the darkness,
> And light dwells with Him.
> I acknowledge and praise You,
> O God of my fathers,
> You who have given me wisdom and power,
> For now You have let me know what we asked of You;
> You have let us know what concerns the king. (2:20–23)

The outcome of this revelation is, in the spirit of Isaiah, both that the gentiles recognize the true God and that, in the process, the Jews prosper. Daniel explains Nebuchadnezzar's dream, stressing to the king that he is able to do so only because "there is a God in heaven who reveals mysteries" and because this God chooses to open the future to Nebuchadnezzar through Daniel. In reply the king says, "Truly your God must be the God of gods and Lord of kings and the revealer of mysteries to have enabled you to reveal this mystery" (2:47), and he showers gifts on Daniel and appoints him and his companions to high public office. God seems, behind the scenes, to have become quite active again, and yet, as we shall see, there is a subtle change.

A part of the literary effect of the Book of Esther is that it is played out entirely in the present, like a movie and indeed like a movie with scarcely any backstory. History and memory are, by sharpest contrast with the rest of the Tanakh, of no consequence in the Book of Esther, and this may be no accident: The Jewish memory was, quintessentially, a memory of the mighty acts of God, and the Jews of the Book of Esther no longer look to God. Daniel differs from Esther by being more typically Jewish, looking both backward and forward and continuing to expect divine action.

Yet for Daniel, history has become more a theater for viewing the action than an arena for taking part in it, and this sometimes seems to go for Daniel's God as well. Ecclesiastes, we may recall, believed that the past and the future, though they could not be known, were entirely predetermined and recurrent. Daniel stops short of asserting complete predetermination, much less recurrence. More autonomy than that is reserved for God. And yet we can discern a nascent sense of history as, to use an anachronistic image, a vast reel of film whose contents can be known before it is projected. That God may have made the film counts for less than that he or his angels can at their discretion either provide a preview of it or, as we shall shortly see, prevent its release indefinitely.

It is the miracle of prediction—fortune-telling at the international level—rather than any battlefield miracle that is expected to humble the gentiles and bring them to the worship of the true God. Thus, in Daniel 4, Daniel predicts a time of personal humiliation and misery for Nebuchadnezzar; and Nebuchadnezzar, after the prediction has come true and the time of trial is behind him, "blesse[s] the Most High, and praise[s] and glorifie[s] the Ever-Living One" (4:31). Pharaoh had to be brought by God's "mighty hand and outstretched arm" to a (temporary) acknowledgment of God. Even when divinely caused disaster does befall a gentile enemy, as it befalls Belshazzar on the night when the famous "handwriting on the wall" appears at his feast, God's power is proven less by the fact that Belshazzar is defeated than by the fact that the defeat was predicted. When Darius the Mede overthrows Belshazzar the Babylonian, the Jews may merely exchange one ruler for another; but if through their God they have unique intellectual access to this and future such changes, they have another kind of mastery over their condition. Increasingly, knowledge is power, and almost more than power.

In the latter six chapters of Daniel, which have no parallel in Esther, this emphasis on knowledge only grows more pronounced. Knowledge was also important to the Psalmist, of course, who found the "thoughts of God" as expressed in Torah "weighty" or "precious." The abiding valuing of the law both as a guide to life and as an avenue to intimacy with God accomplished a kind of rescue from the failure of prophecy. But it was, after all, only the second, restorational half of prophecy that had proven a disappointment. The first, judgmental half had been a success to the extent that the punishments which the preexilic prophets predicted—the defeats, the exile—did come to pass. Those disasters, paradoxically, could continue to be counted among the mighty acts of God, the proofs of his power.

But a new kind of disaster defied that kind of conceptualization. The plausibility of the earlier linkage rested on the fact that disaster had followed upon an undeniable mass apostasy. Later, however, the Jews began to be persecuted *because* they were being faithful to their God. Persecutions of this sort (which took place, historically, when the Greeks succeeded the Persians as rulers of the Near East) are alluded to in Daniel's visions. In these visions, the author draws on the Jews' now extensive experience of empires rising and falling to inscribe their current misfortunes in a larger apocalyptic vision of disaster overcoming a long series of empires until, at length, God and his people are victorious. The vision is consoling, for all its short-term horror, because it eliminates that which always makes pain least bearable—namely, the sense that one has been gratuitously singled out to suffer. "Golden lads and girls *all* must," Shakespeare wrote, "As chimney sweepers come to dust." In Daniel's apocalyptic vision, the golden lads are named Sargon and Nebuchadnezzar and Cyrus and Alexander. The fact that all of them without exception will come to dust makes it more bearable that, at the time of writing, it is Israel that looks like a chimney sweeper.

In the end, of course, what consoles most is not the fall of empires as such but Israel's glorious victory. Daniel 7 is a vision of successive inhuman beasts, one more hideous than the next, until at length "one like a human being" appears. The subhuman beasts are the gentile empires, whose rule is temporary; the triumphant human being is the Jews, whose rule, when it comes, will be eternal:

> The dominion of the other beasts was taken away, but an extension of life was given to them for a time and season. As I looked on, in the night vision,
>
> One like a human being
> Came with the clouds of heaven;
> He reached the Ancient of Days
> And was presented to Him.
> Dominion, glory, and kingship were given to him;
> All peoples and nations of every language must
>   serve him.
> His dominion is an everlasting dominion that
>   shall not pass away,
> And his kingship, one that shall not be
>   destroyed. (7:12–14)

Daniel does not know, until it is explained to him, what this vision means, but the explanation, very notably, does not come from the Ancient of Days—God himself—but from an attendant, who explains to Daniel that the last beast in the series

> will speak words against the Most High, and will harass the holy ones of the Most High. He will think of changing times and laws, and they will be delivered into his power for a time, times, and half a time. Then the court will sit and his dominion will be taken away, to be destroyed and abolished for all time. The kingship and dominion and grandeur belonging to all the kingdoms under Heaven will be given to the people of the holy ones of the Most High. Their kingdom shall be an everlasting kingdom, and all dominions shall serve and obey them. (7:25–27)

In the explanation, what is most remarkable is the phrase "Then the court will sit." Fleetingly, we have heard of or seen a heavenly court before: at the creation, in Isaiah's inaugural vision, in Micaiah's description of the heavenly adjudication of wars between Syria and Israel, in the Book of Job, and on a few other occasions. But action taken by any member of the heavenly court but God himself has been exceedingly rare. Here the "attendant" who explains the vision to Daniel seems to be not just a manifestation of God, as several times in the Book of Genesis, but a distinct being in a heavenly assembly taking collective action.

This impression is both strengthened and complicated in Daniel 8, when, after seeing another vision of the end, Daniel overhears two "holy beings" speaking to each other. He then sees "one who looked like a man" and hears a voice, not necessarily or even presumably the voice of God, call out: "Gabriel, make that man understand the vision" (8:16). The famous angel Gabriel makes here his first appearance in the Bible, and he explains to Daniel that the vision he has seen was a representation of the end of time. Daniel, dismayed, is told to keep the vision a secret since it pertains to far-off days.

In Daniel 9, Daniel has been reading Jeremiah, and at Jeremiah 25:12 he has come upon the prediction that seventy years after the fall of Jerusalem to Nebuchadnezzar, Babylon itself will fall. Having read this passage, Daniel puts on sackcloth and ashes, fasts, and prays at great length to God, confessing abjectly and repeatedly that the disaster is the direct result of Israel's disobedience but imploring God's intervention. And then:

> While I was speaking, praying, and confessing my sin and the sin of my people Israel, and laying my supplication before the Lord my God on behalf of the holy mountain of my God—while I was uttering my prayer, the man Gabriel, whom I had previously seen in the vision, was sent forth in flight and reached me about the time of the evening offering. He made me understand by speaking to me and saying, "Daniel, I have just come forth to give you understanding. A word went forth as you began your plea, and I have come to tell it, for you are precious; so mark the word and understand the vision." (9:20–23)

The visions of Daniel are dated, by the Book of Daniel itself, to just before and after the fall of Babylon to the Persians, but by their placement in the literary sequence of the Tanakh, they are effectively read at a later date. Persia, as we saw in the Book of Esther, is long established, and a group of Jews have returned to Jerusalem as well.

It is for their benefit that the "seventy years" of Jeremiah is reinterpreted by Gabriel as seventy weeks of years, thus saving the text and restoring the hope of a still-future definitive victory for God's holy ones, as they are sometimes called in this book. Gabriel divides this 490-year period for Daniel, alluding to various past or future events. The particulars of the vision are less important, however, than is the fact that scripture as written and consulted has now a divinatory importance matching that of dreams or visions and that, again and still, God himself is inactive and silent. God's Bible is replacing the Bible's God.

Gabriel returns in Daniel 10 in the guise of "a man dressed in linen, his loins girt in fine gold. His body was like beryl, his face had the appearance of lightning, his eyes were like flaming torches, his arms and legs had the color of burnished bronze, and the sound of his speech was like the noise of a multitude" (10:5–6). With him, Gabriel brings news of war in heaven. He had sought to come quickly to Daniel's aid, he says.

> However, the prince of the Persian kingdom [a heavenly being allied with Persia] opposed me for twenty-one days; now Michael, a prince of the first rank, has come to my aid, after I was detained there with the kings of Persia. So I have come to make you understand what is to befall your people in the days to come, for there is yet a vision for those days. . . . Now I must go back to fight the prince of Persia. When I go off, the prince of Greece will come in. No one is helping me against them except your prince, Michael. However, I will tell you what is recorded in the book of truth. (10:13–14, 20–21)

What follows is a long, coded but decipherable account of the rise and fall of several empires in the Near East. Their rising and falling is not attributed to any action by God, nor is it even claimed as part of a vast divine plan. Though Gabriel knows its outcome in advance, he claims no further control over it, even in God's name, until the very end:

> At that time, the great prince, Michael, who stands beside the sons of your people, will appear. It will be a time of trouble, the like of which has never been seen since the nation came into being. At that time, your people will be rescued, all who are found inscribed in the book. Many of those that sleep in the dust of the earth will awake, some to eternal life, others to reproaches, to everlasting

> abhorrence. And the knowledgeable will be radiant like the bright expanse of sky, and those who lead the many to righteousness will be like the stars forever and ever.
>
> But you, Daniel, keep the words secret, and seal the book until the time of the end. (12:1–4)

If, in the Book of Esther, God seems to have abdicated in favor of Esther and Mordecai, in the Book of Daniel, he seems to have abdicated in favor of Gabriel and Michael, the counselor and the warrior prince who, respectively, will guide and defend the nation until its final victory. Clearly, the struggle will be a difficult one. If there is a heavenly "prince of Persia" and a "prince of Greece," presumably there are other princes as well. The time when they were an anonymous flutter of wings about the throne of the single, overwhelmingly dominant God seems to have passed. Satan's assertion of his malign power against Job now seems to have been only a harbinger of other angelic beings to come. Ultimate victory is still assured to the righteous, but there is little hope in the interim for more than an understanding of the stages in the tribulation:

> I heard and did not understand, so I said, "My lord [Gabriel], what will be the outcome of these things?" He said, "Go, Daniel, for these words are secret and sealed to the time of the end. Many will be purified and purged and refined; the wicked will act wickedly and none of the wicked will understand; but the knowledgeable will understand." (12:8–10)

There is something cold about this vision. Though it is a vision of victory, it is scarcely one of reconciliation, world peace, the lion lying down beside the lamb, the nations streaming to Zion to learn the law, and so on. It is not even a vision of idyllic prosperity in a land flowing with milk and honey. The imagining of the end has been, in effect, impoverished by the imagining of stages en route to the end. The righteous may hope to be like the stars of the sky, but the awe that the Psalmist brought to every mention of the stars is missing. God has made his final, silent appearance, and the story that began with his creation of light and of the firmament and of the stars has ended with the stars. "In the beginning" has been projected to the end, the final victory. And just here, on this nominally triumphant but oddly flat note, the biography of God comes to its second ending.

Through to the end of the Book of Daniel, the faint possibility of God's return has remained. Now it is gone. God has done what God had to do. Others, one way or another, will now carry his work forward. There have been moments of triumph; the books of Chronicles are appended precisely to recall them before the Tanakh ends. There have been moments of splendid, blind confidence. There have also been moments of rash anger, of perhaps equally rash repentance, and at least one moment of something like shame.

But there are to be no further such moments, no further links in the chain. The Ancient of Days, as Daniel now calls him, is not dead but old and, by implication, weary. Undefeated, undestroyed, he is, somehow, retired from the scene. The multiplicity that characterized him at his most vigorous does not collapse to unity and then to nullity in his gradual disappearance, but he seems only the more poignantly real for that failure to collapse definitively and cleanly. Nothing that literature contrives, after all, is so artificial as its endings. Real lives never end with artistic finality. Either they are rudely interrupted, as Ecclesiastes says, or they end in a slow fade that has none of the rounded perfection of a well-wrought last page. Real lives end, we might say, just as God's life ends: A supreme effort falls slightly short (the Voice from the Whirlwind), a long period opens in which one has progressively less to say and the devotion of one's friends is slowly overtaken by their silence; a final claim is mounted that one's counsel has always mattered more than one's prowess, and the claim helps—but only somewhat. And then the lights fail.

Scroll
"We Make This Pledge in Writing"
EZRA AND NEHEMIAH

The books of Ezra and Nehemiah resume the narrative broken off at the end of II Kings, and the story they tell is of a reconciliation between the Lord and his chosen people. What is striking, however, is that in these books the roles of the two are nearly reversed. In the days of Abraham, Moses, Joshua, and David, the Lord took mighty action on behalf of Israel. In the days of Ezra and Nehemiah, Israel takes energetic action on behalf of the Lord. They become covenant partners again, but on a distinctly different basis.

Historically, the Babylonian empire proved short-lived; and the Persian empire, which succeeded it, dispatched a group of Judean exiles to Jerusalem to build a temple on the site of the one the Babylonians had destroyed. At that time, the Persian intention may not have been to detach Judea from the larger western province to which it then belonged. This was the eventual outcome, however; and if the books of Ezra and Nehemiah provide less than a full account of the reeemergence of Judea as a distinct, though still subordinate, political unit, they nonetheless provide vivid scenes from the time when this change was under way.

Historically, again, the books of Ezra and Nehemiah may be viewed as footage from the infancy of the Jews as a people distinct from the rest of what had been Greater Israel as well as from the other nations of the world. In these books, we see them assuming for the first time the durable character of a nation whose large diaspora supports a smaller population at home. Noble Jews with influence at the seat of world power begin to assume a key role in assuring the survival and welfare of the nation. We have seen legendary expressions of this ideal: Joseph warning Pharaoh of a coming famine and saving his father and brothers from starvation in the process, Esther and Mordecai foiling the plot of two eunuchs to murder the king of Persia and later foiling a larger plot against the Jews of the empire, Daniel distinguishing himself in the Babylonian court. But Nehemiah, cupbearer to the king of Persia, is the first in whom this ideal is embodied in an unmistakably historical setting.

A third development, religiously as well as historically fateful, is acceptance of foreign rule by the politically ascendant party in Jerusalem and its development of socioreligious self-segregation as an alternative to true political sovereignty. In the books of Ezra and Nehemiah, those who impose this philosophy clearly do so over measurable opposition. Some in-country Judeans refuse the strict observance of endogamy and sabbath rest as the sign and enforcement of collective identity. The diaspora may be resigned to foreign hegemony, but some in the land itself—Judeans as opposed to Jews, we might almost say—continue to be drawn to the messianic vision of the nations of the world streaming to Jerusalem to worship God and/or to the apocalyptic vision of Armageddon as the prelude to this glory. Such views are alluded to even here. But the religiously devout, politically pragmatic path taken by the returning exiles Ezra and Nehemiah will become Judaism as we know it and will prove the salvation of the Jews. As such, it must be recognized as an extraordinarily creative and sagacious response to the kind of national trauma that has ended the national life of countless small nations.

The boldness of these Jewish moves is not accompanied, however, by any return to boldness on the part of the Lord God. The very stress in these books on the devotion of the Jewish leaders to the Lord and the eagerness of the people to please him, repenting as soon as their sin is pointed out to them, has a paradoxical effect. It makes the Lord seem less like the Jews' creator, liege, father, or king and more like their enfeebled but cherished ward. His may be the honor, but theirs is the vigor.

Human virtue and divine vigor are inversely proportional in the Tanakh. The Lord God never seemed more invincible than when conducting the endlessly complaining, recalcitrant, "stiff-necked" Israelites out of Egypt and through the desert to the land of Canaan. The generation of migrants whom we meet in Ezra and Nehemiah is by contrast the picture of piety. He himself, however, in their company, neither speaks nor acts. It is for this reason that this prelude to their story seems a coda to his. Back then, he seemed to be creating them as his people; now, they seem to be preserving him as their God.

Ezra

The Book of Ezra opens promisingly, as it were, when the Lord "rouse[s] the spirit of King Cyrus of Persia to issue a proclamation" authorizing a delegation of Jews to return to Jerusalem and rebuild the destroyed temple. But is the king acting on his own, and is the action just being attributed to the Lord's rousing? The question may seem invidious or "modern," but recall that this situation—captive Israelites about to set out for the promised land—very closely matches the exodus from Egypt. And recall that on that occasion the Lord was so eager to have his own power unmistakably demonstrated that he hardened Pharaoh's heart, deliberately making the Egyptian king refuse to grant the Israelites permission to leave. A victory won over no opposition was not enough for him.

Be that as it may, the Jews respond to the proclamation with goodwill. A substantial delegation leaves for Jerusalem, and those who stay behind in Babylon support the emigrants "with silver vessels, with gold, with goods, with livestock, and with precious objects . . ." (Ezra 1:6). The king himself returns to their custody the precious temple furnishings Nebuchadnezzar had carried off.

Under Zerubbabel, the Persian-appointed Jewish governor, and Jeshua, the priest, regular sacrifice is begun on the site of the old temple even before the foundation for the new one is laid. But at the ceremony consecrating the new foundation, feelings are painfully mixed:

> Many of the priests and Levites and the chiefs of the clans, the old men who had seen the first house, wept loudly at the sight of the founding of this house. Many others shouted joyously at the top of their voices. The people could not distinguish the shouts of joy from the people's weeping. . . . (3:12–13)

This is the moment of which the prophet Zechariah said:

> Zerubbabel's hands have founded this House and Zerubbabel's hands shall complete it. Then you shall know that it was the Lord of Hosts who sent me to you. Does anyone scorn a day of small beginnings? When they see the plummet in the hand of Zerubbabel, they shall rejoice. (Zech. 4:8–10)

As it turns out, the plummet quickly falls from Zerubbabel's hand: Local opposition quickly brings the construction of the temple to a halt.

The opposition, paradoxically, comes from people who want to help in the building of the temple, non-Israelites whom the Assyrian king settled in the land and who have adopted the worship of the Lord. "Let us build with you," they say, "since we too worship your God, having offered sacrifices to Him since the time of King Esarhaddon of Assyria, who brought us here" (Ezra 4:2). The assumption must be that some of the Israelites remained in the land after the Assyrian conquest of the northern kingdom of Israel in 722 B.C.E. Otherwise how would the newcomers have adopted the worship of the Israelite Lord? The further assumption must be that the offer is coming from the descendants of the native as well as the immigrant part of Samaria, as the region is now called, after its capital city. But the Jews decline this offer from the "people of the land" (the phrase used in the Book of Joshua to describe the Canaanite natives whom Israel was to displace):

> "It is not for you and us to build a House to our God, but we alone will build it to the Lord God of Israel, in accord with the charge that the king, King Cyrus of Persia, laid upon us." Thereupon the people of the land undermined the resolve of the people of Judah, and made them afraid to build. (4:3–4)

The Samaritans then denounce the Jews to the Persian king, claiming that the rebuilding of Jerusalem will end in sedition: "We advise the king that if this city is rebuilt and its walls are completed, you will no longer have any portion in the province Beyond the River" (4:16)—that is, west of the Jordan. A successor of Cyrus is persuaded by the denunciation and reverses the decree of restoration: "This city is not to be rebuilt until I so order" (4:21). Armed with this decree, the Samaritans stop the Jews' work by main force.

Some time later, prompted by the prophecies of Haggai and Zechariah, Zerubbabel and Jeshua resume work on the temple. The then Persian governor inquires of the current king whether they have authorization for the reconstruction, and this time a confirmation of the original decree is forthcoming. In short order, "urged on by the prophesying of Haggai the prophet and Zechariah son of Iddo . . . they brought the building to completion . . ." (6:14).

The dedication of the finished temple is an occasion of joy without tears, but what has the Lord God's role been in the reconstruction? He "roused the spirit of King Cyrus" at the start, but does the text include him just as a gesture? If the Lord is the true agent, then why does the work stop when Cyrus's successor wants it stopped and resume when the successor's successor wants it resumed? The Lord seems to lack the power he had when he faced Pharaoh to impose his will for his people over any opposition.

One may also ask whether he has abandoned the ambition he once expressed to have all nations acknowledge him at his temple in Jerusalem. If the Persian king, a non-Jew, may decree the rebuilding of the temple, making it to that extent his own project, why may the local non-Jews, some of them Israelites, not take part as well? It would seem that the Persian king is, at least at the practical level, a more important authority than the Lord God. When the "people of the land" offer to help, the Jews do not say that the Lord God has forbidden this, nor does the Lord appear in person to say, "I forbid this." Instead, Persia is invoked: "We alone will build it to the Lord God of Israel, in accord with the charge that the king, King Cyrus of Persia, laid upon us" (4:3). The devotion to the Lord God of Israel is surely sincere, but these words suggest inescapably that the Lord is now Israel's ward, rather than vice versa.

When Moses led the Israelites out of Egypt, he brought them to Mount Sinai. Never in all his life, as the Tanakh recounts it, did the Lord God seem more overwhelmingly dominant than when through Moses he gave Israel his law. The law is a major sign and memorial of his irresistible will and the fearful violence that then enforced it. It is thus surprising to find at this point that the law, like the temple, has come under the patronage of the king of Persia. Ezra, "a scribe expert in the Teaching of Moses" whose lineage extends back to Moses' brother Aaron, receives a commission from King Artaxerxes:

> For you are commissioned by the king and his seven advisers to regulate Judah and Jerusalem according to the law of your God, which is in your care. . . . And you, Ezra, by the divine wisdom you possess, appoint magistrates and judges to judge all the people in the province of Beyond the River who know the laws of your God, and to teach those who do not know them. Let anyone who does not obey the law of your God and the law of the king be punished with dispatch, whether by death, corporal punishment, confiscation of possessions, or imprisonment. (7:14, 25–26)

In the rest of Ezra's commission, the verses not quoted, the king details his material support for the temple; but his endorsement of the law is more noteworthy. Historical scholarship believes that the law "which is in your care" was a written document—either the Torah or the Book of Deuteronomy. Everything suggests that the king reviewed this written document and simply subsumed it to the law of the empire. Ezra's law, in Artaxerxes' view, "reports" to Artaxerxes' law as Ezra himself reports to Artaxerxes.

The Jewish view of the relationship is only gently different. Ezra says: "Blessed is the Lord God of our fathers, who put it into the mind of the king to glorify the House of the Lord in Jerusalem, and who inclined the king and his counselors and the king's military officers to be favorably disposed toward me" (7:27). The text of the Book of Ezra opened with a brief narrative foundation: "The Lord roused the spirit of King Cyrus. . . ." There is no such narrative foundation for the imposition of Jewish law. We do not read "Then the Lord God put it into the mind of the king to impose the Lord's law. . . ." We have rather an action of the king given a theological interpretation by Ezra.

Pious Israelites have interpreted their lives this way from the very start of the Tanakh. Thus, of the birth of Simeon, one of the sons of Leah, we read (Gen. 29:33): "She conceived again and bore a son, and declared, 'This is because the Lord heard that I was unloved and has given me this one also'; and she named him Simeon." But within the earlier narrative, such interpretations were bolstered by actions reported by the narrator. Thus, two verses earlier in Genesis: "The Lord saw that Leah was unloved and he opened her womb." In the books of Ezra and Nehemiah, no such narrative foundation is laid; and these books acquire, as a result, a peculiarly modern character. Though they never discuss unbelief, they also never present belief as unavoidable in the face of the mighty acts of God.

A moment of unusual candor and self-consciousness about just this point occurs in Ezra 8. A large delegation—in effect, a distinct second emigration—of Jews from Babylon accompanies Ezra, bringing with them a potentially major strengthening of the Jewish colony in Jerusalem. Before they set out, Ezra orders the emigrants to fast and beseech God for a safe journey,

> for I was ashamed to ask the king for soldiers and horsemen to protect us against any enemy on the way, since we had told the king, 'The benevolent care of our God is for all who seek Him, while His fierce anger is against all who forsake Him.' So we fasted and besought our God for this, and He responded to our plea. (Ezra 8:22–23)

How much is from the benevolence of God, and how much from the benevolence of the king? Ezra is acutely aware of this question.

His awareness itself constitutes God's principal presence in the action. In Ezra and Nehemiah, by contrast with several of the books we considered in Chapter 10, God is by no means passed over in silence. He is referred to frequently; devotion to him motivates action, even daring action; and in the process he continues to count. On the other hand, his is an attributed reality and a far cry from the demonstrated reality of old. The change, profound and occasionally poignant, is what makes the books of Ezra and Nehemiah the third ending of the Tanakh. He lives on, yes, but the vitality of the Jews palpably exceeds his own.

If Ezra's interpretations mark the definitive retreat of the Lord God from demonstrated to attributed power, the long prayer that Ezra speaks at 9:6–15 marks a parallel retreat from prophecy to preaching. In classic Israelite prophecy, the Lord speaks to Israel and calls on her to act. In the classic Israelite prayer of the Psalms, Israel speaks to God and calls on him to act. In Ezra 9:6–15, we have a combination of the two: Ezra ostensibly speaks to God, but it is not God but Israel whom he calls on to act. With the returned exiles looking on, Ezra rends his garments, tears his hair, and confesses the grievous sin of those among them who have married local women "so that the holy seed has become intermingled with the peoples of the land" (9:2). But at this point in his prayer, the point where a prophet would have announced God's punishment, Ezra exhorts his congregation by asking a rhetorical question nominally of God but actually of them:

> Now, what can we say in the face of this, O our God, for we have forsaken Your commandments, which You gave us through Your servants the prophets when You said, "The land that you are about to possess is a land unclean through the uncleanness of the peoples of the land, through their abhorrent practices with which they, in their impurity, have filled it from one end to the other. Now then, do not give your daughters in marriage to their sons or let their daughters marry your sons; do nothing for their well-being or advantage, then you will be strong and enjoy the bounty of the land and bequeath it to your children forever." After all that has happened to us because of our evil deeds and our deep guilt—though You, our God, have been forbearing, [punishing us] less than our iniquity [deserves] in that You have granted us such a remnant as

> this—shall we once again violate Your commandments by intermarrying with these peoples who follow such abhorrent practices? (9:10–14)

There are verbal echoes here of the Psalms, but the Psalms are genuinely spoken to God. This prayer, not to call it insincere, is spoken past God to the Jews.

But never underestimate a great preacher. The effect of Ezra's "prayer" is dramatic:

> While Ezra was praying and making confession, weeping and prostrating himself before the House of God, a very great crowd of Israelites gathered about him, men, women, and children; the people were weeping bitterly. Then Shecaniah son of Jehiel of the family of Elam spoke up and said to Ezra, "We have trespassed against our God by bringing into our homes foreign women from the peoples of the land; but there is still hope for Israel despite this. Now then, let us make a covenant with our God to expel all these women and those who have been born to them, in accordance with the bidding of the Lord. . . . Take action, for the responsibility is yours and we are with you. Act with resolve!" (10:1–4)

There follows in this tenth and final chapter of the Book of Ezra a mass divorce and expulsion of children. Scores of Jewish men are listed by name, each of whom had married a non-Jewish woman and in some cases had children by her. All of these women and children are driven out.

By the morality of other peoples and other eras, the repentance that Ezra urged was morally wrong, while the sin he condemned was not. But taking the morality of the Tanakh as one finds it, one must be surprised not that the sinners are punished but that they are punished so mildly. After Israel's mass fornication/apostasy with the priestesses of the Baal of Peor (Num. 25), the Lord slew twenty-four thousand Israelites with the plague and required Moses to execute all who had lain with foreign women, impaling them with their faces to the sun. As for the punishment then inflicted on the Midianites for seducing the Israelites, it was genocidal in character. Nothing so violent as that happens here, and Ezra does not suggest in his prayer that it should. The words of "the prophets" that he quotes are not found as such anywhere in the Tanakh, but their nearest equivalents are injunctions that the Lord gives through

Moses in Deuteronomy. There, Moses speaks of both rewards and punishments:

> When the Lord your God brings you to the land that you are about to enter and possess, and He dislodges many nations before you . . . and the Lord your God delivers them to you and you defeat them, you must doom them to destruction: grant them no terms and give them no quarter. You shall not intermarry with them: do not give your daughters to their sons or take their daughters for your sons. For they will turn your children away from Me to worship other gods, and the Lord's anger will blaze forth against you and He will promptly wipe you out. (Deut. 7:1–4)

Ezra speaks only of rewards or, more precisely, of desirable outcomes. The action taken is in accord with the Lord's wishes, but the happy effect of compliance is built in, and the unhappy effect of noncompliance is simply not spoken of.

The contrast between the recalcitrance of the Israelites under Moses and the docility of the Jewish remnant under Ezra is striking. In the person of Shecaniah, the remnant exhorts the new Moses, Ezra, to discipline them, and they accept his corrective measure—the expulsion of their wives and their "intermingled seed"—without demurral. To a point, they do to themselves what once God would have done to them, taking upon themselves his role as judge. But the action taken is a correction rather than a true punishment.

The effect on the felt reality of the Lord is negative if we measure him against what he was in Numbers. However, that may be the wrong measurement to take. For the past several books, he has been not just vastly less than he was in Numbers but significantly less than he is here as the recipient of Ezra's prayer and the source of the ideal of ethnic purity that Ezra preaches. In human terms, the moment is loosely analogous to the one that comes in a long, several-sided conversation when those who have been doing all the talking take notice of someone—call him Francis—who has been not just silent but totally ignored. The silent partner remains silent but is now included by deferential phrases such as "as I'm sure Francis would agree" or "as Francis has often observed."

In purely sociological or Realpolitik terms, Ezra was surely right that uncompromising self-segregation on the part of the Jews had a great deal to do with their "enjoy[ing] the bounty of the land and bequeath[ing] it to their children forever." This is true even if "the land" is taken metaphorically as the social cohesion or ethnic "locatedness" of Jewry in the world. Just what the "abhorrent practices" of the expelled wives were, the Book of Ezra does not tell us. Historically, it is quite conceivable that the divorcées were, as to their beliefs and practices, like the men who in Ezra 4 offer to assist the returning Jewish exiles in rebuilding the temple—that is, non-Israelite or partially Israelite worshipers of the Lord. Their "abhorrent practices," rather than the practices of a rival religion, would then plausibly be syncretistic deviations in the practice of the one received Israelite religion, in which case a reform rather than a mass divorce would seem to be the proper response.

But if that had been the actual response, the Jews could in short order have been demographically swamped within an enlarged, multiethnic population worshiping the Jewish God. They would have been like a founding family after the family firm has gone public: honored to a point but no longer in control. This is rather exactly what happened five hundred years later to the Jews who founded Christianity as a form of Judaism open to non-Jews. Theological or other more value-laden commentary aside, we may credit Ezra with prescience for taking the action he took when he took it. Without him, a monotheistic world religion open to all may have come into existence five hundred years sooner than it did, but the Jews as a nation would have disappeared.

To attribute to Ezra the Jews' adjustment to their status as a minority in diaspora and a political vassal at home is simply to speak of this complex historical process in the simplified, personalized way that the Tanakh itself speaks of it. Later Jewish tradition was to honor Ezra as a second Moses: "Ezra would have been worthy of receiving the Torah had Moses not preceded him," it would say. Contemporary historical scholarship is not sure whether Ezra ever existed, but it is clear in retrospect that, whatever is said about him, a change like the one he is presented as administering did come about. That is, the Jews did become an endogamous, self-segregating nation. Rules that had quite obviously been flouted for centuries by king and commoner alike began to be strictly observed over enormous initial resistance.

Within the Tanakh read as a work of literature, how does this change function as a chapter in the life of God? The answer, as already suggested, is that the Book of Ezra read as literature functions as part of the ending of the life of God. A secure, honored place for him—decent provision, as we might put it—is arranged during a period of dynamic creativity in the life of his people. In his end is their beginning.

Nehemiah

Nehemiah, the last book of the Tanakh that carries the narrative forward at all (I and II Chronicles review events before the fall of Jerusalem), happens also to be the first and only book in the Tanakh written almost entirely as first-person historical narrative. Ezra 8–9 is also in the first person, but it appears in a work of ten chapters otherwise in the third person. By its terminal placement, the change from third-person to first-person narrative in Nehemiah is pregnant with meaning. In the covenant between the Lord God and Israel, the Lord God was, at the start, very obviously the senior partner. In the Book of Ezra, as we have been at some pains to suggest, Israel begins to become the senior partner. In the Book of Nehemiah, when Nehemiah starts to speak in his own name just at the time when he begins to control the flow of events, a change in the form of the narrative may be said to parallel a change in the character of its divine protagonist:

> The narrative of Nehemiah son of Hacaliah:
>
> In the month of Kislev of the twentieth year, when I was in the fortress of Shushan [the Persian capital], Hanani, one of my brothers, together with some men of Judah, arrived, and I asked them about the Jews, the remnant who had survived the captivity, and about Jerusalem. They replied, "The survivors who have survived the captivity there in the province are in dire trouble and disgrace; Jerusalem's wall is full of breaches, and its gates have been destroyed by fire."
>
> When I heard that, I sat and wept, and was in mourning for days, fasting and praying to the God of Heaven. (Neh. 1:1–4)

There follows an ardent prayer with something of a surprise ending: "I said: 'O Lord, God of Heaven, great and awesome God. . . . Grant Your servant success today, and dispose that man [the king] to be compassionate toward him!' I was the king's cupbearer at the time" (1:5, 11).

The king's cupbearer! Even if we are not to understand by "cupbearer" that Nehemiah is the king's Ganymede, his kept youth, he is presumably a young man and clearly at home in the king's innermost circle. In this, the Book of Nehemiah has something in common with the later, first-person chapters of the Book of Daniel. But those chapters present Daniel's dream-visions of the Ancient of Days and the secret future of the whole world. Though they are in the first person, they are scarcely narrative and by no means historical. When Nehemiah speaks in the first person, it is to tell us of his decidedly worldly and practical actions, not his mystical visions.

What makes this change so important is that it places Nehemiah, a human being, uniquely in charge of the shared history—the condition, if you will—of God and Israel. No one in the Tanakh to this late point, not even King David, controls the flow of events as Nehemiah does. And in a way also quite without parallel in all the earlier books of the Tanakh, Nehemiah, exuding confidence, reveals his purposes to us his readers while concealing them, at least as to their full implications, from his contemporaries.

To the king, he indicates that his project is limited: He wishes to rebuild the wall of Jerusalem, no more, and at the king's request he names his return date. The Persian appointees of the province of "Beyond the River" (west of the Jordan) are suspicious, but Nehemiah arrives armed with letters of protection from the king. Late on his first night in Jerusalem, he conducts, on horseback, his own secret survey of the ruined walls of the city. At this point, the local Jewish leaders do not know what he has in mind.

As it turns out, his project is not just to engage the Jerusalemites themselves in gradually repairing the damage that the Babylonians have done to their city but to draft a labor force from the entire Judean countryside to turn Jerusalem, almost overnight, into a fortified city capable of serving as a regional citadel and thus weakening the control exercised over Judea by Sanballat the Horonite. From Samaria, Sanballat claims jurisdiction over the entire region in the name of the Persian king, and it is not without reason that he asks of Nehemiah, "What is this that you are doing? Are you rebelling against the king?" (2:19). The honest answer, never given, is no and yes: No, Nehemiah is not about to rebel against the king, but yes, he is about to present the king with an irreversible administrative revision of his Transjordanian domain.

In its extreme specificity, Nehemiah 3 reads like a preserved work order from the actual reconstruction project. Task forces from different parts of Judea are assigned different sectors of the wall to rebuild. Reporting one of the taunts of his enemies—"That stone wall they are building—if a fox climbed it he would breach it!"—

Nehemiah interrupts his own narrative with a brief prayer for revenge: "Hear, our God, how we have become a mockery, and return their taunts upon their heads!" (3:35–36). A moment later Nehemiah reports in the unmistakable tone of a natural leader: "We rebuilt the wall till it was continuous all around to half its height; for the people's heart was in the work" (3:38).

Situated on a high promontory with an internal water supply, Jerusalem was eminently suitable for a fortress. As a Jebusite city, it had withstood the Israelites long after they were in control of the rest of the countryside. After David took it, it withstood the Israelites' enemies for centuries, even throwing back one attempt at conquest by the Assyrians. With decent walls, it could emerge as a significant local power again.

Having failed to stop Nehemiah's effort from getting under way, Sanballat puts together a local coalition to halt it by main force, but Nehemiah is ready for him:

> From that day on, half my servants did work and half held lances and shields, bows and armor. And the officers stood behind the whole house of Judah who were rebuilding the wall. The basket-carriers were burdened, doing work with one hand while the other held a weapon. As for the builders, each had his sword girded at his side as he was building. The trumpeter stood beside me. I said to the nobles, the prefects, and the rest of the people, "There is much work and it is spread out; we are scattered over the wall, far from one another. When you hear a trumpet call, gather yourselves to me at that place; our God will fight for us!" And so we worked on, while half were holding lances, from the break of day until the stars appeared. (4:10–15)

The entire force has become, in Nehemiah's casual but revealing reference, "my servants." He promises, rhetorically, "Our God will fight for us!" But he is far more specific in describing his practical solution to the problems of how to have a work gang and an army at the same time and how to muster a defense quickly against an enemy's attempt to breach the wall by concentrating his own forces at a single point.

Confidence in God or self-confidence? To the Deuteronomist, Isaiah, and the Psalmist, Israelite self-confidence is reprehensible: Israel should trust in the Lord, not in its own valor or skill. But

Nehemiah, for all his piety, stands at some remove from this strand of the tradition. That he does so may be seen in his reaction to a last attempt to intimidate him. Sanballat sends him a "friendly" letter with a veiled threat:

> Its text was: "Word has reached the nations, and Geshem [an Arab leader] too says that you and the Jews are planning to rebel—for which reason you are building the wall—and that you are to be their king. Such is the word. You have also set up prophets in Jerusalem to proclaim about you, 'There is a king in Judah!' Word of these things will surely reach the king; so come, let us confer together."
>
> I sent back a message to him saying, "None of these things you mention has occurred; they are figments of your imagination"—for they all wished to intimidate us, thinking, "They will desist from the work, and it will not get done." (6:6–9)

Meanwhile, another feigned friend within the city suggests that an irresistible attack on Jerusalem is at hand and Nehemiah should take refuge in the sanctuary of the temple. Nehemiah replies:

> "Will a man like me take flight? Besides who such as I can go into the sanctuary and live? I will not go in." Then I realized that it was not God who sent him, but that he uttered that prophecy about me—Tobiah and Sanballat having hired him—because he was a hireling. . . . (6:11–13)

As a layman, Nehemiah was barred from entering the sanctuary. The false warning was an attempt to entrap him in sacrilege.

Both parts of Nehemiah's reply count. On the one hand, he is by his own lights a pious Jew who respects the temple rules. But on the other, he is a fighter who trusts in his own valor for his defense even while attributing his success to the Lord. And his self-confidence is evidently well-earned:

> The wall was finished on the twenty-fifth of Elul, after fifty-two days [an extraordinary feat of construction]. When all our enemies heard it, all the nations round about us were intimidated, and fell very low in their own estimation; they realized that this work had been accomplished by the help of God. (6:15–16)

National security now essentially secured, Nehemiah addresses domestic affairs in Jerusalem, regulating indebtedness and conducting a census, with his by now familiar energy. In passing, he says (5:14): "From the day I was commissioned to be governor in the land of Judah—from the twentieth year of King Artaxerxes until his thirty-second year, twelve years in all—neither I nor my brothers ever ate of the governor's food allowance." As the king's cupbearer, Nehemiah was conceivably a man of great personal wealth, serving in the manner of some American millionaires in civic positions without salary. That aside, the commission that Nehemiah received from Artaxerxes at the start of this narrative was definitely not a commission to be governor. As we noted, it was a limited commission to rebuild the city wall and then return to Shushan. But Shushan is a long way from Jerusalem. Did Artaxerxes, in practical terms, retain the power to summon Nehemiah home? Once Jerusalem is back in business as a fortified city, no further mention is made of Persia or its king.

The action instead returns to Ezra and therewith, in a new way, to God. In Nehemiah 8–10, Ezra reads "the scroll of the Teaching of Moses" from a wooden tower "to the men and the women and those who could understand." At the same time, Levites stationed among the crowd "read from the scroll of the Teaching of God, translating it and giving the sense; so they understood the reading" (8:1, 3, 8). Not all of the Jewish population of newborn Jerusalem understands Hebrew; some, presumably, know only Aramaic, the lingua franca of the Persian (and, earlier, the Assyrian) empire.

The reading frightens the people, and they begin weeping. But the religious leaders reassure them: "Go, eat choice foods and drink sweet drinks and send portions to whoever has nothing prepared, for the day is holy to our Lord. Do not be sad, for your rejoicing in the Lord is the source of your strength" (8:10). The leaders then lead the people in celebrating—for the first time in a long while if not quite, as the text says, for the first time since the days of Joshua—the feast of tabernacles or booths: makeshift dwellings like those the nation lived in during its desert wanderings after receiving the law and entering into a covenant with the Lord but before entering the promised land.

After the reading of the law, seven Levites recite a long prayer (Neh. 9–10), rehearsing the history of the nation and ratifying the Teaching of God as just read in the name of the people. The conclusion of the prayer reads:

> Today we are slaves, and the land that You gave our fathers to enjoy its fruit and bounty—here we are slaves on it! On account of our sins it yields its abundant crops to kings whom You have set over us. They rule over our bodies and our beasts as they please, and we are in great distress.
>
> In view of all this, we make this pledge and put it in writing; and on the sealed copy [are subscribed] our officials, our Levites, and our priests. (9:36–10:1)

There follows a listing of names. Then the common people swear an oral oath:

> And the rest of the people . . . all who know enough to understand, join with their noble brothers, and take an oath with sanctions to follow the Teaching of God, given through Moses the servant of God, and to observe carefully all the commandments of the Lord our Lord [literally, "*yahweh* our Lord"], His rules and laws.
>
> Namely. . . . (10:29–31)

And there then follows a list of several items singled out for explicit ratification: the ban on intermarriage, a ban on commerce on the sabbath, the establishment of the seventh year as a sabbatical year and a year when debts are all forgiven, and a set of provisions for support of the Jerusalem temple, ending: "We will not neglect the House of our God" (10:40).

Now that the Jews have committed themselves to observing God's law and ratified their covenant with him, how does the Lord indicate that he has accepted their ratification? It is worth recalling, at this point, how in the Book of Exodus he indicated his acceptance of their ratification at Mount Sinai after the first reading of the law. There we read:

> Early in the morning, [Moses] set up an altar at the foot of the mountain, with twelve pillars for the twelve tribes of Israel. He designated some young men among the Israelites, and they offered burnt offerings and sacrificed bulls as offerings of well-being to the Lord. Moses took one part of the blood and put it in basins, and the other part of the blood he dashed against the altar. Then he took the record of the covenant and read it aloud to the people. And they said, "All that the Lord has spoken we will faithfully do!" Moses took the blood and dashed it on the people and said,

> "This is the blood of the covenant that the Lord now makes with you concerning all these commands."
>
> Then Moses and Aaron, Nadab and Abihu, and seventy elders of Israel ascended; and they saw the God of Israel: under His feet there was the likeness of a pavement of sapphire, like the very sky for purity. Yet He did not raise His hand against the leaders of the Israelites; they beheld God, and they ate and drank.
>
> The Lord said to Moses, "Come up to Me on the mountain and wait there, and I will give you the stone tablets with the teachings and commandments which I have inscribed to instruct them." So Moses and his attendant Joshua arose, and Moses ascended the mountain of God. To the elders he had said, "Wait here for us until we return to you. You have Aaron and Hur with you; let anyone who has a legal matter approach them."
>
> When Moses had ascended the mountain, the cloud covered the mountain. The Presence of the Lord abode on Mount Sinai, and the cloud hid it for six days. On the seventh day He called to Moses from the midst of the cloud. Now the Presence of the Lord appeared in the sight of the Israelites as a consuming fire on the top of the mountain. Moses went inside the cloud and ascended the mountain; and Moses remained on the mountain forty days and forty nights. (Exod. 24:4–18)

The Lord is a menacing and, if for that reason alone, an overwhelmingly real figure in this long passage. Despite the fact that Israel has shouted in unison, "All that the Lord has spoken we will faithfully do," no one knows whether the elders of Israel will be in danger when they enter his presence. They manage to do so safely, however, and look upon him, and eat and drink. The concreteness of these actions of theirs, not to mention the words the Lord speaks or the cloud or the fire, underscores his own concreteness. There is not the slightest question that he is an active partner in the making of the covenant.

At the reading of the law in Nehemiah 8–10, however, the Lord neither says nor does anything in response to its acceptance by the people. In what sense, then, may he be said to be real to them or at all? In what sense, if any, may he be said to be present?

The books of Ezra and Nehemiah present, in effect, both an objectification and a functional incarnation of the Lord God. The mind of God is objectified in his law, which is now written down in multiple copies and interpreted and translated, as may be necessary, for every Jew. After the reading of the scroll,

> Ezra opened the scroll in the sight of all the people, for he was above all the people; as he opened it, all the people stood up. Ezra blessed the Lord, the great God, and all the people answered, "Amen, Amen," with hands upraised. Then they bowed their heads and prostrated themselves before the Lord with their faces to the ground. (Neh. 8:5–6)

The scroll is not an idol; but when Ezra shows it to them, the people do bow down before it as to the Lord. The people are not in the temple. Ezra has read to them from a "wooden tower" or raised podium. It is the sight of the holy scroll that brings this reaction. The divine scroll contains all that God needs to say. He need not speak again and does not.

As for his actions, Jewish leaders who know the law know his mind and therefore may serve as his vicars. From heaven (he is now routinely spoken of as God of heaven and in heaven), he retains the power to influence the course of human events. But he has transferred to Ezra and Nehemiah and their associates his responsibility to make timely civil and military provision for the Jews as his people on earth. Among the de facto delegated powers is the power to accept in his name the Jewish people's ratification of the new covenant.

With the new covenant thus self-ratified, a new march to Zion occurs in Nehemiah 11 in the form of the resettlement in the rebuilt capital of a tenth of the population of each village in the province. In Nehemiah 12, the energetic leader conducts a census of the priests and Levites charged with the administration of the temple, which is now, clearly, to be the commercial as well as the religious center of Judea, and leads them in a great inaugural spectacle, dividing the huge temple corps into two choirs and sending them on a procession with harps, lyres, and cymbals along the top of the new wall and thence to the temple.

Nehemiah then goes back to Persia after all; but in the thirteenth and concluding chapter of the book, he returns to Jerusalem to punish backsliders from the new covenant. He expels an Ammonite whom he finds living in a room of the temple, tightens the enforcement of sabbath restrictions, and cracks down yet again on intermarriage:

> Also at that time, I saw that Jews had married Ashdodite, Ammonite, and Moabite women; a good number of their children spoke the language of Ashdod and the language of those various peoples, and did not know how to speak Judean. I censured them,

> cursed them, flogged them, tore out their hair, and adjured them by God, saying, "You shall not give your daughters in marriage to their sons, or take any of their daughters for your sons or yourselves. It was just in such things that King Solomon of Israel sinned! Among the many nations there was not a king like him, and so well loved was he by his God that God made him king of all Israel, yet foreign wives caused even him to sin. How, then, can we acquiesce in your doing this great wrong, breaking faith with our God by marrying foreign women?" (13:23–27)

Nehemiah's sermon to the scalped and flogged intermarriers mirrors exactly Ezra's sermon/prayer in Ezra 9. And on this note, after Nehemiah's closing cry "O my God, remember it to my credit!" (13:31), the story of Israel reaches the latest point recorded in the Tanakh, and this third ending to the biography of God is complete.

Perpetual Round

"Let Him Go Up"

CHRONICLES

Nehemiah, the cupbearer who would be king, grew ugly and tyrannical toward the end of his career. The action he took—flogging offenders, tearing out their hair—was unprecedented. It was also something of a shock to find King Solomon brought forward yet again as the paradigmatic sinner. Was he, though a sinner, finally a great king? Or was he, though a great king, finally a sinner? One suspects that Nehemiah tilted toward the latter judgment. But such a question simply cannot be left hanging in the air. Something more must be said. That something comes in the books of Chronicles.

The first book of Chronicles opens with nine prefatory chapters of genealogies beginning with Adam and ending with the exiles in Babylon. What then follows, from I Chronicles 10 to the end of II Chronicles, recapitulates Israelite history from the rise of David to the fall of Jerusalem. The second book of Chronicles ends with a one-and-one-half-verse coda noting the return of Jewish exiles to Jerusalem under King Cyrus of Persia. But these words, the very last words in the Tanakh, are, virtually verbatim, the words that open the Book of Ezra:

> In the first year of King Cyrus of Persia, when the word of the Lord spoken by Jeremiah was fulfilled, the Lord roused the spirit of King Cyrus of Persia to issue a proclamation throughout his realm by word of mouth and in writing as follows:
>
> "Thus said King Cyrus of Persia: The Lord God of Heaven has given me all the kingdoms of the earth and has charged me with building Him a house in Jerusalem, which is in Judah. Any one of you of all His people—may his God be with him, and let him go up. . . ." (Ezra 1:1–3a; II Chron. 36:22–23)

Ezra 1 does not stop there, however, but continues:

> ". . . to Jerusalem that is in Judah and build the House of the Lord God of Israel, the God that is in Jerusalem; and all who stay behind, wherever he may be living, let the people of his place assist him

with silver, gold, goods, and livestock, besides the freewill offering to the House of God that is in Jerusalem." (Ezra 1:3b–4)

That the events recounted in Ezra and Nehemiah are chronologically later than those in Chronicles and that a fragment of the opening of Ezra still clings to the end of Chronicles have strongly suggested to historical scholars that the books of Ezra and Nehemiah originally followed Chronicles (as they still do in the Septuagint and the Old Testament) and have been moved to their current position in the Hebrew Bible, the Tanakh, for an editorial reason. Just what that reason may have been is a matter of historical speculation. The books of Ezra and Nehemiah, quite apart from their relation to Chronicles, are an editorial jigsaw puzzle and a historical maze. Written partly in Aramaic, partly in Hebrew, they consist partly of original material and partly of reproduced Persian documents, and they show every sign of extensive disassembly and reassembly. The repetition of the first words of the book of Ezra at the end of II Chronicles may well be an accident, but its effect is nonetheless to turn these last four books of the Tanakh into the literary equivalent of a musical round. A round is a composition that because its last notes are identical with its first can go on in principle forever. ("Three Blind Mice" is the most familiar example, though nobler ones could be named.)

A round is typically composed to be sung by three or four voices simultaneously; and once the voices are all singing, it is impossible to say what is beginning, what middle, and what end. Just as a circle, unlike a line, has no beginning, middle, or end, so this circular form of song, at its exhilarating best, seems to defeat death. The Tanakh may be said to defeat its own death and God's by ending in a literary round read endlessly from Adam at the beginning of Chronicles to David in the middle to "let him go up" at the end to "to Jerusalem that is in Judah" at the beginning of Ezra through Ezra and Nehemiah to Adam again at the beginning of Chronicles to David to "let him go up" to "to Jerusalem that is in Judah," ad infinitum.

If this seems a somewhat far-fetched notion, let us suggest, first of all, that any literary appreciation of the text of the Tanakh as a whole must somehow address the anomalous fact that the end of its text returns the reader to the middle of its story. One may regard the anomaly of an ending that returns to the middle as mere accident and therefore beneath comment; one may claim to have divined the theological or religious intent behind it; or—by a middle path—one may prescind from intent and rationalize the accident, if accident it be, by attending to its de facto literary effect. The first alternative makes the placement mere noise; the second makes it music; the third makes it, to return to a comparison earlier made, aleatory music—that is, an accidental literary round. Given the fact that Judaism, the religion that edited the books into this order, moves, in the cycle of its religious holidays, through an endlessly recurring rehearsal of Israelite history, concluding the Tanakh with a quasi round is appropriate whether or not it was intentional. A scripture edited to pivot eternally on the hinge of the words "let him go up" and a liturgical calendar recurring annually to the phrase "next year in Jerusalem" go well together.

Aesthetically, does this conclusion satisfy? John Keats might have thought so, at least the Keats who wrote in "Ode on a Grecian Urn":

> Fair youth, beneath the trees, thou canst not leave
>   Thy song, nor ever can those trees be bare;
>   Bold Lover, never, never canst thou kiss,
> Though winning near the goal—yet, do not grieve;
> She cannot fade, though thou hast not thy bliss,
>   For ever wilt thou love, and she be fair!

The relationship between God and Israel, like that of the fair youth and his love, is preserved by being frozen. Language is a forward-moving medium. Stop it, hold a syllable, and you turn it into mere sound. To create in this medium of sentences the equivalent of the beautiful frustration created by the holding of a moment on the vase painting, one must turn a continuing story into an endlessly recurring one. This is what the unique ending of the books of Chronicles makes possible.

The achievement of the aesthetic effect depends on more, of course, than just the stopping of the action. One must also ask what kind of action is stopped. Keats would not have been so entranced by the Grecian urn if it had not been a kiss that was interrupted. Where is the kiss in the books of Chronicles?

The kiss—the moment of exquisite beauty and tenderness that the mind may revisit forever without weariness—comes at I Chronicles 28–29, the last words of King David as he surrenders the throne to his son Solomon. All is now in readiness for the construction of a great temple to the Lord, but David explains that the Lord has told him: "You will not build a house for My name, for you are a man of battles and have shed blood." David then recalls the scene at

II Samuel 7 to which we have already drawn so much attention, in which, for the first time, the Lord God speaks of himself as a father: He will be Solomon's father, building a house, a dynasty, for David rather than requiring David to build a house, a temple, for him. David bows to the will of the Lord, but he has had plans for a temple drawn up and materials set aside for its construction. These he now solemnly entrusts to his son in the presence of God, saying:

> And you, my son Solomon, know the God of your father, and serve Him with single mind and fervent heart, for the Lord searches all minds and discerns the design of every thought; if you seek Him He will be available to you, but if you forsake Him He will abandon you forever. See then, the Lord chose you to build a house as the sanctuary; be strong and do it. (I Chron. 28:9–10)

David's fatherly tone with his son, coming just after his allusion to the fatherhood of God, bathes the moment in familial love. After giving Solomon the plans, David continues:

> Be strong and of good courage and do it; do not be afraid or dismayed, for the Lord God my God is with you; He will not fail you or forsake you till all the work on the House of the Lord is done. Here are the divisions of the priests and Levites for all kinds of service of the House of God, and with you in all the work are willing men, skilled in all sorts of tasks; also the officers and all the people are at your command. (28:20–21)

David's long speech is remarkable for the way he speaks by turns and with affecting sincerity to his subjects, his son, and his God. Historically, if we are to judge from the books of Kings, the accession of Solomon to the throne after David's death was a bloody and ugly business in which Solomon owed his eventual triumph less to his father than to his mother, Bathsheba, who read the palace intrigues shrewdly and disposed of her son's rivals ruthlessly. Chronicles tells a very different succession story. David abdicates in favor of Solomon, and David looks on as Solomon is anointed. After building the temple, Solomon will recite his own dedicatory prayers, which repeat, verbatim, prayers found in II Kings. To an extent, the eight chapters that deal with the succession and the dedication of the temple (I Chron. 28–II Chron. 7) are the heart of the story.

But the heart of hearts, the moment that we may call "the kiss," is David's farewell, his parting prayer to the Lord, unrecorded in the books of Kings:

> Blessed art thou, O Lord, the God of Israel our father, for ever and ever. Thine, O Lord, is the greatness, and the power, and the glory, and the victory, and the majesty; for all that is in the heavens and in the earth is thine; thine is the kingdom, O Lord, and thou art exalted as head above all. Both riches and honor come from thee, and thou rulest over all. In thy hand are power and might; and in thy hand it is to make great and to give strength to all. And now we thank thee, our God, and praise thy glorious name.
>
> But who am I, and what is my people, that we should be able thus to offer willingly? For all things come from thee, and of thy own have we given thee. For we are strangers before thee, and sojourners, as all our fathers were; our days on the earth are like a shadow, and there is no abiding. O Lord our God, all this abundance that we have provided for building thee a house for thy holy name comes from thy hand and is all thy own. I know, my God, that thou triest the heart, and hast pleasure in uprightness; in the uprightness of my heart I have freely offered all these things, and now I have seen thy people, who are present here, offering freely and joyously to thee. O Lord, the God of Abraham, Isaac, and Israel, our fathers, keep for ever such purposes and thoughts in the hearts of thy people, and direct their hearts toward thee. Grant to Solomon my son that with a whole heart he may keep thy commandments, thy testimonies, and thy statutes, performing all, and that he may build the palace for which I have made provision. (RSV; I Chron. 29:10–19)

This is the choral finale to which the closing round of the Tanakh forever recurs: God is father, David is king, Solomon is prince regent; and in a land in which the law is not just perfectly but joyously observed, all hands are poised to begin construction of a magnificent temple.

When we last saw the Lord God, at the end of the Book of Daniel, he was looking on from afar, the Ancient of Days, seated on his lofty throne, all-knowing, perhaps, but silent and impassive. As the Ancient of Days, the Lord God makes no final speech. His last words remain his speech to Job from the whirlwind. But David's prayer to him, if we put it in the Lord God's own mouth, has a striking rhetorical similarity to that speech but, of course, mercifully reverses its mood. As spoken by God rather than by David, David's speech would begin "Mine is the greatness, and the power, and the glory, and the victory, and the majesty; for all that is in the heavens and in the earth is mine." Its second half would continue, much in the manner of the God who humiliated Job, "But who are you, and what is your people, that you should be able thus to offer willingly? For all things come from me, and of my own have you given me."

But David does speak to God and offer to him, and he does so with confidence and love. As the Tanakh ends, the mind of God has been objectified in law, the action of God incarnated in leadership, and now, finally, the voice of God transferred to prayer. David's last prayer is the Lord God's farewell speech. The voice is the voice of the old king, but the desire is the desire of the eternal God.

13

POSTLUDE

Does God Lose Interest?

The classic Greek tragedies are all versions of the same tragedy. All present the human condition as a contest between the personal and the impersonal with the impersonal inevitably victorious. If any one of the circumstances that lead so inexorably to the downfall of Oedipus in Sophocles' *Oedipus Rex* had been different—if as an infant he had been abandoned on another road than the one he was actually abandoned on; if Jocasta, his mother, had died before his return to Thebes; if any link in the chain had been broken—then his will to know the truth, his "tragic flaw," would not have been his ruin. But it was foreordained that events should proceed through this and only this course and that his end should therefore be ineluctably what it is. The spectacle is cathartic to the extent that it succeeds in suggesting that all human lives are variations of the collision it presents. Sophocles invites us, by grieving for Oedipus, to grieve for ourselves.

Hamlet is another kind of tragedy. Though we see Hamlet in a set of circumstances that involve, just as those of *Oedipus Rex*, veiled and revealed truth and a tangled, passionate relationship among the protagonist and his parents, the tragic outcome never seems inevitable. Moreover, Hamlet's flaw, endlessly debated, is located somehow in his character and so would remain a flaw in any of a variety of other circumstances. The particularity of the set of circumstances in which we see him does not play the role the comparable set plays in Greek tragedy. The contest is unlike that between doomed, noble Oedipus and an iron chain of events. It is, instead, a conflict within Hamlet's own character between "the native hue of resolution" and "the pale cast of thought."

Centuries of commentary on these two classics will not boil down to a paragraph each. But longer exposition would not change the point to which the comparison tends: The Tanakh, however different from both, is far nearer in spirit to *Hamlet* than to *Oedipus Rex*. Its action originates within the character of its protagonist; and even when he fails to act, his failure lingers as a more important reality than any event or chain of events. No *ananke*, no inexorably functioning fate, proceeding autonomously without him, ever succeeds him as the engine of the Tanakh's forward motion. Even in the books of Ezra and Nehemiah, where in practical matters the initiative passes from him to the leadership of his chosen people, that leadership understands itself to be doing his will. And whether or not their claim is persuasive, the total absence from the conclusion of the Tanakh of any impersonal alternative to the personal God is undeniable. The action right down to the last page of the collection begins either with God or with human beings. There is no third alternative: no Fate, no Nature, no Cosmos, no Ground of All Being.

IMAGINING THE ONE GOD AS MANY

The extent to which the Tanakh is a character-dominated classic may appear to better advantage if we imagine how its action might unfold if the several personalities fused in the character of the Lord God were broken loose as separate characters. When the Lord God's character is parceled out in this way, what results is a story that immediately begins to assume the familiar contours of a more "ordinary" myth. Changing the names slightly, we might imagine the Tanakh unfolding more or less as follows:

> *In the beginning, the god Eloh created the physical world. Then Eloh and his brother Yah set about creating the human race. Eloh, calm and benign, proposed to Yah that they create mankind "in our image." For Eloh, the human creature was to be the crown and culmination of creation. Yah, however, was reluctant to have mankind "be like one of*

us." He claimed the actual making for himself, and he chose to make mankind from dust, though impulsively he breathed his own spirit into his creature. Eloh had sought a male-and-female human race from the outset. Yah, whose action always seemed to precede his understanding, at first made only the male but gradually realized that a companion was required. Eloh had proposed turning the humans loose in the whole of creation. Yah confined them, instead, in a garden, and imposed upon them rules intended to keep them in ignorance.

The reptilian goddess Mot then lured the woman into disobeying Yah, and the woman in turn misled her husband into joining her in sin. Yah, enraged, humiliated Mot, requiring her henceforth to crawl, snake-like, on her belly, but the punishment he imposed on her was less severe than what he imposed on the man and woman: grievous toil, pain in childbirth, and early mortality. They were then expelled from the garden, but as they left, Yah, suddenly tender, covered their nakedness in garments of skin that he himself had made for them.

Despite Yah's punishments, the first human couple was fertile, and the human race multiplied and filled the earth just as Eloh had intended. But their fertility enraged Mot, who turned her sinuous and slimy body into a world-engulfing flood. All that lived—all animals and plants as well as all mankind—perished. Fortunately, Eloh and Yah denied Mot a total victory. Just days before her attack, they warned Noah to build a ship and stock it with a little of everything in creation. Their battle with Mot lasted forty days, but in the end they were victorious. The floodwaters receded, and creation began anew. Eloh declared that the rainbow would be an eternal sign that Mot would never again be permitted to destroy the earth by flood. Mot herself was temporarily mollified by the fragrance of Noah's burnt offering to Yah.

After the lapse of many generations, in a world again filled with people, Abram, a childless, struggling nomad, received a divine visitor, the mysterious but kindly Magen. Magen promised to help Abram become a father and to guide him to a fertile land where his offspring could become a mighty tribe. Abram followed Magen's instruction, went where he was told to go, and submitted to circumcision as a sign of his bond with Magen. Magen fostered marriages and births in Abram's tribe, assisted women as well as men, and intervened in time of famine or other threat, foiling, for example, Mot's attempt to disguise herself as Eloh and demand the sacrifice of Abram's son Isaac. Magen's powers were modest, but his intentions were benignity itself. He attended quietly as Abram's tribe grew in size and prosperity.

In time Abram's tribe, now called Israel, migrated to Egypt, where it grew more numerous than the Egyptians themselves. Mot then turned the mind of Pharaoh, the king of the Egyptians, against the Israelites. Pharaoh enslaved them and began slaughtering their male infants as they were born. At length, the groans of the oppressed Israelites reached the ears of Eloh and Yah, and they sent the ferocious Sab to the rescue. Sab appeared to the Israelite Moses in the form of unquenchable fire and commanded him to challenge Pharaoh. There followed an orgy of violence against Egypt. Punishment was piled upon punishment, the river was poisoned, the land ravaged, and every firstborn male in the country slain. In the climax of the battle, Sab cut Mot's watery body in twain with his sword, and Pharaoh's army drowned in her remains.

Israel was now free from bondage to Pharaoh but required to serve Sab in perpetuity. Sab conducted the horde of freed slaves to the desert volcano where he made his home, and from amid smoke and flame he thundered forth the terms under which, henceforth, they should serve him. In fear as much as in gratitude, they complied. He then led them back through the desert to the land to which Magen had earlier brought Abram. By sharp contrast with the unwarlike Magen, Sab commanded them to exterminate all the inhabitants of the land's central region, lest there be any temptation for them to worship another god.

Initially, they carried out his instructions, but then they faltered and began to consort with the natives of the land. He had promised them wealth and power if they remained faithful to him but warned them that hideous sufferings awaited if they were unfaithful. By degrees, alas, they did become unfaithful. After the deaths of their great kings, David and his son Solomon, Sab turned implacably against them. Using Babylon and Assyria as the tools of his wrath, he destroyed their capital, Jerusalem, expelled them from the land he had conquered for them, and sent them off into exile and slavery.

Eloh, Yah, Mot, and Sab then competed with one another in offering grandiose visions of what should happen next. Sab, enraged because the nations he had used as tools to punish Israel had gone too far, wanted to destroy them as he had destroyed Israel. Eloh wanted to reconstruct a peaceful world order in which a splendidly rebuilt Jerusalem would be a shrine city for all nations. Yah believed that Sab had gone too far with Israel and wanted to comfort the nation, which he suddenly claimed to love as a child or a wife. Magen was in agony: It was a cruel mystery to him how matters could have come to such a pass. He called on Yah to rescue Israel for his sake. Mot, not quite dead after all, reemerged to call for a spectacular new annihilation of the entire world.

In the denouement, none of Sab's or Mot's threats was carried out. Eloh prevailed on the king of Persia to permit a delegation of Jews to return to Jerusalem and build a modest temple in Eloh's honor, though talk of all nations worshiping him there was quietly dropped. With Sab virtually gone from the scene, the law he had imposed was rediscovered and celebrated as the precious thoughts of a god. A brisk, practical, confident mood began to appear among the Israelites, epitomized by the brief but memorable appearances of Sherah, a goddess of creativity, wisdom, and skill.

At this point, as a modest but real stability was starting to take shape, Mot staged a last, desperate attack. Yah, suspicious and suggestible as ever, had boasted to Mot about Job, a man exemplary both in the outward care and in the inward sincerity of his devotion to Yah. But Mot challenged Yah: Job was devoted only because Yah had treated him so well, the evil goddess claimed. Stung, Yah decided to test Job's devotion by inflicting great suffering on him. As predicted, Job persevered in his devotion: "Yah gives, Yah takes away, blessed be the name of Yah." Yah defeated Mot again, as a result, but Job won a moral victory over Yah by exposing Mot's role in Yah's abuse of his servant. Yah restored Job's fortunes, but a great silence ensued. None of the gods ever spoke again, and none except Eloh was ever seen again; he was glimpsed just once, as a monarch seated, white-haired and silent, on a distant throne.

At length, the Israelites took charge of their own lives. Eloh and Yah were still honored, but their home was understood to be in heaven now; little was expected of them on earth. The law of Sab was codified and copied, but it was now a law in firm human custody. Annually, a religious drama was celebrated recalling the epic of Israel and the gods. Its high point would come at Yah's promise to David that Solomon would be Yah's adopted son, and David's promise to Yah that Solomon would build a temple to honor all the gods and preserve the peace now achieved among them.

What this polytheistic retelling of the Tanakh has that the Tanakh lacks is clarity and a sense of relative inevitability. What it lacks is a single, central protagonist. Retold in this way, the course of events, playing roughly the role that the course of events would play in a well-populated Greek myth, is more important than any one actor. As each of the several gods mentioned is reduced to a signature trait or two, the narrative acquires, notwithstanding the turbulence of the action, a certain underlying calm: What will be will be.

Diffuse anxiety, by contrast, is the more characteristic mood of the Tanakh: What will be may not be—it all depends on a frighteningly unpredictable God. In this unique and endlessly influential classic, the plot is, so to speak, trapped within the principal character. Clarity disappears beneath the welter of personalities and functions that are gathered together in him. One never knows what he will do; more disturbing still, one never knows whether he will do anything at all, and events do not flow majestically and impersonally forward without him. The Psalmist's cry "Why do you sleep, O Lord?" names a religious anxiety that is also the literary suspense that pervades the Tanakh, particularly in its last third. When will the Lord God act, or will he ever act? Massively, at the start, and residually, even at the finish, this is the all-defining question. This is the divine maw that swallows and regurgitates the tale.

CREATION AS TRAGEDY

But why in fact is this anxious interest so pervasive at the start, and why is it only residual at the end? The Lord God's life in the Tanakh begins in activity and speech and ends in passivity and silence. That much, by now, is surely obvious. Not obvious is why it should be so. Why does this work take the form of a long decrescendo to silence? Why does it, so to speak, begin with its climax and decline from there?

Our clue lies in the fact that the course of the Lord God's life runs not just from omnipotence to relative impotence but also from ignorance to relative omniscience. The God we saw in the first verses of Genesis was as confident as he was active, but his confidence quickly came to seem blind because he was so immediately surprised by the consequences of his action. Did he know what he was doing in the first place? The God we see in the last chapters of Daniel is a God who knows in stone-cold detail the entire remaining course of history. Silent as the Ancient of Days may be, he *knows*. As the Lord God's knowledge has grown, we must ask, What has he learned that has reduced him to silence?

We may begin with his originating, implicit confession of motive: "Let us make man in our image, after our likeness." That line has commonly been read as a statement about the nobility of mankind, but it may also be taken as a statement about the initial untransparency of God to himself. He wants an image because he needs an image.

When we asked earlier "What makes God godlike?" we noted that he seems from the beginning to have no life unconnected to his human creature. Because there are no other gods, he can have no divine social life. Israelite mythology knows no Mount Olympus, no heavenly country club where a deity may disport with his own kind. True, God is spoken of almost from the start as "the God of Heaven." On the very first occasion when Abraham speaks *of* rather than *to* his God, "God of Heaven" is the label he chooses. But the Lord God is also the God of Earth. Although there is no place that is not his, there is also no place that is uniquely his. At the dedication of the temple, Solomon asks God to hear the prayers of the people from his "heavenly abode." At the beginning of this long prayer, however, Solomon has said: "Even the heavens to their uttermost reaches cannot contain You, how much less this House that I have built!" (I Kings 8:27). God is omnipresent, yes, but his omnipresence is merely another name for his solitude.

There seems effectively to be nobody for him to be with but the creature he has made in his own image. Honoré de Balzac is said to have cried out on his deathbed for the characters he had created in his fiction. But what if, during his lifetime, Balzac had had no company but those characters? He would then be, analogously, in the condition in which, to all seeming, God seems to be at the start of his life. If this analogy is to work, however, we must understand a divine Balzac who is both the only writer in the world and a writer who has never written before. When he first takes pen in hand, how prepared is he for what will ensue?

The Lord God at the start of the Tanakh is a being in whom self-ignorance is joined to immense power—immense talent, we might risk saying, pursuing the Balzac analogy. Key among the things he does not yet know is that his ignorance of himself has something to do with his will to create. Does he create mankind because he wishes to be known or loved or served? In time interaction with his creature will suggest to him that, yes, he does wish all this for himself, but at the start he does not know what he wishes, and he does not know, either, that he needs his creature to find out.

Knowledge precedes God's opening action at only one point—namely, at his decision to create a self-image. Only at that point does he first say what he is going to do and then do it. Until that point, Goethe's famous line "In the beginning was the Deed" characterizes him perfectly. Only at this point does he shed the perfect but illusory confidence of a sleepwalker. And fatefully he endows his creature with the one power over which he has this modicum of conscious control. He gives the man and the woman, the couple made in his image, the power to make images of themselves. He makes them a reproducing species whose offspring will both be and not be a replication of themselves.

By this inaugural action, God sets in motion the chain of actions and reactions that we have already reviewed. We return to this beginning because it brings us as close as we can come to an explanation of why God's story ends in silence. In brief, once God understands what motivated him at the start, his motivation to continue is undercut. It is this that explains why, to put it in one word, he subsides.

THE TANAKH AS THE REFUSAL OF TRAGEDY

The desire for a self-image carries within it a tragic potential. Once you have seen yourself in your image, will you want to keep looking? Or will self-knowledge prove fatal for self-love? Will you lose interest in yourself, much less in any image of yourself, once the image has served its purpose and you know who you are?

If the Tanakh were tragedy, God, having learned the truth about himself through his relationship with mankind, above all his relationship with Job, would end in despair. But the Tanakh is not tragedy, and the Lord God does not end in despair. Tragedy has clarity and finality. The refusal of tragedy typically has neither. The Tanakh refuses tragedy and ends, as a result, in its own kind of muddle, but its protagonist ends alive, not dead. Taken as a whole, the Tanakh is a divine comedy but one that barely escapes tragedy.

Job, by being God's most perfect image, very nearly destroys God. Job seems to offer the Lord not just blameless behavior but also an open and adoring heart:

> When a round of feast days was over, Job would send word to [his seven sons and three daughters] to sanctify themselves, and, rising early in the morning, he would make burnt offerings, one for each of them; for Job thought, "Perhaps my children have sinned and blasphemed God in their thoughts." This is what Job always used to do. (Job 1:5)

The Lord's fantasy was that by wantonly inflicting suffering on Job, he would provoke only a greater, more glorious demonstration of Job's adoring, selfless devotion. Job is pure and innocent; he will do anything, the Lord thinks. But to the Lord's horror, Job turns out to be a more perfect self-image of the Lord than the Lord had planned on. The Lord wants to see what Job is made of. Very well, Job will show him, but Job will also see what the Lord is made of. Job is the supreme image of God's desire to know God, for he accepts his suffering, but he does not accept it silently; he is not resigned to having no explanation for it. And once the Lord, in his climactic speech, attempts to silence Job with raw power, Job has heard as much as he needs to hear. He demands no further self-disclosure by

God. In effect, he loses interest in him. Thereafter, and as a result, the Lord never regains his own interest in himself.

God's exposure at the end of the Book of Job ought to be the moment of truth that becomes the moment of death. Knowing himself to be what Job teaches him that he is, the Lord should find it impossible to go on; and this is almost what happens.

Almost but not quite. In the section of Chapter 9 entitled "Wife," we said that the feminine was not merely absent from the developed character of God but had been actively excluded from it. At the creative start, God spoke of himself in the plural and saw himself reflected in the human couple rather than the human male. But thereafter the female in the divine male was suppressed, suppressed indeed far more thoroughly than the destroyer in the divine creator. When a goddess was brought into God's temple, his reaction was almost suicidally violent, for when he destroyed Jerusalem, as we have seen, he very nearly destroyed himself. Past that point, as we have also seen, the Tanakh loses it superficial narrative continuity: God's story breaks down. But narrative and character are interdependent. We may also say that past that point God's developed character also breaks down. What rescues both God's story and God himself is what does not fit into either.

In the Song of Songs, coming just after the Book of Job, the non-Israelite rest of mankind reenters the story, and a secular spirit pushes not just Israel but also God himself to the margin. The unidentified singer of the Song of Songs is a young woman of playfulness, physical exuberance, and joy. Her effect in the life of the Lord God is powerful precisely because it diffuses an otherwise fatal intensity. If the tragic climax at the end of the Book of Job is not somehow trumped, God's life will be over. Song of Songs is the trump card. It breaks the mood, changes the subject, and saves the Lord's life.

The Song of Songs is followed by the Book of Ruth, confirming and solidifying the new mood. In that book, Naomi, not one to stand on orthodoxy, tells her two widowed daughters-in-law to go home to Moab, worship Chemosh, get married, be happy. But one of the two, Ruth, insists on returning to Israel with her mother-in-law. Naomi acquiesces, but once back home she quickly sets about the practical business of discreetly seducing a wealthy relative into marrying the young woman.

Thus is the otherwise deathly silence of the Lord God covered over by the rising bustle and hum of real life. Through Lamentations,

Ecclesiastes, Esther, and Daniel, the silence of God may continue; but thanks to Proverbs, Song of Songs, and Ruth, the silence *merely* continues. It acquires no new momentum. It does not become deafening. The relationship between God and mankind does not again reach the fatal pitch of the last chapters of the Book of Job.

And then, suddenly, as a motionless, long-beached boat may begin to rock back and forth again on a rising tide, we find ourselves again in a historical narrative. The Lord God has an honored place in the narrative, but he is now a motivating force rather than an actor. His "precious thoughts," so cherished by the Psalmist and linked by the Psalmist to the Lord's still-remembered and acknowledged role as the master of the physical universe, are objectified and placed in the possession of every member of the community—as their constitution, the written law to which they all swear solemn allegiance and in which some actually sign their names. Israel's immediate neighbors are hostile, but they do at least acknowledge that there is no god but the Lord God; and the king of Persia comes close to doing the same. Nehemiah, significantly, shuttles back and forth between Jerusalem and Shushan, the Persian capital. The sons of Israel in their promised land have been succeeded by world Jewry.

Nehemiah may be described as, in person, the first day of the rest of the Lord God's life. Though Nehemiah is male, he has about him the energetic practicality of Lady Wisdom on creation morn. He lacks something in self-consciousness. He is inclined to act first and reflect later (if ever). He tends to recognize a sin only after he sees it committed. He becomes a warrior only when pushed to it. In all this, however, he merely recalls what his creator was in his time of greatest vigor. Nehemiah is not divine. He is not the son of God. But in key regards he is the perfect reflection, the comprehensive self-image, the quasi incarnation, of the young *yahweh ʾelohim*.

DIVIDED GOD, DIVIDED MAN

We began this postlude with the statement that the Tanakh is more like *Hamlet* than it is like *Oedipus Rex*. One might wonder why this should be. After all, the authors of the later portions of the Tanakh were chronological contemporaries of the earliest Greek tragedians. And, direct relations between the societies aside, a number of common material and social realities independently marked both. Both societies kept slaves, for example, both grew olives, both anointed the hair and body with oil, both practiced animal sacrifice, and so on through a long list. *Hamlet*, two millennia later in a society that did none of these things, is nonetheless a closer spiritual relative to the Tanakh than to *Oedipus Rex* because Elizabethan society *read* the Bible far more seriously than it read the Greeks and was descended from a medieval English society that may be said, with only slight exaggeration, to have read little else. It is precisely the profound effect of the Bible on European society that explains why Shakespearean tragedy is as unlike Greek tragedy as it is.

History textbooks commonly draw attention to the fact that the Bible was the popular encyclopedia of the Middle Ages, but the Bible was also a school for the medieval imagination, and within that school the character of the Lord God was the largest, most overwhelming, least forgettable lesson. When monotheism is under discussion, the point may be legitimately made that polytheistic cultures often harbor within them an intellectual elite espousing either monotheism or some form of philosophical monism. Polytheism, in all its color and variety, according to this familiar argument, is properly to be seen as a part of popular culture. The elite know of it, to be sure, and may enjoy it and refer to it casually, but they assign it little or no intellectual importance.

All this may be true, yet the historians of religion who typically make this argument tend to overlook the psychological impact of a monotheism that is imaginative as well as conceptual. A monotheism in which the divine is not just conceived but also imagined as one must have a different effect on its adherents than one in which the divine is conceived as one but imagined—and portrayed in art, drama, and folklore—as many. Other things being equal, protracted exposure to a God in whom several personalities coexist and alongside whom no other god is ever portrayed even for the folkloric fun of it must foster a way of thinking of the self as similarly composite and similarly alone. The gods of polytheistic pantheons are not to be imagined as simple beings, to be sure. They are no monochromatic simpletons alongside the Lord God as a one-god rainbow coalition. Any one of them—Vishnu, for example—may include in his character portions of human experience, amatory experience in Vishnu's case, that the Lord God's character omits. But whatever the inner complexity of or inner conflict within a Vishnu, there is always for the devotee the possibility of imaginative as well as conceptual escape. There is always, in other words, another god to whom, at will, the incompatible may be transferred. It is not so for the devotee of the Lord God. Everything redounds to the Lord God's credit. Everything also redounds to his blame. He has no cosmic opponent but himself. No one can escape him, and he cannot escape himself. To the extent that the Tanakh can be called a tragedy at all, it is a tragedy—like *Hamlet* and explaining *Hamlet*—whose inevitability is this inevitability of character. The Lord God's character is contradictory, and he is trapped within its contradictions.

If he were, for example, either the omnipotent Lord of Heaven or the solicitous Friend of the Poor but not both, he could escape the trap. But he is indeed both, and he cannot escape. What is a problem of theodicy for the poor man whose suffering is not alleviated ("How can a good God . . . ?") is a conflict of identity for the God who does not alleviate it. Again, if he were only the tender, solicitous husband of Second Isaiah and not also the sword-in-hand butcher of Joshua, he could escape. But he is both, and he cannot escape. He is trapped as Hamlet is trapped—in himself.

Western civilization is descended equally from Athens and Jerusalem, and we routinely speak of both kinds of tragedy. The midair incineration of the space shuttle *Challenger*, the horrifying result of a faulty O-ring, was a tragedy in the Greek manner. The torment of a man who is determined to be both a tender father to his children and a careerist athlete of the larger world is a Jewish tragedy. The first tragedy arises from without; the second arises from within. The first is swept forward to an inevitable resolution; the second can have no resolution and for that reason may always be muddled (at worst) or trumped (at best) by some comedic intrusion: the young lovers of the Song of Songs, the cheerful schemer of the Book of Ruth, the busy builder of the Book of Nehemiah.

Both kinds of tragedy are Western, but it is surely the second kind that touches us more deeply. "The intellect of man is forced to choose / Perfection of the life, or of the work," W. B. Yeats wrote. In its poignancy, the line seems quintessentially modern, but it has everything to do with the ancient buried memory of a God who needed to choose but could not. That God is the divided original whose divided image we remain. His is the restless breathing we still hear in our sleep.

Acknowledgments

You think you are alone. Then you raise your eyes, and you are surrounded. This book was written with the help of a generous grant from the John Simon Guggenheim Foundation. Its opening chapters were written at the Gould Center for Humanistic Studies of Claremont McKenna College, its closing chapters on a series of weekend retreats at the Humanities Center of the Claremont Graduate School. Among other institutional debts, I gratefully acknowledge one to the library at the School of Theology at Claremont and another to the Los Angeles *Times*, especially in the person of its editor, Shelby Coffey III, who was willing in James Agee's fine phrase to permit me voyage. At Alfred A. Knopf, Inc., Jonathan Segal was patient but watchful while he waited for a lengthening manuscript, hospitable but rigorous when he received it—an ally as well as an editor. Georges Borchardt instilled confidence at several crucial moments as only someone can do who is more skeptical, about nearly everything, than one is oneself. My wife, Jacqueline, and my daughter, Kathleen, admonished me often to stop doing the things a wife and daughter might more naturally expect of a husband and father and lock myself in, instead, with God. I embrace the memory of those admonitions.

Others helped in other ways, corporal and spiritual, major and minor, passive and active, too various to describe. I gratefully acknowledge Martha Andresen, Elazar Barkan, Daniel Boyarin, Janet Brodie, Susan Brown, Joel Conarroe, Frank Moore Cross, Mary Douglas, Richard Drake, Richard Eder, Howard Eilberg-Schwartz, God, Nicholas Goodhue, Donald Hall, K. C. Hanson, Holly Hauck, Michael Heim, Herman Hong, William LaFleur, Thomas O. Lambdin, Herb Leibowitz, Jon Levenson, William Loverd, Peter Machinist, Burton Mack, John Maguire, Frank McConnell, Ruth Mellinkoff, Mary J. Miles and the League of Irish Fatalists, Thomas Plate, Robert Polzin, Ricardo Quinones, Alex Raksin, Martin Ridge, Philip Roth, Murray Schwartz, Stanislav Segert, Elisabeth Sifton, Jack Stark, and last but very far from least, Mark C. Taylor.

Appendix

The Books of the Tanakh

Torah: The Five Books of Moses

Genesis
Exodus
Leviticus
Numbers
Deuteronomy

Nebi'im: The Prophets

The Former Prophets

Joshua
Judges
I & II Samuel
I & II Kings

The Latter Prophets

Isaiah
Jeremiah
Ezekiel

Hosea
Joel
Amos

Obadiah
Jonah
Micah
Nahum
Habakkuk
Zephaniah
Haggai
Zechariah
Malachi

Ketubim: The Writings

Psalms
Proverbs
Job
Song of Songs
Ruth
Lamentations
Ecclesiastes
Esther
Daniel
Ezra
Nehemiah
I & II Chronicles

Notes

Keynote

6 **"The Lord is one":** The line translated "Hear, O Israel, the Lord is our God, the Lord is one" is now more usually translated, in the light of historical research, ". . . the Lord is our God, the Lord alone." Since Hebrew has no copulative verb, the Hebrew sentence in question, given a maximally literal English translation, would read: "Hear Israel Lord our God Lord one." Depending on where *is* is inserted, a translation will make different kinds of sense.

Theologians have often read the line as an emblematic formulation of monotheism, like Islam's "There is no god but God." Historians, however, believe it originally expressed Israel's exclusive devotion to the Lord rather than the Lord's ontological status as sole deity. They believe that the English words "the Lord" translate a proper name, *yahweh*, which was borne by a deity whom no ancient Israelite would have taken to be two or more deities. In short, the statement "*yahweh* is one" in its original setting would have been either superfluous or absurd.

My own belief is that the line originally had something of a double meaning. Its primary meaning, to be sure, would have been the one that the historians have identified and that most translations now reflect. Its secondary meaning, however, even at the start, could have been ". . . the Lord our God, the Lord is alone," that is, without the consort that most Semitic deities had. Israel's exclusive devotion to the Lord, and the Lord's lack of any other-than-human object for his own devotion would thus have been simultaneously asserted. In short, the mutual fidelity that the line implies makes it, after all, a good emblem for the integrity and inner unity that the Bible is so anxious to predicate of God.

Chapter 1

8–10 **"a recent survey by William Kerrigan":** *Hamlet's Perfection* (Baltimore and London: Johns Hopkins University Press, 1994), pp. 31–33.

12 **"no warrant . . . for any claim that God is immutable":** The Letter to the Hebrews quotes the one passage in the Tanakh that, in my judgment, comes closest to a claim of immutability for God:

> Of old You established the earth;
> the heavens are the work of Your hands.

They shall perish, but You shall endure;
 they shall all wear out like a garment;
 you change them like clothing and they pass away.
But you are the same, and Your years never end.
(Ps. 102:26–28)

In the rest of Psalm 102, however, which begins "A prayer of the lowly man when he is faint and pours forth his plea before the Lord," the overriding concern is not with the Lord's ontological immutability but with his moral reliability. The thought that the Lord who made the heavens must be even more unchangeable than they are only interests the Psalmist as an image for the Lord's moral constancy. Similarly, the only kind of mutability that the Tanakh actively rules out for God is infidelity.

Translators need to be on guard against misleading in this regard. Thus the King James Version misleadingly translates Malachi 3:6: "For I am the Lord, I change not; therefore ye sons of Jacob are not consumed." A better translation would be: "Because I am still the Lord, you children of Jacob have not perished." The Lord's integrity and fidelity guarantee Israel's survival. His mutability or immutability in other regards is a topic that, for practical purposes, is not addressed.

13–14 **"Robert Alter writes in this vein":** *The World of Biblical Literature* (New York: HarperCollins, Basic Books, 1992), pp. 22–23.

15–16 **"Jews and Christians alike":** Cf. Harold Bloom, " 'Before Moses Was, I Am': The Original and the Belated Testaments," *Notebooks in Cultural Analysis 1* (1984), p. 3. In the opening paragraphs of *The Book of J* (New York: Grove Weidenfeld, 1990, p. 3), Bloom makes this point at greater length:

> The Hebrew Bible . . . ought not to be confused with the Christian Bible, which is founded upon it, but which amounts to a very severe revision of the Bible of the Jews. The Jews call their Holy Scriptures Tanakh, an acronym for the three parts of the Bible: Torah (the Teaching, or Law, also known as the Five Books of Moses, or Pentateuch); Neviʾim (the Prophets); and Kethuvim (the Writings). Christians call the Hebrew Bible the Old Testament, or Covenant, in order to supersede it with their New Testament, a work that remains altogether unacceptable to Jews, who do not regard their Covenant as Old and therefore superseded. Since Christians are obliged to go on calling Tanakh the Old Testament, I myself suggest that Jewish critics and readers might speak of their Scriptures as the Original Testament, and the Christian work as the Belated Testament, for that, after all, is what it is, a revisionary work that attempts to replace a book, Torah, with a man, Jesus of Nazareth, proclaimed as the Messiah of the House of David by Christian believers.

Bloom is right that Christians are obliged to believe that alongside God's covenant with the Jews there is now a new covenant, the one they belong to, with the entire human race. They are under no obligation, however, to use *Old Testament* as the name for the first part of their scripture.

I learned the word *Tanakh* in spring 1966, while attending my first Hebrew classes in the main synagogue of Rome. (I was a Jesuit seminarian at the time, though I resigned from the Society of Jesus a few years later.) My first reaction to this acronym was "How clever!" My second was "How handy!"—how handy, that is, to have a word that gave no offense to Jews while being perfectly acceptable to Christians as well. I spent the following academic year, 1966–67, at Hebrew University in Jerusalem, and there I met a number of Christians who had lived in Israel for many years and were completely fluent in Hebrew. When speaking Hebrew even among themselves, they never referred to the Hebrew Bible by any word other than *Tanakh*, though it is perfectly possible to translate the phrase "Old Testament" into Hebrew.

Many English-speaking Jews, I have observed, do not know the word *Tanakh*, and I have had occasion to introduce several to its use. For these and other reasons, I tend to see the Tanakh as rather less beleaguered than Bloom does, but it is possible that I do so because my own serious study of the collection began where and with whom it did. It was in fact when the word *Tanakh* was explained to me in the Rome synagogue that I first noticed that the Jews read the books of the Old Testament in a different order than we did. At the time, the difference struck me as merely curious, but I found myself coming back to it over the years—idly, as one does: I would just find myself thinking about it. Gradually, I began to see this difference as constituting the Tanakh and the Old Testament as two intimately related but ultimately distinct literary classics.

The New Testament is, in Bloom's well-known sense of the word, an extremely "strong" reading of the Tanakh, perhaps the strongest reading of any classic in literary history. But, on the far side of that reading, the Tanakh is still there, no more the New Testament's captive than any other strongly read work is the captive of its strong readers. This is particularly so if one attends, as Bloom fails to do, to the Tanakh's definitive order. In the criticism of English literature, there are some for whom Milton has been in chains ever since his strong reading by Blake. But there are others for whom Milton is forever unchained, an invincibly major English poet alongside whom Blake is an eccentric minor talent. Nothing the mad Blakeans say will change the mind of the noble Miltonians, and so it stands also between the noble Tanakh and the mad New Testament.

The matter would be different, to be sure, if the Christians had suppressed or revised—that is, literally rewritten—the Jewish scriptures. But, remarkably perhaps, in view of all the other harm Christians have done to Jews over the centuries, they have stopped short of this. Here, it would seem, the influence of the Jewish founders—who founded the new religion on their interpretation of one Jew's death in the light of the Jewish scriptures—has been decisive.

16–18 **"What we now call a scroll":** On the codex and early Christianity, cf. T. Keith Dix:

> Christianity brought with it a startling change in ancient bookmaking, namely, the rise of the codex; see Colin H. Roberts and T. C. Skeat, *The Birth of the Codex* (London [Oxford University Press], 1983). A codex—the form of modern books—is a collection of sheets fastened at the back or spine, usually protected by covers. By the second century CE, the papyrus codex had become the exclusive form for the books of the Christian Bible. For the Jewish scriptures, on the other hand, the roll continued to be the only acceptable form; in the case of Greek literature, the codex achieved parity with the roll about 300 CE and then surpassed it in popularity.

Practical considerations of convenience and economy—the scroll is written on just one side, the codex on both—would have commended the new form of text storage to everyone,

> yet they seem insufficient to explain (in the words of Roberts and Skeat) the "instant and universal" adoption of the codex by Christians as early as 100 CE. . . . In whatever way the papyrus codex first came into being and came to be used for Christian texts, Christians may have favored the codex because its use differentiated them from Jews and other non-Christians. (*The Oxford Companion to the Bible*, editors Bruce M. Metzger and Michael D. Coogan [New York: Oxford University Press, 1993], pp. 94–95)

Dix's last point is developed at greater length by C. H. Roberts, who also believes that practical considerations alone cannot explain the "odd addiction" of the early church to the codex. But a further step was in any event taken when the form of text storage thought uniquely proper for Christian sacred writings was extended to the scriptures the Christians had inherited:

> It is this latter development that is the more striking, as it marks the independence of the Church from Jewish traditions and practices and points the way to the formation of the Christian Canon. We possess codices of Old Testament books, or fragments of them, from the first half of the second century. The adoption of the codex for specifically Christian texts (including for example the Third Gospel and Acts, which, being addressed to the Graeco-Jewish world and having some literary pretensions, would naturally have been published in roll form) would have occurred somewhat earlier, the authority attached to Christian texts being such that they determined the format of the Old Testament books used in the Church rather than vice versa. (*The Cambridge History of the Bible, vol. 1, From the Beginnings to Jerome*, editors P. R. Ackroyd and C. F. Evans [London: Cambridge University Press, 1970], pp. 59–60)

18 **"two ancient Jewish canons":** Counting all languages and considering both the Tanakh and the New Testament, more than two biblical canons are attested. For the purposes of this book, however, only two are considered: the Protestant canon of the Old Testament and the Jewish canon of the Tanakh. The position that the Septuagint canon, from which the order of the Protestant canon is derived, is ancient and Jewish in origin is that of Harry M. Orlinsky in his prolegomenon to C. D. Ginsburg, *Introduction to the Masoretico-Critical Edition of the Hebrew Bible* (New York: Ktav, 1966), pp. xix–xx. An equally common view is that extant ancient codices of the Septuagint all reflect Christian influence. Thus, Sid Z. Leiman in *The Canonization of Hebrew Scripture: The Talmudic and Midrashic Evidence* (Hamden, Conn.: Transactions, the Connecticut Academy of Arts and Sciences; Archon Books, 1976), p. 150:

> That [the Septuagint] places the prophetic collection last among the biblical books is patently artificial: such an arrangement can only convey the notion that the prophetic books anticipate the Gospels (which immediately follow in all Christian Bibles), a notion which could not have arisen prior to the birth of Christianity. Note especially that in the two celebrated uncial manuscripts of [the Septuagint]—Codex Alexandrinus and Codex Sinaiticus—the prophetic books precede the poetic books!

I side with Leiman against Orlinsky.

Tanakh: Technically, the name would have to be *Tinkan* (*torah, nebi'im, ketubim, nebi'im*), for the Septuagint division is quadripartite, not tripartite: (1) torah, (2) former prophets, (3) writings, and (4) latter prophets or, to use the Septuagint's own categories, (1) Pentateuch, (2) history, (3) wisdom, and (4) prophecy. Such details aside, what matters for the biography of God is that the Old Testament, in effect, takes the middle of the Tanakh and moves it to the end.

19 **"the translation quoted":** *Tanakh: A New Translation of the Holy Scriptures According to the Traditional Hebrew Text*, editor in chief Harry M. Orlinsky; editors H. L. Ginsberg and Ephraim A. Speiser (Philadelphia: Jewish Publication Society, publication 5746, 1985).

19–22 **"Bible Scholars Versus Bible Critics":** The long-running debate between critics and scholars that, as William Kerrigan shows, has so structured the collective self-understanding of Shakespeare studies has only in recent years begun to do the same in Bible studies. For most of this century, secular students of the

Bible spoke of themselves as and *only* as scholars. There was no struggle between scholars and critics because there were no critics. The somewhat awkward phrase "historical critical scholarship" was used for the combination of extrabiblical (i.e., historical) data recovered by archaeology with a religiously unbeholden (i.e., critical) consideration of the text. I myself in this book sometimes refer to the practitioners of this discipline as "historical critics," but the far more usual term within the guild itself is simply *scholars.*

Depending on the practitioner, history can, of course, be an art rather than a science. It can also be philosophically informed or even philosophically determined. At the turn of the century, Hegelian Bible historians dominated British and American Bible studies just as Hegelian Shakespeare critics such as A. C. Bradley dominated British and American Shakespeare studies. But the trend in American Old Testament scholarship—matching the trend in Shakespeare scholarship and epitomized by the career of William Foxwell Albright—was toward an explicit repudiation of the Hegelian element in German historicism. Though Albright's first language was German (he was born into an émigré community in rural Iowa where that language was still spoken), he was, religiously, a very American kind of Protestant and, intellectually, an Anglo-American empiricist. Albright read the Germans for their philology, not for their philosophy. His students and his students' students have outspokenly done the same. In Kerrigan's terminology, Albright was a pure scholar: a historian as opposed—indeed rather decidedly opposed—to a philosopher or literary critic.

The fact that historical Bible scholarship has proceeded for so long without serious intellectual opposition (by this point, even in Germany) has led, much as one might expect, to an extreme hypertrophy of historical learning. In Old Historicist terms, the erudition brought to the interpretation of the Tanakh utterly dwarfs anything dreamed of in the interpretation of any secular classic, including the plays of Shakespeare. The hardest-nosed, most data-bound Shakespeare scholar has never had to master a non-Indo-European language, much less several such languages, or a nonalphabetic script or such arcane ancillary disciplines as dendrochronology and epigraphy. Small Latin and little Greek will usually do quite nicely. The objective needs of the historical interpretation of the Bible, especially the Old Testament, may require these prodigies of the Bible scholar, but it matters greatly nonetheless that there has not been for Bible scholarship, as there has always been for the scholarship of the Greek and Latin classics, any counterbalancing *secular* aesthetic criticism. To the extent that any aesthetic criticism attracted a large following, it did so from the pulpit—and was pointedly ignored outside church.

Biblical "New Historicism" is even more impressive in the baroque extremes of its development than biblical "Old Historicism." (Bible scholars themselves, it should be noted, never use either phrase.) Kerrigan regards Stephen Greenblatt as a radical for believing, as Kerrigan puts it, that "there are no writers" and that, in Greenblatt's own formulation, "works of art . . . are the products of collective negotiation and exchange." But radical as such views may be in Shakespeare scholarship, they are the stuff of freshman survey courses on the Bible. It has been a given for at least a century that Moses did not write the books of Moses and that the Moses who appears in (four of) the books of Moses is not the historical Moses—if indeed there ever was a historical Moses. The Book of Isaiah is routinely subdivided into Isaiah, Deutero-Isaiah, and Trito-Isaiah, and none of the divisions is taken to be the work of the historical Isaiah, the prophet who appears in II Kings.

Such examples could be multiplied ad infinitum, but the triumph of "collective negotiation and exchange" may be particularly apparent in one example from contemporary New Testament scholarship. The Lord's Prayer (Matt. 6:9–13) reads in the most familiar version:

> Our Father, who art in heaven, hallowed be thy name. Thy kingdom come, thy will be done on earth as it is in heaven. Give us this day our daily bread, and forgive us our trespasses as we forgive those who trespass against us. And lead us not into temptation, but deliver us from evil.

But the "Jesus Seminar," a gathering of recognized New Testament scholars, believes that of the words that make up the Lord's Prayer the historical Jesus spoke only the first two—that is, only *Our* and *Father*. Past that point, every word was collectively negotiated by the early Christian church. Greenblatt, by comparison with this, is conservatism itself.

The conclusions of "New Historicist" Bible scholarship, because they derive from hard-won erudition, are on their own terms beyond refutation. Or rather, they can only be refuted piecemeal and then only by someone willing to do the intimidatingly difficult work necessary to enter the historiographical battle where it is joined. But historicist terms are by no means the only terms available. There are other equally worthy fights to fight, and other legitimate terms on which to engage a received literary classic.

To return to the Tanakh, historical scholarship believes that Joshua never fought the Battle of Jericho because archaeology has proven that the site of Jericho was uninhabited at the time. Fundamentalism might dispute this conclusion, but literary criticism is free to accept it and move on, reclaiming the story of the Battle of Jericho as literature from its relative wreckage as history.

At the Battle of Jericho, the Lord God appears in person as an armed man, sword in hand, ready to wage war:

> Once, when Joshua was near Jericho, he looked up and saw a man standing before him, drawn sword in hand. Joshua went up to him and asked him, "Are you one of us or of our enemies?" He replied, "No, I am captain of the Lord's host. Now I have come!" Joshua threw himself face down to the ground and, prostrating himself, said to him, "What does my lord command his servant?" The captain of the Lord's host answered Joshua, "Remove your sandals from your feet, for the place where you stand is holy." And Joshua did so. (Josh. 5:13–15)

"Remove your sandals from your feet, for the place where you stand is holy ground" is what the Lord said to Moses when he spoke to him from the burning bush (Exod. 3:5). Having promised victory back then, the Lord now comes to deliver it. The victory will be his, he seems to insist, and not just Joshua's. I offer this incident as an emblem: It can have no status as history, but in the life of the Lord God, it is a vivid and thrilling moment and deserves to be discussed as such. In sum, if *Hamlet* criticism is ready to rediscover the Prince, perhaps it is not too soon for Bible criticism to rediscover the Lord God.

20 **traditional historical scholars as close readers of the text:** See Frank Kermode in conversation with Michael Payne in *Poetry, Narrative, History: The Bucknell Lectures in Literary Theory* (London: Blackwell, 1990), pp. 70–71. Payne says:

> There's an attitude that runs from Moulton to perhaps Helen Gardner, that if a literary critic has a weekend free, he or she can perhaps straighten out problems in biblical studies that fusty scholars have not been able to work through.

Kermode, a literary critic, replies:

> I think you're right. There are two things to be said about that. One is that the professional quality of much technical biblical scholarship is very high; I think far higher than we're normally accustomed to in our profes-

sion. You can't really help being struck by that. And since these texts have been minutely examined for a very long time, that scholarship has created a very powerful tradition. That tradition has its bad side as well as its good, I think, and this is my second point. The training that, until quite recently, people have had in biblical scholarship was immensely thorough. For instance, they know a great deal more Greek than most people who aren't biblical scholars, and they have Hebrew and Aramaic and many other things, a lack of which handicaps the non-professional. The force of that tradition has another effect, and that is that it's very hard to look outside it.

20 **"impressive technical studies":** William Foxwell Albright, *Yahweh and the Gods of Canaan* (Garden City, N.Y.: Doubleday, 1968); Frank Moore Cross, *Canaanite Myth and Hebrew Epic: Essays in the History of the Religion of Israel* (Cambridge: Harvard University Press, 1973); Mark S. Smith, *The Early History of God: Yahweh and the Other Deities in Ancient Israel* (San Francisco: HarperCollins, 1991).

23 **" 'My mother was a Jewess' ":** The most famous version of this Jesus jingle is James Joyce's in *Ulysses*. Its opening verse is

> I'm the queerest young fellow that ever you heard.
> My mother's a jew, my father's a bird.
> With Joseph the joiner I cannot agree
> So here's to disciples and Calvary.
> (New York: Random House, Vintage Books,
> 1990; p. 19)

Chapter 2

29–30 **"The Lord God," *yahweh ʾelohim*:** While this might seem to be a combination of two names, in fact *ʾelohim* in the phrase *yahweh ʾelohim* serves only to identify *yahweh* unmistakably as divine. Though I shall use the conventional translation "the Lord God," the effect in Hebrew of *yahweh ʾelohim* is "the Lord (God)" or "Yahweh (God)" or, perhaps best, "divine Yahweh." Once past the second account of creation—that is, starting at Genesis 4—the text of the Tanakh refers to *yahweh ʾelohim* simply as *yahweh*, "the Lord," having clearly established his divinity.

The custom of translating *yahweh* as "the Lord" is hallowed by long usage in English, a usage in which Christians have respected the age-old Jewish tradition. I wish to defer to that tradition. But to understand how the character of God takes shape from book to book of the Tanakh, it is important to take note of what the standard usage conceals.

An example or two from slightly later in the Tanakh may make this clear. Compare Exodus 20:1, literally translated "I am the Lord, your God, who brought you out of the land of Egypt," with Genesis 45:4, "I am Joseph, your brother, whom you sold into Egypt." Grammatically, these two sentences have a nearly identical structure. In both a common noun stands in apposition to a proper name, but only in the second is the common noun apparent as such in the translation. It would be apparent in the first as well if we translated it "I am Yahweh, your god, who brought you out of Egypt."

Countless times in the Tanakh, *ʾelohim* is used as a common noun in explanatory apposition to the name *yahweh* in such phrases as, to use the conventional translation, "the Lord your God," "the Lord, the God of Abraham," and "the Lord, the God of heaven." In all three, the capitalization of "God" obscures the fact that *ʾelohim* at these points is a common noun rather than a proper name. By the same token, the use of the capitalized common noun "Lord" obscures the fact that *yahweh* is, here as always, a proper name rather than any kind of common noun. Technically, these phrases would be better translated as "Yahweh, your god," "Yahweh, the god of Abraham," and "Yahweh, the god of heaven." However, the semantic effect of "Yahweh" for Westerners is to make God seem suddenly not a cosmic stranger but merely an ethnic stranger; in other words, not the august God of our own tradition but some opaque foreigner. My determination to avoid this inconvenience explains why, deference aside, I prefer to use "the Lord" as my ordinary translation of *yahweh*.

The entire matter is complicated, of course, by the fact that ancient Israel had begun to believe in the oneness of God before it had a fully developed, monotheistic intellectual culture to support its belief. Polytheism lingers in various ways in the language of the Tanakh because it was intellectually all but overwhelming in the culture of the time. By sharpest contrast, modern Western intellectual culture, including all modern Western languages, is thoroughly, habitually monotheistic. As a result, it is all but impossible for translations into modern Western languages to capture these ancient echoes of polytheism—and the impression they convey of a monotheism struggling to emerge.

The Hebrew word *yahweh* is a verb functioning as a noun, most likely the abbreviation of an ancient sentence-name. Americans are familiar with such Native American sentence-names as the now famous *Dances with Wolves*. If *Dances with Wolves* were shortened to *Dances*, it would function in English as *yahweh* functions in Hebrew. Like *Dances*, the verb-name *yahweh* has a lexical meaning, not that its meaning has anything to do with dancing. We shall have occasion later to talk about the lexical meaning of *yahweh*. For now it is enough to note that this proper name, like all proper names, could reasonably be transliterated rather than translated. The common English surname *Woods* is not changed to *Bosque* in Spanish translation: It is retained as *Woods*. With the addition of a capital letter (the Hebrew alphabet has no capital letters), an analogous crossing could be managed for *yahweh*. And such a crossing is managed in those translations that use "Yahweh" where we use "the Lord." But if it is reasonable to take that newer translation alternative, it is also reasonable, as already indicated, to retain the older alternative.

There is one further objection to "the Lord" that requires a preliminary comment. Some feminist theologians have objected that "the Lord" is a patriarchal designation and have urged as alternatives to it such secondary biblical God-names as "the Almighty" and "the Holy One." For religious purposes, these substitutions may be perfectly legitimate, but for the special literary purposes of this book they are not. My concern is not—as a theologian's would be—with what the deity is. I am not concerned, in other words, with the deity known by any and all means as a present reality but only with the deity as a character developing from one page to the next in the Bible. In that development femininity arrives late, though only somewhat later, I hasten to add, than fatherhood or kingship. The word *patriarchal*—derived from the Greek words *pater*, "father," and *arche*, "rule"—is descriptively inaccurate for him as he appears in the opening chapters of Genesis because at this point he is neither a father nor a ruler. The better polemical word to use against him, for those who wish a polemic, would be *masculinist*. The unpolemical word would be simply *masculine*. The Hebrew words *yahweh* and *ʾelohim* are both morphologically masculine; and when the deity appears in human form, as he does at a few points in the Book of Genesis, he appears in male form. Elusively, the deity seems neither sexless nor celibate nor neuter. His sexual identity is a complex matter and will require further comment at several points in this book. Suffice it to say, as regards nomenclature alone, that the presentation of *development* in his character would not be served by giving him, right from the start, a sexually neutral, gender concealing name.

31 **" 'This at last / Is bone of my bone' ":** This is my translation. The Hebrew noun for *woman* and another, inflected Hebrew noun meaning *her man* or *her husband* are virtual homonyms.

45–46 **"A destroyer as well as a creator?":** When I compare the Lord or God with a fusion of Marduk and Tiamat, I do not mean to suggest that the history of Israelite monotheism begins in Babylon. The story that the Bible tells, a fit subject for literary criticism, and the story of the telling of the Bible, more properly a subject for ancient history, are not the same. The historical stages through which monotheism passed en route to its full formulation do not necessarily correspond to the periods in the life of the Lord God as they may be followed in the pages of the Bible. What happens early in the life may have been thought late in the history, and vice versa. The literary point that must be made about the protagonist of the flood story of Genesis is that, having been a creator, he now becomes a destroyer as well. Though I believe that this point, about the radical ambiguity of the divine character, can be made with useful clarity by comparing the biblical flood story with the Babylonian one, the point does not depend on that comparison.

Historically speaking, the personalities of several ancient Semitic deities contributed to that of the Lord God of Israel. Marduk's contribution was neither early nor especially large. As for Tiamat, it is obviously difficult to prove, historically, that a goddess of watery chaos and destruction has contributed to the character of Israel's deity by noting her *absence* from the flood story in which he is the protagonist. But my concern is not historiography but characterization. By whatever historical stages the text assumed the form in which we now read it, the deity in its pages may be described as *like* a Marduk who has fused with his Tiamat. To say this is, I hope, to draw some literary benefit from history, but it is not to write history.

61 **"the name ʾ*el*":** El, a high god known by this name throughout the Semitic world, was not altogether identical in every region. Canaanite El had certain personal responsibilities vis-à-vis mankind. He was involved, for example, in mourning. But the broader interpersonal or intimate character of the *relationship* that Abraham and his offspring have with their high god has its nearer analogue in Mesopotamia. It is, above all, the combination of these elements that is unique. On Canaanite El see John Gray, *Near Eastern Mythology: Mesopotamia, Syria, Palestine* (London: Hamlyn, 1969), pp. 70–71, 86.

62 **"Ancient Mesopotamian religion":** Readers interested in the Mesopotamian personal god are referred to Thorkild Jakobsen, *Treasures of Darkness: A History of Mesopotamian Religion* (New Haven, Conn.: Yale University Press, 1976).

71 **" 'O god of my father Abraham' ":** The JPS TANAKH reads, "God of my father Abraham and God of my father Isaac" where I have "god of my father Abraham and god of my father Isaac." Hebrew, as noted already, has no capital letters. I use the lowercase here and at several other points to suggest the humbler character of the deity in question.

83 **"invidious comparison between Judah and Joseph":** Jacob's presumptive heir is, of course, neither Judah nor Joseph but his eldest son, Reuben. Jacob withdraws his blessing from his eldest because Reuben once slept with Bilhah, one of his father's concubines, an episode mentioned in a single verse, Gen. 35:22. The relation among the three remains of concern to the end of the Tanakh. I Chronicles 5:1–2 explains:

> [Reuben] was the first-born; but when he defiled his father's bed, his birthright was given to the sons of Joseph son of Israel, so he is not reckoned as first-born in the genealogy; though Judah became more powerful than his brothers and a leader came from him, yet the birthright belonged to Joseph.

Chapter 4

126 **"God's tabernacle or dwelling tent":** The Hebrew word *miškan* is given the traditional, Latinate translation "tabernacle" in both the JPS and the RSV. This English word is derived from the Latin *tabernaculum*, which means "tent." Over time, the word *tabernacle* has taken on the sacral character of its occupant, but what is being built for the Lord God here must be understood to be a dwelling tent—similar to, though more elaborate than, the tents of the people camping with him in the desert. Unless the residential purpose of the tent is kept in mind, the significance of its construction is obscured.

143 **"the foreskin of your heart":** I use the RSV translation of this passage largely because of its translation of Deuteronomy 10:16: "Circumcise therefore the foreskin of your heart, and be no longer stubborn." The JPS translation of the same verse is "Cut away, therefore, the thickening about your hearts and stiffen your necks no more." It is interesting that the RSV retains the metaphor in the first half of the verse and gives a nonmetaphorical, interpretive translation of the second half, whereas the JPS does just the reverse. I would prefer to retain both metaphors, but in particular the first: Cutting away the foreskin has a moral meaning in the Israelite context that cutting away a "thickening about your heart," whatever that phrase summons up, does not. Clearly, reference is being made in this verse to a change of attitude. If the metaphor of the foreskin is dropped, all cutting should go with it. Thus, "Open your hearts, and be no longer stubborn."

147 **"For covenant love has been preceded by the more mysterious, gratuitous love":** This point is made repeatedly. Thus,

> It is not because you are the most numerous of peoples that the Lord set His heart on you and chose you—indeed, you are the smallest of peoples; but it was because the Lord favored you and kept the oath He made to your fathers that the Lord freed you with a mighty hand and rescued you from the house of bondage, from the power of Pharaoh king of Egypt. (Deut. 7:7–8)

We may note parenthetically how strikingly the national literature of the Jews chastens Jewish pride. But that matter aside, the JPS translation rightly mutes a phrase that could be translated literally "because the Lord loved you" or "out of the Lord's love for you" to "because the Lord favored you."

Why is this a better translation? One might argue, against it, that by stressing how gratuitous the Lord's favor is, Moses has certainly come close to calling it love. But there is a difference between fidelity to a commitment and fondness, and the context includes much about commitment and nothing about fondness. In the passage just quoted, the Lord's love or favor comes linked immediately to "the oath He made to your fathers." The same linkage is to be seen in Deuteronomy 10:12–16, the passage quoted earlier, in which Moses exhorts the Israelites to circumcise their hearts. Why should they do this? Because of what the Lord has first done: "The Lord set his heart in love upon your fathers and chose their descendants after them. . . . Circumcise *therefore* the foreskin of your heart. . . ."

But does this very linkage not suggest that the Lord's original choice of Abraham was an act of love? If in literal circumcision the Israelites lose a part of their penises (symbolically, their reproductive autonomy) to the Lord, are they not exhorted here to lose a part of their hearts (symbolically, their emotional autonomy)? And is that loss not love? Furthermore, if the relationship is as reciprocal as it seems, then has the Lord not by implication lost his heart to Israel? In short, is circumcision of the heart not a clue to the Lord's own emotions?

The answer is no. Recalling that the heart here stands for what we would call the mind, the circumcision metaphor implies spontaneous, unguarded devotion across many generations—devotion that does not stop first and think but acts immediately—but it does not imply anything like emotional communion between lovers. Because the Lord's choice of Israel is gratuitous, Israel's answering devotion is to be similarly gratuitous. And yet, specifically on the Lord's side, the relationship lacks the interiority of love in the fullest sense of the word. Though Moses tells the Israelites, "Circumcise the foreskin of your heart," he never quotes the Lord in any expression equivalent to "I have circumcised the foreskin of my heart." The Lord speaks through his actions and *only* through his actions. He has chosen Israel, yes, and Moses infers from that act that he loves Israel. But the Lord himself, having said so much through Moses in his own name in the Book of Exodus, never says "I love you" through him in the Book of Deuteronomy—where the word *love* is heard so often.

Consider how different the effect of Deuteronomy 7:7 would be if the Lord, rather than Moses, were the speaker, and the words were spoken in the first person: "It is not because you are the most numerous of peoples that I set my heart on you and chose you—indeed, you are the smallest of peoples; but it was because I loved you. . . ." Moses can infer divine favor, in short, but only God can declare divine love. In Deuteronomy, God does not do so, and the omission cannot possibly be an accident.

A similar sensitivity to the Lord seen from within and from without leads the Jewish Publication Society to a relatively cool translation of an often-cited verse, Deuteronomy 10:18–19: "[The Lord] befriends the stranger, providing him with food and clothing. You too must befriend the stranger, for you were strangers in the land of Egypt." The NRSV translation of this verse is "[The Lord] loves the strangers, providing them food and clothing. You shall also love the stranger, for you were strangers in the land of Egypt."

Though I have faulted the JPS translation for its interpretive, half-bowdlerized translation of "circumcise the foreskin of your heart," its choice here of *befriend* over *love* is not the choice of an abstract word over a concrete word but of a word suggesting behavior over one suggesting emotion. As I read the Book of Deuteronomy, *befriend* makes very much the right suggestion. The Lord God will eventually be a lover of a sort, but he is not a lover yet.

Chapter 5

167 **"God has never characterized himself . . . as a king":** I do not mean to make a historical claim that during the life of the Israelite monarchy down to the fall of Jerusalem God was never spoken of as king. King-language is everywhere in the Book of Psalms, and presumably many of the Psalms date from the time of the monarchy. This fact only makes more striking, however, the absence from the Deuteronomistic History (Joshua through II Kings) of king-language as applied to God. In a consecutive reading of the Tanakh, God's first appearance in the guise of a king does not come until the Book of Isaiah, the first book *after* the fall of the Israelite monarchy itself.

Chapter 7

200 **"Egyptian Jewry":** On the relationship between Philonic Judaism and Christianity, see Daniel Boyarin:

> I am going to suggest that there were tendencies, which, while not sharply defined, already separated first-century Greek speakers, who were relatively acculturated to Hellenism, from Semitic speakers, who were less acculturated. These tendencies were, on my hypothesis, to become polar-

ized as time went on, leading *in the end* to a sharp division between Hellenizers, who became absorbed into Christian groups, and anti-Hellenizers, who formed the nascent rabbinic movement. The adoption of Philo exclusively in the Church and the fact that he was ignored by the Rabbis are symptomatic of this relationship through which the Christian movement became widely characterized by its connection with middle and neoplatonism. In fact, this connection (between Philonic Judaism and Christianity) was recognized in antiquity as well, for popular Christian legend had Philo convert to Christianity. (*Carnal Israel: Reading Sex in Talmudic Culture* [Berkeley: University of California Press, 1993], pp. 4–5).

203 **quotations from Isaiah are all from the RSV:** With some mixed feelings, I have chosen to use the Revised Standard Version rather than the Jewish Publication Society Tanakh as my citation text in this chapter. Because I read the books of the Tanakh in the Jewish order, I have elsewhere made the JPS TANAKH my main citation text. However, I consider Isaiah the greatest poet in the Bible, matching the writer of the Book of Job in eloquence and surpassing him in range. Among existing English translations, the RSV strikes me as, poetically, the least unequal to his power.

Because Isaiah is a prophet heavily invoked in the New Testament as prophesying Christ, I may be suspected, as a Christian, of favoring a translation made under Christian auspices. This is not the case. I do hear echoes of Handel's *Messiah* in the RSV Isaiah, echoes that I cannot hear in the JPS Isaiah, but that is no more than a pleasant distraction. As to the interpretation of the Hebrew text, the two translations do not differ greatly. Least of all do they differ polemically in their translation of verses that might seem to lend themselves, polemically, to messianic or unmessianic readings. One of the great and too-little-noticed achievements of contemporary Bible scholarship is that in such matters learning rather than religious affiliation governs the outcome.

To announce a new translation of a great literary classic, as the late John Ciardi once wrote, announcing his stunning translation of Dante's *Divina commedia*, is to announce a defeat. Since all Bible translators begin defeated, no one can claim victory over another. The JPS Isaiah has moments of wonderful power; but, intending no snub, asking, rather, a kind of indulgence, I change horses at this point and ride through Isaiah on the RSV.

212 **"the emergence of the idea of a world state in Assyria":** On the Assyrians as exploiting their prowess as charioteers to "[remove] the boundaries of peoples," see John Keegan:

> . . . the Assyrians solved the besetting problem of Mesopotamian civilisation—the encirclement of its rich but naturally defenceless land by predators—by going over to the offensive, and progressively extending the boundaries of what became the first ethnically eclectic empire to include parts of what today are Arabia, Iran and Turkey, together with the whole of modern Syria and Israel. Thus the legacy of the chariot was the war-making itself. The chariot itself was to be the nucleus of the campaigning army. (*A History of Warfare* [New York: Alfred A. Knopf, 1993], p. 16)

226 **" 'Come and gorge, all you wild beasts' ":** Isaiah 56:6–9 is quoted in the Jerusalem Bible translation. The RSV, like the JPS version, reads it as the opening verse in the section immediately following (56:9–12, on this reading), an indictment of Israel's leaders, its shepherds, for leaving the nation, the flock, defenseless before its enemies, the wild beasts. Either reading is coherent, and both are ironic: The nations are beasts in both. Quite conceivably, the verse has been deliberately given this ambivalent placement.

Chapter 8

243 **"what the Lord God and Frédéric [Moreau] have in common":** A subject of considerable potential interest is the extent to which Flaubert may have modeled his own personality on God's, creating in his characters creators like himself and then forgiving their creative transgressions. See also the discussion of *Hamlet* and the tragedy of character in the postlude to this book.

Chapter 9

256 **"Haggai, Zechariah, Malachi":** Two of the first nine minor prophets, Joel and Jonah, were actually written after the exile as well, or so most historical critics believe; but because those two carry no explicit date in their opening lines, they seem to speak contemporaneously with the explicitly dated, preexilic prophetic books that precede and follow them.

292 **"Pascal's wager two millennia before Pascal":** The seventeenth-century French philosopher Blaise Pascal believed that there was no finally convincing way to determine whether the human species was created by a good God, by an evil demon, or by chance. His own response was to gamble on the first alternative. To quote Richard H. Popkin:

> If there is a God, [Pascal] argued, he is infinitely incomprehensible to us. But either God exists or he does not exist, and we are unable to tell which alternative is true. However, both our present lives and our possible future lives may well be greatly affected by the alternative we accept. Hence, Pascal contended, since eternal life and happiness is a possible result of one choice (if God does exist) and since nothing is lost if we are wrong about the other choice (if God does not exist and we choose to believe that he does), then the reasonable gamble, given what may be at stake, is to choose the theistic alternative. He who remains an unbeliever is taking an infinitely unreasonable risk just because he does not know which alternative is true. *The Encyclopedia of Philosophy* (New York: Macmillan, 1967), vol. 6, p. 54.

Chapter 10

317 **"mock-deferential quotations":** The mock deference of which I speak is similar in important regards to the feigned submission that David Robertson sees in "The Book of Job: A Literary Study," *Soundings* 56 (1973), pp. 446–69, a study that for all its brevity has rightly held a permanent place in all subsequent discussion of the pivotal verses in the pivotal book of the Tanakh.

Greenberg essay: *The Literary Guide to the Bible*, edited by Robert Alter and Frank Kermode (Cambridge: Harvard University Press, 1987), p. 298.

322 **Edwin M. Good:** *In Terms of Tempest: A Reading of Job* (Stanford: Stanford University Press, 1990), p. 371.

323 **Good's interpretation of Job** 42:6: *Ibid.*, p. 26.

" 'The King James and most other versions' ": Stephen Mitchell, *The Book of Job* (Berkeley: North Point Press, 1987), p. xxv.

324 **Job** 42:6**:** In the contested verse, the word translated as "despise myself" is the Hebrew verb *ʾemʾas*. This is a verb whose meaning conveys rejection with a particular note of physical revulsion. Job earlier (19:18) uses the same verb to characterize the instinctive revulsion that children feel when they see his disgusting

body. The context thus makes clear that the root *m's* is a word with deeply physical connotations:

> My odor is repulsive to my wife;
> I am loathsome to my children.
> Even youngsters disdain [*ma'asu*] me;
> When I rise, they speak against me.

The form *'em'as* is transitive; that is, it requires an object to complete its sense. Rather than take *'apar wa'eper,* "dust and ashes," as its object, however, the Septuagint decided that "myself," *though it does not appear in the text,* had to be an understood object of Job's visceral loathing at this point and added the appropriate Greek pronoun, *emauton,* to its version. Most other translations since then have done something equivalent. Thus, the Jewish Publication Society translation, "I recant," implies the object "my words" ("I despise my words" = "I recant"). Only when some such object is supplied can the word *'em'as* be made the predicate in a sentence of recantation or repentance. A reflexive object such as "myself" or "my words" has traditionally been supplied because translators believed that the sense of the verse required one.

In fact, however, the verse does not suggest repentance *apart from* the gratuitous provision of a reflexive object. In other words, unless the reflexive object and with it the repentance are supplied from the translator's mind, they will not appear in the translation. Without the provision of an object such as "myself" or "my words" at this point, the rest of any supposed recantatory sense in the passage vanishes. By simply declining to supplement the meaning of *'em'as* in the traditional direction, we allow the rest of the short speech to subside into radical ambiguity and, thereby, recover its original irony. Translators, in general, must seek to eliminate ambiguity, but irony is a special challenge: It requires ambiguity.

The annotation to 42:6 in the 1991 *New Oxford Annotated Bible* by Samuel Terrien as now revised by Roland E. Murphy admits that the use of *myself* in the translation is without justification: "The meaning is not clear. *I despise myself,* but no object of the verb is indicated in the Hebrew." Unfortunately, despite the annotation, the traditional translation is retained in the NRSV.

The provision of *myself,* translating nothing that is in the text, has a secondary, also destructive effect on the understanding of the verse. The tradition of inserting an understood object after *'em'as* has broken the link between *'em'as* and the immediately following verb, *weniḥamtiy,* translated in the RSV as "and repent." The link between the two is stronger than it can appear in any translation because the second verb is syntactically linked to the first by being "converted" from the imperfect to the perfect form, a change that does not affect the lexical meaning of either verb but does place the pair in narrative sequence. This is poetry, of course, not prose narrative, but Job is nonetheless telling us what occurred in him as a result of the Lord's appearance. The two verbs are to be read as hendiadys—that is, as a single action expressed through two verbs as, in English, "break down and cry" or "rise and shine." When the two are read this way, *'em'as,* the first verb, no longer lacks an object or need be supplied an understood reflexive object but has the same object that *wenihamtiy* has—namely, "dust and ashes." Hebrew poetry works by parallelism. In this case, the two closely linked verbs in the first half of the verse are balanced by the two closely linked nouns in the second. The Stuttgart *Biblia Hebraica,* the standard critical edition of the Hebrew text of the Tanakh, divides 42:6 in this way—that is, the two verbs in the first half of the verse, the two nouns in the second. Translations that insist on providing an understood object for *'em'as* are forced to disregard the poetic shape of the verse being translated.

As for the second verb, *niḥamtiy* (the prefix *we-* is the conjunction "and"), it may mean—when followed by the preposition *'al,* as it is here—either "I am sorry *about,*" and thus also "I change my mind" (whence "repent") or "I am sorry *for.*"

The clue to which meaning is more appropriate in any instance is ordinarily given by the noun that follows the preposition. If that noun names a person, the verb is to be translated "sorry for"; if not, "sorry about." The phrase that follows the preposition *ʿal* in Job 42:6, *ʿapar waʾeper*, "dust and ashes," may represent either kind of object. It may refer to the human being as corruptible—that is, doomed to physical decay—in much the way that the English *clay* does. When Abraham is contending with the Lord over the destruction of Sodom, he says (RSV; Gen. 18:27): "Behold, I have taken upon myself to speak to the Lord, I who am but dust and ashes." If *ʿapar waʾeper* is taken in that sense here, *niḥamtiy ʿal ʿapar waʾeper* can be translated, "I am moved to compassion over mortal clay." As for the effect of *ʾemʾas* as preceding *niḥamtiy*, it intensifies this compassion by predicating of Job the same deeply physical reaction that he predicates of himself when he says at 9:21 (RSV) *ʾemʾas ḥayyay*, "I loathe my life," and, again, the same physical reaction that 19:18 predicates of children when they look upon Job's putrefying body. Revulsion and compassion are not mutually exclusive. Who, seeing photographs from the Nazi concentration camps, has not felt both? Job, knowing what he now knows of God, feels both toward his fellow men.

Dust and ashes are also, however, associated with repentance for sin in the Bible, and this opens another entire line of interpretation. If *ʿapar waʾeper* is taken to mean, by metonymy, repentance for sin, Job could be saying, "I am sorry about the dust and ashes" or, in effect, "I repent of repentance." Edwin M. Good prefers the latter sense and gives the following gloss on his own reading:

> I will grant this to those who think Job repents of some sin. If willfully misconstruing the world is a sin, Job repents of it. If thinking that the issue of sin is important in construing the world is a sin, Job repents of it. If the essence of religion is that it solves the problem of sin, Job repents of religion. (*In Terms of Tempest*, p. 378)

Terrien and Murphy in the 1991 *New Oxford Annotated Bible* prefer the "mortal clay" reading of *ʿapar waʾeper*, though they are in agreement with Good that no ordinary sin is being repented of:

> *Repent*, a verb that is often used to indicate a change of mind on the Lord's part (Ex 32.14; Jer 18.8, 10). Here it does not mean repentance for sin (see vv. 7–8, where Job is said to have spoken *what is right*). *In dust and ashes*, in the sense that this figure expresses his weakness and humanity "since I am but dust and ashes" (see also Gen 18.27; Job 30.19).

Stephen Mitchell, in his *The Book of Job* (see note on p. 425), agrees with Terrien and Murphy with regard to "dust and ashes" but prefers to read *niḥamtiy* in yet another attested sense: "I am comforted"—that is, "I feel compassion for *myself*." The Jewish Publication Society translation is close to this sense, translating *niḥamtiy* as "relent." Mitchell translates the last line of Job's closing speech: "Therefore I will be quiet, *comforted* that I am dust." In Mitchell's effectively Buddhist interpretation of the Book of Job, Job's defeat is a paradoxical surrender coinciding with enlightenment. Job surrenders his narrow insistence on morality and accepts, in a moment of ecstatic release, his own finitude and mortality:

> Once the personal will is surrendered, future and past disappear, the morning stars burst out singing, and the deep will, contemplating the world it has created, says, "Behold, it is very good."
>
> Job's comfort at the end is in his mortality. The physical body is acknowledged as dust, the personal drama as delusion. It is as if the world we perceive through our senses, that whole gorgeous and terrible pageant, were the breath-thin surface of a bubble, and everything else, inside and

> outside, is pure radiance. Both suffering and joy come then like a brief reflection, and death like a pin. (p. xxviii)

In this translation, *ʾemʾas*, the word Mitchell translates as "I will be quiet" rather than as any equivalent of "I despise," staggers badly under its interpretive load; but he is joined in his perfectly defensible interpretation of *niḥamtiy* by Moshe Greenberg in the above-mentioned *Literary Guide*.

No translation of 42:6 can exclude significantly different alternatives, as Good is at pains to admit in advance. But both Good and Mitchell see Job as achieving an intellectual breakthrough in the very last words of his last speech. Given the circumstances, this seems much to expect. Terrien joins them in the 1962 *Oxford Annotated Bible* note to 42:5:

> God has not justified Job, but he has come to him personally; the upholder of the universe cares for a lonely man so deeply that he offers him the fulness of his communion. Job is not vindicated but he has obtained far more than a recognition of his innocence: he has been accepted by the ever-present master-worker, and intimacy with the Creator makes vindication superfluous. The philosophical problem is not solved, but it is transfigured by the theological reality of the divine-human rapport.

Terrien's "intimacy with the Creator," Mitchell's "pure radiance," Good's repentance of "thinking that the issue of sin is important in construing the world"—all three seem to demand something all but superhuman of a man still lying naked on the ash heap, a man still covered with loathsome sores "from the sole of his foot to the crown of his head," and—crushing all other considerations—a man newly in receipt of the devastating news that his condition is incurable: God will not rescue him or vindicate him, only mock him until, at length, he kills him.

Supposing no epiphany in the final verse but only a final perseverance, reading *ʿapar waʾeper* as a reference to mankind in its mortal frailty, reading *ʾemʾas weniḥamtiy ʿal* as two verbs in hendiadys connoting, jointly, revulsion and pity with *ʿapar waʾeper*, referring to mortal man, as their object, we may translate the closing verse, woodenly and literally, "Now my eyes have seen you; therefore, I feel revulsion and compassion over dust and ashes" or, more idiomatically, "Now that my eyes have seen you, I shudder with sorrow for mortal clay."

I am indebted for my interpretation of Job 42:6 to a January 1988 letter from Stanislav Segert, professor emeritus of Semitic languages at UCLA. Commenting on the oldest extant translation of this verse, a fragment of a targum, or translation into Aramaic, found among the Dead Sea Scrolls, Segert writes:

> . . . the oldest targum from Qumran Cave 11 has *ʾtnsk wʾtmhʾ* (with *h* above the line). Van der Ploeg and van der Woude in their 1971 edition translate it as "je suis épanché edissolu"; Sokoloff (1974) as "I am poured out and boiled up," while giving in glossary (216) the meaning "to dissolve" for *mhy*; Pope (1973) gives on p. 349 the text of the 11Q Targum with the translation "I am poured out and dissolved/smitten(?)."

All of these translations, Segert suggests, reflect the targum's syntactic and semantic linkage of two verbs that, in my opinion, a later, extrinsically motivated (and still dominant) translation tradition has wrongly separated into "despise (myself)" on the one hand and "repent in dust and ashes" on the other.

The difficult Hebrew of the Book of Job stands at a certain remove from the Hebrew of the rest of the Tanakh, and twentieth-century scholars have been particularly attentive to the light that may be thrown on Job by comparisons of its prosody with the prosody of the recently (1930) deciphered cognate language of Ugaritic. Segert, the émigré Czech author of a standard grammar of Ugaritic, comments further on the structure of Job 42:6, dividing it in the usual way into 42:6a and 42:6b:

> Since both coordinated adverbial modifiers in 6b are functionally synonymous nouns, corresponding functional synonymity may be supposed for both coordinated verbal predicates in 6a. The perons [*sic*] are identical; the consecutive perfect (not marked by ultima stress because of position in pausa) corresponds to the imperfect, the difference of verbal pattern is caused by lack of qal of *nḥm*.
>
> [However,] division in cola such as in BHS [*Biblia Hebraica Stuttgartensis*]—6a two verbs, 6b two nouns—is followed in [only] a minority of modern translations. . . . The now [usually] preferred division of cola leaves the first verb isolated and connects the second verb with nouns of matters used for expressing repentance. Still the general meaning of both verbs points in the same direction. (Re 6b, cf. Job 30:19 [a verse in which "dust and ashes" refers not to repentance but to Job's humiliating physical vulnerability].)

Segert does not believe that the traditional "repentance" or "change of heart" interpretation can be ruled out on linguistic or prosodic grounds alone, but he confirms my view that technical arguments can indeed be mustered for the alternate interpretation of 42:6 that I propose.

Segert raises a question, however, about my interpretation of the parallel lines in the preceding 42:5. Here I read what Job *sees* of God as the antithesis of what—in the following, parallel hemistich—he has *heard* about God. Antithetic parallelism of this sort is common in Hebrew poetry, but Segert notes that it seems not to occur elsewhere in the Book of Job. He quotes M. Pope: "It is difficult to find a clear case of antithetic parallelism in the Book of Job." Segert comments: "The value of such an antithesis in the very last verse of the poetic section of Job would be significant as a totally unexpected surprise (this device was studied by the Prague structuralists)."

I note that whether 42:5b is antithesis or emphasis of 42:5a, 42:6 may still be read as Job's dismayed judgment on God rather than his defeated judgment on himself. Thus we may translate either:

(42:5b emphasizing 42:5a)
42:5a Word of you had reached my ears,
 42:5b and now that my eyes have seen you,
42:6a I shudder with sorrow
 42:6b for mortal clay.

or

(42:5a reversing 42:5a)
42:5a Word of you had reached my ears,
 42:5b but now that my eyes have seen you,
42:6a I shudder with sorrow
 42:6b for mortal clay.

What changes with the change of "and" to "but" in these two translations (the same Hebrew word can yield either conjunction in English) is only what we must understand Job to have previously thought about God. In the first translation, Job implies long-standing doubts now confirmed. In the second, he alludes to happier reports now refuted. The distinction is important but secondary. What is primary is whether or not God succeeds in forcing Job's attention away from God and back upon Job himself. If God can force Job somehow to stop blaming God and start blaming himself, God wins. If God cannot do that, God loses. In contemporary political language, the question is whether God can make his opponent the issue.

Despite spectacular effort, God, in my judgment, fails in his attempt to do this, and Job becomes as a result the turning point in the life of God, reading that life as a movement from self-ignorance to self-knowledge.

If God defeats Job, in short, Job ceases to be a serious event in the life of God, and God can forget about his garrulous upstart. But if Job defeats God, God can never forget Job, and neither can we. The creature having taken this much of a hand in creating his creator, the two are, henceforth, permanently linked.

Chapter 11

336 **"Transfigured Night":**

> Das Kind, das du empfangen hast,
> sei deiner Seele keine Last,
> o sieh, wie klar das Weltall schimmert!
> Es ist ein Glanz um Alles her,
> du treibst mit mir auf kaltem Meer,
> doch eine eigne Wärme flimmert
> von dir in mich, von mir in dich;
> dir wird das fremde Kind verklären,
> du wirst es mir, von mir gebären,
> du hast den Glanz in mich gebracht,
> du hast mich selbst zum Kind gemacht.
>
> Er fasst sie um die starken Hüften,
> ihr Atem mischt sich in den Lüften,
> zwei Menschen gehn durch hohe, helle Nacht.

These lines, which conclude the poem, are just under half its total length. For the full poem and a discussion of its relationship to Schoenberg's composition, see Walter Frisch, *The Early Works of Arnold Schoenberg 1893–1908* (Berkeley: University of California Press, 1993), pp. 109ff. The translation is mine.

Chapter 12

379 **mass divorce:** The polarity that preoccupied the authors of the Book of Ezra and that has perennially preoccupied commentators is the polarity Jew/gentile. But it is difficult to read about a mass divorce without thinking of another polarity: male/female. Feminist criticism is now a presence in the room whenever a passage such as this one is read. And feminist criticism may be only the earliest developing form of a wave of reader-centered criticism. Ellen Van Wolde of the Theologische Faculteit Tilburg, The Netherlands, writes:

> The study of literature in the twentieth century shows a development that is indirectly reflected in exegesis of the Bible. The idea that meaning in a biblical text is determined by the writer (tradition and redaction criticism) was first replaced by the conviction that the text itself was the main source (close reading, stylistics, structuralism). Subsequently there was a tendency to grant the reader some importance too (rhetorical analysis, reader-response criticism, studies considering the position of narrator or reader). Now it is held that the reader is to a large extent responsible for determining meaning (deconstruction, poststructuralism, ideological criticism). Whereas interest was at first focused on the object (the text), it later moved more and more in the direction of the subject of signification (the reader). At this moment, the subject in his/her ideological definition, in his/her own specific social context (reading as a woman, as a black male, a Chinese female) is regarded by many as the central factor determining the meaning

of a text. ("A Text-Semantic Study of the Hebrew Bible, Illustrated with Noah and Job," *Journal of Biblical Literature*, vol. 113, no. 1, Spring 1994, p. 19)

Van Wolde's capsule history ends with a secular version of Protestantism's individual interpretation of Scripture, a tradition that is alive in the United States in many thousands of Bible study groups where the goal is for each participant to determine what the Bible means to him or her personally. Historical, text-based, author-focused scholarship—also Protestant in its foundation—was to a considerable extent an attempt to provide a brake on the infinite fragmentation that is the logical result of interpretation by each subject "in his/her own specific social context."

The approach taken in this book is reader-centered to the extent that attending to literary effect even when no authorial intent can be established necessarily privileges an imagined single reader by whom the supposed effect is felt. But my own imagined reader is ideal rather than real. He or she no doubt does not escape my social persona, but neither do I actively pursue him or her, insisting on exercising my rights as the "subject of signification." I would defend classic criticism as a middle ground between historical scholarship on the right and political or psychological therapy on the left.

381 **" 'Ezra would have been worthy' ":** Rabbi José in *b. Megilla 16b*. For this and other citations from rabbinic literature, see Jacob M. Myers in *Ezra, Nehemiah*, The Anchor Bible (New York: Doubleday, 1965), p. lxxii.

386 **" 'the scroll of the Teaching of Moses' ":** Because the Book of Deuteronomy is a work superbly suited for public reading, because it is generally believed to be the "book of the law" discovered and read aloud to King Josiah in Jerusalem some decades before its fall (see II Kings 22), and because both that public reading and the reading at Nehemiah 8 produce acute distress on the part of the hearers (the king tears his clothes, the people weep), I myself believe that, historically, there was an Ezra and a reading and that the scroll read (the text says scroll, not scrolls) contained only the Book of Deuteronomy, not the entire Torah.

I imagine the reported reaction, in either event, to have been stimulated by Deuteronomy 28, the concluding chapter of blessings and curses on those who kept or broke the covenant, rather than by Deuteronomy 32, the blessing of Moses, which ends the received text. The blessings and curses, a standard conclusion for an ancient covenant, may well have been the original ending, and the curses are well-suited to induce tears or panic.

The facts that the Torah was surely edited in Babylon and that Ezra returns from Babylon (by then under Persian rule) as a scholar of the law have prompted the thought that the editorial work was substantially complete for the entire Torah by the time of his visit. But given the fact that Babylon remained the intellectual center of gravity for world Jewry even after the reestablishment of a Jewish national life in Judaea, it is at least as likely as otherwise that the editing continued well into the Persian period.

Index

A NOTE ABOUT THE AUTHOR

Jack Miles is a columnist and member of the editorial board of the Los Angeles *Times*. For seven years he was that newspaper's literary editor. A former Jesuit, he pursued religious studies at the Pontifical Gregorian University, Rome, and the Hebrew University, Jerusalem. He holds a doctorate in Near Eastern languages from Harvard University. He was a 1989 Regents Lecturer at the University of California and a 1990 Guggenheim Fellow. The director of the *Times* literary awards program, he has served as president of the National Book Critics Circle, of which he is still a member. Miles writes for a long list of learned and popular publications, notably *The Atlantic Monthly*. He is married with one daughter.

A NOTE ON THE TYPE

The text of this book was set in a digitized version of Bembo, a well-known Monotype face. Named for Pietro Bembo, the celebrated Renaissance writer and humanist scholar who was made a cardinal and served as secretary to Pope Leo X, the original cutting of Bembo was made by Francesco Griffo of Bologna only a few years after Columbus discovered America.

Sturdy, well-balanced, and finely proportioned, Bembo is a face of rare beauty, and extremely legible in all of its sizes.

Composed by PennSet,
Bloomsburg, Pennsylvania

Printed and bound by R. R. Donnelley & Sons,
Harrisonburg, Virginia

Designed by Cassandra J. Pappas